Using

Visual Basic

Michael McKelvy

Using Visual Basic

Library of Congress Catalog No.: 95-70635

ISBN: 0-7897-0266-5

97 96 95   6 5 4 3 2 1

Interpretation of the printing code: the rightmost double-digit number is the year of the book's printing; the rightmost single-digit number, the number of the book's printing. For example, a printing code of 95-1 shows that the first printing of the book occurred in 1995.

Screen reproductions in this book were created using Collage Plus from Inner Media, Inc., Hollis, NH.

Credits

President and Publisher
Roland Elgey

Associate Publisher
Joseph B. Wikert

Editorial Services Director
Elizabeth Keaffaber

Managing Editor
Sandy Doell

Director of Marketing
Lynn E. Zingraf

Senior Series Editor
Chris Nelson

Title Manager
Bryan Gambrel

Acquisitions Editor
Fred Slone

Production Editor
Maureen A. Schneeberger

Editors
Kelli M. Brooks, Patrick Kanouse
Nanci Sears Perry, Damon Jordan
Elizabeth Bruns, Danielle Bird
Caroline D. Roop, Theresa Mathias

Assistant Product Marketing Manager
Kim Margolius

Technical Editors
Jeff Bankston, Brian Blackman
David Fullerton, Gary King
Pamela Wilson

Acquisitions Coordinator
Angela C. Kozlowski

Operations Coordinator
Patricia J. Brooks

Editorial Assistant
Michelle R. Newcomb

Book Designer
Ruth Harvey

Cover Designer
Dan Armstrong

Production Team
Mary Ann Abramson, Steve Adams
Carol Bowers, Georgianna Briggs
Michael Brumitt, Charlotte Clapp
Terrie Deemer, Joan Evans
Judy Everly, Amy Gornik
Mike Henry, Damon Jordan
Ayanna Lacey, Kevin Laseau
Paula Lowell, Steph Mineart
Casey Price, Nancy Price
Brian-Kent Proffitt, Tina Trettin
Susan Van Ness, Mark Walchle
Angelina Ward

Indexer
Cheryl Dietsch

Composed in *ITC Century*, *ITC Highlander*, and *MCPdigital* by Que Corporation.

To my wife, Wanda, and my children, Laura and Eric, for their support, and for their patience with the long hours.

About the Author

Mike McKelvy is the owner and president of McKelvy Software Systems, a software consulting firm in Birmingham, Alabama, which specializes in the development of database applications. Mike has been developing software for business and engineering applications for over 15 years and has written a variety of engineering and financial analysis programs for a number of businesses. Mike has also recently worked on two other books for Que.

Acknowledgments

As with all computer books, this book is the result of the combined efforts of a number of people. I want to express my sincere thanks to everyone involved for the work that they did in making this book a reality.

I would especially like to thank Fred Slone, my Acquisitions Editor, and Joe Wikert, Associate Publisher, for giving me the opportunity to write this book. It has been a great experience and, most of the time, a lot of fun.

A special thanks also to Maureen Schneeberger and Bryan Gambrel for all their work in editing and developing the manuscript, respectively. Both of them provided me with many ideas to put things in just the right phrase to make them more understandable to the reader. This book would also not have been possible without the help of Kelli Brooks and Patrick Kanouse (who also worked on the editing of the book). And, thanks to Angela Kozlowski and Michelle Newcomb.

I would also like to extend my thanks to my wife, Wanda, who provided encouragement through the entire project, as well as helped me proofread the manuscript.

We'd like to hear from you!

As part of our continuing effort to produce books of the highest possible quality, Que would like to hear your comments. To stay competitive, we *really* want you, as a computer book reader and user, to let us know what you like or dislike most about this book or other Que products.

You can mail comments, ideas, or suggestions for improving future editions to the address below, or send us a fax at (317) 581-4663. For the online inclined, Macmillan Computer Publishing has a forum on CompuServe (type **GO QUEBOOKS** at any prompt) through which our staff and authors are available for questions and comments. The address of our Internet site is **http://www.mcp.com** (World Wide Web).

In addition to exploring our forum, please feel free to contact me personally to discuss your opinions of this book: I'm **75230,1556** on CompuServe, and I'm **bgambrel@que.mcp.com** on the Internet.

Thanks in advance—your comments will help us to continue publishing the best books available on computer topics in today's market.

Bryan Gambrel
Title Manager
Que Corporation
201 W. 103rd Street
Indianapolis, Indiana 46290
USA

Table of Contents

Introduction

1 Learning Your Way Around Visual Basic   7

What's in a program?   9

Meet the tools of your trade   11

Where are my tools?   13

It all begins with a clean form   14

Dropping controls on your form, not on your toes   14

The Visual Basic toolbox   16

You can change properties from the Properties window   18

How do I keep track of all the pieces?   18

New project or old, the file menu is the place to start   21

Save your project so you don't lose your stuff   22

Summary   23

2 It All Begins with Designing Your Program   25

Building the perfect beast   26

How do I decide what I want my program to do?   27

Start with a plan   27

How do I develop a plan?   29

Why is a plan important?   30

Putting your ideas on the screen   31

Common interface pieces   31

Interfaces in an instant   32

Telling others how it works   33

The rest of the creation process   33

Summary   34

3 Time to Build Your First Program!   35

Define what you want your program to do   36

Data input—food for your program   37

Connect the dots...   37

Can I name my text box George?   39

I want my data   42

Bet you can't draw just one   44

Bad location? Controls can move   44

Identify the inputs? How?   46

Is it running, or sitting on idle?   48

I want to add a command button to the form   48

Run, command button, run   49

Find out if you can afford the loan   51

Put your ideas on the screen now...

see page 31

How do I run the program?   52
Don't forget to save your work!   53
Summary   54

4 Letting the User Enter Text   55

One line of text? No problem!   56
Words and short phrases   57
What happens at the end of the box?   57
Can a text box handle multiple lines of text?   58
Ahh, to create a masterpiece...   58
Scroll, scroll, scroll your box...   60
Can I limit the amount of text that can be entered in a text box?   63
Do I have to retype a whole line if I make a mistake? No way!   65
Now how do I use this input in a program?   66
Set boundaries on what the user can enter   68
Adding the Masked Edit control   69
Hey, only some of your characters are allowed   70
Pot holders? No, place holders   71
Getting the information from the Masked Edit control   73
Summary   75

5 Making Your Words Look Good   77

Introduction to fonts   78
How do I control the fonts in a program?   80
This font is everywhere   80
You're not stuck with just one font   82
Change fonts while the program is running!   83
That is an attractive program!   87
You can set the color of controls during design   87
You can also change colors with code   89
Summary   92

6 Create Fancier Text with the RichTextBox Control   93

What can the RichTextBox do?   94
How does it work?   95
It's like the standard text box   95
The effects of formatting   96
Need text effects? RichTextBox to the rescue   96
The formatting options   97
Setting the initial font   97
Changing the appearance of words   98
Move to the right   101
Shifting paragraphs   102
Saving your work for posterity   103
I wanna make more changes   103

*How can
I get
information
from the
user?*

see page 56

The search is over   104
Summary   105

7 Adding Pictures to Convey More Information   107

What can I do with pictures in my programs?   108
How do I add the pictures?   109
Adding a picture to a form   109
How and when do I use the Picture control?   111
What the Image control can do   113
The best way to display pictures   114
Changing a control's picture with code   115
Copy this, copy that   117
I want to create picture buttons and toolbars for
my program   117
Setting up the picture button   118
Letting the user push the button   119
Summary   121

8 Limiting Input with Checkboxes and Option Buttons   123

Why do you need to limit the user's choices?   124
Am I limiting your choices? Yes or no?   124
Creating a checkbox   125
And the user chooses...   127
Pick a button, any button   129
Gimme some option buttons   129
Which button is selected?   131
Allowing the user to select from multiple groups   133
My option buttons have been framed   134
Put yourself in this picture   135
Determining selected buttons   135
How do I know when to use which multiple option
grouping?   136
Summary   136

9 Allow More Input Choices with List Boxes and Combo Boxes   139

Can I offer users lists of information to choose from?   140
How do I make a list?   140
Setting up the list box   141
Make changes to the item list from your program   142
How can I sort the list?   145
How do I let the user make selections?   146
What did you pick?   147

A picture box is worth a thousand words...

see page 108

Choose one, and only one, of the following option buttons

see page 129

Giving list boxes different looks 147
Can I create a list box with multiple choices? 148
When it's not on the list 151
When space is at a premium, try a drop-down list 151
What does the combo box do? 152
You must choose which item will be selected initially 152
How do I get the input from a combo box? 153
Users can add new items to a combo box 153
Summary 155

10 Group Your Controls into Containers 157

What is a container used for? 158
Add framing to make your work much clearer 158
How do I create a frame? 159
How do I place controls in the frame? 160
I want to use multiple frames 161
The picture box is also a container 164
Separate your data even more with tabbed dialogs 164
Begin by drawing the Tab control 165
Now, what do I do with the Tab control? 169
Summary 171

11 Use Scroll Bars and Spin Buttons for Entering Numbers 173

How does a scroll bar work? 174
Setting up the bar 175
How should I use a scroll bar to show the user the most information? 177
Entering numbers with a spin.
Spin button, that is… 180
Adding a spin button 180
How do I change numbers with the spin button? 181
Going full circle with the spin button control 182
Summary 184

12 Other Controls You Should Know About 185

Add labels to identify areas 186
Use single and multiple line labels 187
You can let the user change label text at runtime 188
You can change a label's appearance 189
Taking command of your programs 191
Add order to your buttons 192
Controlling the Enter and Esc keys 192
You can designate access keys 193
Changing tasks? Change the command buttons 194

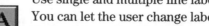

Let your controls hang out in groups

see page 158

Adding timing to your programs   195

How do I set up the Timer control?   196

Creating a screen saver   197

Graphics take shape   199

Highlight your forms with graphics controls   199

Drawing shapes   200

Drawing lines   201

New controls for 32-bit systems   202

Sliding into first   202

Am I making any progress?   203

Summary   204

13 Enhance Your Program with Custom Menus   207

You can add your own menus!   208

Why use a menu?   208

What are the essentials of a menu?   209

What items go in each menu?   210

How do I build a program menu?   211

It all starts with the Menu Editor   211

Choose the menu items carefully   211

A menu should have levels   212

Add those separator bars for clarity   214

Let's create a menu   214

Now let's modify an existing menu   216

Making the menu respond to the user   216

Adding code to perform a task   217

Is it on or off?   217

Keyboard access   218

Access keys for menu items   219

Shortcut keys for common functions   219

Adding limits to where people can go   220

Controlling what the user can run   221

Out of sight, out of mind?   222

Enhancing your program with pop-up menus   223

Creating a pop-up menu   223

Invoking the pop-up menu   224

Summary   226

14 Communicating with the User Through Dialog Boxes   227

Tell me more about dialogs   228

Giving information to the user   229

Why use the message box?   230

What the message box can't do   230

Now for some fun. Let's create a screen saver

see page 197

Use the Menu Editor to add full menus to your programs

see page 211

Make your applications look like the expensive ones you buy at the store by adding the common Windows dialog boxes

see page 250

How to create a simple message   230
    Specifying the message   231
    More than just a single line   232
    Information in the title   233
Adding information with pictures   234
Giving the user choices   235
    What choices does the user have?   236
    Specifying the buttons   237
    Setting a default button   238
Dealing with the choices   239
Getting information from the user   241
    Setting up and running the input box   242
    Checking for an answer   243
Summary   244

15 Use the Common Dialog for Specialized Information   247

What is the Common Dialog?   248
    How do I use the Common Dialog in my program?   249
    You can create custom titles for the Common Dialog   250
Using the Common Dialog with the file functions   250
    Opening an existing file   252
    Saving files   252
    Making use of the filename entered by the user   253
    Specifying file types using the *Filter* property   254
Use the Common Dialog with the font functions   256
    Set up the dialog to retrieve font information   256
    Use the font information   257
Let your users specify colors   258
Working with printers   259
    Selecting a printer with the dialog   260
    Using the information   261
Summary   261

16 Creating Your Own Custom Dialogs   263

Why do you need a custom dialog?   264
Setting up the form for the dialog   264
    Let's start simple—a label and one command button   265
    Adding text boxes for user input   266
Running the dialog you created   267
    Setting it up and presenting it to the user   268
    How do I remove it from the screen?   270

I want pictures   271

Including space for an icon   271

Use control arrays to store icon choices   271

Adding custom icons   273

Give me better buttons   273

Handling the changing number of buttons   274

Captions you design   275

Getting the user's responses   275

Summary   276

17 Adding Variables to Your Programs   277

Why store data in variables?   278

What's in a name?   278

Telling the variable what to store   279

What type of information can a variable hold?   281

You must tell the program what the variable can hold   283

You can assign values using literals   288

You can also use the variant variable   289

Constants—some things never change   291

Why use a constant instead of the value it represents?   291

Constants supplied by Visual Basic   292

Creating your own constants   292

Summary   294

18 Power Up Your Visual Basic Programs with Some Basic Math   295

Introduction to math operators   296

Addition and subtraction   296

Multiplication and division   298

Exponents   301

Order of operations   302

Using parentheses to ensure order   303

Variable types are important when performing math   304

How to use math in your programs   306

Manipulate dates and times with math   307

Determining the number of days between dates   308

Other date and time functions   310

Using more advanced math functions   311

General math functions   311

Trigonometry   312

Summary   313

Can my program remember information?

see page 278

19 Handling Strings of Data   315

Tying strings together   316

Changing the appearance of text in a string   320

In either case—upper or lower   320

Justifying the text   321

Getting pieces of a string   322

Determining what is in the string   323

Determining the length of the string   326

Getting rid of spaces   326

Carving out certain characters   327

Replacing characters in a string   329

Combining strings and numbers   331

Summary   332

20 Making Decisions Based Upon Data Comparisons   335

Comparisons are logical operations   336

You can compare numbers   336

Are these values equal?   337

Which one is bigger?   338

You can compare strings   339

Do these strings match?   339

Which string comes first?   340

Sorting upper- and lowercase letters together   342

Checking a string to see if it fits a pattern   344

You can even compare conditions!   346

How do I use the *And* operator?   346

How do I use the *Or* operator?   346

What is *Xor*?   347

What are parenthetical groups for?   347

Can I make sure something is *False*?   348

Summary   349

21 How Can I Manage Lots of Data? Use Arrays!   351

How is an array different from a simple variable?   352

Start with a simple array   354

How do I set up an array?   354

How do I get to the elements of the array?   355

Where does the array start?   358

Most real-world arrays are multidimensional   361

I didn't make the array big enough!   364

Changing the size of the array   364

Change the array's size with variables   365

Regaining your memory   367

Summary   368

Which weighs more? A ton of bricks or a ton of feathers...

see page 336

I didn't make the array big enough!

see page 364

22 Conditional Loops: Keep Going Until I Tell You to Stop 369

Keep looping while you wait   370

How can I check the condition   371

I want to always run the loop at least once   373

Keep looping until it's time   376

Which type of loop should I use?   379

Can I quit a loop early?   380

How to avoid getting stuck in an endless loop   382

What causes an infinite loop?   383

Be careful that your loops don't keep Windows (3.1) waiting   385

What happens in a long loop?   385

Let other applications have some time   386

Summary   387

23 Counter Loops: How Many Times Will This Occur?   389

What's different about counter loops?   390

The basic *For* loop   391

How the *For* loop works   391

What not to do inside the loop   394

Exiting the loop   395

Can I change the step size?   397

Can I count down in a loop?   398

Loops can be flexible   400

You can create multiple combinations of loops   401

Nesting *For* loops   401

Nesting other loops and decisions   403

Improper nesting   404

Summary   405

24 If I Go This Way, Where Will I End Up?   407

I only care if the results are *True*   408

How to use a single line *If* statement   409

How to use multiple commands for a condition   411

What if the results are not *True*?   412

How to use the *Not* operator   413

How to handle *True* and *False* conditions   414

You can set up a loop to evaluate many conditions   416

How do I handle conditional values?   419

Summary   421

25 *Select Case*: The Right Tool for Making Major Decisions   423

Making a selection   424

All I need is a simple comparison   425

How can I do more?   427

Which type of loop should I use?

see page 379

You can create multiple combinations of loops

see page 401

If A is greater than B and C is less than B, is A greater than C?

see page 429

For real power, try multiple comparisons   429
   You can use specific values   429
   You can use ranges of values   430
   Try using different conditions
   in the same block   434
Should I use *Select Case* or *If/Then/ElseIf*?   436
Summary   437

26 Basic Building Blocks: Procedures and Functions   439

Modular construction   440
   Why use a procedure?   440
   How does a procedure work?   441
How do I build a procedure?   442
   Starting construction   442
   Passing data to the procedure   446
   Working with passed arrays   448
   Exiting a procedure early   450
Where do I put a procedure?   451
   Storing a procedure in a form file   451
   Using a module file for procedures   452
What does a function do?   452
   Creating a function   452
   Calling a function   453

Useful functions you can create...

see page 454

Useful functions you can create   454
   String functions   454
   Math functions   458
   Array functions   458
Does my procedure work throughout the whole program?   459
   Scope of procedures   460
   Scope of variables   460
   What is a *Static* variable?   461
Summary   462

27 Storing Your Information in Files   463

How does sequential file access work?   465
   How do I open the file?   466
   How do I read the file's contents?   467
   How can I add new information to be stored in a file?   471
How does random file access work?   474
   Defining the record variable   474
   Opening a random access file   476
   Reading and writing information in a record   477
Close it when you're finished   478
File management   478
Summary   480

28 Creating a Database 481

What is a computer database? 482
How does Visual Basic work with databases? 484
    What kind of data can I store? 485
    What else can a Jet database do? 485
Planning is required 486
    What data do I need? 487
    Organizing the data into tables 487
    Tables for the inventory application 492
Time to build your own database 493
    Using the Data Manager application 493
    Using the Data Access Objects 499
Summary 500

What is a Visual Basic database?

see page 484

29 Accessing Databases 501

What is needed to access a database? 502
    Making it easy 502
    Bound controls 504
How do I use the Data control? 504
    A simple database setup 505
    Advanced Data control options 509
Setting up the bound controls 512
    The basic controls 513
    Make your choice 514
Advanced controls 515
    Data-bound lists 515
    Data-bound grids 517
Let Visual Basic build your forms 518
Summary 520

What is needed to access a database?

see page 502

30 Getting the Most from Your Database Application 523

Writing code to enhance your database application 524
How do I add and delete records? 525
    Adding data records 525
    Discarding data records 527
Will the data please come to order? 528
How do I go about searching for data? 531
    Finding records in a table 531
    Finding records in a dynaset or snapshot 534
    Returning to a specific record 537
Summary 538

Let Visual Basic build your database forms...

see page 518

31 Working with More Than One Table: Using SQL and the Data Control   539

Doing more with the Data control   540
Structured Query Language (SQL) to the rescue   541
 I only need one table   541
 I need multiple tables   550
How do I change the recordset?   553
How can I test my SQL statements?   555
Summary   556

32 Printing the Results of Your Programs   557

All I really need it to do is just print!   558
 Where does my printing go?   558
 Putting words on paper (or screen)   559
How can I liven up a dull report?   563
 Can I choose another font?   563
 Spice things up with a little color   565
I need to make sure everything fits   567
 How big is my print space?   567
 What size is the piece I need to print?   569
 Put it where you want it   572
How can I control the printer?   573
How do I clear the screen?   574
I want to print it all   575
Summary   576

33 Adding Graphics to Your Programs   577

Where can I draw?   579
How do I add lines and boxes?   579
 From point A to point B   580
 Line patterns and widths   582
 Inside the box   584
 Half full or half empty   584
How do I add circles and curves?   587
 Perfect circles   588
 Not-so-perfect circles   589
 Want some pie?   590
What's the point?   592
What can the graphics controls do?   593
Summary   593

34 Finding Bugs in Your Programs   595

Keys to successful bug-hunting   596
Avoid syntax errors   596

*Now, how do
I print this?!*

see page 558

*Add your own
drawings to
your
programs*

see page 579

When you encounter an error   598
How the Debug window works   599
   You can determine a variable's value   600
   Running commands   602
   How did I get here?   602
Stop it—Pausing the program's execution   603
One step at a time   604
Summary   605

What to do when you encounter an error...

see page 598

35 Error Handling: Anticipating Mistakes that Users Will Make   607

Only give people access to what they need   609
   Start by disabling and hiding controls   610
   You can also prevent users from editing fields   611
An ounce of prevention...   613
   Is the data in range?   613
   Wrong data types   614
Handling errors you can't avoid   615
   The basic error handler   616
   You can ignore some errors   619
Summary   620

Sometimes you can't avoid errors, but you can prepare for them

see page 615

36 When One Form Isn't Enough   621

Juggling multiple forms   622
   Adding a new form   622
   Nothing but code   623
   Importing an existing form or module   624
   Working with the different forms   625
   How do I display forms other than my startup form?   625
Making a new start   626
Take control of your environment   628
   Options to customize your design mode   629
   Saving your toolbox   631
Summary   632

Where do I go from here?

see page 636

37 The Search for More Help Continues   633

There's no need to reinvent the wheel   634
   Controls you already have   634
   Other controls you can get   635
Hungry for more?   636
   Printed material   636
   More printed material   637
   The on-line community   637
Summary   638

A Answers to the Quizzes   639

Introduction

Computers are great tools capable of performing a variety of tasks. But, in order to perform these tasks, a computer must be programmed. All of the major applications (such as Word, Excel, Project) were written by programmers who slaved away for months writing thousands and thousands of lines of code.

This book's purpose in life

For most tasks, I know that you don't have months to devote to accomplishing your goal. That is why you chose Visual Basic to do programming, and why this book was written. Visual Basic provides the easiest way for you to create programs that run in the Windows operating system. Its forms and controls save you from most of the headaches associated with showing and updating Windows, so you can concentrate on the important things.

This book takes the same approach. While there are more detailed books on the market, this book is designed to get you up and running quickly. It shows you the basic stuff you need to know to create a Visual Basic program for your task. The information is organized to make it easy to find just what you need without having to wade through thousands of pages, or seemingly infinite levels of Help files.

It was also the intention of the publishers to provide you with enough depth of information that you could accomplish fairly sophisticated tasks, not just simple ones. While this may not be the only reference you ever need for Visual Basic, I hope you find it one of the most useful.

A look at the pieces

There are several logical categories that this book covers. Each category contains a number of chapters related to the subject at hand.

Where do I begin?

Chapters 1-3 provide you with a tour of the Visual Basic desktop to familiarize you with the different tools at your disposal. These chapters also discuss program design and walk through an example program to show how some things are done.

What the user will see

Chapters 4-12 discuss many of the Visual Basic controls that you use for your user interface. These controls help you gather and display data, perform tasks, and make selections. Most controls are grouped according to their function, which allows you to see the benefits and drawbacks of different controls for each task.

When you need more than a simple screen

Most programs require you to do more than just get a few pieces of data from the user and display information. Programs have a large number of complex tasks. Chapters 13-16 show you how to use menus to organize your program's tasks, and how some of Visual Basic's built-in tools can make your programming easier.

Processing information

Chapters 17-21 explain all you need to know about variables, those objects that hold data for you in a program. These chapters also explain how Visual Basic programs can manipulate numbers and text and explain how logical statements work in a program.

Getting things done

Want to know how to make the computer perform repetitive tasks or make decisions? Chapters 22-25 is the place for you. These chapters cover how loops are used to do things over and over. They also cover several methods of allowing the computer to choose courses of action based on decision information that you provide.

Building your program in blocks

Chapter 26 shows you how to build procedures and functions. These program elements allow you to build and test your code in small pieces. They are also reusable, so once you create the perfect routine in one program, you can use it in others. Also in this section are several procedures and functions which provide you with capabilities not included in Visual Basic's internal functions. I have found these functions to be quite useful in my work.

Getting information in and out

At some point, every program must either read information in or write information out. Chapters 27-33 deal with storing information in files and with getting the information out onto paper in the form of reports and graphs. A large part of this section deals with the creation and use of database files. Databases are being used more often than ever before for more and more tasks.

Other stuff you might need

Finally, chapters 34-37 contain several other topics that I thought you should know. These topics include finding and preventing errors in your code, managing your programming project, and using third-party controls and add-ins.

Nuggets of information

This book contains a number of special elements that are designed to make it easier to read and to help you find information more quickly. There are also a few parts that are set up to help reinforce the information you just learned.

Speaking of Visual Basic

This element shows you the syntax of the commands that are used in Visual Basic and explains all the parameters of the commands.

TIP **Tips describe shortcuts and secrets that show you the best way to** get a job done. This is information that is often left out of the Visual Basic documentation.

CAUTION **Cautions warn you about potential problems that might arise from** a particular action.

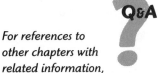

Q&A *What are Q&A notes?*

For references to other chapters with related information, look for this cross-reference in the margin.

These are notes cast in a question and answer format. Some are just additional information. Others discuss solutions to common problems. Many of the problems are easy-to-make but hard-to-find coding mistakes.

Listing 1.1 This is an Example of Program Code

```
For I = 1 To 11
    Xpsn = lmarg + ((I - 1) * 10 * SclX)
    Chart.CurrentX = Xpsn
    Chart.CurrentY = bmarg + 5
    Chart.Print Right(Str((I - 1) * 10), 3)
    Chart.Line (Xpsn, bmarg)-(Xpsn, bmarg - 40)
Next I
```

After each code listing, look for the magnifying glass to identify the paragraph that explains the code listing. Everything you need to know about the preceding code listing is discussed here.

❝ *Plain English, please!*

These elements are used to translate Visual Basic **terms** and **jargon** into English. **❞**

How do I use this in the real world?

These are program examples that show you how to perform a real task that you might use in your work.

Catch the bug

This simple exercise consists of a flawed code segment relating to the material you just covered. Your job is to find these errors, to help solidify the concepts in your mind.

In addition to these elements sprinkled throughout the chapter, at the end of each chapter you will find a set of review questions and review exercises. The questions are designed to test your knowledge of the terms and concepts that you just covered. The exercises ask you to apply this understanding, by either modifying an existing code segment from the book or writing your own code from scratch. You will find that these questions and exercises get more difficult as you proceed.

Also, throughout the book you'll run across text that is in a different typeface. **Bold** is for new terms or text that you type.

Every once in a while, you'll see <u>underlined</u> letters in commands, pressing these letters while holding down the Alt key is a faster way to use the commands. For example, press Alt+F to display the <u>F</u>ile menu.

`Monospace` is used to identify Visual Basic code listings. The following conventions are followed in monospace:

- Words with an initial capital letter are Visual Basic keywords that need to be entered exactly as they are shown.

- Words in lowercase represent parameters for which you provide values.

- Items enclosed in square brackets [] are optional items that you may choose to exclude.

- Items separated by a vertical bar (|) indicate that you must choose one or the other of the items.

- All other punctuation marks (such as parentheses, commas, periods, etc.) should be entered exactly as shown.

1

Learning Your Way Around Visual Basic

● **In this chapter:**

- What's a program made up of?

- Parts is parts. The parts of the Visual Basic screen

- How do I start a programming project?

- How do I save my work?

With Visual Basic, the power of Windows programming is available to even beginning programmers . . . . **>**

█f you want to be able to write programs for Windows, you've come to the right place. Visual Basic is designed to make it easy for users to write Windows programs. Visual Basic makes development easy by providing you with a lot of tools to accomplish the many tasks that are required in a program. These tools let you avoid having to know about all the details of programming—like how to get a keystroke or paint something on the screen.

For example, you may be familiar with bitmap files, those files that contain pictures that you can use for your Windows wallpaper (among other uses). You can use those pictures in your programs, even though you may know nothing about how the pictures are stored or how to draw them on the screen. You can use them because Visual Basic provides you a tool that will handle all the details for you and just put the picture where you want it.

You may be thinking, "If it's so easy to use, it must be limited in what it can do, right?" Wrong! With Visual Basic, you can write a very simple program—such as one that gets a user ID and password for network login—or you can write very complex programs that handle the payroll for a 100,000 employee company. Or, you can develop a word processor geared to writing reports for astronomers. Figure 1.1 shows examples of two Visual Basic programs.

Fig. 1.1
You can use Visual Basic to create a wide variety of programs.

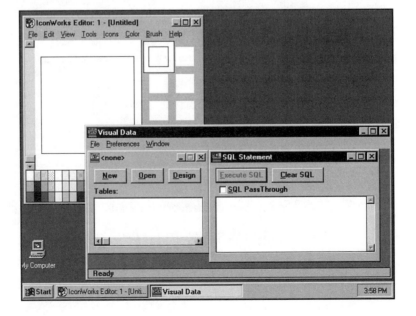

Granted, there are a few limits in Visual Basic, and as with any program development tool, there are other programming languages that do a better job in certain areas. However, it is a very powerful tool, as well as being easy to use.

What's in a program?

To begin your introduction to Visual Basic, let's first look at the pieces that make up a program. Every computer program is made up of a **user interface** which gets and displays information, and program code which processes the information. In Visual Basic, the user interface and some of the code is contained in a **form**.

 Plain English, please!

The **user interface** of a program is the visible part of the program that presents information to the user and gets input from the user. There are many types of user interfaces. The dashboard of your car is a user interface that uses dials and lights to present mechanical information to the user—you.

The user interface of a Windows program is much more robust. It typically will contain a menu, one or more toolbars (a series of picture buttons) for shortcuts, and a work area, such as a document or spreadsheet. This is the type of interface that will be of most interest to you in program development.

A **form** is what creates the window(s) that your users see in your program. **99**

Most Visual Basic programs are made up of at least one form (see fig 1.2). As you can see, it looks like the window of any other Windows program. A new form provides you with a clean work area for your program, somewhat like how an artist's new canvas provides a place for his or her masterpiece.

Fig. 1.2
A form provides the view of your program that is presented to the user.

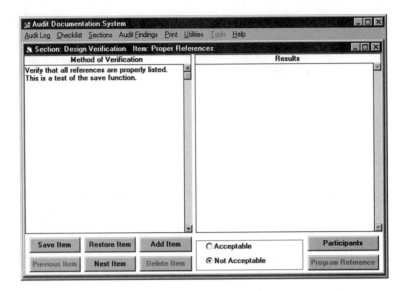

But a form is more than just a pretty picture to display information. It also provides a means for the user to interact with your program by entering data and starting program activities. Forms contain all the user interface elements that will be needed for your program.

While the visual interface is important in the development of your program, it doesn't do a whole lot for you by itself. You also have to have some **code** in your program to make it actually do something. You can think of it this way—a form without code is like a car without an engine; it may look very pretty, but you can't go very far in it.

 Plain English, please!

Code is the language you use to communicate with the computer. A computer cannot understand English; it only understands machine language, a series of on and off circuits. To tell the computer what to do, you need to translate English commands into computer language. The code is like a foreign language dictionary. It uses a specialized set of words and a translator (the **compiler**) to put instructions into the machine language that the computer can comprehend. **99**

Listing 1.1 is an example of some program code. This particular code segment is used to draw labels on a chart.

Listing 1.1   Example of Program Code

```
For I = 1 To 11
    Xpsn = lmarg + ((I - 1) * 10 * SclX)
    Chart.CurrentX = Xpsn
    Chart.CurrentY = bmarg + 5
    Chart.Print Right(Str((I - 1) * 10), 3)
    Chart.Line (Xpsn, bmarg)-(Xpsn, bmarg - 40)
Next I
```

Meet the tools of your trade

As stated previously, Visual Basic is a great tool for developing Windows
programs. Of course, as with any tool you use in life, you need to become
familiar with how it works before you can use it effectively. Showing you
how things in Visual Basic work is obviously the focus of this book. But
before we start with how all the individual tools work, let's take a tour of the
desktop where your programming work will be done (see fig. 1.3).

Fig. 1.3
The Visual Basic
desktop is where you
develop your programs.

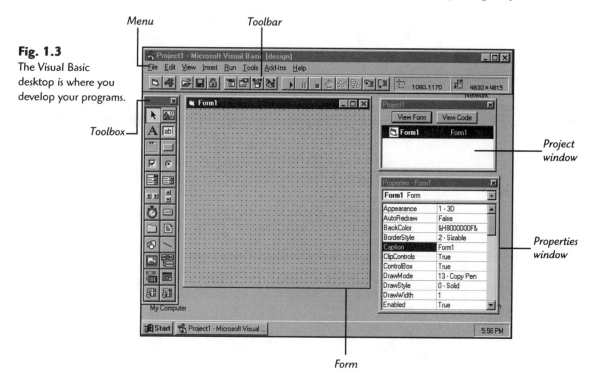

As you can see, Visual Basic shares alot of elements with other Windows programs. There is a **menu bar**, a toolbar which contains buttons for the most commonly performed tasks, and a work area where you actually create your programs. Even a few of the menus are the same: File, Edit, Help, and others.

Each of these menus contains several familiar menu options. The File menu allows you to open, save, and close files. The Edit menu contains the Cut, Copy, and Paste commands. The Help menu provides you access to the Visual Basic help system. In addition, there are some familiar **shortcut keys** that work the same in Visual Basic as in other programs. This similarity of menus and keystrokes makes it easier to learn how Visual Basic works. Table 1.1 lists several of the more commonly used shortcut keys.

 Plain English, please!

A **shortcut key**, or **hotkey**, is a key or key combination that performs a task more quickly than selecting the appropriate command from a menu. For example, to remove some text, you would have to choose the Cut option from the Edit menu. Or, you could press Ctrl+X, the shortcut key. 〞

Table 1.1   Get Straight to Your Task with Shortcut Keys

Menu Item	Shortcut Key	Description
Edit, Cut	Ctrl+X	Removes text or a control from its current location and copies it to the Clipboard.
Edit, Copy	Ctrl+C	Makes a copy of text or a control in the Clipboard.
Edit, Paste	Ctrl+V	Pastes the contents of the Clipboard to the form or code window.
Edit, Undo	Ctrl+Z	Undoes the last change.
Edit, Find	Ctrl+F	Finds a piece of text.
File, Open	Ctrl+O	Opens a project.
File, Save	Ctrl+S	Saves the current file.
File, Print	Ctrl+P	Prints the current form or module.

Where are my tools?

As mentioned earlier, one of the pieces of the desktop is the toolbar (see fig. 1.4). This provides you with quick access to some of the most often-used functions in Visual Basic.

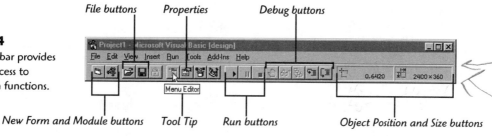

Fig. 1.4
The toolbar provides quick access to common functions.

The toolbar in Visual Basic follows the standard used by the latest generation of programs in that it provides you with Tool Tips to tell you what each button is. A Tool Tip is a little yellow "balloon" with a description in it (refer to fig. 1.4). These pop up if you leave the cursor on a button for a few seconds.

Most of the buttons on the toolbar will be addressed in detail later in the book. Two other areas on the toolbar deserve special mention. At the far right of the toolbar are two blocks with a pair of numbers in each block. These two blocks show the position and size of the form or control with which you are working. The two numbers in the first block indicate the horizontal and vertical positions, respectively, of the upper left corner of the current object. These numbers are the Left and Top properties of the object. If you are working with a form, these positions are in relation to the top left corner of the screen. If you are working with a control, the positions are in relation to the top left corner of the current form (or current container if the control is inside a picture box or frame).

The two numbers in the second block show the horizontal and vertical dimensions, respectively, of the current object. These dimensions are the Width and Height properties of the object. Both the position and dimension information is given in **twips**.

Plain English, please!

Twips are screen measurements used by Visual Basic. There are approximately 1440 twips in a logical inch. (A logical inch is the screen size of an object which would be one inch long on a printed page.)

 Q&A *Can I change the appearance of the toolbar?*

While you can choose whether or not to display the toolbar (by selecting Toolbar from the <u>V</u>iew menu), you cannot add, remove, or arrange buttons on the toolbar itself.

It all begins with a clean form

As I stated earlier, most Visual Basic programs contain at least one form. Just as an artist paints on a blank canvas, the Visual Basic programmer draws the elements of the user interface on a blank form. The form holds all the pieces of your user interface. You visually design the interface by drawing controls on the form.

The form is part of the desktop and is your primary work area for creating your program. If you look back closely at the form in figure 1.3, you will notice that the form has dots on it that form a grid. This grid is there solely to help you position your controls on the form. When you run your program, the grid is not visible. You can control the spacing of the grid dots from the Environment Options **dialog box**. You can also choose not to display the grid at all.

 Plain English, please!

A **dialog box** (or simply a **dialog**, for short) is a special form that is used to get information from the user. Dialogs are often used to allow the user to specify a file to retrieve or to give a saved file a name. Many of a program's options are presented in a dialog box.

Dropping controls on your form, not on your toes

Another major part of the desktop in Visual Basic is the **control toolbox**. This toolbox contains all the **controls** that you have available for use in your program. These controls are what make Visual Basic so powerful and yet easy to use. There are controls that allow you to perform all kinds of tasks in your program. Figure 1.5 shows the basic control set that is available when you first start Visual Basic. The toolbox can be moved around on the screen to a location that is convenient to you. You move it by clicking and dragging on the bar at the top of the box.

Fig. 1.5
Here are all the controls you need in a neat toolbox.

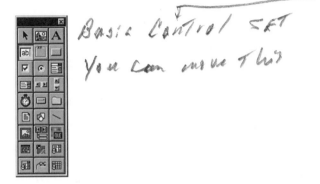

Basic Control SET
You can move This

 Plain English, please!

Controls are the basic building blocks of all Visual Basic programs. Controls provide a way of performing tasks in a program without forcing you to code all the little details required to make things happen.

Some controls (like text boxes, scroll bars, list boxes, checkboxes, and option buttons) are used to get user input. Other controls, such as command buttons, let the user initiate actions in the program. Command buttons behave like buttons on your TV's remote control. You press a button and the TV changes channels, adjusts the volume, or turns off.

Q&A Sometimes when I work on a program, the toolbox gets covered up by my form. What can I do about it?

If the toolbox is hidden, you can bring it to the top by selecting Toolbox from the View menu. If you want to make sure that the toolbox is always on top, you can select Options from the Tools menu, select the Environment Options tab, and check the Toolbox On Top box in the dialog box (see fig. 1.6).

The Visual Basic toolbox

Here is a brief explanation of each of the controls in the basic set:

Pointer
Allows you to select or activate a control on the form.

Picture Box
Allows you to display and edit graphics images.

Label
Displays text.

Text Box
Allows you to display and edit text, numbers, and dates.

Frame
Provides a method for grouping other controls.

Command Button
Provides a means to start a program function.

CheckBox
Displays or allows input of a two part choice, such as Yes/No or True/False.

Option Button
Displays or allows a choice among multiple items.

ComboBox
Allows the user to select an entry from a list or enter a new value.

ListBox
Allows the user to select an entry from a list.

Horizontal Scroll Bar
Allows the user to input numerical information.

Vertical Scroll Bar
Allows the user to input numerical information.

Timer
Provides a means for an action to be taken on a timed basis.

Drive ListBox
Displays and allows a user to choose from available disk drives on the computer.

Directory ListBox
Displays and allows a user to choose from available directories or folders from the selected drive on the computer.

File ListBox
Displays and allows a user to choose from available files in the current directory or folder.

Shape
Displays geometric shapes on the form.

Line
Displays lines on the form.

Image
Displays graphics images.

Data Control
Provides a link to database files.

OLE Container
Provides the user with connectivity to other applications.

Common Dialog
Provides user interface dialog boxes for a variety of choices such as font selection, color selection, printer options, and file options.

RichTextBox
Allows the user complete formatting control over text.

Data Bound ListBox
Allows the user to choose items from a list contained in a database file.

Data Bound ComboBox
Allows the user to choose items from a list contained in a database file or enter a new value.

Sheridan Tab Control
Allows the user to create notebook style pages for an application.

Data Bound Grid
Allows the user to edit multiple rows of database information.

Fig. 1.6
Change your desktop with the Environment Options dialog box.

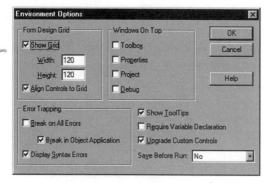

You can change properties from the Properties window

The Properties window is another part of the Visual Basic desktop. This window shows all the available properties for the current form or control. These properties determine how a form or control will look and how it will perform in a program. Figure 1.7 shows the Properties window with several key elements called out.

Fig. 1.7
The Properties window provides access to the features of a form or control.

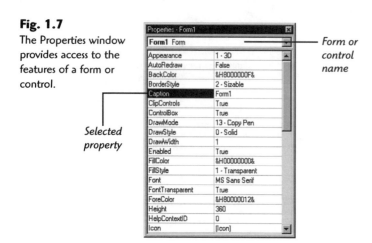

Form or control name

Selected property

How do I keep track of all the pieces?

The final piece of the desktop is the Project window. This window shows all the forms and code modules that are used in your program. Each program that you build in Visual Basic is known as a **project**. When you want to create a new program, you start a new project.

For many of your programs, you will have only a single form, and there will be only one entry in the Project window. For other programs, such as the VISDATA sample program, there are a number of forms and code **modules**. Figure 1.8 shows an example of a simple Project window and a more complex Project window.

Fig. 1.8
The Project window organizes all the pieces of your program. The first Project window contains a new project; the second Project window contains a project with many files.

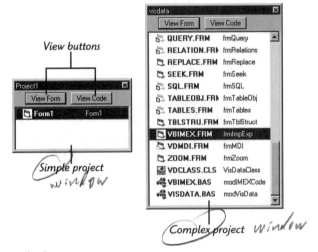

Plain English, please!

A **project** is a collection of all the pieces that make up your program, including the forms, the code modules, and any custom controls that you may be using.

You have probably heard the term "project" used in other contexts, such as the art project you worked on in school. What pieces did you need for that art project? A canvas, paints, brushes, and maybe a photo or model as your design. You probably kept all these pieces in a box or a locker so you could find all the pieces easily when you were ready to work on your masterpiece. A Visual Basic project works in much the same manner. The project file keeps track of the location of all the pieces of your program.

A **module** is a collection of pieces of code that are used by your program. This collection is stored in a separate file and may be used by more than one program.

By using a project file, Visual Basic protects you from having to remember where every piece is when you want to work on your program. You simply retrieve the project file, and Visual Basic handles the rest by loading all the form and module files, and adding any custom controls to the toolbox. And while this may not seem important for a program with only one form, it becomes vital for a large program. When you compile your program, a single executable file (.exe) is created for the project.

Q&A *Is the project file the only file stored by Visual Basic for my program?*

No. A project file only stores the location (the subdirectory or folder) of the other files that make up your program. The information that makes up a form is stored in a form file. This file contains information about the size of the form, its starting position on the screen, and the fonts that the form uses. The form data file also contains similar information about each user interface component on the form. The form data files are stored in text format so you can easily view the form information and the underlying code. The file extension for the form data file is FRM. You may also have FRX files if your forms contain any picture boxes or other graphics pieces.

To learn more about modules, please see Chapter 36, "When One Form Isn't Enough."

Your project may also contain a collection of functions and procedures stored in a module file. This file uses a BAS extension.

Q&A *Can the same file be used in more than one project?*

Most definitely, yes! If you have developed a form to get a person's name, address, and phone number, you can and should use it in any programs that require that information. You can use it both in your personal address book program and in a program for tracking church membership.

From the Project window, you can select a form with which to work. Then you can view the visual part of the form, with all the controls and properties, or you can view the code which is contained in the form. The Project window will also allow you to select a code module (if your program has one) and view the code contained in it. When you select a form or module to view, this allows you to edit the information contained in it.

You can select any form or module in the Project window by clicking it with the mouse. Once you select a form, you can view the form itself by choosing the View Form button at the top of the window. You can view the code in the selected form or module by choosing the View Code button. If you choose to view the code, you will be presented with the code editing window (see fig. 1.9).

The figure shows you the continuous code view, where all your procedures are shown in a scrolling window. You may also choose to only view one procedure at a time, as shown in figure 1.10. You can set the view you prefer by using the Environment Options dialog.

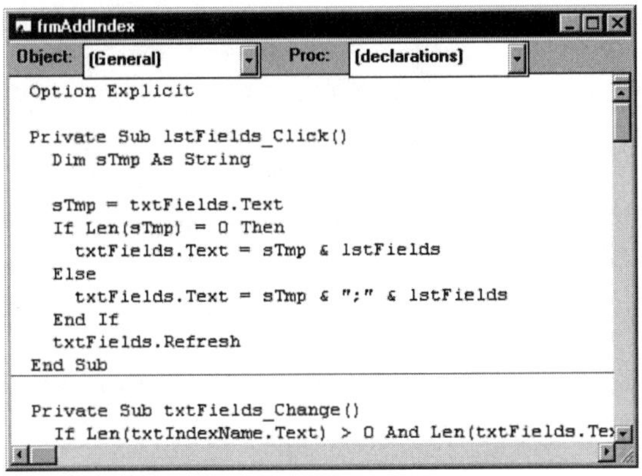

Fig. 1.9
The code editing window allows you to enter or change the code used by your program.

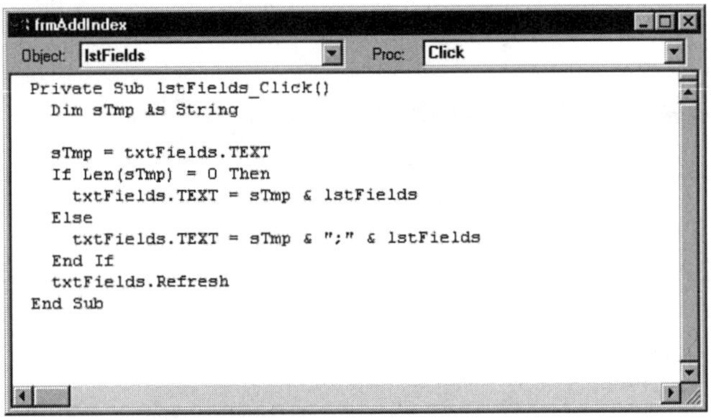

```
frmAddIndex                                    _□X
Object: (General)          Proc:  (declarations)
    Option Explicit

    Private Sub lstFields_Click()
       Dim sTmp As String

       sTmp = txtFields.Text
       If Len(sTmp) = 0 Then
          txtFields.Text = sTmp & lstFields
       Else
          txtFields.Text = sTmp & ";" & lstFields
       End If
       txtFields.Refresh
    End Sub

    Private Sub txtFields_Change()
       If Len(txtIndexName.Text) > 0 And Len(txtFields.Te
```

Fig. 1.10
You can also choose to view procedures one at a time.

```
frmAddIndex                                    _□X
Object: lstFields          Proc:  Click
    Private Sub lstFields_Click()
       Dim sTmp As String

       sTmp = txtFields.TEXT
       If Len(sTmp) = 0 Then
          txtFields.TEXT = sTmp & lstFields
       Else
          txtFields.TEXT = sTmp & ";" & lstFields
       End If
       txtFields.Refresh
    End Sub
```

TIP **Double-clicking a form name will perform the same function as** the View Form button.

New project or old, the file menu is the place to start

When you want to work on a project, you can either start a new project or work on an existing one. When you first start Visual Basic, a new project is opened. This project contains one form which is the starting point of your program.

You can also start a new project from within Visual Basic by selecting <u>N</u>ew Project from the <u>F</u>ile menu. If you have made any changes in the project on which you are currently working, Visual Basic will ask you if you want to save the changes to that project before opening a new one. When the new project is opened, your desktop will look just like it did when you started Visual Basic.

When you want to work on an existing project, you can open it from the Open Project dialog box shown in figure 1.11. You can access this dialog by selecting <u>O</u>pen Project from the <u>F</u>ile menu, choosing the Open button on the toolbar, or pressing Ctrl+O. All three methods work the same. The Open Project dialog box lets you change disk drives and/or directories to find your project file.

 TIP **All project files have a file extension of VBP. This extension is the** default in the File Open dialog box.

Directory selection

File selection

Fig. 1.11
The Open Project dialog box allows you to search your disk drives for your project file.

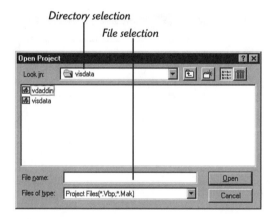

 TIP **Your four most recently used projects (the latest ones you worked** on) can be selected directly from the File menu.

Save your project so you don't lose your stuff

When you have finished working on a project, you will need to save it. You can save your work by selecting <u>S</u>ave Project from the <u>F</u>ile menu or by choosing the Save button on the toolbar. When you tell Visual Basic to save your project, it will save the changes to each of the form and module files that you modified since the last save. It will also save the project file if it has been changed. For any new file that you created, Visual Basic will present you with the Save File dialog box where you can specify the location of the file and the name you want to use for it (see fig. 1.12).

Fig. 1.12

Tell the computer where to put your files with the Save File dialog box.

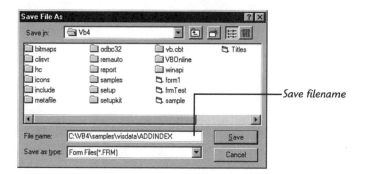

Save filename

CAUTION **Make sure you are putting your files where you want them. The** default directory for the Save File dialog box may be the VB subdirectory.

When you save a new project for the first time, you will be presented with the Save File dialog box once for each form and module in the project, and once for the project file itself.

Summary

As I stated in the beginning of the chapter, Visual Basic provides an easy way to develop Windows programs. Its ease of use is due in great part to the way the Visual Basic desktop works. As you work on developing programs, you will find that the desktop provides a number of shortcuts to get your work done faster. I will try to point out many of these shortcuts during the course of this book.

Review questions

1 What are shortcut keys?

2 How can you find the relative position and size of a control?

3 Where are the Visual Basic controls located?

4 What is the quickest way to re-open the project you last used?

2

It All Begins with Designing Your Program

● **In this chapter:**

- **Building your plan from the ground up**

- **What goes into the program and what comes out?**

- **Gotta have a plan**

- **What should I include on my program's screens?**

Building a good program begins with a good design. Trying to build a program without a good design is like trying to build a house without a blueprint. . . . . ❯

To most people, a computer program comes in a box from the store. They load the disks, read the documentation (some people do this, don't they?), and get to work. You, however, have decided that what you can buy off the shelf doesn't fit your needs, is too hard to use, is too expensive, or all of the above. So you decide to create your own program.

Building the perfect beast

Building a computer program is like building a house; except in building a program, you are the architect, carpenter, plumber, and electrician. Like building a house, to successfully build a computer program, there are several things you must do:

- Decide what the program should do and how it will do its job.

- Design the appearance of the program.

- Gather the materials to build the program.

- Create the pieces of the program.

- Put the pieces together.

- Test the program.

- Fix any problems.

- Write the documentation.

If this list appears daunting, don't worry, it isn't. This book is devoted to making these tasks as easy as possible for you. And just to reassure you that some of it is easy, let's deal with one of the items quickly—gathering the materials.

For information about custom controls and other resources, see Chapter 37, "The Search for More Help Continues."

For many of the programs you will create, you have already gathered all the materials you need. You have a copy of Visual Basic loaded on your machine, and you have a copy of this book within easy reach. You can do a lot with these tools. On some occasions, you will need specialized tools for particular tasks. I will even help you find those. (Now that wasn't so bad, was it?)

How do I decide what I want my program to do?

The first step in creating a program is to decide what you want it to do. Obviously, if you have decided to create a program, you have a need that must be filled. Perhaps you need a specialized data entry system to handle telephone surveys, or you need a sophisticated model to calculate the distribution of airborne pollutants. You may just want a simple database to keep up with your Christmas card list. This need defines the task or goal of the program as a whole.

If your program will need to accomplish multiple tasks, you need to define each task that should be accomplished. Also, if one task depends upon the completion of another task, you need to establish the task order within your program. For example, when you calculate your taxes, you must determine your taxable income before you can find out how much you owe.

Start with a plan

The next part of designing your program is to create a plan for how the program will do what you want. A plan is simply a method for achieving a goal. You create plans for a wedding, plans for your vacation, and plans for your retirement. For example, if you were taking a cross-country trip going from New York to Los Angeles, you would make plans for where and when you would stop for the night, how often you need to stop for gas, and so on. The plan covers the details of how you will get things done.

Creating a computer program requires a plan, too. For a simple program, the plan can be quite short, explaining briefly what information goes in, what calculations are performed, and what information comes out. You can even put this information in the form of a chart, as shown in figure 2.1. Complex programs, such as a payroll program, require a much more detailed plan.

Fig. 2.1
A simple flowchart can serve as your design plan for a simple program, and can help with the plan for a complex program.

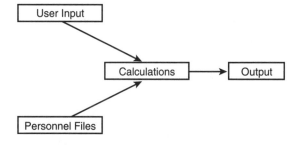

So what should be included in your plan? Your plan for a computer program should include the description of the problem to be solved or the job to be performed. The plan should also be able to answer the following questions:

- Who will be using the program?

- What information will need to be input into the program?

- What results should the program output?

- What information will the program store, and how will it store that information?

- How will the program handle errors?

Let's briefly look at each of these questions. First, you need to have some idea of who the users of the program will be. A program designed for a novice computer user will tend to have a different interface than one designed for a power user. For one thing, you will need to include more instructions for the novice user, possibly in the form of additional prompts, or through the use of **cue cards** and **wizards**.

 Plain English, please!

A **cue card** is a small window that stays on top of your application. This window contains step-by-step instructions for accomplishing a given task. Some word processors use cue cards to tell you how to do a mail merge, for example.

A **wizard** is actually a small program that automates a task for you. To accomplish the task, you run the wizard and respond to the prompts issued by the program. Visual Basic uses a wizard to help you with the creation of distribution disks for your program. Some spreadsheets and other programs that create charts include a chart wizard to help you with that task.

What about input and output? The **input** of the program includes data that will be entered by the user, data that resides in data files, and data from other programs. The input may also include options that the user may set to control a particular part of the program, such as whether a long or short report should be printed. You not only need to know what the inputs are, but also where they will come from.

The **output** of the program is the results, usually in the form of information on the screen, a printed report, or a data file. You need to know what the output will include and in what form the user expects it.

 Plain English, please!

Input is any information that is entered by the user for a program to do its work. If you developed a program to add any two numbers, the numbers entered by the user are the inputs to the program.

Output is, in essence, the answers that the program provides. This can be a single word or number or a 100-page report, depending on the purpose for which the program was designed.

File handling will be discussed in Chapter 27, "Storing Your Information in Files," and Chapter 28, "Creating a Database."

Handling and preventing user errors will be covered in Chapter 35, "Error Handling: Anticipating Mistakes That Users Will Make."

You also need to decide if your program will store information in files. If so, how many files? And what type of files will you need? Programs that store a small amount of data may only require the use of text files. Other programs that create a large amount of data that is shared with other programs and users may need the power of a database management system.

Finally, you need to decide how to handle errors that come up in your program. These are not the errors that you make while you develop the program, but errors that the user might make—such as trying to write a file to a floppy disk but forgetting to put one in the floppy drive, or trying to read from a file that does not exist.

How do I develop a plan?

If you are creating a program for yourself, you probably just need to sit down for a few minutes and think about the program. What do you know that is necessary to solve the problem, and where is this information located? The answer to this question will provide the input to the program.

The output of the program will be determined by what question you want the program to answer. For example, if you ask yourself, "How much money did I spend last year?" the answer would depend on whether you wanted a total for the year, totals by month, totals by expense category, or other information. Also, would you want numerical answers, or would you prefer a graph? Figure 2.2 shows some of the different outputs that could be used to answer the question.

Fig. 2.2

Depending on the question you want answered, the output of your program can come in many forms.

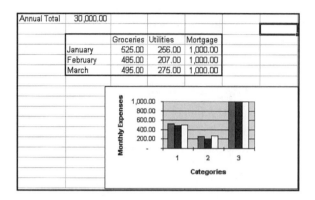

If you are creating a program for someone else, the best way to develop the program plan is by talking to them. Find out if they have any existing reports or other information you can use to get a better idea of their tasks. You will also need to find out how information will be entered into the program. Do they have it in data files already and, if so, what form are they in?

No matter who the program is for, or how simple the program is, write down the information that you gather during the design phase. This way, you will always be able to refer back to the information to make sure you haven't omitted anything.

Why is a plan important?

A plan provides information that you can refer to throughout the programming process to make sure that you are accomplishing what you intended. Trying to build a program without a good design is like trying to build a house without a blueprint. If you don't have a blueprint, your windows and doors will be in the wrong place, your roof may leak, and your electrical system may not work.

If you are developing a program for someone else, the plan provides a way of agreeing on exactly what the program will do and how it will do its job. This helps to eliminate any misunderstandings between the programmer and the client.

A good written plan can also provide milestones for the expected completion of different phases of the programming project. This helps make sure that you stay on schedule and deliver your program when it is expected.

Putting your ideas on the screen

The user interface is often what distinguishes a great program from a good program. The reason is that people expect a program to do a job and to do it right. Both Word and WordPerfect will create great letters and reports, right? What sets them apart from each other is the user interface.

For the programs you write, you want the user interface to provide all the necessary information without being cluttered. You also want commonly performed tasks to be easy to find, such as a Save button to save a file. Also, make sure you provide a sufficient work area for your users to perform their tasks. A word processor that can only show two lines at a time is not very useful. Take a look at several of the programs you use, and see which features of the user interface you like best. You can reproduce most of these features in your program using Visual Basic.

Common interface pieces

While your user interface may differ from other Windows programs, there are some things that it needs to have in common with them as well. These days, users rarely read the "getting started" sections of manuals. They want to get right to work. If your interface has some common elements with other Windows programs, the users will be able to start using the program almost immediately.

Some of these common elements are:

Creating a menu is covered in Chapter 13, "Enhance Your Program with Custom Menus."

- The File menu, where you can open, save, and close files. The program's Exit function is also expected here.

- The Edit menu, where the cut, copy, paste, and clear operations reside.

- The Help menu, where the user can look when they get lost.

Creating a toolbar is discussed in Chapter 7, "Adding Pictures to Convey More Information."

- A toolbar, where picture buttons are used as shortcuts to common tasks.

If you take a look at any major Windows software package, you will see how these common elements are used to make it easy for the user to work with multiple programs.

Interfaces in an instant

While you probably can't create a good interface quite that quickly, Visual Basic does make it easy for you to design your user interface. You can quickly and easily add controls and a menu to the screen. You can move things around, try out different controls, and in general, play with the interface until you get it the way you want. Then, once you have the interface design set, you can make the rest of the program work.

This is particularly useful when developing a program for another person. You can sit down with the user and show different screen design concepts. You can then get feedback from the user and quickly make changes in response to the comments. This process is known as **prototyping**.

How can I use this in the real world?

Prototyping can be very valuable in getting your programming project off to a good start. A club membership application I developed required the ability to keep track of each members' personal information, as well as when they visited the club and what services they used. After the initial meeting with the client, several screens were quickly developed to show the flow of information and how data would be entered. These were shown to the client the day after the initial meeting.

For one of the screens, the member check-in screen, the client's first response was "We don't do it that way!" This generated further discussion on the best way to accomplish the task. Had rapid prototyping not been available, this problem would not have surfaced until much later and would have required changing a lot of code to fix it. The instant feedback of the prototyping probably saved a week's worth of work.

Telling others how it works

One of the points mentioned in the program development process was writing the program documentation. This is one of the most important and yet often-neglected parts of creating a program. The documentation is important so that you can communicate to others all the wonderful benefits and features of your program. It is also essential to being able to maintain your program and add features to it later. Take it from someone who knows; without the documentation, you will end up spending a lot of time going back over your code trying to determine what you did and why you did it that way.

While the documentation is the last bullet in the list in the section "Building the perfect beast," it should by no means be saved until all other programming tasks are completed. You should be writing your documentation throughout the programming process. As you create a feature, just write down a few notes about what it does and how to use it. To help yourself maintain your code in the future, include plenty of **comment lines** in your code.

 Plain English, please!

A **comment line** is a line in your program that does not perform any function, but is there to tell you what is going on at a particular point. A comment line starts with the single quote (`'`) and can be placed just about anywhere in your code. 99

The rest of the creation process

So far, we have covered the first three items in the program development process. The rest of the items will be covered in other parts of the book. Much of the book deals with creating the pieces of a program, from the parts of the user interface to the actual calculations, as well as how the pieces fit together. As for testing your program and fixing any problems, Chapter 34, "Finding Bugs in Your Programs," discusses these topics at length.

Summary

Design plans are important. They help keep you on track toward creating a program that works well and makes things easy on the user. Some time spent developing a good initial design will save you a lot of time later in the programming process.

Review questions

1 What are the steps in the program development cycle?

2 Why should you develop a design plan?

3 What common user interface pieces should you include in most of your programs?

Exercises

1 Create a design plan for a mailing list program.

2 What information would you need for the club membership program discussed in the "How can I use this in the real world?" section?

3 Design a program for a medical office where a receptionist would enter appointment information and a doctor would enter medical history and notes.

3

Time to Build Your First Program!

● **In this chapter:**

- **What goes where on the form?**

- **How does a user enter information for a program?**

- **The answer is right in front of you**

- **Telling the program what to do**

Unlike what you might imagine, designing a program in Visual Basic that allows user input is as easy as the click of a button . . . . ➤

C hapter 2, "It All Begins with Designing Your Program," discussed the main steps of program design. The first of these steps was to define the task that you want the program to perform. Next you needed to define the input to the program and the output you wanted from the program.

Define what you want your program to do

For your first program, you are going to develop a specialized calculator that will tell you the monthly payment on a loan. The loan calculation program will need to perform three tasks:

- Get information about the loan amount, term, and interest rate

- Calculate the monthly payment

- Display the monthly payment to the user

In developing this program, you will need to use several Visual Basic controls. You will need controls to accept input, a control to display output, and a control to tell the program to run the calculation. As you develop this application, you will learn more about what controls are and how they work. You will also learn concepts that will be used in every program you will write.

The basic set of controls that you see when you start Visual Basic is shown in figure 3.1. This set of controls is the Visual Basic toolbox.

Fig. 3.1
Controls in the toolbox
provide the basic
building blocks for all
your programs.

Data input—food for your program

The first thing needed in the program is a way for the user to enter information. While there are numerous ways to obtain user input (you will look at a number of these through the course of the book), the main workhorse for getting information is the **TextBox control**.

If you have ever filled out a form, such as a job or credit card application, you have used the pencil and paper equivalent of a text box's input functions. On a job application, for example, there are blank spaces for you to enter information such as your name, your date of birth, and the number of years you attended school. Each of these blanks could be a text box on a computerized form.

A TextBox control provides two functions—it displays information and it accepts user input. Without something like a TextBox control, displaying a piece of information on the screen would be quite complicated. Your program would have to determine where to position the information on the screen, determine the size of the display area, and then print the information to the desired spot. With a TextBox control, you just tell the control what to display, and it does the rest. If you don't like where the information was displayed, you simply move your text box. No coding is required. Similarly, if you don't like the appearance of the text box, you can easily change the text font or the colors.

Accepting user input works the same way. The TextBox control handles all the hard tasks for you, such as the following:

- Getting the character keystroke
- Placing the appropriate character in the display
- Handling cursor movement, delete, and backspace key functions
- Handling text insertion or overstrike functions
- Storing the information in memory

Connect the dots...

The first step in using a text box is to select it from the toolbox and draw it on the form. You select any control by clicking it in the toolbox. The selected control will be shown in the toolbox as a depressed button.

As you can see, drawing a text box, or any other control, on a form is like drawing objects with the Windows Paintbrush program.

After you have selected the TextBox control, move your mouse back over to the form. You will notice that the mouse cursor has changed from an arrow to a cross. This indicates that you are in the drawing mode. To draw a control, follow these steps:

1 Place the mouse cursor at the first corner of the area where you want the control.

2 Press and hold the left mouse button.

3 Drag the mouse to the opposite corner of the area where you want the control. You will notice that a "rubber band" box is shown as you drag the mouse. This rubber band box shows you the area that the control will occupy. This area may be a single line or multiple lines (see fig. 3.2).

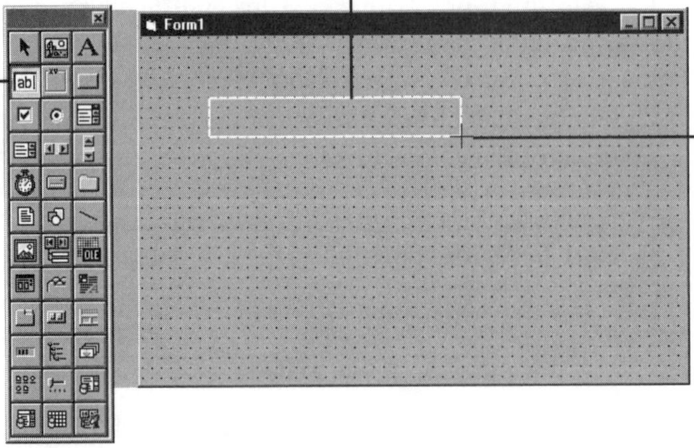

Fig. 3.2
You can create any size text box. Just stretch the rubber band to the desired size.

Selected control (TextBox)

"rubber band"

Cross cursor

4 Release the mouse button. The control will be drawn in the size and location that you specified with the drawing operation (see fig. 3.3).

Fig. 3.3
Once drawn on the form, the text box is ready for user input.

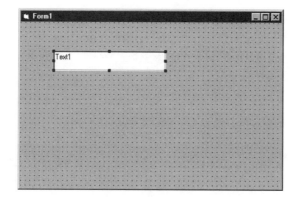

Can I name my text box George?

After you create the text box on your form, you need to assign it a name. The name is what your program uses to identify which text box it is working with at any given time. Without the name, the program cannot communicate with the control. The name for a text box works like the license plate for your car. While there may be a number of cars that look like yours, none of them will have the same license plate as yours. By the same token, while several text boxes may look alike and even contain the same information, each is identified by a unique name.

Just in case you forget to assign a name to a text box, Visual Basic initially assigns one for you. For the first text box on the form, this default name is Text1. For the second text box, the name is Text2, and so on. You could just use the default name, but it is good programming practice to give the text box a name with some meaning to you. This will make it easier to maintain your program when you need to make the inevitable changes. For instance, if part of your program gets a person's first and last names and middle initial in three separate text boxes, it is easier to remember which text box is which if they are named txtLname, txtFname, and txtMid rather than Text1, Text2, and Text3.

TIP   **You will notice that the names I assigned all had the prefix txt.**
A good programming practice is to use prefixes to identify what the controls are. In another program, I might use labels to display the information, in which case I would call them lblLname, lblFname, and lblMid.

Using the prefix to identify the control will help you keep track of what can be done with the control, as each control has different functionality. You will find a list of the suggested prefixes for many of the Visual Basic controls in table 3.1.

Table 3.1 Identifying Prefix for the Control Type

Control Type	Prefix
CheckBox	chk
ComboBox	cbo
Command Button	cmd
Common Dialog	cdl
Data	dat
Data Bound ComboBox	dbc
Data Bound ListBox	dbl
Directory ListBox	dir
Drive ListBox	drv
File ListBox	fil
Frame	fra
Grid	grd
Horizontal ScrollBar	hsb
Image	img
Label	lbl
Line	lin
ListBox	lst
Menu	mnu
OLE Container	ole
Option Button	opt

Control Type	Prefix
Picture Box	pic
Shape	shp
TextBox	txt
Timer	tmr
Vertical ScrollBar	vsb

The name of an object is one of its **properties**. An object's properties control its look and its functionality.

 Plain English, please!

Properties of a control help define the appearance of the control. This is like describing your car. How would you describe your car? Two-door, bright red, convertible sports car with gray leather interior? (Aren't you lucky?) Each part of the description tells you something about the car's appearance, such as the number of doors, the color of the paint, the color of the interior, and the type of roof.

In the same manner, properties such as Font, Forecolor, and Backcolor tell you something about the appearance of the control. Other properties (such as Top, Left, Height, and Width) tell you about the size and position of the control on the form.

To assign a name other than the default to the text box, you will need to change the Name property of the text box. To do this, make sure the text box is selected on the form, and then press the F4 key to access the Properties dialog box as shown in figure 3.4. Select the Name property, and then type in the name you want to use for the control. For the example we are creating, enter the name **txtPrincipal**.

 TIP   **You can go directly to the Name property of an object by** pressing Ctrl+Shift+N.

Fig. 3.4
The Properties dialog
box allows you to
change the name of
the text box, as well as
other attributes of the
control.

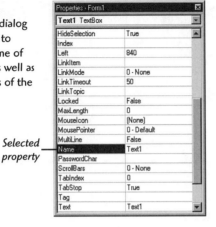

Selected
property

 TIP **You can also get to the Properties dialog box using the mouse, if**
you prefer. You can either click the dialog box itself, or click the Properties
button on the toolbar. The advantage of using the F4 key is that it will take
you directly to the Properties dialog even if it is covered up by another
window.

To get to a specific property, hold down the Ctrl and Shift keys and press
the first letter in the property name.

Q&A *Are there any restrictions or requirements when*
assigning names?

There are three restrictions that must be followed when naming controls:

- The name must begin with a letter.

- The name can only contain letters, numbers, or the underscore (_)
  character—nothing else.

- The name can only be up to 40 characters in length.

I want my data

Obviously, if you want to use the information that a user enters in a text
box, you have to have a way to call up the information. The information in a
text box is stored in the Text property. To reference the information, you
need to specify both the name of the text box and the Text property using
dot notation.

❝ *Plain English, please!*

Dot notation is a means of identifying the control whose property you want to change or retrieve as well as the name of the specific property. Since each text box has a Text property, you must identify the control as well. In your code, the control name and property name are separated by a period, or "dot."

If the control you want to change is on a different form, you will also need to specify the form name. The form name is separated from the control name by the ! operator. ❞

For example, the following line would retrieve the Text property of the txtLastName text box on the frmMember form:

```
lname = frmMember!txtLastName.Text
```

In addition to being able to retrieve the value of a property, you can also change the value of one or more properties of a control from within your program. This is done using an assignment statement in the program. The syntax for an assignment statement is:

```
formname!controlname.propertyname = value
```

Many of the properties of controls can be changed in this manner. A few properties, such as the Name property, can only be changed in the design mode. They cannot be changed by an assignment statement. For a complete list of the available properties of a control, you should refer to the Visual Basic help topic for the control.

The following example shows how to change the Text property of the txtPrincipal text box previously created:

```
txtPrincipal.Text = 100000
```

Speaking of dot notation

Using the dot notation, the property of a control is specified as follows:

```
formname!controlname.propertyname
```

In using this notation, you must specify the controlname and the propertyname. The formname may be omitted; however, if you do not include the formname, the current form is assumed. Usually, you will assign the value of the property to a variable for further processing, or pass the value to a function.

Catch the bug

What is wrong with the following assignment:

```
txtPrincipal.Text 1000
```

Answer: *When assigning a value, you must include the equal sign (=) as follows:*

```
txtPrincipal.Text = 1000
```

For more on the use of variables, see Chapter 17, "Adding Variables to Your Programs."

To learn about functions, refer to Chapter 26, "Basic Building Blocks: Procedures and Functions."

Bet you can't draw just one

Now that we've gone through the details of setting up one text box, I'll let you set up the rest of the ones needed for the loan payment calculator on your own. (Don't panic, I'll give you some guidance.)

You will need to draw three additional text boxes using the method described previously. As you draw each box, give it a name as follows: txtTerm for the first one, txtRate for the next, and txtPayment for the last one. When you are through, your form should look something like the one in figure 3.5.

Fig. 3.5
You need one text box for each input variable in the loan calculation.

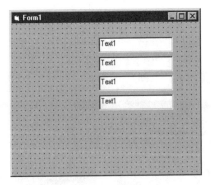

Bad location? Controls can move

What? You say your form doesn't look anything like figure 3.5? If you're like me, when you drew those four text boxes, they weren't all quite the same size and they weren't lined up very well. This is not a problem. With Visual

Basic's design environment, it is easy to change the size or location of a control.

To change a control's size, select the control on the form by clicking it with the mouse. You will see stretch points appear on each side and at each corner of the control (see fig. 3.6). If you place the mouse cursor on one of these points, the cursor will change to a double-headed arrow. Now press and hold the left mouse button, and drag the mouse to change the size of the control. This works exactly the same way as stretching a window in Program Manager or other Windows programs.

Fig. 3.6
The currently selected control has eight points around it which allow you to resize the control.

Stretch points

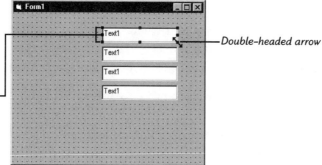

Double-headed arrow

If you are more comfortable using the keyboard, you can *resize* a control by holding down the Shift key and pressing the appropriate arrow key. To *move* a control, hold down the Ctrl key and use the arrow keys. Also, using the keyboard may be easier than using the mouse to make minute adjustments.

If you want to move the control with the mouse, click the mouse pointer somewhere on the control (anywhere but one of the stretch points) and drag the control to its new position while holding down the mouse button.

CAUTION If you have multiple controls on your form (which you will for most programs), you will need to be careful about placing the control you are moving on top of any others. If you cover up one control with another, the user can't get to the underlying control and your program may not work correctly.

If you want, you can also remove a control from the form completely. To delete the control from your form, just click the control to select it, and then press the Delete key. The control will disappear from your form.

What if I delete a control by mistake?

Visual Basic will allow you to perform an "Undelete" immediately after you have deleted a control. This will recover the control that you deleted. However, this will only work if you haven't done anything else since you deleted the control. The easiest way to do this is to press the Ctrl+Z hot key combination.

Identify the inputs? How?

You identify the input with label controls. After you have created the text boxes where the user can enter data, you also need to place information on the screen that tells the user what information to enter in each box. The easiest way to do this is to place a label control next to each text box. The Label control can contain a description of the data to be entered.

In many respects, a Label control is very similar to a text box. It can contain letters, numbers, or dates. It can contain a single word or an entire paragraph. Figure 3.7 contains several Label controls that illustrate the diversity of appearances that can be achieved. Using the earlier analogy of a job application, the labels are like the words printed on the form to tell you where to write your name or other information.

The key difference between a Label control and a text box is that a Label control can't be edited by the user. Also, the Label control does not have a Text property. Instead, the information you see in the Label control is stored in the Caption property.

To add a Label control to your program, follow these steps:

1 Select the Label control from the toolbox.

2 Draw the Label control on the form near the top text box.

3 Change the Name property of the label to lblPrincipal.

4 Change the Caption property to Amount of Loan.

By adding this label, you have now made the program easier to use by telling the users where to enter the amount of the loan. As with the text boxes for the program, I will let you create the rest of the labels. You will need to create one for each of the other text boxes. Table 3.2 lists the recommended Name and Caption property settings. When you have finished, your form should resemble figure 3.8.

Fig. 3.7
The *Alignment* property controls the position of the text in a Label control.

Label control

Three different labels

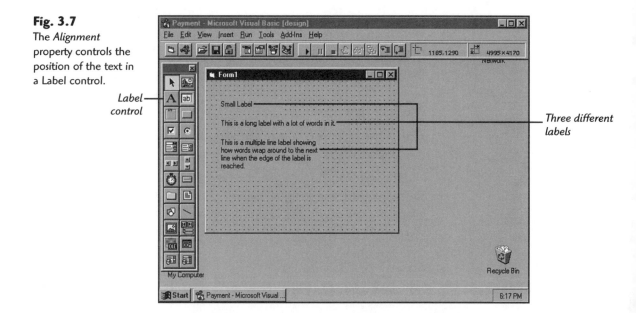

Table 3.2　Labels to Identify the Input

Label Name	Caption
lblTerm	Length of Loan (Years)
lblRate	Interest Rate (%)
lblPayment	Monthly Payment

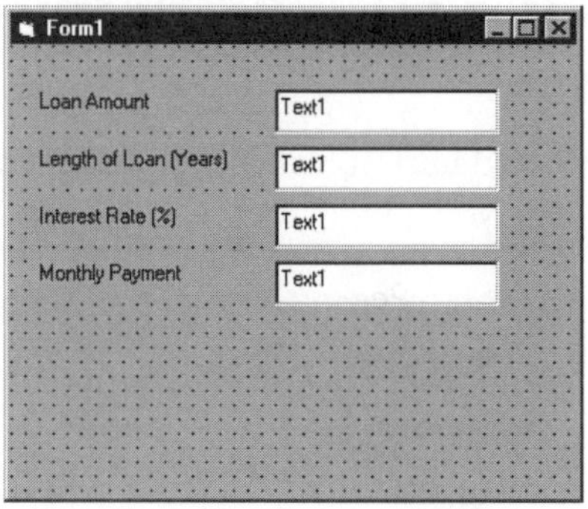

Fig. 3.8
Labels on the loan payment calculator tell the user what to enter.

When I entered the information in the Caption ***property, all of it did not show up on the form. Why?***

The information you entered is in the Caption property, but the Label control is not large enough to display all of it. Just resize the control until your entire text appears.

Can I set a label's Caption ***property only from the Properties dialog?***

No. The Caption property, like the Text property of the text box, can also be set from your program using an assignment statement. In fact, many programmers use the Label control to display calculation results since the user cannot change them.

Is it running, or sitting on idle?

If you ran our program now, you would see a form with labels and text boxes on it. You could enter anything you wanted in the text boxes, but that would be as far as you could go. You haven't told the program to do anything else.

So how do you make the program do something useful? You add Visual Basic code to your program and provide a means for the user to activate the code. This is often done using a command button. The command button is the main way of telling the program to do something. The command button is sort of the programming equivalent of the ignition switch in your car.

I want to add a command button to the form

To make use of a command button, you will first need to add it to the form. You do this the same way you added the text boxes and labels:

1 Select the command button control from the toolbox.

2 Click and drag the mouse on the form to define the area that the command button should occupy.

3 Release the mouse button to draw the command button.

As you did for the text box, you need to assign a unique name to the command button. Again, press F4 to display the Properties dialog, select the `Name` property, and enter the name `cmdCalcPayment`. This name will be used in the program to reference the command button.

The command button, like the Label control, also has a `Caption` property. When you created the command button, you probably noticed that the word `Command1` showed up on the command button. This text is the default value of the `Caption` property for the command button. I recommend changing this to something more meaningful, so select the `Caption` property and enter **Calculate Loan Payment**. Your screen should now look like the one in figure 3.9.

Fig. 3.9
Adding a command button allows the user to initiate program actions.

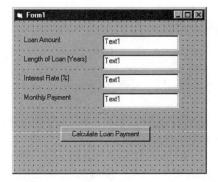

Run, command button, run

Now you have a command button on the form, but you still haven't told it to do anything; that is, you haven't told the program what action to take. To make the command button perform an action when it is clicked, you need to add code to the `Click` **event** of the button. To add code, double-click the command button. This will bring up the code entry window as shown in figure 3.10.

TIP If you prefer using keys instead of the mouse, pressing F7 will also bring up the code entry window.

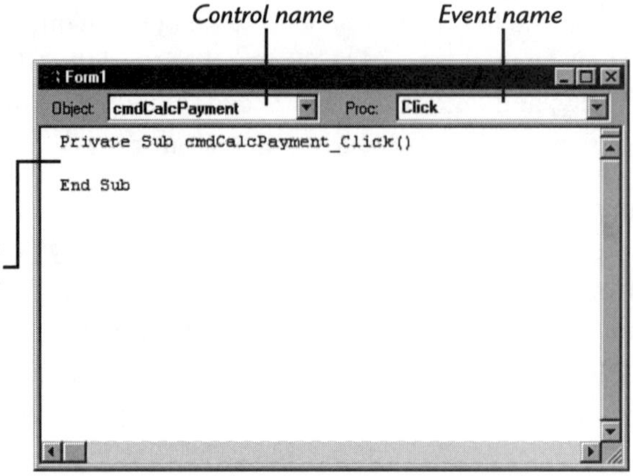

Control name   Event name

Fig. 3.10
The code entry window
allows you to enter
code to respond to
various events.

Input code
here

```
Private Sub cmdCalcPayment_Click()

End Sub
```

❝ ❝ *Plain English, please!*

In Visual Basic programming, an **event** is an action to which the program
can respond. Examples of events are a user clicking a button, the value of
a control changing, or a specified amount of time elapsing. ❞ ❞

There are two types of events that can occur. One is a user-initiated event.
This is like pressing a button on your radio. When you press a channel
button, you initiate a "program" which changes the radio station. The other
type of event is an environmental event. This is similar to the operation of
the thermostat in your home. When the temperature drops below a certain
point, a program is initiated which starts the heater.

For your programs, each control has been set up to recognize certain types
of events. Some controls can respond to mouse clicks and double-clicks.
Other controls can respond to changes in their values. If you want the
control in your program to respond to a specific event, you must place code
in the event procedure for that control. Otherwise, your program will ignore
the event. In other words, if you want your program to change radio sta-
tions, per se, you must tell it how to do so.

When you first open the code window, you will see two lines of code separated by a blank line, illustrated as follows:

```
Private Sub cmdCalcPayment_Click()

End Sub
```

To learn more about procedures, see Chapter 26, "Basic Building Blocks: Procedures and Functions."

The first line of code defines the beginning of the procedure that will be used for the `Click` event of your command button. Notice that the procedure name, `cmdCalcPayment_Click`, contains both the name of the command button and the name of the event. The last line of code defines the end of the procedure. Between these two lines is where you place the code you want run when the user clicks the command button.

Find out if you can afford the loan

You will use the following code to calculate the loan payment based on the information entered by the user:

```
intrate = txtRate.Text / 1200#
nmonths = txtTerm.Text * 12
fctr1 = (1 + intrate) ^ nmonths
clcpay = txtPrincipal.Text * ((intrate * fctr1) /
(fctr1 - 1))
txtPayment.Text = Int(clcpay * 100) / 100
```

The first line of code gets the annual percentage interest rate from the `txtRate` text box and converts it into a fractional monthly rate. This value is stored in the variable `intrate`. The second line gets the number of years of the loan from the `txtTerm` text box and converts it to months. This value is stored in the variable `nmonths`. These two lines of code set up the values of the variables you need for the calculation.

The next two lines of code perform the actual calculation. The math operations used in these two lines will be discussed in detail in Chapter 18, "Power Up Your Visual Basic Programs with Some Basic Math."

The final line of the code performs a round-off calculation, then assigns the result to the `txtPayment` text box. The assignment statement is what allows the result to be displayed in the text box.

TIP **When you are entering code, type everything except variable** names in lowercase letters. Then, when you move to the next line, Visual Basic will automatically change your code to reflect the proper capitalization of command and property names. This provides an indication that you entered the code using the correct syntax.

Catch the bug

The following code will not display the payment. Why?

```
intrate = txtRate.Text / 1200#
nmonths = txtTerm.Text * 12
fctr1 = (1 + intrate) ^ nmonths
clcpay = txtPrincipal.Text * ((intrate * fctr1) /
(fctr1 - 1))
```

Answer: *The problem is that the results were never assigned to the* txtPayment *text box as follows:*

```
txtPrincipal.Text = clcpay
```

How do I run the program?

Now that all the controls have been placed on the form and the calculation code has been entered, it is time to run the program. You can run the program by pressing the F5 key (or you can select <u>S</u>tart from the <u>R</u>un menu). Once the program is running, you can enter values for the loan amount, term, and interest rate. Then, click the Calculate Loan Payment command button to see the results. If everything works correctly, entering the following values—amount=15000, term=5, rate=7—will calculate a payment of 297.01. Try running the calculation several times, using different values for the given variables.

When you are finished running calculations, you can click the Close box of the window to end the program. You can also choose <u>E</u>nd from the <u>R</u>un menu at the top of the screen.

Q&A ***How can I make the text box blank when the program first starts?***

Since the information shown in a text box is stored in the Text property, you can set it to anything you want while in the design mode (the mode in which Visual Basic starts). Whatever value you set will show up as the initial value of the control when the program is in run mode (when your program is running). To make it blank, select the Text property of the control, and erase whatever words appear there.

Don't forget to save your work!

When you have finished working on your program, you will want to save it so you can use it again. In fact, it is a good idea to save your work often in case of a power failure or other problem. Just as you would save a report or a spreadsheet, it is also good practice to save your program before you run it. This way if your program causes your system to crash, you won't lose all your changes.

 TIP **You can have Visual Basic automatically save your program before** you run it by selecting the File Save option in the Environment Options dialog box.

When Visual Basic saves a program, it saves each form in a separate file, saves any procedure files you may have, and saves a project file which identifies all the pieces of the program. For a large program, you could end up with quite a few files. For the loan calculator program, there are only two files, the form file and the project file.

To save your program, click the Save button on the Visual Basic toolbar. This will start the save process. The first time you save a program, Visual Basic will present you with a Save File As dialog box (see fig. 3.11). From this dialog, you can choose the drive and directory where your files will be saved, and you can give each file a name. Form files have an extension of FRM, while project files have an extension of VBP. The Save File As dialog box will be presented once for each file that needs to be saved.

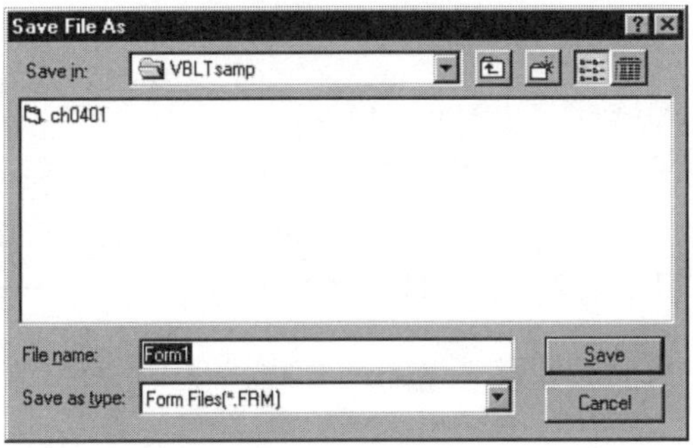

Fig. 3.11
The Save File As dialog box appears the first time a file is saved.

Save File As	? X
Save in: VBLTsamp	
ch0401	
File name: Form1	Save
Save as type: Form Files(*.FRM)	Cancel

After you save a program once, clicking the Save button will save all modified files in the project. You will only be presented with the Save File As dialog box if you have created any new files.

Summary

This chapter presented you with the basics of creating a program in Visual Basic. You learned how to prompt the user for input, get the input values, and use the input to perform a calculation. You have also seen how this was done with a minimum of programming (you only entered five lines of code).

The rest of the book will go into much more detail on the various aspects of programming and the capabilities of controls. As you can see, though, a lot can be done with only three types of controls.

Review questions

1 What are the two functions that a text box can perform?

2 Which property of the TextBox control stores the information entered by the user?

3 Why must each control have a unique name?

4 How are a Label control and a TextBox control similar? How are they different?

5 What type of statement sets the value of a control's property?

Exercises

1 Change the loan payment calculation program to display the output in a label instead of a text box.

2 Change the program to calculate the principal that can be borrowed for a given loan payment. The formula is:

```
Principal = Payment * (fctr1-1) / (intrate*fctr1).
```

Letting the User Enter Text

● **In this chapter:**

- **Psst. I want a single piece of information**

- **In twenty-five characters or less...**

- **Can I control what the user enters?**

- **I want to enter lots of text**

- **How can the user manipulate text?**

The text box is the most versatile data entry control available in Visual Basic—and one that you'll use in just about every program you design . . . . **>**

To learn how to manipulate text in your program, see Chapter 19, "Handling Strings of Data."

Most people use computers to do one of two things—well, three, if you count play games—process numbers (as in a spreadsheet) or work with words (as in a word processor). Therefore, it makes sense that a large portion of many of your programs will be devoted to getting and manipulating numbers and text (words). The manipulation part is left until later in the book. For now, let's just concentrate on how you can get the information from the user.

One line of text? No problem!

For help with handling numbers in your program, see Chapter 18, "Power Up Your Visual Basic Programs with Some Basic Math."

In Chapter 3, I said that the workhorse for getting text and numbers into the system was the TextBox control, and we used several text boxes to get the numbers for the loan payment calculator. A text box, though, is capable of much more than getting or displaying a single word or number. It can handle large amounts of information, such as sentences or paragraphs, or even entire book chapters. In fact, a text box can hold up to 64,000 characters of information. For comparison, the chapter you are now reading contains about 50,000 characters. Figure 4.1 shows a variety of text boxes that can be used to gather input.

Fig. 4.1
Text boxes can be used in a variety of ways to get information from a user.

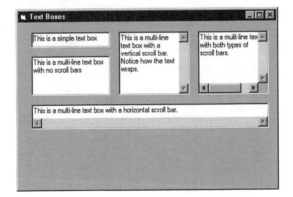

Q&A *I often see computer capacities referred to in bytes. How does that relate to a character?*

In Windows 3.1, if you are dealing with files that contain only text (i.e., letters, numbers, and punctuation marks), then characters and bytes are approximately the same. That is, if you create a file with a single letter in it, the file will be one byte long. In 32-bit environments (Windows 95 and Windows NT), each character will take up two bytes.

Words and short phrases

The simplest text box is used to get a single piece of information from the user—a word, a number, a date, even a single letter. To allow a user to enter this information, you just draw a single-line text box on the form and assign it a name (using the Name property). Then when the program is run, the user simply types the information in.

To demonstrate what you can do with the simple text box, let's draw three small ones on a form. Draw the text boxes so that they look like the one in figure 4.2, large enough to hold one or two small words. Then, run the program and try typing different things into the text boxes, such as your first name in the first text box, your date of birth in the next box, or how many years you went to school in the last box. You'll see that the text box can handle any of the information, and in fact, doesn't care what you type in it.

Fig. 4.2
You can make a text box any size you want.

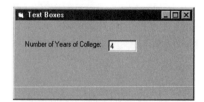

 TIP To draw several controls of the same type without having to reselect the control, hold down the Ctrl key when you select the control. This way, your cursor will remain in the drawing mode after you finish the first box. This allows you to draw additional boxes.

What happens at the end of the box?

If you typed enough information into this text box, you might have reached the end of the box and noticed that the text started scrolling out the left end of the box. Everything that you typed is still stored in the Text property of the text box, but you are only seeing the portion of it that can be contained in the box. This is like looking at the world with binoculars. Even though you can only see a small part of the total view, the rest of it is still out there. If you turn your head to the left or right, you will see another part of the view.

The text box works the same way. If you have a text box that will display 20 characters, you can type as much as you want. But you will only be able to look at 20 characters at a time—which 20 characters will depend on the position of your cursor. To look at the text beyond the edges of the box, you can use the cursor movement keys to move the cursor and therefore change the view.

TIP **Like many other programs, the right and left arrow keys will move** you one character at a time. Holding the Ctrl key and pressing the right or left arrow keys will move you one word at a time, while pressing the Home or End keys will move you to the beginning or end of the text, respectively.

Can a text box handle multiple lines of text?

If you have an application where your users will need to enter a lot of text in a single field, you probably don't want them to have to look at their information a few characters at a time. Fortunately, a text box is also capable of presenting a view of multiple lines of text at once.

Ahh, to create a masterpiece...

To allow a user to enter multiple lines of text, you need to do two things that are different from creating a simple text box. First, you need to draw a box that is large enough to show several lines of information. As an example, draw a text box on your form that is about half as tall as the form itself. (If you still have the text boxes on the screen from the previous section, select one of them and stretch it by clicking and dragging one of the stretch points, and then delete the other two text boxes.) When you are finished, your form should look like the one in figure 4.3.

Fig. 4.3
Use a big box for lots of text.

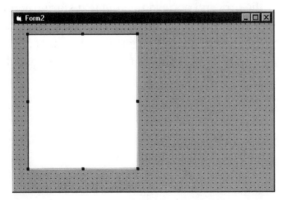

The other thing you need to do is tell Visual Basic that you want the text box to accept multiple lines of text. This is done by setting the text box's MultiLine property to True. To set the MultiLine property, switch to the Properties dialog box, and then select the MultiLine property (see fig. 4.4). At the right end of the property input area, you will see an arrow pointing down. Clicking this arrow will give you a choice of all the available values for the property—in this case, True or False. Select the True value. Now your text box can accept multiple lines.

How can I use this in the real world?

There are a number of reasons why you would want to be able to have the user enter more information than will fit on one line of text. For example, if you had a program that collected comments about the quality of restaurant service, you might have text entry areas for what people liked best and least about the restaurant.

Another example would be a patient information form for a doctor. When you see a doctor for the first time, you usually have to fill out a form on which you provide information such as your name, address, insurance company, any drug allergies, and a description of the problem. While this form usually gives you a small space for your name and address, there are usually several lines available for you to list your allergies and describe your symptoms. The following figure shows you what a patient information form might look like as part of a computer program.

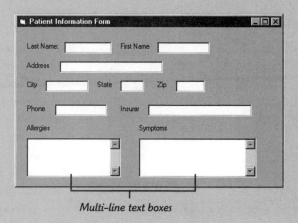

Multi-line text boxes

Fig. 4.4
Multiple text lines are
automatic with the
MultiLine property set
to *True*.

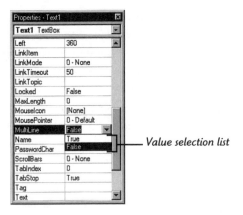

Value selection list

If you run your program now and try typing in some text, you will find that
as you get to the end of a line, the text automatically starts on the next line.
This is called **word wrapping**. If you type enough information that fills the
entire text box, you will see that the earliest information entered starts
scrolling out the top of the box. As with the single line text box, the information is still all there. You are just seeing only a portion of it.

Q&A *How does word wrapping affect my text?*

When the text box is set up for multiple lines of input, a new line is started
as the user's text reaches the end of a line. The new line always starts at the
beginning of a word; words are never split in the middle. If you increase
the size of the text box, it will hold more words on each line. While the
text box shows the information on multiple lines, no line breaks are
contained in the value of the Text property unless you press Enter to
insert a line break.

Scroll, scroll, scroll your box...

Once you have set up a text box for multiple lines, you can also add **scroll
bars** to it. Scroll bars provide you with two benefits. First, the position
button of the bar provides the user with a visual indication that there is
more text than is currently shown in the text box. Second, and more importantly, the scroll bar provides an easy way to move from one part of the text

to another. If you have ever used a word processor such as Microsoft Word, you are familiar with how scroll bars work. Scroll bars are also found in the Program Manager and File Manager when you have more stuff than will fit in the window.

 Plain English, please!

Scroll bars are the long, narrow boxes with arrows at each end, located at the right side or the bottom of the text box. The arrows, the button, and the bar are used with the mouse to move around the text box. The button also indicates the relative position of the cursor in the text box. Scroll bars can only be used in multi-line text boxes.

Catch the bug

If you wanted to write a Visual Basic program that produced the following output as shown in Image 1, which of the following properties are set incorrectly?

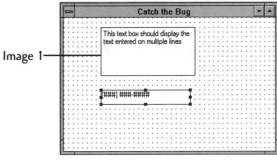

Image 1

- Alignment = 0-Left Justify
- MultiLine = False
- ScrollBars = 0-None

Answer: *The* MultiLine *property should be set to* True.

For those of you not familiar with scroll bars, here's a brief explanation. Clicking the mouse on the arrows at either end of the scroll bar will move you a small step in the direction of the arrow. For a vertical scroll bar, this small step is typically one line. Clicking the scroll bar between the position button and an arrow will move you a large step in the direction of the arrow. Finally, you can move to a specific position in the text box by clicking and dragging the position button. The position of the button in the scroll bar shows the percentage position in the text box. In other words, if the button is about halfway down the scroll bar, you are at about the middle of the text.

There are two types of scroll bars available for the text box—a horizontal scroll bar and a vertical scroll bar (see fig. 4.5). These bars are a part of the text box, and should not be confused with the scroll bar controls covered in Chapter 9.

Fig. 4.5
Scroll bars in a text box indicate that more text is available than is currently shown.

Click here for large steps

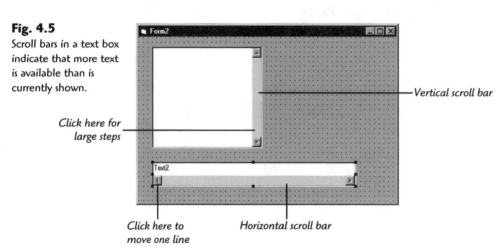

Vertical scroll bar

Click here to move one line

Horizontal scroll bar

Each of the two scroll bars works differently. The horizontal scroll bar does not support word wrapping. Any text you type will be displayed on a single line until you press Enter. Pressing Enter will start a new line of text. The scroll bar allows you to move left and right within the text box.

With the vertical scroll bar, word wrapping is supported, and the text is automatically shown in multiple lines within the text box. This control bar allows you to move up and down in the text box.

If you want, you can use both scroll bars together. When using both, word wrapping is not supported. For almost all situations, it is probably better to use the vertical scroll bar, as this will be more familiar to the users of your program.

To add a scroll bar to your text box, you must first make sure that the MultiLine property is set to True. Then, select the ScrollBars property, and click the down arrow at the right side of the entry field. This will provide you a selection list of None, Horizontal, Vertical, or Both as shown in figure 4.6. Choose the type of scroll you want from the list.

Fig. 4.6
Pick either or both types of scroll bars for your text box.

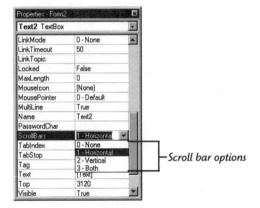

— *Scroll bar options*

Can I limit the amount of text that can be entered in a text box?

I have talked about how to handle a lot of text in a text box, but what about limiting the amount of information a user can enter? Well, a text box can handle this, too. The TextBox control includes the MaxLength property. The purpose of this property is to allow you to enter the maximum number of characters that the user will be allowed to enter.

For more on using database files in a program, see Chapter 29, "Accessing Databases."

Setting the maximum number of characters is quite easy. Just select the `MaxLength` property of the text box, and type in a number. If you want to allow the user an unlimited number of characters (the default setting), then enter zero (0) for the value.

TIP **The amount of text that can be entered in a text box is not truly** unlimited. If the `MaxLength` property *is* set to zero, the user can enter up to 32K of text. For any amount of text above 32K, you must enter the appropriate value in the `MaxLength` property. The absolute maximum amount of text that can be entered is 64K.

So what happens when the user is entering data and gets to the maximum number of characters? At that point, the text box stops accepting additional characters and beeps each time another character is typed. You can try this for yourself. Place a text box on a form, and set the `MaxLength` property to 10. Then run the program and start typing in the letters of the alphabet. You will see that *a* through *j* are accepted, but when you type *k*, the text box does not accept it. This occurs even if there appears to be plenty of additional space to the right of the text you entered.

How can I use this in the real world?

There are a number of reasons why you might want to limit the number of characters a user can enter. In many programs, you will be dealing with IDs that are a fixed length. For example, an inventory program might use part numbers that are 10 characters long, or a personnel information system might use a social security number, which is, by definition, nine characters long. Limiting the social security number text box to nine characters helps prevent the staff from accidentally creating a new account because a digit was entered twice.

Another need to limit the length of a text field comes in when connecting to database files. Most fields in a database file have a specific length. If you allow your user to enter more characters than can be stored in the field, information will be lost or an error may be generated.

Do I have to retype a whole line if I make a mistake? No way!

We have looked at how to create various types of text boxes, but how can users edit what they enter? Are they limited to just straight typing of information? Fortunately, no.

If you have used any Windows word processor, you are already familiar with how to edit the text in a text box. Just like a word processor, you can highlight text with the mouse or with the cursor keys. You can then cut, copy, or paste text using the shortcut keys defined for those functions. You can even undo your last change by pressing Ctrl+Z.

To select text in a text box with a mouse, just place the cursor at the beginning of the text you want, click and hold the left mouse button, and drag the mouse to the end of the desired text. The text will be highlighted as you move the mouse. To select text with the cursor keys, you again place the cursor at the beginning of the desired text. Then, holding down the Shift key, use the cursor keys to select the desired text. Using these techniques, you can move text around within a text box or between text boxes.

Let's take a closer look at selecting and moving text with the following example. Start by adding two text boxes to a form, then running the program. Enter a few words in the first text box, then select one of the words as previously described. Press Ctrl+X to cut the text from the first text box. You will notice that it disappears from the box. Now press the Tab key to move to the next text box, and then press Ctrl+V. The text that you removed from the first box now appears in the second. Figure 4.7 shows a before and after view of an editing operation.

Fig. 4.7
You can easily move text from one box to another.

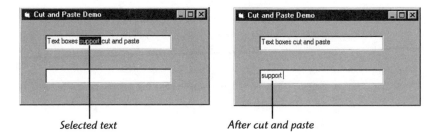

Selected text   After cut and paste

TIP **To select a single word in a text box, double-click the word with** the mouse.

For more about using fonts and colors, see Chapter 5, "Making Your Words Look Good."

One editing feature that is not automatically supported by the text box is the drag-and-drop editing that you find in most word processors. You can, however, implement drag-and-drop using program code. Text boxes are also limited to one font and one color of text within each text box. Therefore, you cannot do any real formatting.

Now how do I use this input in a program?

So far, I have talked quite a bit about how to let a user enter text using a text box. However, that information does you little good if you can't use it in the program. By using the information, I mean that it can be manipulated, added to other information, stored in a file, or printed.

The text box provides you with two properties that can retrieve the information that a user entered. The first is the Text property. As you will recall, all the information that a user enters is stored in the Text property. The information can be used in a program by referencing the Text property. For example, the following code will take a user's name from the text box (named FirstName), add the word "Hello" to the text, and display the result in a message box:

```
dsptxt = "Hello, " & FirstName.Text
MsgBox dsptxt
```

To retrieve the information from a text box, you must specify both the text box (control) name and the name of the property containing the value. The control name and the property name are separated by a dot (.). The first line of the previous listing retrieves the text, adds the string Hello, and assigns the result to the variable dsptxt.

TIP **The Text property of a text box is its "value" property. This means** that to access the information in the text box, you need only specify the control name.

The second line tells the program to show the contents of the variable dsptxt in a message window.

The Text property is the most often used way of handling information in a text box. There is, however, a second property that can be used to reference all or some of the information in a text box. This property is the SelText property. This property contains any text in the box that has been selected by the user. To see how this SelText is different from the Text property, create a text box on the form and give it the name TestSel. Then, create a command button on the form and change its Caption property to Print Text. Access the code window for the command button by double-clicking the button, and then place the following code in the Click event:

```
Form1.Print TestSel.Text
Form1.Print TestSel.SelText
```

TIP **When you double-click a control, the code window is opened with** the default event for that control selected for editing. The default event for a command button is the Click event.

Run the program by pressing F5, and then type a few words in the text box. Select one of the words using the mouse or cursor keys, and then click the command button. When you click the command button, two lines will be printed in the top left corner of your form. The first line will contain the entire contents of the text box, while the second line will contain only the word you selected (see fig. 4.8).

Fig. 4.8
The *Text* and *SelText* properties allow you to retrieve all or part of the information typed into a text box.

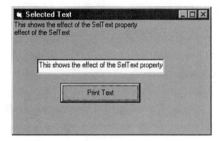

TIP **The SelText property will return a blank string if no text is** selected.

The SelText property is very useful if you are developing any type of word processing capabilities in your program.

Catch the bug

You want to move the text selected by the user from one box to another. You have used the following code, but it doesn't work like you expect. What's wrong?

```
txtDest.Text = txtSource.Text
```

Answer: The Text *property contains the entire contents of the text box. The* SelText *property is the correct one to use, as shown:*

```
txtDest.Text = txtSource.SelText
```

Set boundaries on what the user can enter

While limiting the number of characters that a user can enter is one way of controlling the input, it is often necessary to also control the type of characters that can be entered (i.e., letters, digits, or punctuation marks). In addition, there may be times when you want to change the appearance of the text box to include familiar place holders for the data entry, such as the parentheses in a phone number or hyphens in a social security number. While you could use a standard text box and use program code to accomplish this, there is an easier way.

Visual Basic provides a number of custom controls that are not among the standard set present when you start Visual Basic. Among these custom controls is a Masked Edit control (see fig. 4.9). This control allows you to specify the number, type, and position of characters in the data entry field. It also allows you to use place holder characters within the field.

Fig. 4.9
The Masked Edit control lets you provide visual cues to the user for entering information.

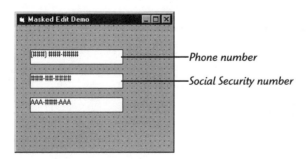

Adding the Masked Edit control

Since the Masked Edit control is not part of the standard control toolbox, the first step in using the control is telling Visual Basic to make the control available to you. This is done through the Custom Controls dialog box shown in figure 4.10.

Fig. 4.10

The Custom Controls dialog box allows you to add controls to the toolbox, or remove them if desired.

Click here to select

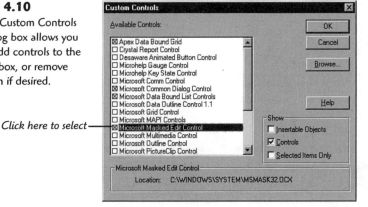

You access the dialog by choosing Custom Controls from the Tools menu. Once the dialog is on the screen, you can add a control by clicking the check box to the left of the control name. For the examples in the rest of this section, go ahead and check the box for Microsoft Masked Edit Control. (When the control is selected for use, an X appears in the checkbox. Any controls with blank checkboxes will not appear in the control toolbox.) After you have selected the control, click the OK button on the dialog to close it and to add the selected control(s) to your toolbox. Your toolbox should now look like figure 4.11, and the Masked Edit control is available for your use.

Now that you have added the Masked Edit control to your toolbox, you are ready to work with it in your program. As with any other control, to add a Masked Edit control to your form, you select it from the toolbox and then draw it on the form where you want it. A Masked Edit control will only support one line of input instead of multiple lines like a text box, so you will need to draw it wide enough to contain all the characters to be entered.

Fig. 4.11
The Masked Edit
control is now
available for use.

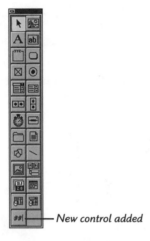

— New control added

 TIP **The Masked Edit control is capable of handling a maximum of 64** characters. While this is quite sufficient for most needs, if your program requires a larger field, you will have to use a standard text box.

Hey, only some of your characters are allowed

The key feature of the Masked Edit control is its ability to control what characters are entered and where they are placed in a field. For instance, if your program requires users to enter zip code information, you would like to ensure that they only enter numbers in the field. The same thing is true for phone numbers or Social Security numbers. Other times, you will need your users to enter a date in a specific form, such as Jan-25-95, or a time (8:06 a.m.). In these cases, you want to make sure that only certain characters are entered at certain locations.

The Masked Edit control has a property called the Mask property, which allows you to tell the Masked Edit control what characters you want where. If the Mask property is blank (the default setting), then the Masked Edit control behaves like a simple text box. To specify what characters are allowed and where they can be placed, you specify character codes in the Mask property. The character codes also specify how many characters can be entered in the field. If you only put five codes in the mask, then no more than five characters can be entered by the user. Table 4.1 shows the different character codes that can be used in the Masked Edit control.

Table 4.1   Allowable Characters Set by the Character Code

Character code	What you can type
#	Any digit 0-9, space, plus or minus (+ or -) signs
?	Any letter a-z or A-Z
A	Any letter or digit
&	Any character or space
.	Decimal placeholder (i.e., 10.001)
,	Thousands separator (i.e., 10,000)
/	Date separator (i.e., 07/06/95)
:	Time separator (i.e., 08:21)

Using these control characters, you can develop input masks for any type of data. For example, the mask for a five-digit zip code would be #####. If you wanted a mask for state abbreviations, it would be ??. This mask only allows letters to be entered, and only two letters may be entered.

To see how this works, draw a Masked Edit control on a form and set the Mask property to either the zip code mask (#####) or the state mask (??). Then run the code and try entering the information. You will see that the control stops accepting characters when you have typed in as many as you specified codes for. You will also notice that if you try to type a letter in the zip code or a number in the state abbreviation, the control will not accept the invalid character.

Pot holders? No, place holders

In addition to the character codes, you can also place any other characters in the mask for use as place holders, including (but not limited to) asterisks (*), dollar signs ($), parentheses, hyphens, and commas. For example, the typical notation for a phone number is (212) 555-1234. Within this notation, the parentheses, the space, and the hyphen are all place holders. To represent this in an input mask, you would set the Mask property to (###) ###-####. Try this for yourself. Using the Masked Edit control from the previous section, select the Mask property and set it to this phone number mask. After you have set the mask, run the program and enter your phone number in the Masked Edit control. Your form should look like figure 4.12.

Fig. 4.12
The Masked Edit control allows you to control what the user enters, and where it is entered.

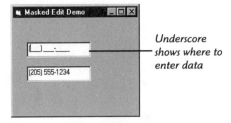

Underscore shows where to enter data

When you first look at the Masked Edit before you type, you will notice that there are underscore characters (_) in every location that you had entered a character code in the Mask property. This tells you, or the user, what locations are available for typing. As you type your phone number, you will notice that the first three numbers you type are entered between the parentheses, then the input skips to the three entry locations in front of the hyphen. In other words, the Masked Input control automatically skips the place holders.

Using the characters' codes and place holders, you can create many kinds of custom input fields. A few examples are shown in table 4.2.

Table 4.2   Input Masks That Make Data Entry Easier

Data to be entered	Mask	Example
Zip Code	#####	35242
Phone Number	(###) ###-####	(205) 555-7575
Social Security Number	###-##-####	123-45-6789
Month–Day–Year	AAA ##, ####	Jan 25, 1995
Date	##/##/##	01/25/95
Time	##:## AA	02:31 p.m.

Getting the information from the Masked Edit control

Like the text box, the Masked Edit control supports both the `Text` and `SelText` properties. This allows you to access the entire contents of the field, or just the part that the user selected.

Catch the bug

You want a field to accept a telephone number, as shown in Image 2, but your Masked Edit control won't allow numbers. What is wrong with the following `Mask` property?

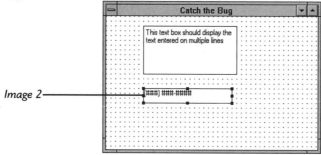

Image 2

```
Mask = (AAA) ???-????
```

Answer: *For entering a number, the correct control code is the pound sign (#). The question mark (?) will allow numbers, but the capital A will not. Either of the following masks is acceptable:*

```
Mask = (???) ???-????
```

```
Mask = (###) ###-####
```

There are a few differences in the behavior of these properties that you should be aware of. The Text property contains all the information that the user entered, plus any place holder characters that were in the Mask property. For example, the phone number mask that you entered contained parentheses, a space, and a hyphen. When a user enters a phone number, only the digits are entered, but the Text property contains all the digits and the place holders. That is, if the user entered 2055550770, the Text property would contain (205) 555-0770.

There is also another property that can be used to reference the information in the Masked Edit control. This property is the ClipText property. This property, in conjunction with the ClipMode property, will allow you to retrieve only the information that the user typed, with or without the place holder characters. The ClipMode property has two settings, Include Literals and Exclude Literals. Setting this property to Exclude Literals allows you to retrieve just the user information, no place holder characters.

To see how this works, start with the phone number example used previously. Set the ClipMode property of the Masked Edit control to 1 - Exclude Literals. Then, add a command button to the form and enter the following code in the Click event:

```
Form1.Print MaskEdBox1.Text
Form1.Print MaskEdBox1.ClipText
```

Now run the program. After entering your phone number, click the command button. The two different values will be printed in the upper left corner of your form. Notice that the first line (the Text property) contains the place holder characters, while the second line (the ClipText property) does not. Figure 4.13 shows the screen after the Text and ClipText values have been printed.

Fig. 4.13
The *Text* and *ClipText* properties return different parts of the entered information.

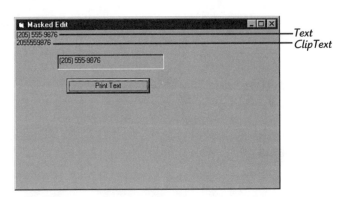

Why is the `ClipText` property important? Because with many types of numerical entries, such as dates, times, and phone numbers, you want to provide the place holders for ease of data entry for the user, but you do not want to store the numbers with all the place holders. Also, the `Mask` property can display numbers with commas separating the thousands, millions, and other groups (i.e., 1,000,000). When the number is used for calculations, you cannot have the commas present.

Summary

As you can see, the text box and the Masked Edit control are very versatile tools for handling the input and display of text, numbers, dates, times, and other information. The text box allows you to work with large amounts of data or get a single entry. The Masked Edit control allows you strict authority over the information being entered. Together, these two controls will probably be able to handle the majority of your data input needs.

Review questions

1 Which property of the text box allows the user to enter more than one line of text?

2 Why would you use scroll bars in a text box?

3 Which property of the text box allows you to limit the number of characters the user can enter?

4 Which property of the Masked Edit control manages what the user can type?

5 Which property of the text box as well as the Masked Edit control stores the information entered by the user?

6 What input mask would you use to enter a part number that consisted of three letters followed by a hyphen and three numbers?

Exercises

1 Change the Masked Edit for the zip code to one that will support the "zip+4" code.

2 Create a text box that will only accept two characters for an abbreviation field.

3 Using the Cut and Paste example shown in figure 4.7, add a command button to automatically copy the selected text in the first box to the second box.

4 Using labels, text boxes, and Masked Edit controls, create the patient information form shown in the "How can I use this in the real world?" example.

5

Making Your Words Look Good

● **In this chapter:**

● **I want to jazz up my text**

● **How big can fonts get?**

● **A rainbow of colors at your fingertips**

● **Color can inform as well as entertain**

You probably use different fonts and colors in your reports and papers to draw the reader's attention; the same can be done in your programs. . . . . ▶

I f you have worked at all with a word processor, you have probably done some work with fonts. A font describes how the letters and numbers you use will look. Figure 5.1 shows you several different fonts in different sizes. Fonts are like different styles of handwriting. Some people print in block capital letters, other people write in script, and some very talented people produce beautiful calligraphy.

Fig. 5.1
Fonts control the appearance of the text on your screen.

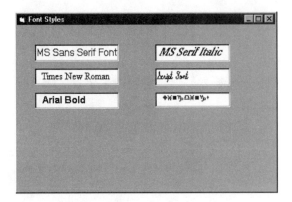

Introduction to fonts

Actually, there are several characteristics involved in the definition of the fonts used in your programs. First, there is the base font which determines if your letters look like typewriter letters, look handwritten, or have a futuristic look.

Once the base font has been defined, several other **attributes** control the final appearance of the letters you see on the screen. One attribute controls whether or not a font is bold. Characters may also be italicized or underlined. Finally, you can have strikethrough characters.

 Plain English, please!

Attributes are used to describe the appearance of an object. People often refer to physical attributes when describing a person, such as his or her height, hair color, or eye color. Attributes for fonts simply describe the physical appearance of the font. **"**

The final attribute is the font size. With most fonts used in Windows—and therefore in Visual Basic—you can specify the size of the letters being displayed. In a typical setup, the default font size is in the range of eight to 12 **points**. If desired, though, you can set the font size anywhere between one and 2,048 points, though I wouldn't recommend either extreme. (A one-point font would be the ultimate in contract fine print.) A point size below eight becomes difficult to read, and a point size of 250 will cause just a few characters to fill the entire screen. Figure 5.2 gives you some idea of the different point sizes.

Fig. 5.2

Fonts can range in size from tiny to jumbo.

6-point font

66 Plain English, please!

The height of text is measured in **points**. One point is equivalent to 1/72 of a logical inch. Therefore, using a 12-point font, approximately six lines of text would fit in a vertical inch. 99

The idea behind using different fonts and font attributes is to increase the readability of the information on the screen or to add emphasis to a particular piece of information. The proper use of fonts can greatly enhance the programs you create.

CAUTION **It is easy to get carried away with using different fonts, and this** can cause some problems. Too many different fonts on a single screen can make the text look disorganized and confusing. It is best to choose one or two fonts, then use the attributes to achieve effects. This will give your programs a cleaner look.

How do I control the fonts in a program?

To learn more about printing, see Chapter 32, "Printing the Results of Your Programs."

Visual Basic lets you control all the attributes of fonts in your programs. You can specify a font for an entire form or for individual controls. You can even control the fonts used for information that is printed out by your program.

Visual Basic allows you to set up fonts during the design phase of your program. It also gives you the ability to actually change them while the program is running. This means that you can allow your user to select fonts for certain parts of the program. Or, you can set up the program so that the fonts change in response to some event in the program, such as a change in the value of a text box.

This font is everywhere

The default font for Visual Basic programs is called MS Sans Serif. This is the font that you see in the title bars of all Windows programs. Unless you change the font for a control, this font will be used in every control that you add to your program. Figure 5.3 shows you some of the base fonts that are available to you.

If you want to use a single font for all the parts of your program, you can set the form's font to the one you want, before you place any controls on the form. Whatever font is used for the form will also be used for any control that is added to the form.

How can I use this in the real world?

There are several reasons why you might want to use fonts or font attributes in your programs. For me, one big advantage of being able to control font sizes is to make them more readable on laptop, or portable, computers. If you use a laptop often, you know what I mean. The ten- or 12-point font that looks great on your 15" desktop monitor can be difficult to read on the 9" screen of your portable computer. Therefore, I typically use a larger font size for the portable. When I write programs, I also give users the capability of changing the font size to their liking.

TIP **Changing the font used for the form will not affect any controls** already on the form, only new controls which are added to the form. Also, the font setting does not affect the font used for the form's caption (the text in the title bar). This font is controlled by the Windows setting.

Fig. 5.3
Use different fonts to
liven up your programs.

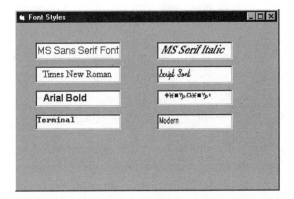

To set the font for your form, you need to make sure the form is selected (instead of one of the controls), and then access the Properties dialog box. When you select the Font property in the dialog, a button with an ellipsis (...) will appear at the right edge of the input area. Clicking this button will bring up the Font dialog box (see fig. 5.4).

Fig. 5.4
If you're bad with
names, use the Font
dialog box to choose
a font.

This dialog box contains controls enabling you to easily select a font and its attributes. This dialog also contains a sample window which shows you what your selection will look like.

The first list in the dialog box allows you to select the base font that you want to use. The fonts in this list are taken from the available fonts that you have installed on your system. You can use the cursor keys or the scroll bar to scroll through the list to find the font you want.

 TIP   **If you know the name of the font, or part of it, you can start** typing the name in the text field above the list. As you type each letter, the list moves to the appropriate entry. This can help you scan the list more quickly, especially if the font list is long.

After you have selected the base font, you can select the font style from the next list. The selections in this list determine whether the bold and italic attributes are on or not. You might notice that some fonts do not support all the possible attributes.

The third list lets you select the font size. This list typically ranges from about eight to 72 points. Not all possible sizes are represented in the list, so if you need a different size, just type it in.

When you have selected the base font and its attributes, you click the OK button in the dialog box to make the change. To abort the change, simply click the Cancel button.

 CAUTION   **If you are creating programs for others to use on their machines,** be careful of the fonts you choose. Others using your program may not have the same fonts as you. Your program will attempt to find a similar font on the user's machine, but the results may be unacceptable. Windows will always find an equivalent font for MS Serif and MS Sans Serif. Other fonts that are found on most machines are Arial, Courier New, and Times New Roman. These three are TrueType fonts.

You're not stuck with just one font

In addition to setting the font for the form, you may want to set a different font, or different attributes, for a single control or group of controls. For example, you may want to give all of your labels one font and all your text boxes a different font. Or you may decide to use one font for controls containing numbers and another font for those containing letters.

You can change fonts for individual controls the same way that you changed them for the form. This is done by using the Font dialog box to set the font properties. Each control has a font property and, in fact, you could use a different font for each control on your form, though I wouldn't recommend it.

To change a font for a control, select the font by clicking the control, and then access the Properties dialog box. Next, select the Font property and press the ellipsis button to bring up the Font dialog box. From the dialog, you can then specify all the font properties for the control.

 TIP **You can select multiple controls by holding down the Shift key** and clicking each control. You can then change the font for all the controls at the same time.

Change fonts while the program is running!

Since the fonts used by a control or form are defined by properties, they can be changed from within a program. There are seven properties which control the appearance of text in a form. These properties are as follows:

- Name, which specifies the base font.
- Bold, which determines whether or not the text will appear in boldface type.
- Italic, which determines whether or not the text will appear in italics.
- Underline, which determines whether or not the text is underlined.
- Size, which specifies the size of the type in points.
- StrikeThrough, which determines whether or not the text shows a strikethrough line.
- Weight, which determines the thickness of the letters in the text.

How do I change the base font?

You are not limited to defining fonts only while you design your program. You can also change the base font of an object using an assignment statement.

TIP **You can find the names of the fonts installed on your system by** looking at the choices in the Font dialog box.

Quick change the appearance of a font

After the base font is specified, the `Bold`, `Italic`, and `Underline` properties can be used to change how the font looks. Each of these properties has two possible values, `True` or `False`. If the value is set to `True`, the base font is modified by the property. The following code turns on all of these properties for the `FontDemo` control:

```
FontDemo.Font.Bold = True
FontDemo.Font.Italic = True
FontDemo.Font.Underline = True
```

To turn the properties off, you would simply set the values to `False`.

Speaking of base fonts

To change your base font, you assign a value to the `Name` property of the Font object, like the following:

```
FontDemo.Font.Name = "Times New Roman"
```

The first word, `FontDemo`, is just the name of the control whose font is to be changed. The second word, `Font`, tells the program that we are changing one of the properties of the font for the control. The third word, `Name`, specifies the particular property that is being changed.

After defining which property is being changed, a value is assigned to the property. This value is the name of the font itself. The `Name` property is expecting a value in the form of a string; therefore, the name of the font must be enclosed in quotes. Some of the fonts typically found in Windows setups are Arial, Courier New, MS Sans Serif, MS Serif, and Times New Roman (refer to fig. 5.3).

Bigger is better

The final property that affects the font is the `Size` property. As mentioned before, the value for the `Size` property can be any integer between 1 and 2,048. (Refer to fig. 5.2 to see examples of font sizes.) The `Size` property is set using an assignment statement just like the other properties as shown in the following code:

```
FontDemo.Font.Size = 16
```

CAUTION **When you change the font size in code, the control using the font** may not be able to adjust to accommodate the new size. Therefore, part of the text in the control may not be visible to the user. If you want to make sure that the new size will fit, you can use the `TextWidth` and `TextHeight` methods of the control to determine the actual size of your text. You can then adjust the `Width` and `Height` properties of the control accordingly.

How do the properties work?

To effectively demonstrate the behavior of the font properties, let's build a quick example. First, create a text box on the form and change its `Name` property to `FontDemo`. (You just *knew* I specified that name in the code listings for a reason.) Next, add five command buttons to the form using the `Caption` and `Name` properties defined in the following table. These command buttons will be used to implement font changes in the text box.

Caption	Name
Change Font	ChngFont
Bold	MakeBold
Italic	MakeItalic
Underline	UndLine
Increase Size	MakeBig

When you have finished adding the command buttons, your form should look like figure 5.5. After you have set up the form, you will need to add a line of code to the `Click` event of each command button. These lines are the same ones that were explained previously. Table 5.1 shows which line of code to add to each button. These button names correspond to the ones specified in the previous table.

Fig. 5.5
Changing fonts on
the fly.

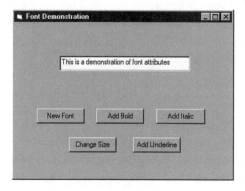

Table 5.1   Code Actually Changes the Font Appearance

Button Name	Code
ChngFont	FontDemo.Font.Name = "Times New Roman"
MakeBold	FontDemo.Font.Bold = True
MakeItalic	FontDemo.Font.Italic = True
UndLine	FontDemo.Font.Underline = True
MakeBig	FontDemo.Font.Size = 16

After you have entered the code for each Click event, run the program. Type a few words of text into the text box, then click the command buttons to see how the text changes.

Catch the bug

Why did this statement cause an error when you tried to run the program?

```
txtFontDemo.Font.Name = MS Sans Serif
```

Answer: *Since the Name property expects a string, the name of the font (MS Sans Serif) must appear inside quotation marks as follows:*

```
txtFontDemo.Font.Name = "MS Sans Serif"
```

That is an attractive program!

Using different fonts is one way to change the appearance of information in your programs. The other way to change appearances is through the use of color. Color can be used to grab a user's attention, to convey important information, or just to make an application more visually appealing. Think of it like watching the TV news. You get the same information whether you watch it on a black and white set or a color set, but which would you prefer?

You can set the color of controls during design

As with fonts, you can set color properties for your form and for individual controls. In fact, most controls allow you to set two colors. You can set the background color using the `BackColor` property, and you can set the foreground or text color using the `ForeColor` property.

How can I use this in the real world?

One beneficial use of font attributes is to highlight information. For example, when you develop a form, you could use bold type for the labels of all the required information. Then, as the user enters information in the associated text box, change the font to normal (not bold) to indicate that the required field has been filled. The font could be changed back to bold if the user erases the information.

In a member tracking system, information such as a person's first and last names, address, and phone number would be required. Other information such as a birthdate or occupation would be optional.

To try this out, place a label and a text box on a form. Make sure the label is using bold type and that the text box is empty. Placing the following code in the Change event of the text box will achieve the results described:

```
If Len(Text1.Text) > 0 Then
    Label1.Font.Bold = False
Else
    Label1.Font.Bold = True
End If
```

Run the program and watch what happens as you enter and erase text.

TIP **Unlike setting a font for the form, the color setting for your form** does not carry forward to other controls.

The default setting for each of the color properties is based on the Windows system color settings. The default setting of the BackColor property is the Windows background color, usually white. The default setting of the ForeColor property is the color of the text in Windows menus, usually black.

TIP **If you use the default color settings and then change your** Windows colors, the colors for your program will also change.

There are two ways to set the colors of your form and controls during the design process. You can use either the color palette, or you can select colors from a list from the Properties dialog. You can also, of course, set color properties using code.

Set colors with the color palette

The color palette is one of the tools available to you in Visual Basic's design mode. The color palette is accessed by choosing Color Palette from the View menu (see fig. 5.6).

Forecolor selection

Fig. 5.6
The color palette allows you to easily choose the foreground and background colors of your controls.

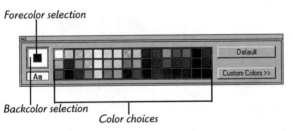

Backcolor selection

Color choices

The color palette consists of a property selection area (two concentric squares), a series of color indicators, and two command buttons. To change the color properties of one of your controls, select the control and then, using the mouse, just select either the foreground (click the inner box) or background (click the outer box). Next, click the color that you want in the color indicator boxes. As you choose the colors, you will immediately see the results both in the color palette and in your control. If you want to return your control's colors to their default values, just click the default button.

Set colors with the color list

The other way to set the colors of a control is to set the individual properties from the Properties dialog box. To set a color, select the property (either ForeColor or BackColor), and then click the arrow button at the right of the property value. This will bring up the color picker. Choose the color you want by clicking the appropriate square (see fig. 5.7).

Fig. 5.7
Change colors with the click of a mouse.

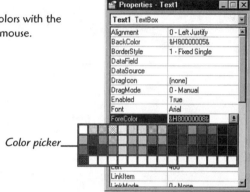

Color picker

What are the funny numbers displayed in the property value of the colors?

Those numbers represent the color in hexadecimal (base 16) format. As you read the number from the right, the first two characters represent the amount of red in the color. The next two characters represent the amount of green in the color, and the last two characters represent the amount of blue. Each of more than 16,000,000 possible colors is represented by varying amounts of red, green, and blue (RGB). The ampersands (&) and the *H* in the number tell the program that the number is hexadecimal.

You can also change colors with code

As with most everything else, the ForeColor and BackColor properties can be changed with code in your program. You do this, of course, with an assignment statement where you tell the program what control and property to change, and what the new value of the property is. But what are the values? Can you just say, "Make this red?" Well, almost.

As described previously, every color is a combination of some amount of red, green, and blue. If you are a glutton for punishment, you can figure out

To find out how constants work, see Chapter 17, "Adding Variables to Your Programs."

how much of each goes in a particular color and convert that into the right numerical value. Fortunately, it is much easier than that. Visual Basic provides a set of constants for many of the most common colors. These constants contain the numerical value that you need for the color (see table 5.2).

Table 5.2   Color Constants You Can Use in Your Code

Color	Constant	Numerical value
Black	vbBlack	0
Red	vbRed	255
Green	vbGreen	65,280
Yellow	vbYellow	65,535
Blue	vbBlue	16,711,680
Magenta	vbMagenta	16,711,935
Cyan	vbCyan	16,776,960
White	vbWhite	16,777,215

To use one of these color constants, you simply enter its name in the assignment statement. The following code will display yellow text on a blue background:

```
ColorDemo.ForeColor = vbYellow
ColorDemo.BackColor = vbBlue
```

Catch the bug

What is wrong with this assignment statement used to change the color of a control?

```
txtColor.ForeColor = "Light Blue"
```

Answer*: Color values must be entered using a number or a color constant. The correct statement would be:*

```
txtColor.ForeColor = vbCyan
```

How can I use this in the real world?

You've probably heard of red ink in discussing finances, especially if you follow government budgets. You can set up your applications to actually show negative numbers in red, positive numbers in green, or anything else you want.

First, draw a text box on the form and delete the information in the Text property. Next, go to the code window and place the following code in the Change event of the text box:

```
If Val(Text1.Text) < 0 Then
    Text1.ForeColor = vbRed
Else
    Text1.ForeColor = vbGreen
End If
```

When you run this program, type different numbers into the text box, some positive and some negative. The negative ones will show up in red, and the positive ones will show up in green.

Summary

Using colors and font styles other than the defaults can add a lot to your applications. Hopefully, you have seen how easy it is to incorporate different colors and fonts in your designs.

Review questions

1 What are the seven properties that define a font?

2 What is a good size for a typical font?

3 Why should you avoid using lots of fonts?

4 What three colors are used to define all screen colors?

5 What two color properties control the appearance of a control?

Exercises

1 Using the example in the section "How do the properties work?," add another command button to restore the font properties to their original values.

2 Create a program containing command buttons to change the color of text in a text box to red, green, blue, yellow, etc.

6

Create Fancier Text with the RichTextBox Control

● **In this chapter:**

● **Differences between the RichTextBox and the standard text box**

● **What kind of formatting can I do with the RichTextBox?**

● **Can I really have multiple fonts in the box?**

● **Storing information in the box**

The RichTextBox allows you complete formatting control over your text . . . . ➤

What can the RichTextBox do?

Prior to this version of Visual Basic, text processing was limited to the use of the text box. This meant that only a single font or color could be used for all the text being edited. The implication of this was that, without the use of a third-party control, true word processing capabilities were beyond the easy reach of Visual Basic programs.

Now, however, Visual Basic includes the RichTextBox control. This control allows the user to apply different fonts, font attributes, and colors to different sections of the text being edited. The user can also control the justification of text and create such effects as indents or **hanging indents**. All these effects will be covered later in this chapter.

 Plain English, please!

A **hanging indent** is where the first line of a paragraph starts at the left margin, but the remaining lines are indented by some amount.

The RichTextBox control accomplishes all these functions by providing support for the **Rich Text Format** (**RTF**) language. The control will interpret RTF codes and apply the proper formatting to the text (see fig. 6.1). The control also has the capability of importing and exporting RTF files.

 Plain English, please!

Rich Text Format (RTF) is a set of codes that are included in a text file to provide formatting information. Since all of the codes are comprised of ASCII characters, RTF files can be handled and edited by any program capable of editing text files. However, only programs with RTF support will show how the formatting appears on the screen.

Fig. 6.1
The format information
is identified by braces
({}).

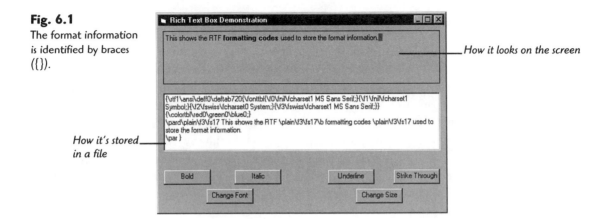

How it looks on the screen

*How it's stored
in a file*

How does it work?

In many ways, the RichTextBox works the same way as the standard text box. It shares many properties with the TextBox control. In fact, the RichTextBox supports all properties that are supported by the text box. This makes it easy to substitute the RichTextBox for any text boxes in your program. Simply delete the text box and place a RichTextBox in its place with the same name. You will not need to change any of your program code to handle this. You will, however, want to add new code to take advantage of the additional capabilities of the RichTextBox.

It's like the standard text box

*For information on
binding controls to
a database, see
Chapter 29,
"Accessing
Databases."*

Like the TextBox control, the RichTextBox supports single and multiple line display and editing of text. (Multiple line editing is enabled by setting the MultiLine property to True.) Both controls support the use of scroll bars for multiple line editing (using the ScrollBars property). Both controls can be locked (by setting the Locked property to True) to provide a read-only display of information. Both controls support Cut and Paste or Copy and Paste operations for editing. And finally, both can be bound to a Data control for use in database applications.

Due to this similarity, I will only focus on the unique capabilities of the RichTextBox in this chapter. To learn more about the properties shared with the text box, see Chapter 4, "Letting the User Enter Text."

The effects of formatting

The RichTextBox allows the user to select a portion of the text in the control and apply special formatting to it. The user can change the font of the selection, make the selection bold or italic, or underline the selection. When the user applies any or all of these formats to the selection, the new formatting is shown on the screen. In addition, formatting codes (which are not shown on the screen) are placed in the text of the control. These codes allow the formatting information to be stored then used by other programs that support RTF format codes. This means that you can export your formatted text to a word processor or other program and retain the formatting.

Need text effects? RichTextBox to the rescue

The RichTextBox is one of the custom controls that comes with Visual Basic. This control is not normally available in the toolbox when you first start Visual Basic. To add the RichTextBox to the toolbox, you need to choose Custom Controls from the Tools menu. This will display the Custom Controls dialog box. You then select the control by clicking the box next to the Microsoft Rich Text Custom Control. When an X is shown in the box, the control is selected for use. Choosing the OK button adds the control to the toolbox and returns you to the Visual Basic design environment.

To start working with a RichTextBox control, you choose it from the toolbox and draw it on the screen just like any other control. Figure 6.2 shows a RichTextBox drawn on a form. As always, after you draw the control on the form, you should give it a unique name.

Fig. 6.2
You probably won't use the RichTextBox for small editing jobs.

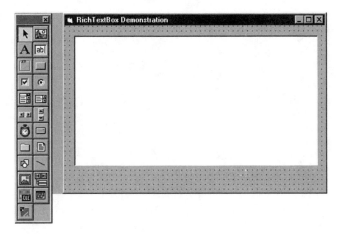

The formatting options

The thing that makes the RichTextBox a very powerful tool for creating programs for editing text is that it allows you tremendous control over the formatting of the text it contains. We will look at many of the effects which are possible with the RichTextBox in this section.

One thing that all the formatting options have in common is how they affect the text in the control. If you set a format property while some text is selected, only the selected text is affected by the new property value. If, however, you set a new format value with no text selected, the property will affect all text typed at the insertion point until the property value is again changed. This works exactly like the formatting options in your word processing program.

Setting the initial font

After you have drawn a RichTextBox on your form, you can set the initial text characteristics of the control from the Properties dialog box. Just select the Font property, and click the ellipsis button at the right of the line. This will bring up the Font dialog box (see fig. 6.3). From this dialog box, you can choose the font, font style, size, and effects that will initially be used in the RichTextBox.

Fig. 6.3
You can choose the initial font settings for the RichTextBox from the Font dialog box.

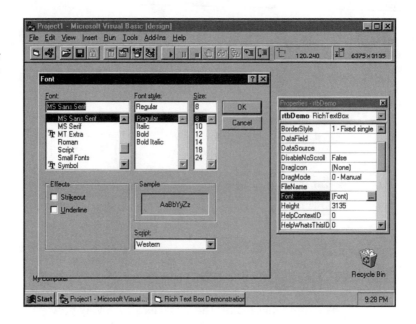

For more on fonts and colors and how to set them, see Chapter 5, "Making Your Words Look Good."

You can also set the initial properties with assignment statements when the form containing the RichTextBox is loaded. These properties are set the same way as for any other control.

When you set the initial values of the Font properties, you also set the initial value of the SelBold, SelFontName, SelFontSize, and SelItalic properties that are used by the RichTextBox for formatting.

 TIP   **If you change the value of the** Font **property or any of its** attributes, it will affect all text that has not had any special formatting applied.

Changing the appearance of words

Once the initial font has been set and the user is entering text, formatting of individual words and phrases can be accomplished by setting one or more of the following properties:

- SelFontName—Changes the font of the selection.

- SelBold—Makes the selection bold.

- SelItalic—Makes the selection italic.

- `SelFontSize`—Changes the size of the selection's type.

- `SelUnderline`—Underlines the selection.

- `SelStrikeThrough`—Shows the selection in strikethrough mode.

Each of these properties can be set using an assignment statement. One way to apply some of these properties is through the use of command buttons, which will set the properties. Figure 6.4 shows a form containing a RichTextBox control and command buttons to turn on the `Bold`, `Italic`, `Underline`, and `StrikeThrough` properties of the selected text. The form also contains command buttons to change the font to Times New Roman and to change the font size to 14 points. Listing 6.1 shows the code for each of the command buttons on the form.

Fig. 6.4

You can set the font properties of a selection using command buttons containing the proper code.

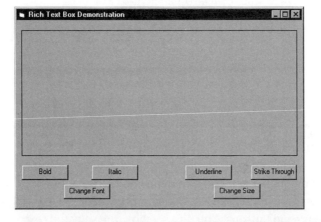

Listing 6.1 Setting the Properties of the Selected Text

```
'***********************************************
'This command button turns on the Bold setting
'***********************************************
Private Sub cmdBold_Click()
    rtbTextEdit.SelBold = True
End Sub
'***********************************************
'This command button turns on the Italic setting
'***********************************************
Private Sub cmdItalic_Click()
    rtbTextEdit.SelItalic = True
End Sub
```

continues

Listing 6.1 Continued

```
'****************************************************
'This command button turns on the Underline setting
'****************************************************
Private Sub cmdUnderline_Click()
    rtbTextEdit.SelUnderline = True
End Sub
'****************************************************
'This command button turns on the StrikeThrough setting
'****************************************************
Private Sub cmdStrikeThrough_Click()
    rtbTextEdit.SelStrikeThrough = True
End Sub
'*****************************************************
'This command button changes the font of the selection
'*****************************************************
Private Sub cmdFontChange_Click()
    rtbTextEdit.SelFontName = "Times New Roman"
End Sub
'*****************************************************
'This command button changes the size of the selection
'*****************************************************
Private Sub cmdNewSize_Click()
    rtbTextEdit.SelFontSize = 14
End Sub
```

You can create this form yourself by placing the RichTextBox control and the command buttons on a form and placing the appropriate assignment statement in each command button. Then run the program and type some text in the RichTextBox. Select a portion of the text and press one of the command buttons. You will see how the selected text is changed, but all other text is left alone (see fig. 6.5). This is in contrast to working with the standard text box where all the text in the box received the same change.

Fig. 6.5
Select the text by clicking and dragging the mouse.

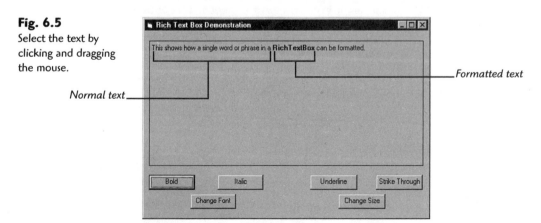

Catch the bug

The following code is supposed to change the selection to boldface. Why didn't it work?

```
rtbTextEdit.Font.Bold = True
```

Answer*: This code will change the base font to bold. The correct property for the selected text is the* SelBold *property as follows:*

```
rtbTextEdit.SelBold = True
```

Move to the right

In addition to the ability of the RichTextBox to change the font characteristics of words, the control also allows you to use indents and hanging indents in your text. A standard indent causes the left edge of the selected paragraph to be shifted in from the left edge of the RichTextBox control. This type of indent is invoked using the SelIndent property of the control. You can also shift the right edge of the paragraph in from the right edge of the control using the SelRightIndent property. Finally, you can create a hanging indent, where all lines after the first line of the paragraph are indented, using the SelHangingIndent property. Figure 6.6 shows each of these text effects. You can also apply multiple indent types to the same paragraph.

Fig. 6.6
Select a paragraph to indent by triple-clicking anywhere in the paragraph.

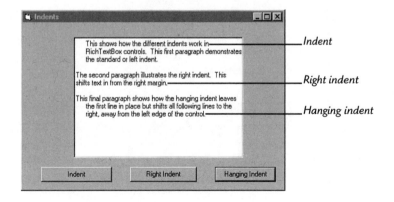

Shifting paragraphs

With the RichTextBox, you can change the alignment of paragraphs in your text. You can have the paragraphs aligned along the left edge of the RichTextBox (the default), along the right edge, or centered in the box (see fig. 6.7). The property that controls the alignment of the paragraph is the SelAlignment property. This property can have one of three values, shown in table 6.1.

Fig. 6.7
Changing the *SelAlignment* property changes the position of the paragraph.

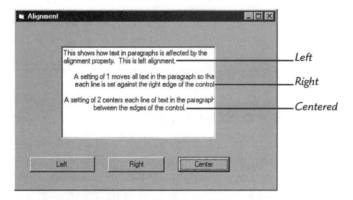

Speaking of *SelIndent*

You cannot set the indent features of the RichTextBox from the design mode. They can only be set from code. The following code shows how the *SelIndent* property is used to shift a paragraph in from the left edge of the control. The same syntax is used for the SelRightIndent and SelHangingIndent properties:

```
controlname.SelIndent = value
```

controlname is the name of the RichTextBox containing the text you want to indent. SelIndent (or SelRightIndent or SelHangingIndent) specifies the property name, which determines the type of indent to be used. value is an integer number which specifies the amount of the indent. The value is the number of scale units (usually twips) that you want the text indented.

Table 6.1   Controlling the Alignment of the Paragraph

Property Value	Effect
0	Sets the beginning of each line flush with the left side of the box.
1	Sets the end of each line flush with the right side of the box.
2	Centers each line between the edges of the box.

Saving your work for posterity

In order for you to save the formatting information that is used in the RichTextBox, you must save not only the text, but the formatting codes as well. This information is saved in ASCII text files. Fortunately, you don't have to know how to save or read the files necessary for the formatting support. The RichTextBox has control methods which can do this for you.

To save the text in a RichTextBox, you use the `SaveFile` method, like the following:

```
rtbname.SaveFile = filename
```

The argument *rtbname* is the name of the RichTextBox whose contents you want to save. *filename* is the name of the file where the information is to be saved. The *filename* argument can include the path (drive and directory) of the file. If the path is omitted, the current directory will be assumed. `filename` can be a literal string enclosed in quotes or a string variable which contains a valid filename.

I wanna make more changes

Typically, you will not create the perfect document on the first try. This means that you will want to retrieve your text for additional editing at some time in the future. In order to retrieve RTF text into the RichTextBox, you need to use the `LoadFile` method of the control like the following:

To retrieve text from a file and place it in a RichTextBox, you use the LoadFile method, like the following:

```
rtbname.LoadFile = filename
```

The argument `rtbname` is the name of the RichTextBox where you want to place the contents of the file. `filename` is the name of the file containing the text you want to edit. The `filename` argument can include the path (drive and directory) of the file. If the path is omitted, the current directory will be assumed. `filename` can be a literal string enclosed in quotes or a string variable which contains a valid filename.

The search is over

Another great feature of the RichTextBox is that you can search its contents for a string of text with the `Find` method. You can choose to have the search confined to the selected text or to a specific section of the text. You can also have the search look through the entire contents of the RichTextBox.

Speaking of *Find*

The `Find` method is used to find a text string in the RichTextBox, like the following:

```
rtbname.Find(searchstr, start, end, options)
```

As with the other methods, `rtbname` identifies the RichTextBox that you want searched. The `searchstr` parameter identifies the string that you want to find. This can be a literal string, a variable, or a string function. `start` and `end` are integer values that specify the scope of the search by character position. The first character in a RichTextBox is located at position 0. If both parameters are included, the search will be performed on all text between the two points. If `end` is omitted, the entire contents of the RichTextBox will be searched. If both parameters are omitted, only the selected text will be searched.

`options` is the parameter that determines whether case matching is performed and whether the match is based on the whole word or a piece of the word. If the match can be based on a piece of a word, then "the" and "there" would be a match. An option value of 2 forces whole word matching, while a value of 4 forces case sensitive matching. If you want to use both options, set the value to the sum of the individual feature values (in this example, 6).

Another option that is available for the search is whether to match the case of the search string. If case matching is not required, the strings "The" and "the" would be considered to be a match. If case matching is required, the strings would not match because one contains a capital letter while the other does not.

Summary

The RichTextBox control takes text editing into realms into which it has never gone before in Visual Basic. You can now format text easily and create your own word processing capabilities.

Review questions

1 What can the RichTextBox do that a text box cannot?

2 What is the effect of setting a formatting property while text is selected?

3 What is the effect of setting a formatting property when no text is selected?

4 How is the formatting information saved in a file?

5 What methods are used to store and retrieve information for a RichTextBox control?

Exercises

1 Set up buttons to change the attributes of the selected text from bold or italic back to normal text.

2 Set up the buttons to toggle back and forth between bold and normal or italic and normal. Hint, you will need to check the initial settings of the properties.

3 Create the code for the indent example shown in figure 6.6.

4 Create a full text editor that includes font changes, paragraph alignment, and indent capabilities.

Adding Pictures to Convey More Information

● **In this chapter:**

● **What a pretty picture. Can I use it in my program?**

● **You can use pictures in several different places**

● **You don't have to use the whole picture**

● **Can I create picture buttons like other programs have?**

● **Looks can be deceiving**

There are some times when words just won't convey what you have in mind; for just these cases, Visual Basic allows you to include pictures in your programs . . . . ⊘

As the old saying goes, a picture is worth a thousand words. But when only a picture will do, no number of words can replace it. So, when you need to incorporate pictures in your program, what can you do?

In Visual Basic, you have two controls available that can display pictures—the Picture control and the Image control. One of these controls, the Picture control, will even let you edit or annotate pictures. You can add a picture directly to your form to provide a background for your program that can be either entertaining or informative. Figure 7.1 shows an example of using a picture (in this case, a flow diagram) as a form's background.

Fig. 7.1
A picture in the background can add information to your program.

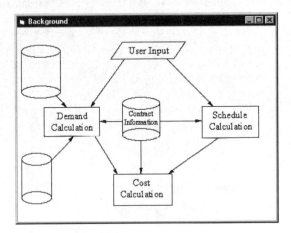

What can I do with pictures in my programs?

So what kinds of pictures can be displayed using Visual Basic? The Picture and Image controls can display pictures that are stored as bitmap files, icons, or Windows metafiles. These files have extensions of BMP, ICO, and WMF, respectively. Any other graphics file formats must be converted to one of these types before they can be used in your program. The same types of files can be displayed on a form.

 TIP There are many third-party graphics programs that can convert pictures from one file format to another. The Paint program that comes with Windows has some limited ability to perform this function.

How do I add the pictures?

You can add pictures to your program by loading a picture onto your form. You can also add a picture by placing a Picture or Image control on the form and loading the picture into the control. While the form, Picture control, and Image control all handle pictures a little differently, the basic method for adding a picture to them is the same.

When you are in design mode, you can add a picture by setting the `Picture` property of the form or control to the name of the file containing the picture. To set the `Picture` property, select it in the Properties dialog box, and then press the ellipsis button in the property input field. This will bring up the Load Picture dialog box (see fig. 7.2). From this dialog box, select the file that you want shown on the form or in the control.

Fig. 7.2
You can double-click the *Picture* property to bring up the Load Picture dialog box.

If you want to remove the picture completely, set the `Picture` property to `(none)`. This is done by highlighting the contents of the `Picture` property and pressing the Delete key.

Adding a picture to a form

When you add a picture directly to a form, it creates a background for your program. The entire picture contained in the file is loaded onto the form, starting at the upper left corner of the form. If the picture is smaller than the form, then white space (or whatever your background color is) will be visible to the right and below the picture, as shown in figure 7.3. This is just like placing a 5×7 photograph in a picture frame that is 8×10.

Fig. 7.3
If you want, you can resize your form to fit the picture.

———— *Small picture*

Of course, the picture may also be larger than the form. In this case, you will only see the upper left portion of the picture that fits within the form. However, the entire picture is still loaded, and if you increase the size of the form, you will be able to see more of the picture. This is like looking out a window in that your view is limited. But unlike a real glass window, your form can be stretched.

How can I use this in the real world?

The use of pictures in a program can greatly improve the program's effectiveness, and in some cases, is absolutely necessary. The possibilities are as endless as they are diverse! For example, a security program may contain a picture of each employee in a company. As an employee passes his badge through a reader, the computer displays the picture of the employee, which a security guard can match to the person. In real estate, an agent could use a program that contains pictures and statistics about houses to show to prospective buyers.

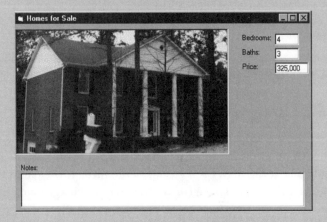

Another application that might be able to use pictures is an airline's reservations program, where a seating chart of the plane would be shown to assist the ticket agent with seat selections.

TIP **Information about the size of a picture or the stretching of a** picture applies to pictures contained in bitmap or icon files. Pictures contained in Windows metafiles will automatically adjust to fit the size of their container. This container can be the form itself or a picture box or Image control.

Q&A *If my picture is larger than my form, will scroll bars be added to the form?*

No. Visual Basic does not automatically include scroll bars to let you view more of the picture.

Since the picture is in the background of the form, any controls that you place on the form will appear above the picture. The background will not show through any controls except the Label and Shape controls. Notice the difference in the background of the Label control and text box in figure 7.4. The background picture on the form shows through the Label control but not the text box.

Fig. 7.4
The background on a form will show through a Label control, but not a text box.

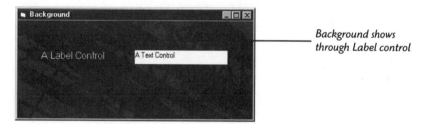

Background shows through Label control

How and when do I use the Picture control?

The Picture control displays pictures in a manner similar to the form. That is, the picture (or the portion that is visible) is displayed exactly the way it was drawn. It is neither stretched nor compressed to fit the control. To use a picture in a picture control, you first draw the control on the form, then assign a picture to the `Picture` property using the Load Picture dialog box described previously.

One difference between the Picture control and a form is that the Picture control can be set up to automatically adjust to the size of the picture being displayed. This is done by setting the `AutoSize` property to `True`. The default value of the `AutoSize` property (`False`) specifies that the Picture control remain the same size (the initial size that you drew) no matter what the size of the picture it contains (see fig. 7.5).

Fig. 7.5

The *AutoSize* property determines whether or not the Picture control adjusts to fit the picture being displayed.

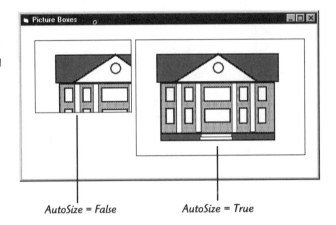

AutoSize = False   AutoSize = True

 TIP   **When the Picture control expands or contracts, the top left** corner of the control remains in the same location where it was originally placed.

 Q&A   *Can I set up a control so that the picture fits the space I define?*

Hey! You're getting ahead of me. Yes, you can do this with the Image control as you'll see in a minute.

You can try this for yourself. Place a Picture control on the form, and then set the `AutoSize` property to `True`. Now try setting the `Picture` property to different pictures. There are a number of bitmaps you can use in the subdirectory where Windows is installed. Watch how the Picture control adjusts to fit the picture that you load.

 Q&A   *What happens if the picture I want to display is larger than the form that will contain the Picture control?*

Only the portion of the picture that fits in the form will be shown. The form's size will not be adjusted.

The Picture control can also be used to hold other controls. In the Visual Basic parlance, it can be used as a container. As you draw other controls on top of a Picture control, they become a part of the control. Then if you move or hide the Picture control, all the controls it contains are moved or hidden right along with it. In this way, the Picture control can be used as a form within a form.

What the Image control can do

The final way that you can get a picture on a form is by using the Image control. Just like the Picture control, you draw an Image control on your form and then assign a file to its `Picture` property. The Image control, however, handles pictures in a slightly different manner than the Picture control or form does.

The default behavior of the Image control is to change size to fit the picture being displayed. You can change this behavior by changing the setting of the `Stretch` property. The default setting of the property is `False`. If you set the `Stretch` property to `True`, then the picture being displayed will be stretched or compressed to fit the size of the control.

 TIP **No matter what setting you use for the `Stretch` property, the** entire picture will be displayed in the Image control.

You can imagine how this works if you think of drawing a picture on a balloon. If you draw a picture while the balloon is deflated and then blow it up, the picture is stretched right along with the balloon itself. Likewise, if you draw on an inflated balloon and then let the air out, the picture will get smaller.

This works fine as long as the height and width of the Image control is proportional to the height and width of the original picture—sort of like moving from a 21" TV to a 50" big screen. However, if the height and width are not proportional, the **aspect ratio** is changed and the picture will be distorted. Figure 7.6 shows several Image controls with the same picture to illustrate the effect of the `Stretch` property.

Fig. 7.6
The *Stretch* property can affect the appearance of a picture in an Image control.

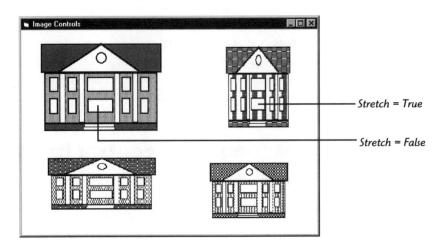

Stretch = True

Stretch = False

66 *Plain English, please!*

The **aspect ratio** is simply the ratio of the vertical size of a picture to the horizontal size. If you keep the contents of the picture the same, increasing the vertical size will cause objects in the picture to appear taller and thinner. The same thing happens if you decrease the horizontal size. 99

As you did with the Picture control, try out the Image control by placing one on the form and loading various pictures. Try it with the `Stretch` property set first to `False`, then to `True`.

One difference between the Image control and the Picture control is that the Image control cannot contain or hold other controls. This means that any controls that are placed on top of the Image control are not moved when the Image control is moved; rather, they stay in their original locations.

The best way to display pictures

There *is* no best way to display pictures. As with many other design decisions, the best method to use depends on what you are trying to accomplish. For example, if you need to place other controls over the picture, the picture must be contained in either a picture box or the form itself. If you want to display more than one picture at a time, you cannot display them directly on the form. You must use Picture box controls or Image controls since you can have as many of them on your form as you want. To help you with your decision on which control to use, table 7.1 summarizes some of the key features of each.

Table 7.1   Features that Help Determine Where to Display a Picture

Feature	Present in Form	Picture	Image
Can display bitmaps, icons, and metafiles	Yes	Yes	Yes
Can contain other controls	Yes	Yes	No
Can automatically adjust to fit picture size	No	Yes	Yes
Can fit entire picture in any space (bitmaps and icons)	No	No	Yes
Can be used to edit picture	No	Yes	No

Changing a control's picture with code

Most of the programs described in the previous "How can I use this in the real world" section require that the program be able to change pictures as the data changes. For instance, with the real estate program, you would have to load a new picture for each house selected for viewing. This means that you have to be able to load the pictures with code.

To learn more about using variables in code, refer to Chapter 17, "Adding Variables to Your Programs"

There are two ways to use code to place a picture in a control or form. You can use the LoadPicture function to import the picture from a file, or you can copy a picture from another control or the form.

To show you how this works, place a Picture control (named SlideShow), a text box (named PictName), and a command button (named ShowPict) on a form so that it looks like figure 7.7. Now place the following code line in the Click event of the command button:

```
SlideShow.Picture = LoadPicture(PictName.Text)
```

Fig. 7.7
You can load pictures
from code using the
LoadPicture function.

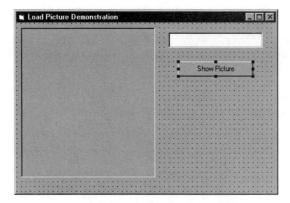

Now run the program. Enter a filename, such as C:\WINDOWS\ARCHES.BMP, in the text box and then click on the command button. For each filename you enter, a different picture will be displayed.

Using the LoadPicture function, you can also delete the picture in a control. To do this, simply call the function with no filename given, like the following:

```
SlideShow.Picture = LoadPicture()
```

Speaking of *Load Picture*

To assign a picture to a Picture control, an Image control, or a form, use the
LoadPicture function as follows:

```
object.Picture = LoadPicture(filename)
```

In this syntax, object refers to the name of the form or Picture or Image control
where you are displaying the picture. Picture is the name of the property that
will contain the picture information. LoadPicture is the name of the function
itself.

Finally, filename represents the name of the file that contains the picture to be
displayed, such as ARCHES.BMP. You must specify the filename and the extension
of the file. If the file is not in the current directory, you must also specify the
complete path to the file. You may either enter the file directly, or you may use
a string variable which contains the name of the file. If you use the file directly,
you must enclose the name in double quotation marks ("").

In the example program, you would do this by blanking out the contents of the text box and then clicking the command button.

Copy this, copy that

The other way to get a picture into a control or onto a form is to copy it from another control. You can copy a picture from one control to another using a simple assignment statement. For example, the following statement would copy the picture from one Image control (`Image1`) to another (`Image2`):

```
Image1.Picture = Image2.Picture
```

Why would you want to do this? Well, the ability to copy a picture from one control to another is the basis of simple animation. You create the animation by copying successive pictures in a series to a control at set time intervals. I won't go into the details of how to do this, but if you are interested, take a look at the `REDTOP` project in the sample applications that came with Visual Basic.

I want to create picture buttons and toolbars for my program

Even if you don't need to display pictures of houses or people in your programs, you may still want to use the Image control. The Image control provides you with a way to create picture buttons like the ones found on the toolbars of most programs.

Catch the bug

This code attempts to place a picture into an Image control. Can you tell what is wrong with the code?

```
imgPretty.Stretch = False
imgPretty.Left = 1000
imgPretty.Picture = "C:\BITMAPS\PUPPY.BMP"
```

Answer: *You cannot assign a file directly to the* `Picture` *property of a control. You must use the* `LoadPicture` *function as shown:*

```
imgPretty.Picture = LoadPicture("C:\BITMAPS\PUPPY.BMP")
```

The advantage of using picture buttons is that they can give the user an idea of the function of the commands run by clicking the button. Also, making use of the same buttons as other programs lets the user learn your applications more quickly. For example, if you include a button with a diskette on it, most people will assume that clicking that button will save their files. You can use a series of Image controls to create a toolbar.

Setting up the picture button

The first step in creating a picture button is to place an Image control on the form. To do this, select the Image control from the Visual Basic toolbar and position it on the form.

Once you have placed the Image control on the form, you will need to assign the picture of a button to the Image control. The picture can be assigned at designtime using the Load Picture dialog box previously described. As the picture is loaded, the Image control will automatically be resized to fit the button picture (remember the default setting of the `Stretch` property). You can then place the button anywhere you want on the form by clicking it and dragging it to its final location.

TIP **There are a number of toolbar style bitmaps provided with Visual** Basic for use in your programs. They are located in the `\bitmaps\toolbar` subdirectory under the Visual Basic main directory. If none of these bitmaps suit your needs, you can create your own with Paintbrush or another graphics package.

You can use a series of Image controls to create your own toolbar. Figure 7.8 shows a toolbar that could be used for a number of programs.

Fig. 7.8
A toolbar provides a
visual cue of the
functions it invokes.

To activate the buttons of the toolbar, you need to place code for the desired function in the `Click` event of each Image control you use. This is equivalent to placing code in the `Click` event of a command button, as was discussed in Chapter 3, "Time to Build Your First Program!". When your application is run, the user will access these functions simply by clicking the button for the function.

Letting the user push the button

If you have worked with an application containing a toolbar, you have probably noticed that many buttons change appearance when they are clicked. Typically, they show one image when the button is "up," then a different image when the button is depressed. The button is depressed when the mouse button is pushed down. This activity often happens quickly, but if you press and hold the mouse button, you can see the other image.

You can make your toolbar do the same thing by using multiple pictures for each Image control and using the MouseDown and MouseUp events of the control to change the pictures.

To create this two-state button, you will need to place three Image controls on the form for each button you want to present to the user. One Image control will be the actual button on the toolbar. The other two Image controls will contain the pictures for the two button states, one for the "up" state and one for the "down" state. You will need to set the Visible property of these latter two Image controls to False, so that they do not show up in the actual application. Figure 7.9 shows the form as it looks in the design mode. (The toolbar, as it looks in the run mode, was shown in figure 7.8.)

Fig. 7.9

The controls containing the button images need to be hidden when the application is run.

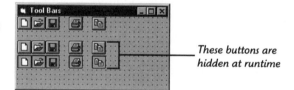

These buttons are hidden at runtime

Changing the state of the button requires changing the picture in the Image control presented to the user. This is done by setting the Picture property of the Image control shown to the user with the picture in one of the other Image controls. The down button is loaded in the MouseDown event, while the up button is loaded in the MouseUp event. This code is shown in listing 7.1. Notice that the initial setting of the button is loaded in the Form_Load event.

Listing 7.1 **Change Pictures Using the *Picture* Property**

```
'*****************************************************
'The button is initially loaded with the up picture.
'*****************************************************
Private Sub Form_Load()
    Image1.Picture = Image2.Picture
End Sub
'*******************************************************
'When the mouse button is pressed, the down button is shown
'*******************************************************
Private Sub Image1_MouseDown(Button As Integer,
Shift As Integer, X As Single, Y As Single)
    Image1.Picture = Image3.Picture
End Sub
'*********************************************************
'When the mouse button is released, the up button is shown
again
'*********************************************************
Private Sub Image1_MouseUp(Button As Integer,
Shift As Integer, X As Single, Y As Single)
    Image1.Picture = Image2.Picture
End Sub
```

Listing 7.1 consists of three assignment statements placed in individual events. The first event, the Load event for the form, occurs when the program first starts. The statement loads the picture from the Image2 control, which contains the up state of the button, to the Image1 control, which is the one shown to the user. This assures you that the up button is shown as the initial condition.

When the user presses the mouse button down, the second event is triggered, the MouseDown event. The code in this event assigns the picture of the down state of the button to the image shown to the user. As long as the mouse button is down, this picture will be shown.

The final event is the MouseUp event. This event occurs when the user releases the mouse button. The code in this event restores the original up state of the button. You will notice that this code is the same as the code in the Form_Load event.

The code in listing 7.1 and the different pictures provide the appearance that the button is actually being pressed. The up and down appearance of the button is shown in figure 7.10.

Fig. 7.10

Using a two-state button gives the user the impression of actually pressing a button on the screen.

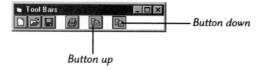

Button down

Button up

Summary

In this chapter, you have seen a few ways in which pictures can be used as part of your programs. You have seen how to add pictures during design and during program execution. You have even learned how to create a toolbar using Image controls. As you have seen, pictures in various forms can be an integral part of your programs.

Review Questions

1 What three objects can display pictures in your program?

2 How can you make the Picture control change size to fit the picture being displayed?

3 What happens to a picture in the Image control when the `Stretch` property is set to `True`?

4 What can a Picture control do that an Image control can't?

Exercises

1 Change the example for using the `LoadPicture` function to use an Image control instead of a Picture control. Try it once with each setting of the `Stretch` property.

2 Using the method explained for a single button, create a toolbar of Image controls.

3 Using multiple pictures, create an animation sequence by copying different pictures to a single control.

4 Use a Windows metafile to create a background for an application.

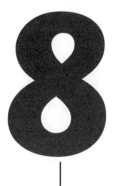

Limiting Input with Checkboxes and Option Buttons

● **In this chapter:**

● **Yes or no? Let the users make up their minds**

● **Multiple choice is not just for exams anymore**

● **You picked option number 1**

● **Pick one from each category**

If you want to control the information your users can enter, then checkboxes and option buttons might be just what you need . . . . ➤

Previously, you have seen how to get input from a user with the use of a text box. This works well for a number of data-gathering needs. But what if you just want to ask a simple piece of information such as, "Do you own a car?" or "What is your marital status?" In these cases, the answer you want is limited to, at most, a few choices.

Why do you need to limit the user's choices?

While a text box will work for getting simple information, what is the user supposed to enter? For a Yes or No choice, do you want the user to type out the entire word or just use the first letter? Or would you prefer True or False responses? By the same token, what should a person enter for marital status? Are you looking for just married or single, or do you want to include divorced and widowed?

These differences may not seem like much on the outside, but they can have a critical difference in how you write a program. If you set up a program to handle only the words "Yes" and "No," your program will have a problem if users type in "Maybe," or if they mistype a word.

You can eliminate the problem and provide the user with more direction on the responses you seek by giving them a specific set of choices. This can be accomplished through the use of checkboxes and option buttons.

Am I limiting your choices? Yes or no?

A checkbox is one of the controls in Visual Basic. It is used to get an answer of either Yes or No from the user. It works like a light switch. It is either on or off; there is no in-between. When a checkbox is on, a checkmark (✓) is displayed in the box. This indicates that the answer to the checkbox's question is "Yes." When the checkbox is off, the box is empty, indicating a "No" answer. Figure 8.1 shows a checked (on) and unchecked (off) box.

 TIP   **The checkmark is used in Windows 95 programs. Windows NT or** Windows 3.1 programs will show an X in the checkbox.

Fig. 8.1
Click the box or the prompt to change the value of the checkbox.

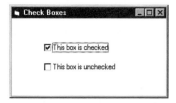

The prompts used in a checkbox do not necessarily have to be in the form of a question. If you have looked at some of the option dialog boxes used for programs, you have seen checkboxes used to specify which options should be turned on. The **prompt** for the checkbox is simply the option name, instead of a question. Figure 8.2 shows the Environment Options dialog box for Visual Basic, which shows this type of use.

66 *Plain English, please!*

A prompt is simply a name for the text used to tell the user what to enter, or in the case of a checkbox, what question the Yes or No answer refers to. **99**

Fig. 8.2
Checkboxes are everywhere.

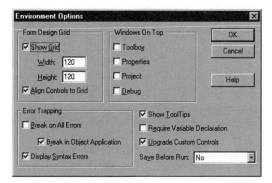

Creating a checkbox

As with other controls, the first step to using a checkbox is to draw it on the form. By now, you are probably familiar with the process—select the CheckBox control, place the mouse cursor at one corner of the box area, click the left button, drag the cursor to the opposite corner, and then release the button.

The Name property and suggested naming conventions were discussed in Chapter 3, "Time to Build Your First Program!"

Now you have a checkbox on the form that has a prompt of Check1. Since this will have absolutely no meaning to a user, you will need to change the prompt to something more useful. The prompt of a checkbox is contained in the Caption property of the box. Select the Caption property from the Properties dialog box and change it to "Are we having fun yet?" While you are working on the properties, don't forget to change the Name property of the control.

Controlling the appearance

You can change the appearance of the checkbox by changing the font used for the text, or by changing the colors used for the foreground and background. You can also change the appearance by changing the **text justification** of the box using its Alignment property.

 Plain English, please!

Text justification is used to describe the position of the text within an area. The three typical choices for text justification are **left-justified** (text lines up against the left edge of the area), **right-justified** (text lines up against the right edge of the area), and **centered** (there is equal space on both sides of the text). **"**

Unless you specifically change the Alignment property, a checkbox will appear with the box immediately to the left of the prompt in the left-justified position. By selecting Right Justify for the Alignment property, you change the appearance of the checkbox so that the box is at the right side of the prompt (see fig. 8.3).

Fig. 8.3
Be consistent in the placement of the box to avoid confusing your user.

 CAUTION **If you use right justification for the checkbox, make sure that** the control is sized so that the box is next to the prompt. Otherwise, a misalignment (like the one in figure 8.3) can cause confusion for the user.

Setting the initial value

The final thing you will need to do in setting up a checkbox is to set the initial state for the control, either checked or unchecked. Whether the checkbox is checked or not is controlled by the Value property. If you want the checkbox to be checked when the program starts, set the Value property to 1—checked; otherwise, leave the property with a setting of 0—unchecked—which is the default value.

 TIP **There is a third possible setting for the checkbox Value property.** The setting is 2—grayed. When set to this value, the checkbox will show a gray checkmark in the box. This indicates that the value of the checkbox has yet to be defined. This setting can only be set at designtime or by code. The user cannot set the checkbox to this value.

And the user chooses...

When a checkbox is shown on a form, the user can change the value of the checkbox by clicking it with the mouse. The user can also use the Tab key to move to the checkbox, and then press the Space Bar to change the value of the checkbox. One click of the mouse or one press of the Space Bar will **toggle**, or change, the value from checked to unchecked, or vice versa. A second click will return the checkbox to its original setting.

For most programs, you will want to determine whether or not the checkbox is checked in your code. You do this by looking at the Value property. The code in listing 8.1 looks at the Value property of the "Are we having fun yet?" checkbox, and then prints an appropriate message based on the value. The code is placed in the Click event of the checkbox so that it is executed each time the checkbox is changed.

Listing 8.1   Find Out What the User Chose

```
Form1.Cls
If RealFun.Value = vbChecked Then
    Form1.Print "This is a blast"
Else
    Form1.Print "This is a real bore"
End If
```

To learn more about conditional statements, see Chapter 24, "If I Go This Way, Where Will I End Up?"

The first line of code in the listing clears the form of any text that may have been printed on it previously. The `Cls` method has no effect on controls on the form. The next line determines the setting of the checkbox's `Value` property. (Substitute the name of your checkbox for the name `RealFun` when you try this.) If the `Value` property is set to `1` (checked), the condition is `True` and the first statement, `This is a blast`, is printed. If the `Value` property is `0` (unchecked), the condition is `False` and the second statement, `This is a real bore`, is printed.

Catch the bug

The checkbox in the figure doesn't match the property values listed below. Can you tell which ones are wrong?

```
Alignment = 0 - Left Justify
Caption = Married
Value = 0 - Unchecked
```

Answer: For the box shown, the properties should have been:

```
Alignment= 1 - Right Justify
Caption = Married
Value= 0 - Unchecked.
```

How can I use this in the real world?

You can use checkboxes for gathering information, such as on a job application. For this task, you might need to know things like, "Do you have your own transportation?" or "Can you work weekends?" You can probably think of a number of other Yes/No questions that would benefit from using a checkbox.

Pick a button, any button

The other way to let the user make choices is with the use of option buttons. Option buttons are never used singly. The value of option buttons is to use them in a group, to allow a user to select a single value from multiple choices (see fig. 8.4).

Option buttons work like the speed selection buttons on a blender. If you press one button down, all the other buttons come up. The option buttons work the same way in that when you check one button, all the other buttons are automatically unchecked.

Fig. 8.4
When you pick one button, the others are cleared.

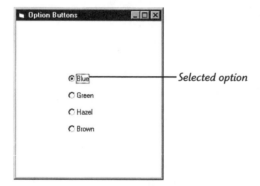

Selected option

Gimme some option buttons

To use option buttons, you need to create a button for each possible choice that the user can select from. For instance, you might have the user select eye color from the choices blue, hazel, green, or brown. For this, you would need four option buttons.

Where do I place these babies?

To create the set of option buttons, you draw each button on the form and set its properties. Like the checkbox, the prompt for the option button is contained in the `Caption` property. To create the form shown in figure 8.4, draw four buttons on the form and set the caption of each button to one of the four eye colors. For other programs, you may have more or fewer options. You can create as many option buttons as you need to allow for all the choices you want to present to your user.

Q&A ***Can I include an option for "Other" and have a blank for the user to fill in?***

While this cannot be done with an option button alone, you could use an option button in conjunction with a text box to provide this. The text box would serve as your entry blank. See the following figure as an example.

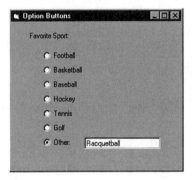

Setting the initial value

Once you have placed all the required buttons on the form, you will want to make one of the buttons the initial choice. To do this, select the button you want, and set its Value property to True. You will notice on your form that the circle associated with this button becomes a filled circle. All the other buttons on the form will change to empty circles. (Remember, only one option button can be selected at a time.)

Controlling the appearance

Option buttons have the same capabilities for controlling the appearance of an individual button as checkboxes. You can, of course, choose different fonts for the prompts, and different colors, too. Like the checkbox, you can also change the Alignment property of the option buttons to place the circle to the right or the left of the prompt.

TIP **The foreground color you choose for an option button affects the** circle in the button (whether filled or unfilled) as well as the text in the prompt.

One additional factor in the appearance of option buttons is the arrangement of individual buttons within the group. You can arrange buttons in either a horizontal group or a vertical group (see fig. 8.5). My personal preference is to use vertical groups so that all the circles in the buttons are aligned.

 The groups of buttons shown in figure 8.5 are placed in separate containers. This technique will be covered in the later section, "Allowing the user to select from multiple groups."

Fig. 8.5
Option buttons may be arranged in either horizontal groups or vertical groups, depending on your preference.

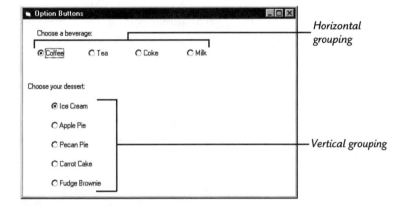

Horizontal grouping

Vertical grouping

 I have trouble getting all the option buttons lined up correctly. What can I do?

Let's look at lining up the buttons in a vertical group. The property that controls how far a control is from the left side of the form is the Left property. By setting the Left property of all the option buttons to the same number, they will be perfectly lined up.

 An easy way to line up the buttons is to select all the buttons at once. Then, setting the Left property in the Properties dialog box will set it for all the buttons.

Which button is selected?

When the option buttons are displayed in your program, the user can choose one by clicking it with the mouse. A button may also be selected by using the cursor keys. Whichever option button has the **focus** will be the one that has the filled circle. The filled circle indicates the choice on the screen.

Plain English, please!

The **focus** is the dotted rectangular box that indicates which control is active. This box moves from control to control as you enter information or click buttons on the form.

Since your program can't see the screen to tell which option button has the filled circle, you need to use another method to tell it which button the user picked. The `Value` property tells you whether or not a particular button was picked. The property will be set to `True` for the selected option and `False` for all others. Therefore, you need to examine the `Value` property of each option button to find the one that is `True`.

Looking at the example of eye color, the code in listing 8.2 will examine the `Value` property of the option buttons and print out the appropriate eye color on the form. To be able to run this code, I added a command button (named `ColorChoice`) to the form. The code is contained in the `Click` event of the command button.

Listing 8.2   Finding the Selected Button

```
Private Sub ColorChoice_Click()
    Form1.Cls
    If BlueEyes.Value Then
        Form1.Print "Your eyes are blue"
    ElseIf GreenEyes.Value Then
        Form1.Print "Your eyes are green"
    ElseIf HazelEyes.Value Then
        Form1.Print "Your eyes are hazel"
    ElseIf BrownEyes.Value Then
        Form1.Print "Your eyes are brown"
    End If
End Sub
```

The first line is used to clear any printed text from the form. The second line starts the process of checking for the selected option button. This line checks the `Value` property of the `BlueEyes` button. If the `Value` is `True`, indicating that this is the selected button, the code will move to the next line, print the statement `Your eyes are green`, and skip the rest of the statements. If the `Value` is `False`, the code will proceed to the first `ElseIf` statement, which checks the `Value` of the `GreenEyes` button. This process continues until the code finds the selected button.

Allowing the user to select from multiple groups

I previously said that only one option button on a form could be selected at a time. This is true, but there is a way to allow you to give your users choices from several groups of buttons at the same time. Grouping your buttons allows users to select items cafeteria style, like one entree, one vegetable, one dessert, and one drink. When the buttons are properly grouped, the user can select one, but only one, button from each group of buttons (see fig. 8.6).

Fig. 8.6
The border around the buttons visually groups the buttons for your user.

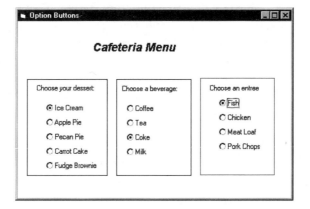

The secret to creating button groups is the use of a Container control. There are two controls that can be used for this purpose—the Frame control and the Picture control. Each of these controls can hold other controls within their borders. Any controls contained by either a Frame or Picture control are treated as a part of the container. This means that when a container is moved, all the controls within it move, too. Likewise, if a container is disabled, none of the controls in it are accessible.

TIP   **Any control can be placed inside a container. You can even place** a container within another container, like the stacking barrels you played with as a kid.

The purpose of using a container with option buttons is to segregate the buttons within it from buttons that are on the form or in another container. This means that you can select one button from the group within each container and can create as many containers as you need.

Q&A **Can I have multiple groups within a container?**

No. Just like a form can only support one group of buttons, no matter how they are arranged on a form, each container can only support one group of buttons.

My option buttons have been framed

The sole purpose of the Frame control is to provide a container to group other controls. To use a Frame control as a container, first draw a frame on your form (the same way you draw any other control), and then draw the other controls on top of the frame. In order for a control to be contained in the frame, it must be drawn on the frame to begin with. Once a control is drawn, it cannot be dragged onto the frame from another part of the form, nor can it be dragged out of the frame. To move a control into or out of a frame, you must use the Cut and Paste selections of the Edit menu.

TIP **To verify that a control is contained by the frame, try moving the** frame. If the control moves with it, then it is part of the frame.

A frame is initially drawn with a single line border around it and a caption in the upper left corner. You can change the `Caption` property to identify the group of controls in the frame, or you can delete the `Caption` property to give you an unbroken border around the controls (see fig. 8.7). The only other thing you can do for the appearance of the frame is to change the foreground and background colors.

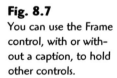

Fig. 8.7
You can use the Frame control, with or without a caption, to hold other controls.

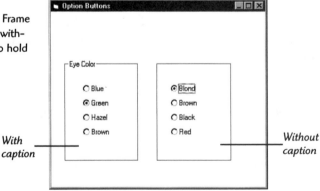

Put yourself in this picture

We discussed picture controls in Chapter 7, "Adding Pictures to Convey More Information," as a way of displaying and editing pictures in files. It was also mentioned that you could place other controls in a Picture control. When you do this, you are using the Picture control as a container for the other controls.

To use a Picture control as a container, you perform the same steps that you did to use a frame. Specifically, draw the Picture control on the form and then draw the other controls on the Picture control.

What are the advantages to using a Picture control instead of a Frame control? There are two main ones:

- A Picture control allows you to eliminate the border around the group if you want to. You cannot eliminate the border in a Frame control.

- You can load a picture into the Picture control to serve as a background for the rest of the controls. You can use a background to help identify how the option buttons are used, such as placing a picture of food items as the background for cafeteria choices.

Figure 8.8 shows a Picture control with a background picture, one with just a border, and one with no border, each containing a group of option buttons.

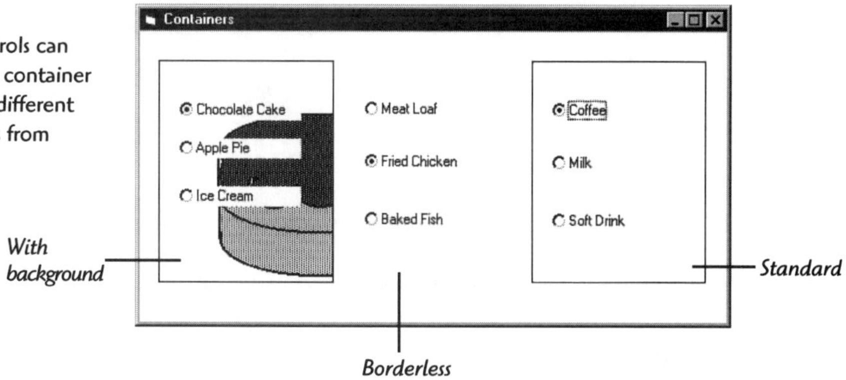

Fig. 8.8
Picture controls can be used as a container to give you different visual effects from a frame.

Determining selected buttons

Finding out which buttons were selected by the user is the same for button groups as it was for having all the buttons on the form. For each group of buttons (a group being within a container), you will need a set of conditional statements like the ones in listing 8.2.

How do I know when to use which multiple option grouping?

For most applications, it is probably best to use a frame to contain the option buttons. A frame uses fewer system resources than a Picture control. However, if you want a borderless container or a background for your option buttons, the Picture control is the only way to go.

Summary

This chapter introduced you to providing choices to your users with either checkboxes or option buttons. It has also introduced you to the concept of using containers to hold groups of controls. As you have seen, checkboxes and option buttons can facilitate data entry for the user and eliminate potential problems for the programmer.

Review questions

1 What is a checkbox used for?

2 How does the `Alignment` property affect the appearance of a checkbox?

3 What are the three possible settings of the `Value` property for a checkbox?

4 How many checkboxes can be selected at the same time?

5 Can you use a single option button by itself?

6 How many option buttons can be selected at the same time?

7 What is the purpose of a container?

Exercises

1 Add code to the `Click` property of a checkbox that will turn it red if it is checked, or blue if it is unchecked.

2 Change the eye color example so that the chosen color appears in a text box.

3 Using the eye color example as a starting point, add a set of option buttons to allow the user to select hair color as well.

4 Create the groups of option buttons for the cafeteria example.

9

Allow More Input Choices with List Boxes and Combo Boxes

● In this chapter:

- **What do I do if I need more than a few choices?**

- **Create a list of choices**

- **Lists can be sorted to make items easy to find**

- **Can the user add items to the list?**

- **Select more than one item from the list**

Offer your users a longer list of options to choose from than checkboxes and option buttons—use list boxes and combo boxes. . . . . ►

I t seems like our lives are full of lists—a grocery list, a list of weekend chores, a guest list for a party. Some people even go so far as to have a list of lists. I'm going to add a few more lists for you to keep up with. Hopefully, though, these lists will help you organize some of the others.

Can I offer users lists of information to choose from?

You saw in Chapter 8 that you can use checkboxes and option buttons to make choices. These controls are great for many purposes, but they are inadequate for handling large numbers of choices. Can you imagine how cluttered your form would be if you provided option buttons to allow a user to choose the state where they live?

Fortunately, Visual Basic provides you with several types of lists to handle these large numbers of choices. Lists can be used to get a single choice or multiple choices. Some lists even allow the user to enter values that are not on the list. You'll take a look at all of these in this chapter.

How do I make a list?

To see how to allow a user to easily enter numbers, refer to Chapter 11, "Use Scroll Bars and Spin Buttons for Entering Numbers."

Figure 9.1 shows a simple list used to pick a state abbreviation for use on a mailing label. This simple list shows you all the components that make up the list box. Let's take a look at the parts of this simple list box. First, look at the list of items. These items are the choices from which the user will select. The items in most lists are groups of related objects, such as state abbreviations, fruits, or job classifications. They are also typically text items. List are not frequently used for numerical input.

Fig. 9.1
A simple list box contains a series of choices for the user.

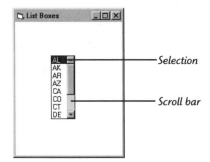

The next component of note in the list box is the scroll bar. When the scroll bar is present, it indicates that there are more items on the list than will fit in the box and provides the user with an easy way to view the additional items.

The selected item is the one chosen by the user. The selected item is indicated by a highlight bar, a blue bar with white text on most systems.

To the user, using the simple list box is like choosing channels on your TV. The cable company decides what channels to put on the selection list. You can then pick any of these channels; but if you don't like any of them, you can't add one to the list. With the list box, the choices are set up by you, the programmer, but the user can only select from the items you decide should be available.

Setting up the list box

When you first draw a list box on the form, it only shows the border of the box and the text List1 (for the first list box). There are no scroll bars present and, of course, no list items. The scroll bars are only added to the list box when you have more items than will fit. This is done automatically by the program. Figure 9.2 shows you the initial appearance of a list box. Also, when you draw the box, you should make it at least tall enough to handle four or five items; otherwise, there will be no room for the scroll bars if they are needed. Figure 9.2 also shows you a list box that is drawn too small to allow for the scroll bars.

Fig. 9.2

The initial appearance of a list box can be quite different from its final appearance.

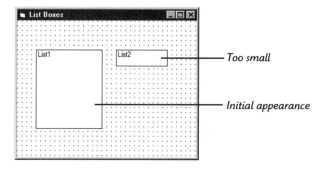

To learn about arrays and how they work, see Chapter 21, "How Can I Manage Lots of Data? Use Arrays!"

After you draw the list box, you will want to add items to the list. These will be the choices available to the user. The list items are stored in a string array in the List property of the list box. Each list item is an element in this array. To add items to the list, select the List property from the Properties dialog box. You will see the text (List) and a down arrow in the property field. Click the down arrow to access the list item input area (see fig. 9.3).

Fig. 9.3
Items will appear in the list in the order in which they are added.

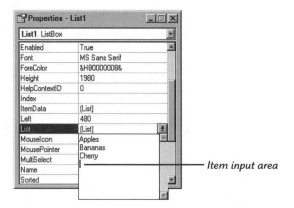

— Item input area

To add an item to the list, just type it into the item input area and then press Enter to accept the list. After you accept the list, the list box will show the items you entered and, if necessary, will display the scroll bar at the right of the list.

TIP To enter more than one item at a time, press Ctrl+Enter after each item to move to the next line of the input area. Press Enter when you have finished entering all the items.

After you enter your list of items, you may notice that your list box is not wide enough to show full text of certain items, or that the scroll bar obscures part of the text. If so, you can widen the list box by dragging one of the stretch points.

Make changes to the item list from your program

There may be programs where you want to modify the list of items displayed in the list in response to events in the program or the user of the program. For example, if you are using a list box to display food items, you might want to set up the list so that meat items are not displayed for a vegetarian user.

To accommodate this, the list box allows you to add items to or remove items from the list box as the program is running. You can place code to accomplish this in any control event. If you want, you can even place code in the Load event of your form to set up the initial list instead of typing the entries in through the Properties dialog box. To add items to the list, you will need to use the AddItem **method**.

 *Plain English, please!*

A **method** is a pre-programmed part of a control that tells it how to perform a function. For example, when you go to start your car, you don't have to give it instructions of start the fuel flow, engage the starter gear, and supply power to the spark plugs; you just turn the key. The car is already set up to do the rest. So, you could say that your car has a Start method. Each control in Visual Basic has different methods that let it perform certain functions. These methods make your programming job easier.

The `AddItem` method is used to add a list item to a list box or combo box control. The `AddItem` method performs the same function as you writing a new item on your grocery list. The `AddItem` method is used as follows:

```
Listname.AddItem listitem [, index]
```

In this statement, `Listname` refers to the control name of the list box or combo box to which the item will be added. `AddItem` is the name of the method. The word `listitem` refers to the particular item you are adding. This can be a word, a number, a group of words, or any other text. If the item is anything but a number, it must be enclosed in double quotation marks (`""`).

The `index` is an optional entry which specifies the position in the list that the new item will be placed. (Note that the first item in a list has an index of 0.) For example, say you had a list consisting of orange, apple, lemon, and pear, and entered the following line:

```
Fruits.AddItem "Tangerine", 1
```

Tangerine would be placed in the list between orange and apple. Figure 9.4 shows the list before and after the insertion of the item. If you include the index, it must be separated from the item by a comma. If you do not include the index, the item will be placed at the end of the list, or in the proper sort order if the `Sorted` property is `True`.

To delete an item from the list, equivalent to using the eraser on your grocery list, you use the `RemoveItem` method as follows:

```
Listname.RemoveItem index
```

Fig. 9.4
You can add and
remove items with
program code, or you
can delete the entire
list.

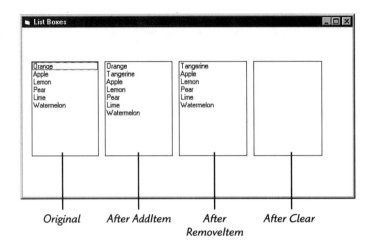

Original   After AddItem   After
RemoveItem   After Clear

In the case of the RemoveItem method, the index must be entered. This is the only way for the program to know which item to remove. The following code removes the first item of the list. Figure 9.4 shows the list after the following command was run:

```
Fruits.RemoveItem 0
```

TIP   **If you want to remove all the items in a list, use the Clear meth-**od, (i.e., Fruits.Clear). This method, in essence, throws away your entire list.

To set up the list you saw in figure 9.4, you could place the following code in the form's Load event. The series of AddItem statements would create your list of choices.

```
Fruits.AddItem "Orange"
Fruits.AddItem "Apple"
Fruits.AddItem "Pear"
Fruits.AddItem "Lemon"
Fruits.AddItem "Lime"
Fruits.AddItem "Watermelon"
```

Catch the bug

Given the input list on the left, which of the two output lists on the right will be the result of the following code line?

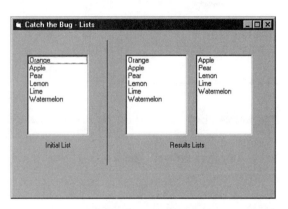

```
Fruits.RemoveItem "Orange"
```

Answer: *You do not specify the name of the item to remove it. You must specify its index. Therefore the list would remain unchanged, like the first output list.*

How can I sort the list?

Often, when you present a list to the user, you want the choices in some sort of order. This makes it easier for the user to find the choice they are looking for. Figure 9.5 shows two lists, one sorted and the other unsorted. In which list is it easier to find the word *apple*?

Sorting a list in a list box is very easy. You just set the Sorted property of the box to True. This will arrange the list in **ascending order**. This sorts all items that you put in the list from the Properties dialog box and displays them in the sorted order. In addition, any new items that you add using the AddItem method will automatically be placed in the correct position in the order.

Fig. 9.5
Setting the *Sorted* property of a list places items in alphabetic order.

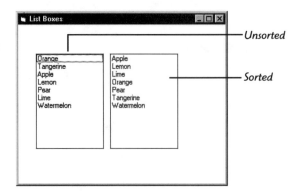

> **TIP** The Sorted **property has no impact on the order of the list dis-**
> played in the design mode. The list box will show the items in the order in
> which they were entered. The Sorted property only works during program
> execution.

You can set the Sorted property in design mode from the Properties dialog box. You can also set the Sorted property from code by using the following statement:

```
Fruits.Sorted = True
```

How do I let the user make selections?

When the user is presented with a list, how does he or she make a choice from the list? There are two ways you can choose an item from the list. The most direct method is to click the item with the mouse. When you click an item, the highlight bar will appear on it indicating your selection. If there is a scroll bar on the list, you can move up and down through the list by clicking above or below the position button, or by clicking and dragging the button itself. These operations are shown in figure 9.6.

Fig. 9.6
Selecting an item is as simple as a mouse click.

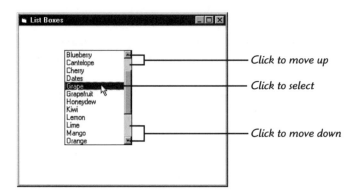

If you prefer using keys to make your selection, just use the up and down cursor keys to move the highlight bar to your choice. Whether you use the mouse or the keyboard, the highlight bar indicates which item was selected.

What did you pick?

For most programs, you will want to get the user's selection and do something with it. To find out what the user selected, you will need to work with two properties of the list box, the `ListIndex` and the `List` properties.

The `ListIndex` property tells you the index number of the item that was selected. You can then retrieve the actual item from the `List` property using the index number. The following code will display the selected item in a text box:

```
idx = Fruits.ListIndex
ChosenFruit.Text = Fruits.List(idx)
```

The first line of this code sets a variable (`idx`) to the value of the `ListIndex` property. This value tells you the position of the item in the `List` array. (A list array is a type of variable array.) In the second line, you specify the position of the item in the `List` array in order to retrieve the item. This is the part of the statement to the right of the equal sign. The rest of the statement tells the program to place the list item in the `Text` property of a text box.

Giving list boxes different looks

Arrays are described in greater detail in Chapter 21, "How Can I Manage Lots of Data? Use Arrays!"

The list you have been working with is only one way to present the list information. You can change how the list looks using the `Columns` property. The default value of the property is `0`. This gives you the standard list box that you have been working with. Setting the property to 1 causes the list to be presented one column at a time, but to scroll horizontally instead of vertically. Setting the property to greater than 1 will cause the list to be displayed in the number of columns specified by the property (i.e., a value of 2 will display the list in two columns). When the list is displayed in multiple columns, the list scrolls horizontally. These various looks for the list box are shown in figure 9.7.

No matter which look you choose to use, the list box works the same way, and user selections are made and retrieved in the same manner.

Fig. 9.7
You can display a list box in a single column or in multiple columns.

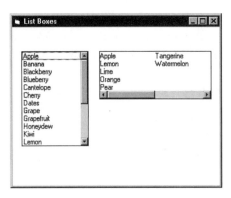

Can I create a list box with multiple choices?

There are occasions when you will need to allow the user to select more than one item from a list. The list box supports this with the `MultiSelect` property. This property has three possible settings: 0 (None), 1 (Simple), and 2 (Extended).

How can I use this in the real world?

One great use of the multiple item selections is in an order entry system. When a person places an order with a company, he or she is usually buying more than one item. A multiple selection, list like the one in the following figure, allows the salesperson to select all the items for the order, and then process the entire order at once.

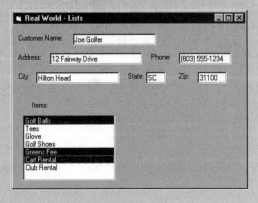

A setting of 0 (None) means that multiple selections are not allowed, and the list box can accept only one selection at a time. This is the default setting. The other two settings both allow multiple selections; the difference is in how they let the user make selections.

Select multiple items one at a time

With a setting of 1 (Simple), you can click an item with the mouse to select it, or click a selected item to deselect it. If you are using the keyboard to make your selection, use the cursor keys to move the focus (the dotted line border) to an item, and then press the space bar to select or deselect it. Figure 9.8 shows a list with multiple items selected.

Fig. 9.8
You can select multiple items from a list with the proper setting of the *MultiSelect* property.

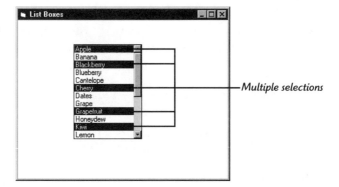

Multiple selections

Select a bunch of items at once

The final setting of `MultiSelect`, 2 (Extended), is the most complex. In this mode, you can quickly select a range of items. With the mouse, click the first item in the range. Then while holding down the Shift key, click the last item in the range. All the items between the first and last item will be selected. If you want to add or delete a single item, hold down the Ctrl key while you click the item with the mouse. Figure 9.9 shows a before and after shot of selecting a range.

Fig. 9.9
If the *MultiSelect* property is set to 2, you can select an entire range of items with two mouse clicks.

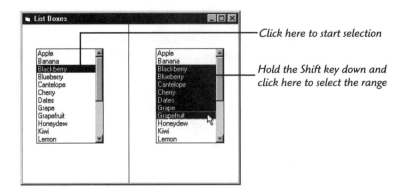

Click here to start selection

Hold the Shift key down and click here to select the range

How do I read all the selections as input?

Getting the selections from a multiple selection list box is a little different than for a single selection. Since the `ListIndex` property will only work for a single selection, you can't use it to process multiple selections. Instead, you have to examine each item in the list to determine if it is selected.

Whether an item is selected or not is indicated by the `Selected` property. This property is an array that has an element for each item in the list. The value of the `Selected` property for each item is either `True` (the item is selected) or `False` (the item is not selected).

You will also need to know how many items are in the list so you can make sure you check them all. This information is contained in the `ListCount` property. The following code prints the name of each selected item on the form:

```
numitm = Fruits.ListCount
For I = 0 to numitm - 1
    If Fruits.Selected(I) Then Form1.Print Fruits.List(I)
Next I
```

To check all the items in the list box, you need to know how many items there are. The first line of the code gets this value from the `ListCount` property and stores it in the variable `numitm`.

To learn more about counter loops and conditional statements, see Chapters 23 and 24 respectively.

The second and last line of the code are the end points of a `For ... Next` loop. You tell the loop to start counting from `0` since the index of the first item is `0`. Then, since the index of the last item is one less than the number of items, you set the end of the loop to `numitm-1`.

The `If` statement inside the loop is used to check the value of the `Selected` property for each item. If the item is selected, it is printed on the form. If it is not selected, the print operation is skipped.

When it's not on the list

The other control that allows you to present lists to the user is the combo box. The combo box can be used in three different forms—the drop-down list, the simple combo box, and the drop-down combo box (see fig. 9.10).

Fig. 9.10
The combo box provides a compact way of presenting a list of items.

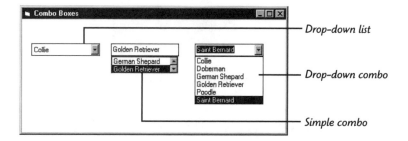

The combo box has many things in common with the list box. Both use the `AddItem`, `RemoveItem`, and `Clear` methods to modify the contents of the list. Both can present a sorted or unsorted list. There are, however, some things that one can do but that the other cannot.

The main thing lacking from the combo box is support for multiple selections. The key advantage of the combo box, though, is that it allows the user to enter a choice that is not on the list. This works like an election ballot, where you can choose a candidate from the list of those running, or write in your own.

When space is at a premium, try a drop-down list

You can create a drop-down list by drawing a combo box on the form and then setting the `Style` property to 2 (Drop-down List). The main difference between the drop-down list and the standard list box is that the drop-down list takes up less room. When the drop-down list is created, it is only tall enough to show one item.

TIP **The drop-down list style of the combo box does not allow the user** to enter items that are not in the list.

When you want to select an item from the list, click the down arrow at the right of the box to extend the list. You then make your selection by clicking it. After you make your selection, the list retracts like a window shade, and your selection is shown in the box. Figure 9.11 shows a drop-down list in both the extended and retracted state.

Fig. 9.11
The drop-down list retracts the list out of your way when you are not making a selection.

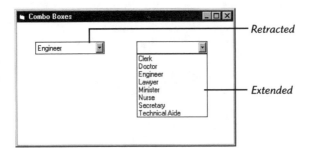

What does the combo box do?

The combo box that allows you to enter choices other than those on the list comes in two forms, the simple combo box and the drop-down combo box. The difference between these two is in the way you access items already in the list.

The simple combo box is set up by drawing the control on the form and then setting the `Style` property to 1 (Simple Combo). With the simple combo, you can only access the items in the list using the cursor keys to move up and down through the list. This shows you only one item at a time. Because of this, you would probably only want to use this style for a short list. If you don't find what you want on the list, you can type in a new choice.

The drop-down combo box works like a combination of the drop-down list and the simple combo box. You select an item from the list the same way you would for a drop-down list, but you can also enter a value that is not on the list. The drop-down combo box is created by setting the `Style` property to 0 (Drop-down Combo). This happens to be the default setting of the combo box control.

You must choose which item will be selected initially

Depending on your application, you might want to set the initial item for a combo box. An example of setting the choice would be in a program that needed to know your citizenship. You could provide a list of choices, but set the initial value to "U.S. citizen" since that would be the selection of most people in this country.

You set the initial value using the ListIndex property as shown in the following code:

```
Fruits.ListIndex = 3
```

This statement causes the fourth item in the list to be displayed when the combo box is first shown. (Remember, the list indexes start at 0.) Setting the initial choice will work with any of the three combo box styles. If you do not set an initial choice, the first item in the list will be displayed.

How do I get the input from a combo box?

Getting the user's choice from a combo box is different from getting the choice from a list box. With a combo box, you have to be able to handle the possibility of the user entering a value that is not on the list. You can get the user's choice with the Text property of the combo box. The Text property will hold any value that is typed in by the user, or will hold the item selected from the list. The following line of code would print the user's selection:

```
Form1.Print cboFruits.Text
```

Users can add new items to a combo box

If you include a combo box as part of a data entry form, you may want to have the ability to take any new items entered by the user and add them to the list of choices. That way, when the user enters another record, he or she won't have to type the same choice again.

The combo box does not have a specific method to handle this function, nor does the addition of a new item trigger a particular event. You can, however, take advantage of the fact that there will be more than one control on the form that the user must enter data into. A typical data entry form for a personnel application is shown in figure 9.12. The combo box that you want to add to is the one for "College." As the user enters new colleges, they are added to the list, so they only have to be entered one time.

In almost all cases, after you have entered the college name, you will move to the next field to enter more information or will click a command button to execute a task. Either way, the focus will move from the combo box to another control. This will trigger the LostFocus event. Therefore, you can use this event to add new items to the list using the following code:

```
If cboFruits.ListIndex < 0 Then
    newchc = cboFruits.Text
    cboFruits.AddItem newchc
End If
```

Fig. 9.12
The combo box lets the user choose from a list of colleges or enter one of their own.

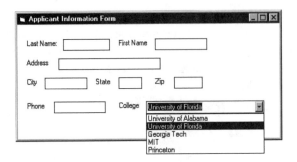

 This code is fairly simple. The first line checks the value of the combo box's `ListIndex` property. If the `ListIndex` is -1, no item in the list is currently selected. This means that the item in the `Text` property is a new item entered by the user, and you want to add it to the list. If the `ListIndex` is 0 or greater, then the item already exists in the list and you don't want to add it again.

The second line of code retrieves the user's input from the `Text` property of the combo box and assigns it to the variable `newchc`. Finally, the third line of the code uses the `AddItem` method to add the new item to the list.

Catch the bug

The following code is used to set up a drop-down list for selecting a type of pet in a pet shop. Can you tell which line of the code is incorrect?

```
cboDemo.Style = 2
cboDemo.AddItem "Puppies"
cboDemo.AddItem "Kittens"
cboDemo.AddItem "Canaries"
cboDemo.MultiSelect = True
```

Answer: *The last line should not be used on a combo box since it does not support multiple selections.*

Summary

You covered a lot of ground in this chapter. You have seen how to create a list box and determine which item was selected by the user. You have also seen how a combo box gives more flexibility to the user to enter items that may not be on the list. Now, let's see how much you remember.

Review questions

1 How do you add or remove items from a list while the program is running?

2 What property controls the appearance of a list box?

3 How can you set up a list box to handle multiple choices?

4 Is there any easy way to find out how many items are in the list?

5 What property determines how a combo box will work?

6 How is the user's selection determined for a list box? For a combo box?

Exercises

1 Change the form Load event which sets up the fruit list to make it a sorted list.

2 Change the fruit list to make it a drop-down list.

3 Change the list so the user can add their own fruits.

4 Set up a list of names so a person could select multiple names to receive a form letter.

10

Group Your Controls into Containers

● **In this chapter:**

- **How can I get more controls on a form when I run out of space?**

- **Containers—not just Tupperware anymore**

- **How can I create those neat tabbed dialogs that I see in commercial applications?**

- **Customize those tabs to your liking**

Just as the food in your refrigerator is organized in containers, the controls on your form should be grouped into containers. You'll get more use out of the limited space available on the form . . . . ❯

A s you develop more and more complex programs with Visual Basic, you will find that space on a form is one of the most limiting factors in your program design. There are only so many controls that you can place on a form before you run out of room. One solution to the problem is to place some of the controls on other forms and call these forms as you need them. For many applications, this is the best solution, especially if the data on the different forms is not closely related.

Handling multiple forms in a project is covered in Chapter 36, "When One Form Isn't Enough. "

But consider the case of an application that has a large amount of related data. For this type of application, it would be very inconvenient to have to move back and forth between multiple forms to enter all the data. So what do you do?

What is a container used for?

There are several controls in Visual Basic that allow you to show and hide groups of controls all at the same time. This gives you the ability to place all the controls on one form, but only display the ones that you need to work with at the moment. You can then use command buttons to switch back and forth between groups of controls. These controls are called containers because they are able to hold other controls.

For a discussion of containers as a way to group option buttons to allow multiple selections, see Chapter 8, "Limiting Input with Checkboxes and Option Buttons. "

There are three container controls that come with Visual Basic. These controls are the following:

- Frame control

- PictureBox control

- Sheridan Tabbed Dialog control

Add framing to make your work much clearer

The Frame control is truly a container. The sole purpose of the Frame control is to hold other controls. The Frame control is the simplest of the container controls and is also the one that uses the least resources. Unfortunately, this also means that the Frame control is the most limiting of the container controls. But it will do the job for many of your applications.

How do I create a frame?

Creating a frame to hold other controls is quite simple. You select the Frame control from the Toolbox and draw it on the form in the size you want. Then you set its `Name` property to a unique value and enter any caption that you want to appear on the Frame. The Frame will appear on your form as a single line border with the caption in the upper-left corner. If you want to have an unbroken border, just delete all text in the `Caption` property. Frames with and without a caption are shown in figure 10.1.

The other property that affects the look of the Frame control is the `Appearance` property. You can set this property to `0` to give the frame a flat appearance, or `1` to give it a 3D look. These two looks are also shown in figure 10.1.

How can I use this in the real world?

Two applications that require large amounts of related data are loan applications (as shown in this figure) and personnel data applications. For each of these, you need not only the basic information about a person (name, address, phone number, etc.), but also a large amount of other information (such as previous job experience, education, or citizenship status for a personnel application). You can use these applications to demonstrate how to handle the large amounts of data with the container controls.

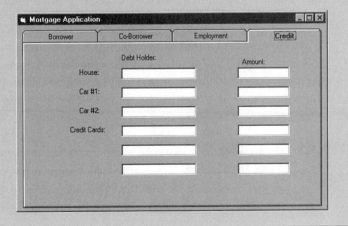

Fig. 10.1
The Frame control's properties can be set to give you several appearances.

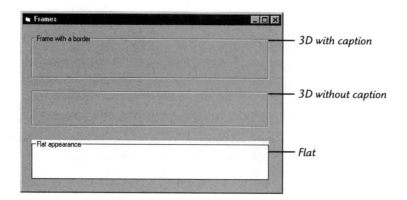

— *3D with caption*

— *3D without caption*

— *Flat*

TIP **One of the great things about Visual Basic is that its tool set can** be extended by using **custom controls**. Some custom controls merely allow you more control over their appearance than the standard controls. Others provide you with capabilities that are not available in any of Visual Basic's controls.

One of the custom controls—accessed through the Custom Control option from the Tools menu—is a 3D frame by Sheridan Software Systems. This frame is almost identical to the standard frame, but allows you to control the placement of the caption and the type of shadowing to use for the 3D effect.

How do I place controls in the frame?

You can place any other controls in a frame or other container control. You can even place other containers within the frame.

To place controls in a frame, just select the control you want and draw it in the frame just like you would draw it on the form. You need to make sure that the cursor is inside the frame when you start drawing the control. Otherwise, the control will not be contained by the frame. Figure 10.2 shows several controls for a personnel application drawn on a frame.

TIP **If you want to make sure a control is in the frame, try moving the** frame. If the control moves with it, the control is part of the frame. If the control does not move with the frame, you can use cut and paste to move it into the frame.

Fig. 10.2

Make sure your cursor is inside the frame before you start to draw a control.

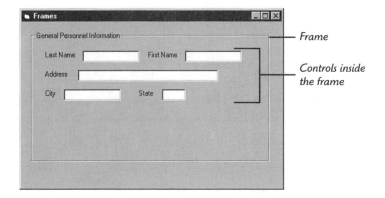

Frame

Controls inside the frame

There are a couple of things you need to be aware of. First, any control that is already on the form will not become part of the frame, even if the frame is drawn over the control. Second, you cannot move a control into a frame from the base form simply by dragging it onto the frame. You can drag the control over the frame and it will look like it is part of the frame, but the control is not contained by the frame.

Q&A *Is there any way I can get a control from the base form into the frame?*

While you cannot use drag-and-drop to place a control in the frame, you can use cut-and-paste editing. First, select the control on the form. Then, cut it from the form by pressing Ctrl+X or choosing Cut from the Edit menu. Next, select the frame by clicking it. Then, paste the control into the frame by pressing Ctrl+V or choosing Paste from the Edit menu. The control will now be part of the frame.

I want to use multiple frames

At the beginning of the chapter, I said that you could use containers to display groups of data as needed. Now, we get to the methods you use to accomplish this. Starting with the form shown in figure 10.2, you will add a second Frame control to the form. In this frame, you place controls to handle previous job experience (see fig. 10.3). You will notice in the figure that the two frames overlap while you are setting them up. This is to provide easy access to either frame.

Fig. 10.3

You can create multiple "pages" using multiple frames.

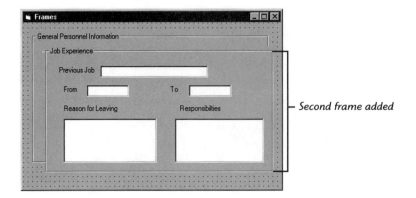

— *Second frame added*

After the layout of both frames is done to your liking, line the frames up so that they are exactly on top of each other. Now you need to add a way to switch back and forth between the two frames. Switching between the frames is accomplished by setting the Visible property of one frame to True while the Visible property of the other frame is set to False. When the Visible property of a container is set to False, the container and all the controls it holds disappear from the form. When the Visible property is set to True, the container reappears.

First, the following code is placed in the Form_Load event of the form to set the initial condition of the two frames:

```
fraGeneral.Visible = True
fraJobExp.Visible = False
```

This code causes the Job Experience frame to be hidden on startup of the application. Next, you need a Command button to switch between the two frames. The code in listing 10.1 shows how the switch is accomplished. This code is placed in the Click event of the Command button.

Listing 10.1   Switch Frames Using the *Visible* Properties of Each

```
If fraGeneral.Visible Then
    fraGeneral.Visible = False
    fraJobExp.Visible = True
    cmdSwitch.Caption = "Show General Information"
Else
    fraGeneral.Visible = True
    fraJobExp.Visible = False
    cmdSwitch.Caption = "Show Job Experience"
End If
```

 **code** An If statement is used to determine which of the frames is visible at the time the command button was clicked. If the Visible property of the fraGeneral frame is True, the general information frame is shown. You, therefore, want to hide this frame and show the fraJobExp frame. This is done by appropriately setting the Visible properties of the two frames. And since the job experience information will be visible, change the caption of the command button to "Show General Information" to indicate what will happen the next time the button is clicked.

If the Visible property of the fraGeneral frame is False, this means that the job experience information is visible. Therefore, you want to reverse the process in the first part of the If statement, by hiding the fraJobExp frame and showing the fraGeneral frame.

Figure 10.4 shows the General Information frame, while figure 10.5 shows the Job Experience frame.

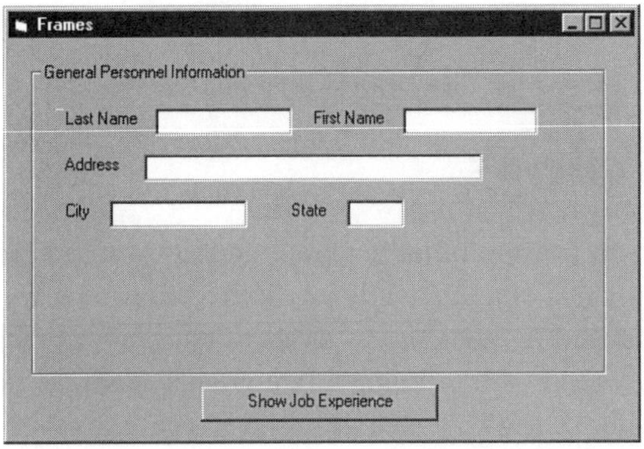

Fig. 10.4
The general employee information is shown before the switch.

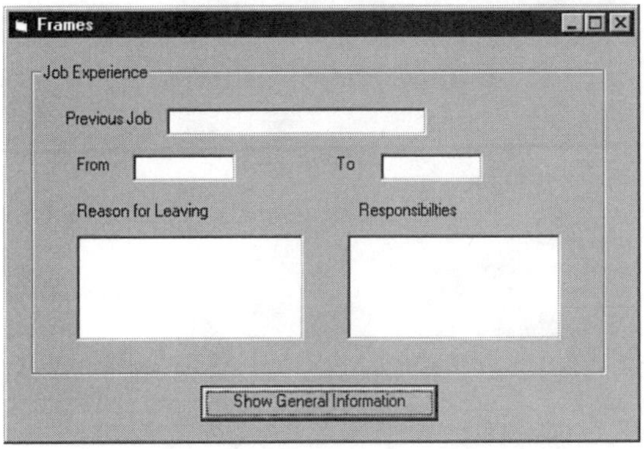

Fig. 10.5
The job experience information is shown after the switch.

The picture box is also a container

The PictureBox control can also be used as a container. Used in this way, it works the same as a Frame control with a few minor cosmetic differences, such as:

- The picture box does not display a caption on its border.

- You can set up a picture box with or without a border shown. A frame always has a border.

- You can place a picture in the picture box to serve as a background for the other controls.

To learn how to set up a picture box, refer to Chapter 7, "Adding Pictures to Convey More Information."

Once you have set up the picture box, you can draw controls on it like you did for the Frame control. You can also show and hide the picture box using similar code to that shown in listing 10.1. (Only the control names would be different from the code used for the frames.)

Separate your data even more with tabbed dialogs

Another way to present large amounts of information on a single form is through the use of a tabbed dialog. You have probably already seen this type of control used in the latest versions of your favorite programs. If not, you can look at the Options dialog box in Visual Basic (choose Options from the Tools menu) to see how tabs are used to present information (see fig. 10.6).

Fig. 10.6
Tabs allow you to place a lot of information on a form and allow your users easy access to the information.

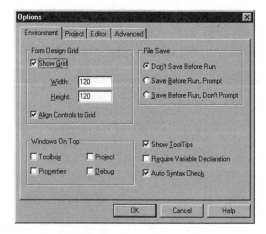

The Tab control can best be compared to the use of file tabs or index tabs in a notebook. Each tab can have a label on it to indicate its contents. Each of the tab pages functions like a Frame control to separate the controls on the current page from the controls on other pages. The Sheridan Tabbed Dialog control is one of the custom controls that comes with Visual Basic. To be able to use it, you must first select it from the Custom Controls dialog box. Once you have selected it, the Tab control will be added to your toolbox.

Begin by drawing the Tab control

To start setting up the Tab control, select it from the toolbox and draw it on your form just like any other control. The initial setup of the Tab control shows three tabs in a single row (see fig. 10.7).

Fig. 10.7
The Tab control is initially drawn with three tabs.

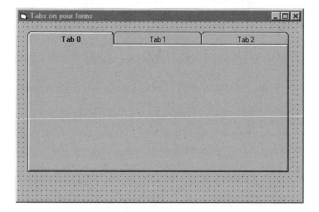

You can manipulate the number of tabs in the control and the number of tabs on a row by the `Tabs` and `TabsPerRow` properties' settings, respectively. Changing the setting of the `Tabs` property increases or decreases the number of tabs from the initial value of three. The `TabsPerRow` property tells the control how many tabs to display on each row of the Tab control. If the number of tabs is greater than the number per row, additional rows will be added to accommodate all the requested tabs. Figure 10.8 shows how the control would look with a setting of six for the `Tabs` property and two for the `TabsPerRow` property.

Fig. 10.8
You can change the
control to show six
tabs on three rows.

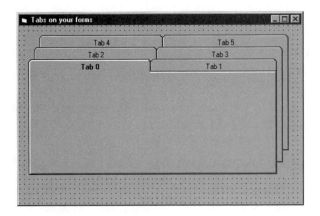

Change the appearance of the Tab control

In addition to being able to set the number of tabs and the number per row, you can control many aspects of the appearance of the Tab control through its properties, which include the following:

- Style—Controls whether the tabs look like those in Microsoft Office applications or the ones in Windows 95.

- TabHeight—Controls the height (in twips) of the tab portion of each page. A larger height allows more information to be printed on the tab.

- TabMaxWidth—Sets the maximum width of each tab in twips. If this property is set to 0, the tabs will be sized to fit the space on a row.

- TabOrientation—Controls whether the tabs appear on the top, bottom, left, or right of the control.

- WordWrap—Controls whether the text in the Caption property can use multiple lines to print.

The Style property can be set to 0 for Microsoft Office (for Windows 3.1) tabs or 1 for Windows 95 tabs (see fig. 10.9).

The TabOrientation property can be set to one of the following four values: 0 (tabs at the top), 1 (tabs at the bottom), 2 (tabs at the left), or 3 (tabs at the right). Figure 10.10 shows tabs at the top and at the right of the Tab control.

Fig. 10.9
You can choose either of two styles of tabs for the Tab control.

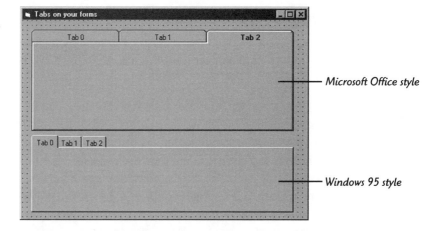

Microsoft Office style

Windows 95 style

Fig. 10.10
You can choose where to position the tabs on the control.

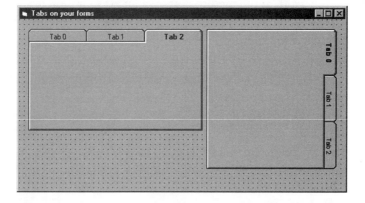

TIP **Figure 10.10 shows the captions of the tabs running vertically for** the tabs at the right of the control. This is only possible if a TrueType font is used for the control.

The WordWrap property (when set to True) allows the text of the Caption property to occupy multiple lines. This assumes that the TabHeight property is set to a sufficient amount to accommodate the multiple lines. If the TabHeight property cannot accommodate multiple lines, information will be lost. If WordWrap is set to False, only the center portion of the caption (for a long caption) is shown on the tab.

Add descriptive captions for each tab

You can set a different caption for each of the tabs in the Tab control. In addition, you can add a picture to the tab to help the user in identification of the tab.

If a picture is used, the Tab control will place as much of the picture on the tab as possible. The picture is centered vertically and horizontally on the tab. If the picture is taller than the `TabHeight`, both the top and bottom of the picture are cropped. From side to side, the picture and the caption are centered together. This means that the caption text will appear to the right of the picture and the total width of the picture and the caption will be centered. The picture is not cropped on the sides unless the picture is wider than the width of the tab. For pictures smaller than the width of the tab, the full width of the picture is shown and the caption is given the remaining space. Figure 10.11 shows a Tab control with pictures and captions set for each tab.

Fig. 10.11
Pictures on the tabs can indicate the information they contain.

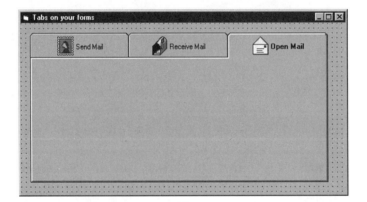

To set the text shown on a tab, you must first select the tab, either by clicking it or by setting the `Tab` property. Once you have selected the tab, you enter the text in the `Caption` property. This property can be different for each tab. If you want to have a picture on the tab, you can select a picture from the Load Picture dialog box accessed by clicking the ellipsis button at the right of the `Picture` property.

Q&A ***How can I change the caption and picture on a tab while the program is running?***

While you set the text and picture in design mode using the Caption and Picture properties, the values for each tab are actually stored in the TabCaption and TabPicture property arrays, respectively. These arrays are the properties you would access to set the text and pictures at runtime.

How do I use the customization dialog?

In addition to using the Properties dialog box to set up the Tab control, you can also access the properties through the Sheridan Tabbed Dialog Control Properties window (see fig. 10.12). This window is accessed by clicking the ellipsis button next to the Custom property in the Properties dialog box. This window gives you easy access to every tab in the control. Whether you use this window or the Properties dialog is a matter of personal preference.

Fig. 10.12
The customization dialog may make it easier for you to set up your Tab control.

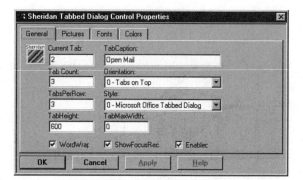

Now, what do I do with the Tab control?

After you have set the number of tabs and have gotten the appearance of the Tab control set the way you want it, you need to add controls to the individual tab pages. For each tab page, you select the tab by clicking it, and then draw the controls on the page just like you did for the Frame controls. As with the Frame control, you can place any type of controls on the tab page, including text, pictures, and frames. Figure 10.13 shows the personnel application as it would look using the Tab control.

Fig. 10.13
The Tab control can be used to handle the multiple pages of the personnel application.

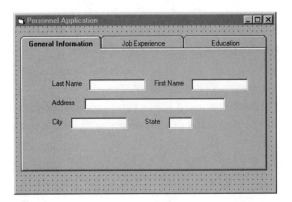

Q&A *Can I place any control on a Tab page?*

For the most part, yes. However, you need to be careful when using option buttons. While the Tab control is a true container, the individual tab pages are not. If you place option buttons on the tab pages, all the option buttons in the entire control are considered to be part of the same group. This means that only one button in the Tab control may be selected at a time. This is true even if the buttons are on different pages. As with forms, the only way to have the option buttons behave as multiple groups is to place the option buttons for each tab page inside a frame on the page. This allows you to select one option button from each group (i.e., each tab page). This configuration is illustrated in the following figure.

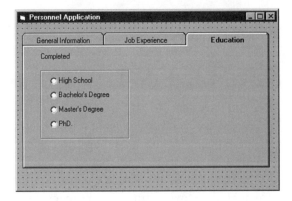

Summary

Container controls let you create multiple pages of information on a single form. This maximizes your use of available space and can make the information easier for your users to access.

Review questions

1 What is the simplest container control?

2 What happens to controls in a container when the container is hidden?

3 What is one of the main benefits of using a picture box instead of a frame as a container?

4 Which properties of the Tab control affect the number of rows of tabs?

5 What special requirement is there for option buttons with the Tab control?

Exercises

1 Starting with the frames shown in figures 10.4 and 10.5, add a third page to the personnel application and add the command buttons to switch between the three pages.

2 Using the same technique as the personnel application in Exercise 1, use picture boxes to develop a loan application.

3 Set up a Tabbed dialog similar to the Options dialog box in Visual Basic.

Use Scroll Bars and Spin Buttons for Entering Numbers

● **In this chapter:**

- ● **Enter numbers with a scroll bar**

- ● **What numbers can I enter with a scroll bar?**

- ● **What does a spin button do?**

- ● **Advantages of using scroll bars or spin buttons instead of text boxes**

With scroll bars and spin buttons, entering numbers becomes a breeze . . . . ▶

n Chapter 3, "Time to Build Your First Program!," you used a series of text boxes to get the numbers needed for a loan payment calculation. Using a text box is a very flexible way of getting numerical input from the user. Users can enter any number they want in a text box. However, a text box is not the only way to enter and display numerical information, as you can see from figure 11.1.

Fig. 11.1

There are many different controls in Visual Basic that can be used to enter and display numbers.

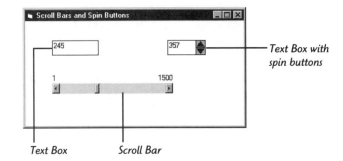

Text Box with spin buttons

Text Box   Scroll Bar

Many programming situations require more control over the numbers being entered than is available with a text box alone. This control can be over the type of numbers entered or the range of acceptable numbers. Scroll bars provide one means of achieving this control. A scroll bar allows the user to input a number within a certain range using the mouse. This accomplishes two purposes—greater control over the numbers and easier number entry for the user.

A second means of entering numbers is with spin buttons. These buttons do not enter numbers directly, but work with a text box or other control to enter the numbers. The spin buttons do, however, provide a measure of control over the numbers and, like the scroll bars, make it easier for a user to enter numbers.

How does a scroll bar work?

You have seen scroll bars used in a text box for multiple line editing in Chapter 4, "Letting the User Enter Text," and in lists to access long lists of items in Chapter 8, "Limiting Input with Checkboxes and Option Buttons." While they look basically the same, these scroll bars are different from the scroll bar controls in Visual Basic.

Scroll bars work like a slide switch on the equalizer of your stereo system. Each switch on the equalizer has a minimum level setting and a maximum setting. The slider bar allows you to set any level in the range. Scroll bars also have minimum and maximum settings, and allow you to use a slider to set a value anywhere in the range.

  Visual Basic provides two types of scroll bars for entering numerical data—the vertical scroll bar and the horizontal scroll bar (see fig. 11.2). The two scroll bars controls are referred to in the documentation as VScrollBar and HScrollBar, respectively.

Fig. 11.2
Scroll bars can be used to enter any number in a range.

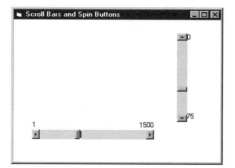

The only difference between these two controls is the orientation of the bar on the form. All the methods, events, and properties of the controls are the same. In this discussion, you will be looking at the HScrollBar control, but the discussion applies equally to the VScrollBar.

Setting up the bar

If you've read any of the other chapters on controls, you've heard the familiar tune, "start by drawing the control on the form and give it a unique name." Now that we have that out of the way, we can look at what is different about setting up a scroll bar.

The scroll bar is capable of accepting whole numbers (integers) anywhere in the range of –32,768 to 32,767. It is capable of that range, but most of your programs will require a much smaller range. One typical range is from 0 to 100, where the user would be entering a number as a percentage.

For the rest of the discussion in this chapter, go ahead and draw a horizontal scroll bar on the form, and give it the name hsbPercent. The bar should look like the horizontal bar in figure 11.2.

Controlling the boundaries

The range of values that can be entered with the scroll bars is determined by the settings of the Min and Max properties. The Min property sets the lower bound of the value range and has a default setting of 0. The Max property sets the upper bound of the range and has a default value of 32,767. You can change the settings of these properties from the Properties dialog box, or through the use of code statements as shown below. For the example we are building, use the Properties dialog box to set the Min property to 0 and the Max property to 100, as follows:

```
hsbPercent.Min = 0
hsbPercent.Max = 100
```

Big changes and little changes

If you have used a scroll bar in a word processor or other program, you know that clicking the arrow at either end of the bar moves you a short distance, and clicking between an arrow and the position button moves you a bigger distance. The scroll bar controls work the same way, and you get to set how much the numbers will change with each kind of move. The number selected by the user in a scroll bar is contained in the Value property. This property changes every time you click the scroll bar or drag the position button, as indicated in figure 11.3.

How can I use this in the real world?

There are many applications for scroll bars in your programs. Using them to set a percentage is one use. You can also use them to control the speaker volumes in a multi-media application or font size in a desktop application, like the following figure.

If you have fooled with the colors in Windows, you have seen the scroll bars that allow you to enter the amount of red, green, and blue that will appear in a color. These bars have a range of 0 to 255, the possible values of the color settings.

Click arrows for small changes

Fig. 11.3
Clicking various parts of the scroll bar will change its value by different amounts.

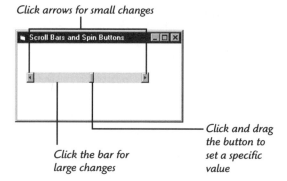

Click the bar for large changes

Click and drag the button to set a specific value

The amount that the `Value` property increases or decreases when an arrow is clicked is controlled by the `SmallChange` property. This property is used to give you very fine control over the numbers being entered. Its default value is 1, which is probably a good number to use for most purposes.

When you click between the arrow and the position button, the `Value` property can change by a different amount than if you click an arrow. The amount of this change is set by the `LargeChange` property. The default setting of the `LargeChange` property is 1. The setting you use will depend on your application. For the example, a value of 10 is the number we will use.

TIP **A good rule of thumb is to set the `LargeChange` property to a** number about 5 to 10 percent of the total range (i.e., a value of 50 for a 0 to 1000 range).

How should I use a scroll bar to show the user the most information?

A scroll bar by itself is not all that useful. The user cannot tell what the range of numbers is. Without knowing the range, making a guess at the actual value of the scroll bar is fruitless. There are several ways of displaying additional information about the scroll bar value that will make scroll bars easier for the user to work with.

Label the ends

The first thing you can do to make the scroll bar easier to use is to tell the user what the minimum and maximum values are. You can do this by adding label controls above each end of the scroll bar as shown in figure 11.4.

Fig. 11.4
Labels inform the user of the range of numbers that can be entered.

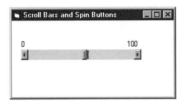

Showing the actual value

While labels help you see approximately what the value is, you still cannot see the exact value. Take another look at figure 11.4. You can tell that the value is around 50 since the position button is about halfway between 0 and 100. But is the actual value 51, 48, or 55? You don't know.

The only way to know the actual value of the scroll bar is to display it in another control such as a text box (see fig. 11.5).

Fig. 11.5
If the actual value of a scroll bar is important, put it in a text box.

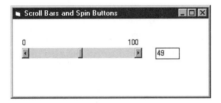

Assigning the value of the scroll bar to a text box is easy. You use a code statement like the following:

```
txtActValue.Text = hsbPercent.Value
```

The statement itself is the easy part. The tricky part is knowing where to put the statement. In order to show the value at all times, you will actually have to place this statement in three events.

The first event is the Load event for your form. Placing the assignment statement in this event displays the initial value of the scroll bar.

The second location for the statement is the Change event of the scroll bar. This event is triggered each time the user clicks one of the arrows or on the bar. The Change event is also triggered when you release the mouse button after dragging the position button to a new location.

Unfortunately, the Change event is not triggered while the position button is being dragged. If you want to be able to see the changes in the Value property while you drag the button, you will need to place the code statement in a third location—the Scroll event of the scroll bar.

When you have entered the code in all three events, your code entry window should look something like figure 11.6.

Fig. 11.6
You must use code to display the actual value of the scroll bar.

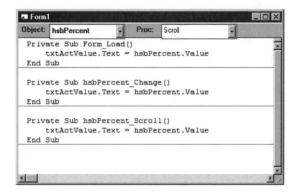

 Q&A *Does using the scroll bar prevent the user from entering a number directly into the text box?*

No. The user can still enter any number, or any other text for that matter, into the text box. If you want to prevent this and have the user only enter data with the scroll bar, you will need to set the ReadOnly property of the text box to True. Then the text box will only display data, but will not accept data entry.

Catch the bug

The following code is used to set up a scroll bar to allow a user to select a percentage. Can you find what is wrong with the code?

```
hsbPercent.Min = 0
hsbPercent.Max = 100
hsbPercent.Value = 250
```

Answer: The Value property cannot be outside the range defined by the Min and Max properties. Any value between 0 and 100 would be acceptable. For example:

```
hsbPercent.Value = 75
```

Entering numbers with a spin. Spin button, that is...

Another way to input numbers in a controlled manner is to use a set of spin buttons. Spin buttons work like the channel changer buttons on your TV remote control. As you press the channel button, the channel is moved one number either up or down. When you get to the last channel, the TV automatically loops to the first channel.

Spin buttons cannot work by themselves. They can only be used to change the value of another control. Spin buttons are most often used in conjunction with a text box. The spin button works by triggering an event when you press either the up or the down button of the spin control. It is up to you to place code in these events to cause the buttons to change the value of another control.

Adding a spin button

The spin button is not one of the basic controls in the Visual Basic toolbox. It is a custom control that must be selected for use from the Custom Controls dialog box (see fig. 11.7). This dialog box is accessed by choosing Custom Controls from the Tools menu, or pressing Alt+T, then C.

Fig. 11.7
Spin buttons can be used for numerical input.

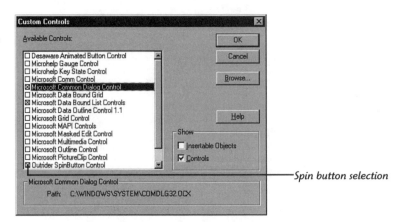

Spin button selection

From the Custom Controls dialog box, choose the Outrider SpinButton Control by clicking the box next to the control name. After a check appears in the box, click the OK button. The control will now appear in your toolbox, ready for use.

To use the control in your program, you will need to draw both a text box to contain the value and the spin buttons to change the value. It is best for aesthetic purposes to draw the buttons so that they are the same height as and adjacent to the text box (see fig. 11.8).

Fig. 11.8

To use a spin button, you must place both the button itself and a control to hold the value on the form.

In addition to drawing the text box and spin button and naming both controls, you will have to set the Text property of the text box to a numeric value. If the text box contains anything other than a number, an error will occur when you try to use the spin buttons.

How do I change numbers with the spin button?

It was previously stated that to make the spin buttons work, you need to add code to the events in the button. There are two events that you will work with, the SpinDown and SpinUp events.

The SpinDown event is triggered when the down arrow of the spin button is clicked. This event is usually set up to decrease the value of the associated text box. The following code shows how the value is changed in the SpinDown event:

```
newval = txtSpinner.Text - 1
txtSpinner.Text = newval
```

The code changes the value of the text box in two steps. The first step retrieves the current value of the text box, subtracts 1 from the value, and stores the result in a variable named newval. I chose to subtract 1 in this case, but you can subtract any value that you want. The second step assigns the value of the variable newval to the Text property of the text box.

The SpinUp event is triggered when the up arrow of the spin button is clicked. This event is usually set up to increase the value of the associated text box. The code for this event is identical to the code for the SpinDown event except that you add a number to the old value of the text box instead of subtracting a number from it. The `SpinUp` event code is shown as follows:

```
newval = txtSpinner.Text + 1
txtSpinner.Text = newval
```

Going full circle with the spin button control

Remember your TV remote control, where the channel changer starts over at the first channel after you reach the last channel? You can do this with the spin buttons as well. You still need to place the code in the `SpinUp` and `SpinDown` events, but the code is a little more complex than that shown previously, which just changes numbers.

For the code you develop, you want the spin buttons to change the value of the text box within the range of 1 to 10. That is, you don't want the number to ever be greater than 10 or less than 1. The following code is a modification of the `SpinDown` event code previously developed:

```
newval = txtSpinner.Text - 1
If newval < 1 Then newval = 10
txtSpinner.Text = newval
```

Basically, all you did was add one line of code to the event. The first step still retrieves the current value of the text box, subtracts 1 from the value, and stores the result in the variable `newval`.

The second line is the new statement. This line uses an `If` statement to see if the value of `newval` is less than 1. If it is, `newval` is assigned the value of 10. If `newval` is not less than 1, it is left alone.

The final step again assigns the value of the variable `newval` to the `Text` property of the text box.

The effect of this code is that when the value of the text box is 1, pressing the down button will change the value to 10. This way, the spin buttons act like a roulette wheel, continually going around and around repeating the same numbers.

For the `SpinUp` event, the code is again similar. In this case, when the value reaches 10, the spin button will loop back down to 1. The code for the `SpinUp` event is as follows:

```
newval = txtSpinner.Text + 1
If newval > 10 Then newval = 1
txtSpinner.Text = newval
```

If you don't want the buttons to loop, but want to make sure that the value of the text box doesn't go below or above a certain number, you can modify the code as follows:

```
newval = txtSpinner.Text + 1
If newval <= 10 Then txtSpinner.Text = newval
```

In this case, as long as `newval` is less than or equal to 10, the text box value will be updated. Otherwise, the assignment statement is ignored.

Catch the bug

The following code was used to set up a spin button, but the buttons work the opposite of the way you expect. Can you see what is wrong?

```
Private Sub Spinner_SpinUp()
    txtSpinner.Text = txtSpinner.Text - 1
End Sub
Private Sub Spinner_SpinDown()
    txtSpinner.Text = txtSpinner.Text + 1
End Sub
```

Answer: The events are reversed. The code to increase the number is in the SpinDown *event and vice versa. (I put this in because it happens to me on occasion.) The correct code is as follows:*

```
Private Sub Spinner_SpinUp()
    txtSpinner.Text = txtSpinner.Text + 1
End Sub
Private Sub Spinner_SpinDown()
    txtSpinner.Text = txtSpinner.Text - 1
End Sub
```

Summary

You have seen that scroll bars and spin buttons can be used as an alternative to a text box to enter numbers. You have also seen how they can provide you with greater control over the numbers entered by the user.

Review questions

1 How do you set the range of numbers for a scroll bar?

2 What kinds of numbers can you enter with a scroll bar?

3 What controls the amount that a spin button changes a number?

4 What is the advantage of using scroll bars over using a text box?

Exercises

1 Change the `hsbPercent` scroll bar to handle a range of 1 to 1,000.

2 Change the spin button example to handle decimal numbers (i.e., 10.1, 3.5, etc.).

3 Set up a spin button so that clicking the buttons updates a scroll bar as well as the text box.

12

Other Controls You Should Know About

● **In this chapter:**

● Displaying information on the screen

● Can I only access a command button by clicking it?

● How to make things happen at specific times

● What can I do to highlight information on my forms?

Visual Basic tools let you add flash to your applications and even run some tasks without the user . . . . ➤

Before you completely leave the section on controls, there are a few other controls that you will probably need from time to time in your programs. Two of these controls—the Label and the Command Button—were mentioned briefly in other chapters. Here, you look at some other things you can do with these two controls. I will also introduce you to three other controls—the Timer control, the Shape control, and the Line control.

Add labels to identify areas

Label controls are used to convey information to the user (see fig. 12.1). You come across labels everyday that provide information to you. For example, there are labels on food items that tell you about calorie counts, ingredients, and methods of preparation. You even have labels on your TV remote or your car radio to tell you the purpose of each button. You have labels on your files so you know what is in them.

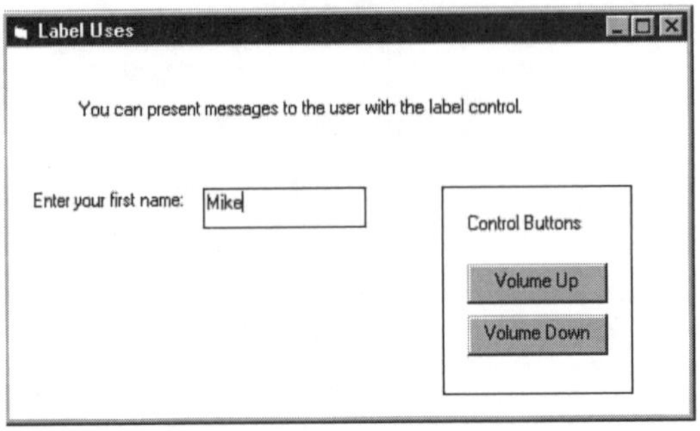

Fig. 12.1
Labels are used to identify other controls or present information.

Labels in your programs provide these same functions. Some labels provide you with general information, either about the program itself (like the labels on soup cans) or as a way to display the program's results. Other labels tell you about the contents of another control. You saw this in Chapter 3 where labels were used to tell the user what to enter in a text box. And like on the remote control, labels can be used to tell you what buttons to push.

You can also use labels on a form to present information like text is used on a billboard. You can use different fonts and colors to highlight information and catch the user's attention.

If you remember the discussions in Chapter 4, you know that you can also use a text box to display and edit information. So, why should you use a Label control if a text box will do the same thing? The biggest reason is that a label uses fewer **system resources** than a text box. In simple terms, this means that your program will be smaller and more efficient if you use labels to display any information that does not need to be edited.

 Plain English, please!

> **System resources** basically refers to the available memory for your program. Each control you place on your form uses a little of this memory. And the more functions a control is capable of, the more memory it uses. This is why a text box uses more resources than a Label control. To make your programs work efficiently, you want to conserve system resources like you conserve electricity in your house. 99

Use single and multiple line labels

Like the text box, you can use labels to display a single word or number. You can also use Label controls to display entire paragraphs of information. The information for a Label control is stored in its `Caption` property. You can display almost any amount of information in a Label control—up to 64,000 characters or the size of your form, whichever is smaller.

The real limitation on displaying information in a label is that all the information must fit within the control. There is no mechanism for the user to scroll through the data like there is for a text box. Figure 12.2 shows what happens to the text if the control is not large enough.

Fig. 12.2
Text gets cut off if a Label control is not large enough.

This is not a problem while you are designing your form, as you can easily resize the Label control to fit the information. As you type the information into the Caption property, you will see that the text automatically wraps to the next line as you hit the end of the control. When you exceed what the control will display, you can still enter information; it just doesn't show up in the control until you increase the control's size.

You can let the user change label text at runtime

When you set the contents of the Label control at designtime, you know exactly how much information there is. Therefore, you can design the control accordingly. If, however, you are using a Label control to display different text as the program runs, the text can be any number of different sizes. The way to handle the changing size is through the use of the WordWrap and AutoSize properties. Consider the following code, which assigns some text to the Caption property of a Label control:

```
lblSmall.Caption = "This text is too big to fit in original
label."
```

If lblSmall is a Small Label control, this text will not fit in the label, and only the first part of the sentence will be displayed. If both the AutoSize and WordWrap properties are set to True, the label will expand or contract vertically to fit the text. The width of the Label control will remain the same. If you set only the AutoSize property to True (leaving the WordWrap property set to False), the label will expand in the horizontal direction but will only be one line high (see fig. 12.3).

Fig. 12.3
The *AutoSize* and *WordWrap* properties control whether a label can change size to fit the text.

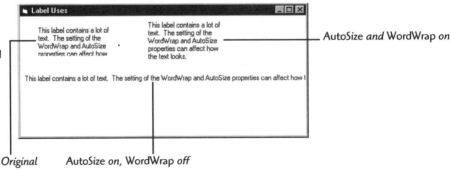

Original   AutoSize on, WordWrap *off*

CAUTION To preserve the original width of your Label control, you must set the WordWrap property to True before setting the AutoSize property. Otherwise, when you set the AutoSize property to True, the Label control will adjust to fit the current contents of the Caption property.

Q&A *I thought word wrapping was automatic with a Label control. Why do I need to set the WordWrap property?*

The WordWrap property only has an effect on the control if the AutoSize property is set to True. If the AutoSize property is False, word wrapping is automatic, but the label will not change size to fit different text sizes.

TIP If you have very limited space on your form, use the text box with scroll bars to show information. To prevent users from changing the information, set the Locked property of the text box to True.

You can change a label's appearance

To learn how to control fonts and colors, see Chapter 5, "Making Your Words Look Good."

A Label control not only provides you with a means to display text on your form but provides ways to change the appearance of the text. As with most controls, you can change the font and color of the information in the label. But with a Label control, you can also change how the text is lined up and control the background and border of the control (see fig. 12.4).

How can I use this in the real world?

One use of the Label control for conveying information would be to display a product description in an order entry application. As salespeople enter item numbers, the application displays the product description for them to make sure that the right item was entered like in the figure. Salespeople do not need to be able to change the product description, just read it to verify that the item number specified by the customer is the right item.

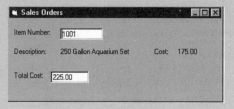

Fig. 12.4
Different label
appearances can be
used to highlight
information.

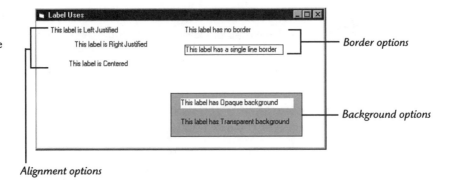

Border options

Background options

Alignment options

Lining up the text

You can align the text in a Label control in one of three ways—left-justified
(the default behavior), right-justified, and centered. (These are all shown in
figure 12.4.) You will notice that the alignment you choose affects all the
lines of text in the control. The alignment of the label's text is controlled by
setting the `Alignment` property of the control. The settings of the `Alignment`
property are `0` for left-justified, `1` for right-justified, and `2` for centered.

Letting other objects show through

You can also adjust the background of the Label control to one of two
styles—opaque (the default setting) or transparent. This style is set using the
`BackStyle` property. When `BackStyle` is set to 1 (opaque), the background
of the Label control is a single, solid color. Nothing that is behind the control
shows through. (Notice that the color of the background is set by the
`BackColor` property.) However, when you set the `BackStyle` property to `0`
(transparent), whatever is behind the label is shown with the label's caption
superimposed over it, as shown in figure 12.4.

Make a run for the border

Finally, you can choose to have a single-line border surround the Label
control by setting the `BorderStyle` property to 1 for Fixed Single. This is
also shown in figure 12.4. If you do not change the setting of the
`BorderStyle` property, its default value—`0` for None—is used, and no
border is placed around the control.

TIP **If you are setting the value of the** `Alignment, BackStyle,` **or** `BorderStyle` properties from code, you only use the numeric portion of the setting. The setting descriptions are only used when setting the values from the Properties dialog. For example:

```
lblBordered.BorderStyle = 1
```

Also, Visual Basic provides symbolic constants that you can use in your code so that you don't have to remember numbers. You can find these constants using the Object Browser.

Catch the bug

| Company Name |

The label control above does not match the property settings below. Can you find the incorrect settings?

```
BorderStyle = 0
Alignment = 1
AutoSize = False
WordWrap = False
```

Answer: *The errors on this control are that the* `BorderStyle` *should be set to 1 to get a single line border, and the* `Alignment` *property should be set to 2 for centered text. Even though the text does wrap around, the* `AutoSize` *and* `WordWrap` *properties may be set to* `False`*. Remember, word wrapping is automatic if the* `AutoSize` *property is* `False`*.*

Taking command of your programs

Other chapters have already discussed how a command button can be used to start a Program function. By now, you know a little about events and that it is the `Click` event that is most often used to "launch" a task. Our discussion so far, though, has focused on using a single command button. This section will focus on the organization of multiple command buttons and assigning keys to the command buttons.

Add order to your buttons

When you place a command button or any other control on a form, that control can be accessed at any time by clicking it with the mouse. But you can also move between the controls using the Tab key. When you use the Tab key, you will access each control in the order in which it was placed on the form.

This works well if you design a perfect form every time. But if you're like me, after you first design the form, you decide that you need to add another button or that a text box would really look better in the bottom corner. Pretty soon, the left-to-right, top-to-bottom order that you use for reading isn't even close to the order in which you placed the controls. Then, when the program is run, pressing the Tab key causes the focus (the Active control) to jump back and forth across the screen instead of proceeding in an orderly manner. This is like adding files to a file cabinet in the order in which they were created instead of alphabetically.

There is a cure for this problem. The order in which a control is accessed is determined by the TabIndex property. This property has a value of 0 for the first control placed on the form. Then, for each control you add, the TabIndex is increased by one. For example, if you place ten controls on the form, their TabIndex values will range from 0 to 9. To change the order of a control, simply set its TabIndex property to a new value. For example, if you want the control to be first, set its value to 0. When you do this, the TabIndex of any controls with a value equal to or greater than the new value is incremented by one. This way the controls are repositioned in the new order.

Controlling the Enter and Esc keys

Often in a program, there is one command button that you expect will be used more frequently than the others. In a data entry application, this might be the button to add a new record. To keep your users from constantly having to switch back and forth between the mouse and the keyboard, you can set up this command button as a default button. That way when the user presses Enter while on any control (except another command button), the Click event of this default button will be triggered. You set up this button by setting the Default property of the button to True.

You can also set up a button that will be triggered if the user presses the Esc key. For this button, you set the `Cancel` property of the button to `True`. There can be only one default and one cancel button on any one form. As you set the value of the `Default` or `Cancel` property of one button to `True`, the `Default` or `Cancel` property of all other buttons are set to `False`.

You can designate access keys

Many users prefer accessing commands through the keyboard instead of having to use the mouse. This is often the case for data entry intensive programs. To accommodate these users, you will want your program to trigger command button events when certain keys are pressed. You can do this by assigning an **access key** to the command button. When an access key is defined, the user can hold down the Alt key and press the access key to trigger the `Click` event of the command button. The access key for each command button must be unique in order for it to work correctly.

You assign an access key in the `Caption` property of the command button. You simply place an ampersand (&) in front of the letter of the key you want to use. For example, if you want the user to be able to press Alt+P to run a Print command button, you would set the `Caption` property to `&Print`. The ampersand does not show up on the button, but the letter for the access key is underlined. Figure 12.5 shows several command buttons with different access keys. The figure also shows the Properties dialog box with the `Caption` property of one of the buttons.

Fig. 12.5
Access keys provide shortcuts to your command buttons.

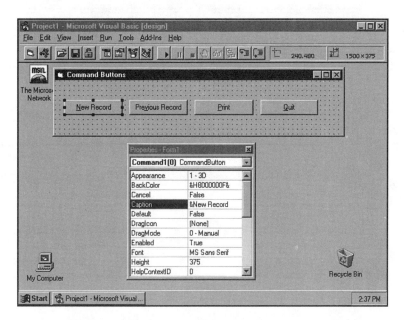

Q&A ***Am I constrained to using only letters for access keys?***

No. You can also use numbers for the access keys.

Changing tasks? Change the command buttons

You can change the `Caption` property (among others) of the command button at runtime. To do this, simply use an assignment statement, such as the following. You can also set an access key when setting the new caption:

```
cmdEdit.Caption = "&Save"
```

The code in listing 12.1 shows how the Add command button would be changed to a Save command button—as discussed in the "How can I use this in the real world?" section—and the appropriate function performed based on the caption of the button.

How can I use this in the real world?

You can use a single set of command buttons for an application and change the captions to fit the current functions of the application. For example, in a database application, such as one for a video store checkout system, you might have command buttons to add a new record or edit the existing one. When you press one of these buttons, you are placed in an edit mode, and it no longer makes sense to have the add and edit options available. You can change these buttons to Save and Cancel to either save changes that you make or to discard them.

The following figure shows the switch between the buttons. The only difference between the two screens is the captions on the command buttons.

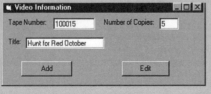

Listing 12.1   The Command Button Caption Changes as the Task Changes

```
If cmdAddrec.Caption = "Add" Then
    Testdata.Addnew
    cmdAddrec.Caption = "Save"
Else
    Testdata.Update
    cmdAddrec.Caption = "Add"
End If
```

Catch the bug

The value of the Caption property shown above doesn't produce the result shown in the figure. What is wrong with the property setting?

```
Caption = Print
```

Answer: *The caption shown on the button indicates that the P is an access key. However, the Caption property does not define an access key by placing an ampersand in front of the P. The correct setting of the Caption property would be "&Print".*

Adding timing to your programs

Another control that comes in handy on occasion is the Timer control. This control works like the cooking timer on your microwave oven. It counts down a specified number of seconds and then takes some action. The action, of course, depends on what code you tell it to run when time has elapsed.

The timer works by counting the number of milliseconds (thousandths of a second) that have elapsed since it was started or since the Timer event was last fired. When the count reaches the amount set by the Interval property, the control triggers the Timer event and runs whatever code is present. This works like the cooking timer on your microwave oven.

How do I set up the Timer control?

You set up a Timer control by first drawing it on the form. Unlike most other controls, the Timer control will show up as an icon on the form, no matter how large you draw it to begin with (see fig. 12.6). The Timer control is not visible on the form when your program is running. It is only seen in the design mode.

Fig. 12.6
The Timer control works in the background and is never seen by the user of your program.

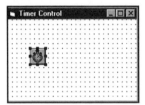

After you draw the control, remember to give your timer a unique name. To make the control work, there is only one property that you need to set. This property is the Interval property. You can set the Interval property for any value between 0 and 65,535. A setting of 0 disables the Timer control. Any other setting specifies the number of milliseconds that should elapse before the Timer event is triggered. The minimum setting, 1, is about the blink of an eye. The maximum setting is just a little longer than a minute. If you want ten seconds to elapse, set the Interval property to a value of 10,000.

Since the maximum value of the Interval property corresponds to about a minute, how can you set up longer time intervals? You set up code within the Timer event that tracks how many times the Interval has elapsed, as shown in listing 12.2.

Listing 12.2   Get Beyond the One Minute Maximum Setting of the
***Interval* Property**

```
Private Sub tmr_Timer()
    Static ElTime
    If ElTime >= 20 Then
        MsgBox "Time's Up!"
        ElTime = 0
    Else
        ElTime = ElTime + 1
    End If
End Sub
```

The declaration of variables is covered in Chapter 17, "Adding Variables to Your Programs."

The first line of the code defines the variable that tracks the number of times the interval has elapsed. The word `Static` means that the value of the variable is maintained even while other code is running.

The conditional statement determines whether the timer has elapsed 20 or more times. If so, a message box is displayed informing the user. The number of times is then reset to 0 to start the cycle over again. If the number of times is less than 20, one is added to the `ElTime` variable, and the procedure is exited.

By adjusting the `Interval` property of the timer and the number of times it elapses, you can make the Timer control count any amount of time.

Creating a screen saver

One of the useful functions that can be accomplished with the Timer control is to blank the screen after a specified period of time. Screen-saving routines were originally used to prevent damage to the screen from having the same image displayed for long periods of time. The more current usage is for security reasons. Many times, people will be in the middle of an application and leave their desk for a few minutes to attend to other tasks. If the users are not careful, sensitive information can be left on the screen for anyone to see. Screen savers provide a way to hide this information if there is no program activity for a specified period of time.

You can use the Timer control to create a simple screen saver for use with your programs. To start, add a Timer control to your main form. Set the `Interval` property of the timer to the desired amount of time. (For demonstration purposes, let's set the timer to 10 seconds, or an `Interval` value of 10,000.)

The next step is to add a second form to your program. You can add another form by pressing the New Form button at the left of the toolbar. You will then need to change the `BackColor` property of the new form to black, and change the `BorderStyle` property to `0` (None). This will give you a black form with no borders, captions, or buttons when the program is run. You will then need to add the following line of code to the form's `Load` event:

```
Form2.WindowState = 2
```

This code will cause the form to be maximized as it is loaded, covering the entire screen.

Now all you need is code to activate the blank form and to deactivate it. The code to activate the form is placed in the `Timer` event of the Timer control on the first form. The code is as follows:

```
Form2.Show
```

This causes the form to be loaded and displayed when the `Timer` event is triggered. Finally, to deactivate the blank form, place the following line in both the `Click` and `KeyDown` events of `Form2`:

```
Form2.Hide
```

This code causes the blank form to be hidden when a key is pressed or the mouse is clicked while the blank form is displayed. When the form is hidden, the original form and the rest of the screen will once again be displayed. Now, run the code and try it for yourself.

To add to the security of the screen saver, you could add a password routine to the code that hides the form. This way, the user would have to enter a password before the screen would be displayed again. You might also want to have the application terminate after a set period of time instead of just having the screen go blank.

Catch the bug

The following property values are used to set up a Timer control. Which of these properties is incorrect for the timer?

```
Name = TimeOff

Interval = 100000
```

Answer: *The* `Interval` *property is incorrect. The maximum allowable value of the property is 65,535.*

Graphics take shape

The last two controls you want to take a look at are the Line and the Shape controls. These controls are used solely to enhance the look of your forms. They can be used to highlight information, separate groups of controls, or just add a little spice to your form.

For information on using containers to group controls, see Chapter 10, "Group Your Controls into Containers."

There are two important things that these controls cannot do. First, they cannot respond to any events. That is, you cannot assign code to perform a function when someone clicks a line or shape. Second, the Shape control can only be used to indicate groups of controls. It cannot be used as a container like the Frame or Picture control.

Highlight your forms with graphics controls

The primary use of graphics controls is to break up information on your form to make it look more orderly. Figure 12.7 shows a form containing a lot of information, with no breaks anywhere on the form. Figure 12.8 shows how the form can be made more readable with the addition of a few graphics controls (shapes and lines).

Fig. 12.7
When a lot of information is presented, a form may look cluttered and be hard to read.

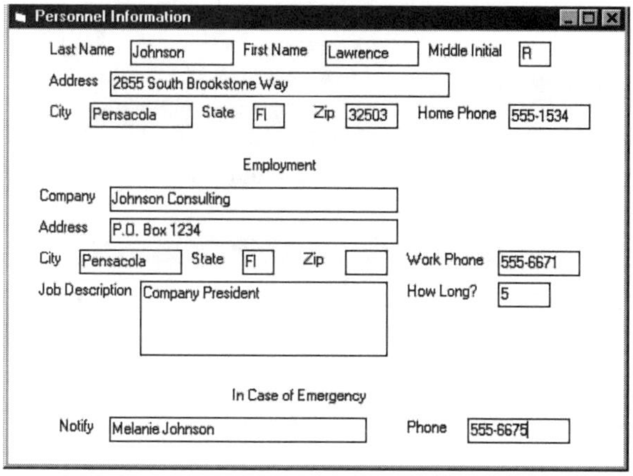

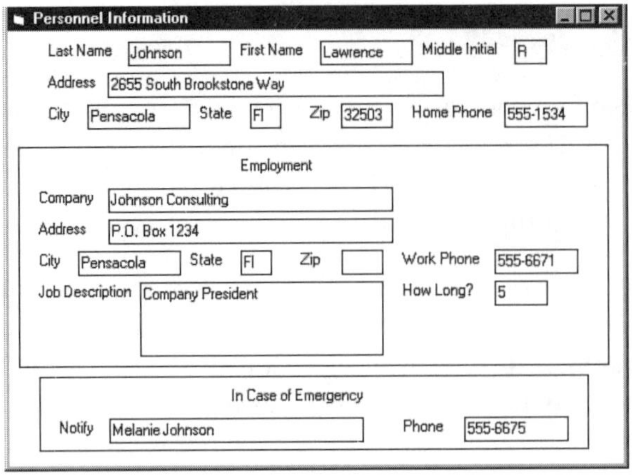

Fig. 12.8
Bring order out of
chaos with the Shape
and Line controls.

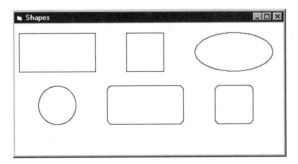

To add graphics controls to your form, you just select the controls from the
toolbox and draw them on the form, just like any other control.

Drawing shapes

The Shape control allows you to surround an area of the form with one of
six shapes:

- A rectangle
- A circle
- A square
- A rounded rectangle
- An oval
- A rounded square

These shapes are shown in figure 12.9. The shape that is used is controlled
by setting the Shape property to the desired value.

Fig. 12.9
The Shape control
surrounds an area of
the form.

You can control not only the shape of the control, but you can control other aspects of the shape's appearance using the properties listed in table 12.1.

Table 12.1 Appearance Properties of the Shape Control

Property	Controls
BorderColor	Sets the color of the line surrounding the shape.
BorderStyle	Sets the line pattern used for the border. This can be any of the seven patterns described for the Line control.
BorderWidth	Sets the width of the line used for the border.
FillColor	Sets the color used for any patterns inside the shape.
FillStyle	Sets the pattern used to fill the shape to one of the eight patterns shown in figure 12.10.

Fig. 12.10
You can use patterns to change the appearance of the Shape control.

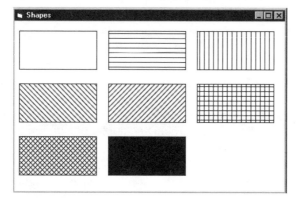

Drawing lines

The Line control serves the same purpose as the Shape control—it separates various parts of the form. The Line control can be used to draw horizontal, vertical, or diagonal lines anywhere on your form. The Line control's appearance is based on the BorderColor, BorderStyle, and BorderWidth properties. These properties function the same way as for the Shape control as defined in table 12.1. The seven possible BorderStyle settings are shown in figure 12.11, along with several different BorderWidth settings.

Fig. 12.11
The Line control can be used with a variety of line patterns and widths to place a line anywhere on the form.

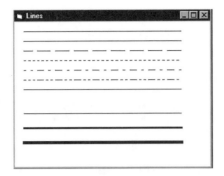

New controls for 32-bit systems

One of the great things about the latest version of Visual Basic is that you can write programs for both 16-bit operating systems (Windows 3.1 and Windows for Workgroups) and 32-bit operating systems (Windows 95 and Windows NT 3.51 or higher). Most of the controls you've seen so far work the same for programs in any of the operating systems. A few controls, however, can only be used in the 32-bit operating systems. The RichTextBox control (covered in Chapter 6) is one of these controls. This section tells you about a few of the other 32-bit controls.

Sliding into first

One of the new controls is the Slider control. The Slider control works like the slider switches on a graphic equalizer of a stereo system. The Slider control is a window that contains the slider button and optionally shows tick marks. The Slider control can be used either horizontally or vertically. Figure 12.12 shows several examples of the Slider control. Table 12.2 lists the properties that control the appearance of the Slider control.

Fig. 12.12
Use the Slider control to set a single value or range of values.

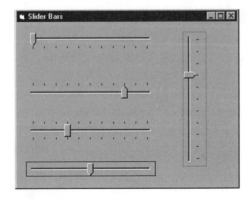

Table 12.2 Appearance Properties for the Slider Control

Property	Settings
BorderStyle	0 for no border, 1 for a single line border.
Orientation	0 for horizontal control, 1 for vertical control
TickStyle	0 for below or right of the slider, 1 for above or left of the slider, 2 for both sides of the slider, 3 for no tick marks
TickFrequency	Sets the number of increments between tick marks, can be any valid positive number

To set a value with the Slider control, you simply move the slider to the desired value. In this manner, the Slider control is very similar to the scroll bars discussed in Chapter 11, "Use Scrollbars and Spin Buttons For Entering Numbers." However, the Slider control has one big advantage over the scroll bars. The Slider control also allows you to set a range of values. To enable the Slider control to set a range, you must first set the SelectRange property to True. The user can then set a range by clicking and dragging the slider while holding down the Shift key. When the range is set, the starting point of the range is contained in the SelStart property, while the size of the range is contained in the SelLength property.

Am I making any progress?

Another of the 32-bit controls is the Progress bar. This control can be used to show the percentage completion of a lengthy operation in your program. The Progress bar is quite easy to set up. After drawing the control on your form, you need to set the Min and Max properties to set the upper and lower bounds of the range of values. Then you set the Value property to a number within the range to indicate your programs progress. By repeatedly updating the Value property, your users see how an operation is progressing. Figure 12.13 show a Progress bar with about 50% of an operation completed. Listing 12.3 shows how you might use a Progress bar to show the completion percentage of a database operation.

Fig. 12.13
The Progress bar gives your users an idea how long an operation will take.

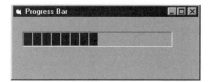

Listing 12.3   Showing How Much of a Database Operation Is Finished

```
Data1.Recordset.MoveLast
numrecs = Data1.Recordset.RecordCount
ProgressBar1.MIN = 1
ProgressBar1.MAX = numrecs
ProgressBar1.VALUE = 1
Data1.Recordset.MoveFirst
For I = 1 To numrecs
    Data1.Recordset.MoveNext
    ProgressBar1.VALUE = I
Next I
```

The first two lines of code are used to determine the number of records in the Recordset. The next three lines set the Min property of the Progress bar to 1, the Max property to the total number of records, and the Value property to 1 for the beginning of the operation. The rest of the code starts with the first record of the database and moves through the entire database using a counter loop. As each record is accessed, the Value property of the Progress bar is set to the loop index to show the percentage completion of the operation.

Summary

Using the right control can make your programs easier to use and your forms easier to read. With the right controls, you can also add greater flexibility to your programs.

Review questions

1 What effect do the AutoSize and WordWrap properties have on the Label control?

2 What control should you use to display a large amount of text in a restricted amount of space?

3 Which properties, other than Font and Color, affect the appearance of the Label control?

4 What do the Default and Cancel properties of the command button do?

5 How do you assign an access key to a command button?

6 What event is triggered when a timer's interval elapses?

7 What control is used to contain other controls?

8 What can the Slider control do that the scrollbars cannot?

9 What are the three key properties of the Progress bar?

Exercises

1 Using the database example, add code that changes both the Edit and Add New command buttons when either is clicked.

2 Write a program routine that assigns a caption to a Label control, then sets the appropriate properties to have the label automatically adjust to the size of the caption.

3 Set up a Timer control that calls the screen saver after five minutes.

13

Enhance Your Program with Custom Menus

● **In this chapter:**

● **Create a menu for programs**

● **What items must I include in the menus?**

● **How a menu starts a task**

● **Assignment access keys and shortcut keys to menu items**

● **Can I selectively make menu items available to different users?**

Powerful menus aren't just found in expensive programs. You can make your programs look very professional by adding menus that provide quick and easy access to all the functions of your program . . . . ➤

Most programs you write will need to perform more than a single function. And for every task that your program will perform, you must have a way for your users to start the function. You could create a command button for each function, but you would end up with a crowded screen that allowed little room for actual work. Of course, you could always use very small command buttons.

You can add your own menus!

A better way to provide access to all the functions of your program is to use a menu. You can handle a very large number of functions with a menu. For example, the menu for Microsoft Word, as I am working with it, contains about 115 menu items. That's a lot of functions. Your own menus may not be this extensive, but you get the idea. Figure 13.1 shows you a typical menu from a program.

Fig. 13.1
The menus for many programs contain the same basic set of functions.

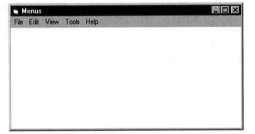

Why use a menu?

Why is a menu such a great way to access functions in your program? There are two main reasons. First, menus use space very efficiently. When you need to get to a function, a couple of mouse clicks or keystrokes starts it running. When your menu is not needed, it rolls up out of the way and takes up almost no space on the screen.

The second reason is familiarity for the user. A properly set-up menu organizes groups of functions in much the same way that you organize rooms in your house. In a house, you have separate rooms for various activities, such as bedrooms for sleeping, a kitchen for cooking, and a dining room or breakfast room for eating. When a guest comes into your house, they have an idea of what activities are done and what furnishings are located in each room, even though they may have never seen the house before. A menu can work the same way. When a user first starts your program, he or she may see a file menu (see fig. 13.2).

Fig. 13.2
A well-designed menu will group like functions under the same menu.

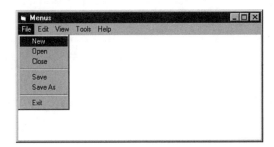

From this menu, users expect to be able to create new files, open existing files, close files, save files, and maybe even copy or delete files. Your users will be familiar with the menus because they have used similar menus in other Windows and even DOS programs.

This means that if your program uses a "standard" menu system, first-time users already have a head start on understanding how to use your program. They will already know how to do the basics and will be able to concentrate on the other functions that make your program unique and hopefully valuable to them.

What are the essentials of a menu?

There are no requirements that you have particular menu items in your program. You don't have to have a menu in your program at all. There are, however, a few standard functions and menus that are included in many programs and are recommended by Microsoft. These standard menus are as follows:

- File—This menu contains any functions related to the opening and closing of files used by your program. Some of the typical menu items are New, Open, Close, Save, and Save As. If your program works extensively with different files, you may also want to include a list of the most recently used files for quick access. If you include a File menu, the program Exit command is usually located in this menu. Also, the Print command is usually contained in the File menu.

- Edit—The Edit menu contains the functions that are related to the editing of text and documents. Some of the typical Edit menu items are Undo, Cut, Copy, Paste, and Clear.

- View—The View menu may be included if your program supports different looks for the same document. A word processor, for example, might include a normal view for editing text and a page layout view for positioning document elements. A database program might have a view for looking at multiple records and a view for detailed examination of a single record. The View menu may also be used to hide and show program objects.

- Tools—This menu is a catch-all for auxiliary programs. For example, a spell checker, grammar checker, or equation editor may be included for a word processor.

- Window—This menu is typically included if your program supports editing multiple documents, databases, or files simultaneously. The Window menu is set up to allow users to arrange multiple documents or switch rapidly between them.

- Help—The Help menu contains the access to the help system for your program. It will typically include menu items for a Help index (a table of contents for help), a Search option (to let the user quickly find a particular topic), and an About option (which provides summary information regarding your program). Any tutorials in a program are also found under the Help menu.

You can use these six menus as a basis for creating your own menu system. You can include any or all of them as needed by your program. If you need to add other menu groups, feel free. You are not bound to use only these options. It is recommended, however, that if you need these functions, you place them in the menus as identified here. Otherwise, you may confuse and frustrate your users.

What items go in each menu?

The first step in setting up a menu is deciding what functions to include in the menu. You will probably want to have access to every major function of your program included in your menu. These functions can include some of the essential functions described above, as well as additional functions unique to your program. If your program consists of multiple forms, you will probably want a menu choice that accesses each of the forms.

Some things you may want to exclude from the menu are items that are specific to a single form or are trivial in nature. For example, in a data entry application, you may not want to include menu items for the next record or a previous record, though you may want menu items to add and delete records.

Once you have decided what you want to include, the next step is assign the menu items to groups. If an item fits easily in one of the essential groups, then place it there. For functions that do not fit in any of these groups, you should try to organize functions into groups of between three and ten items. Having fewer than three items in a menu tends to waste space; having more than ten items in a group can tend to make the menu cluttered.

How do I build a program menu?

Visual Basic allows you to place a menu on any form in your program. If you have multiple forms, you can have a separate menu for each of them. This can give you a great amount of flexibility in creating menus for your programs.

To create a menu on any form, you must use the Menu Editor dialog. This dialog allows you to create menu items and submenus. It also gives you the ability to hide or disable individual items, item groups, or an entire menu.

It all starts with the Menu Editor

To get the Menu Editor dialog box, you click the Menu Editor icon on the toolbar or choose Menu Editor from the Tools menu (see fig. 13.3). (If you like shortcut keys, press Ctrl+E.)

Choose the menu items carefully

Once you have started the Menu Editor, you can begin entering the items that will make up your menu systems. For each menu item, there are two required components—the caption and the name. The caption and the name are properties of the menu item just like the `Caption` and `Name` properties of a command button. The caption contains the text that the user will see when accessing the menu, such as File, Edit, Cut, Copy, and so on. The name is used to identify the menu item to the program for handling the item's `Click` event and other properties of the item like `Enabled`, `Checked`, and `Visible`.

Fig. 13.3
The Menu Editor dialog box is where you create the menu for your program.

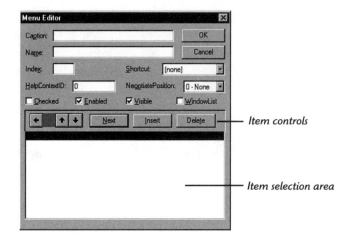

For each menu item that you want in your menu system, enter descriptive text in the Caption field of the editor, then press the Tab key and enter a unique name in the Name field. After you have entered the caption and name, you can press the Enter key to add the item to the menu list. (Alternatively, you can click the Next button to add another item.) As each item is added, it will appear in the item selection area identified in figure 13.3.

A menu should have levels

As you probably know from working with Windows applications, menus can have several levels of menu items. Almost all menus have at least two levels. The top level of the menu includes the items that you see listed in the menu bar at the top of the screen. These items are usually the names of menu groups, and they are rarely used to actually run an individual task. As you click one of these items, a menu list will drop down, revealing the second level menu items (also known as a **submenu**) for that group (see fig. 13.4).

Fig. 13.4
Lower level menus are shown as a menu item is selected.

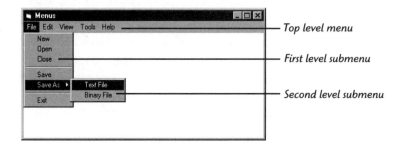

If a second level (or lower level) menu item has a submenu, a right arrow symbol will be displayed to the right of the item. Clicking this item will expose the submenu.

 TIP **Though it is rare to use more than two levels of submenus, Visual** Basic allows you to create up to four submenu levels.

To create a submenu, first create the parent item (the one you will click to access the submenu) as described previously. Next, enter the caption and name of the first item in the submenu, and then click the right arrow button on the Menu Editor (for you keyboard fanatics, press Alt+R). This will indent the menu item in the selection area, indicating that the item is part of a submenu (see fig. 13.5). This looks and works very much like creating an outline in a word processor. In fact, the menu creation process is similar to creating document outlines in the organization of items and groupings.

Fig. 13.5

Pressing the right arrow indents a menu item, making it a submenu of the item above it.

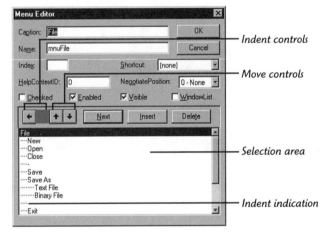

After you have created the first item in the submenu, additional items are automatically indented, making them part of the submenu as well. Now, what do you do when you are ready to enter another main level item? Simply enter the name and caption as usual, then click the left arrow (Alt+L for the keyboard) to promote the item back up one level.

 TIP **For the Name property of submenu items, it is helpful to include** the name of the parent item, such as FileOpen for the Open item of the File menu. This makes it easier to identify the menu item when you access it in code.

After you have finished entering all the items for your menu, click the OK button on the Menu Editor and you will be returned to the form design mode. Notice that you now have a menu at the top of your form, as shown in figure 13.6.

Fig. 13.6
Your menu is created at the top of the form when you exit the Menu Editor.

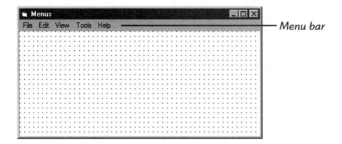

Menu bar

Add those separator bars for clarity

When you have a large menu, like the File menu of many programs, it is useful to break up the menu into smaller groups by using separator bars. A **separator bar** is the solid line that you see across a menu at certain points. Take the File menu, for example. Since it has a large number of items, you will typically see all the File Open commands in a group, followed by a separator bar, then the Save commands followed by another separator bar. Finally, you will usually see the Exit function separated out by itself.

Adding a separator bar to the menu is easy. When you get to a point where you want a bar, simply enter a single hyphen (-) in the Caption field of the Menu Editor. You will also have to enter a Name for the item, even though the user cannot click the separator bar. I usually use names like Bar1 or Junk1 so that I know I don't need to add code to these items.

Let's create a menu

To get you more familiar with the process of creating a menu, let's walk through the development of a simple menu. You'll create a menu with two top-level groups, File and Edit. Each of these items will have several sub-menu items. To get started building the menu, you first need to start the Menu Editor.

For the first item, enter **File** in the Caption field and **mnuFile** in the Name field, then press Enter. This creates the top-level item for the File menu. Next, enter **New** in the Caption field and **FileNew** in the Name field, and then click the right arrow button to tell the editor that this is a submenu item for the File menu. After clicking the right arrow button, press Enter to add the item to the list. Enter two more items, **Open** and **Close**, the same way. (You don't need to click the right arrow for these additional submenu items.) Next, create a separator bar by entering a hyphen in the Caption field and **Bar1** in the Name field. Finally, enter menu items for Save and Save As. This will complete the File menu.

To create the Edit menu, enter **Edit** in the Caption field and **mnuEdit** in the Name field, and then click the left arrow button to indicate that this item is a top-level menu item. To create items under the Edit menu, use the same technique that you used for the File menu items, and enter items for Cut, Copy, and Paste. When you finish, your Menu Editor screen should look like the one in figure 13.7.

Fig. 13.7
The Menu Editor contains the sample menu.

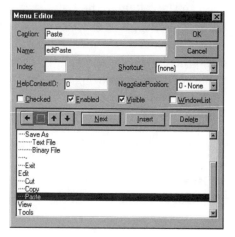

You can click the OK button to exit the editor and create the menu on the form.

Q&A   *When I tried to exit the Menu Editor, I got the message* `Menu control must have a name.` *What happened?*

If you got this message, you forgot to enter a name for one or more of your menu items. When I get this message, I typically forgot to name a separator bar. Fortunately, Visual Basic helps you find your error. When you click the OK button in the message dialog, the Menu Editor automatically places you at the offending item.

Now let's modify an existing menu

If you are not completely happy with the final look of your menu, or you realize that you left out a few items, that is no problem. The Menu Editor also lets you modify your menus after they have been created.

Using the menu you just created, let's go back in and make a few changes. First, delete one of the items you entered. To delete an item, click the item in the selection list to select it and then click the Delete button on the Menu Editor.

CAUTION **When you delete an item, Visual Basic does not verify the dele- tion, it just does it. Also, there is no undelete feature in the Editor. So make sure you really want to delete an item before you do it.**

Next, you want to add an Undo item to the Edit menu, but you want to add it ahead of the Cut item. To do this, simply select the item that will follow the new item (in this case, Cut), and then click the Insert button. This will give you blank Caption and Name fields to enter the information for the new item, and move all following items (starting with the Cut item) down in the selection list.

If you want to move an item in the list, simply select it and click the up or down arrow to move it to a new location. When you have finished making all the changes you want, click OK to accept the changes. Likewise, if the menu item is at the wrong level, you can select the item and then change its level by clicking either the right or left arrow button.

Making the menu respond to the user

Now you've entered all the items you need for your menu. You've got it looking perfect, the best menu ever built. But there's still something missing. You still need the menu to do something. Well, to make the menu items start tasks or set options, you need to add code to the menu.

The menu items only support one event, the `Click` event. This event is triggered by the users when they click the item with the mouse, or when they highlight the item and press Enter. (Users can also access certain menu items using a shortcut key, which is covered in a moment.)

Adding code to perform a task

To add code for a menu item, you use the Code editing window, like you did previously for other events. For a menu item, the easiest way to access the code editing window is to click the item with which you want to work. The code editor will be started, and you will be placed in the `Click` event procedure for your menu choice. You can then enter any valid code in the procedure. For example, the following listing gets a filename from the user and opens the file for input:

```
GetFile.ShowOpen
inpfile = GetFile.Filename
Open inpfile For Input As #1
```

To learn how the Common dialog works, see Chapter 15, "Use the Common Dialog for Specialized Information."

This code makes use of the Common Dialog box (the Common Dialog is named `GetFile`) to get a file name from the user. The first line of code displays the File Open portion of the dialog box. The second line retrieves the filename and assigns it to a variable.

The last line of the code uses the Open statement to actually set up the requested file for input.

Is it on or off?

In addition to being used to start program tasks, the menu items can be used to set options in a program. For example, in the Visual Basic View menu, there are options that let you choose whether the toolbar and the Color Palette are shown. When you have options like this in the menu, you want to be able to indicate to the user whether the option is off or on. (Whether the toolbar and Color Palette are shown is fairly obvious, but many other options may not be.)

Handling file operations are covered in Chapter 27, "Storing Your Information in Files."

To indicate whether an option is off or on, use the menu item's `Checked` property. The `Checked` property will cause the menu to display a checkmark to the left of the menu item if the property is `True`, or show a blank if the property is `False`. Look at the View menu of Visual Basic, at the toolbar item. Click the item a couple of times and watch the effect on the menu, as well as on your screen.

You can set the Checked property of an item while you are in the Menu Editor by clicking the Checked box at the left of the screen. You can also change the value of the Checked property from code to indicate the status of your choice. Listing 13.1 displays and hides a second form used as a toolbox for a program. The code also updates the Checked property of the menu item accordingly.

Listing 13.1   The *Checked* Property Indicates Menu Status

```
If ViewTools.Checked Then
    ToolForm.Hide
    ViewTools.Checked = False
Else
    ToolForm.Show
    ViewTools.Checked = True
End If
```

 The first line of the code is a conditional statement that determines whether the Checked property is set to True. If the property is already True (i.e., the toolbox is displayed), you want to hide the toolbox. This is accomplished in the second line of the code. After the toolbox is hidden, you want to update the menu to indicate this; therefore, set the Checked property to False.

If the Checked property is initially False, the conditional statement branches to the code following the word Else. In this case, the toolbox is hidden, so you want to display it. This is accomplished with the Show method. After displaying the toolbox, update the menu by setting the Checked property to True.

Keyboard access

Everything you have done so far creates a menu that allows the user to perform tasks and select program options by clicking the menu items with a mouse. What about people who want to use the keyboard to access the menus? Your menus can support this as well.

There are two ways to allow keyboard access to your menu items. You can use access keys (also known as **hot keys**), shortcut keys, or both.

Access keys for menu items

When you have access keys defined for your menu, the user can select a top-level menu item (the ones in the menu bar) by holding down the Alt key and pressing the access key. This will cause the submenu for that item to drop down, showing the items for that group. The user can then press the access key defined for the desired item to start the task. For example, the user could press Alt+F, then N for the New item of the File menu.

What is the access key for a menu item? The access key is indicated by an underscore beneath the letter in the item caption (i.e., the F in File). You create an access key by placing an ampersand (&) in front of the letter in the Caption property. For the File menu, the Caption would be &File. You can create an access key for any or all the items in your menu.

To create an effective set of access keys, you need to specify a different key for each of the top-level menu items. Then you need to specify a different key for each of the items in the submenu. You could conceivably have up to 36 access keys, one for each letter of the alphabet and one for each of the ten digits, but you would run out of screen space for the choices before you run out of letters.

 You can use the same letter for submenu items in different groups. For example, the Close item in the File menu and the Copy item in the Edit menu can both use C as an access key. However, if you use the same key for two items within a menu, such as trying to use C for both the Cut and Copy items in the Edit menu, only the first item will be accessed.

 If possible, use the first letter of the menu item as the access key, as this is typically expected by the user.

Shortcut keys for common functions

In addition to access keys, you can assign shortcut keys to some of the more commonly used functions in your program. Shortcut keys provide you with direct access to a function through a single key (such as Delete) or a key combination (such as Ctrl+S). Users who know the shortcut keys can quickly perform these tasks without having to walk through the menu items.

To assign a shortcut key to one of your functions, you simply select the menu item for which you want a shortcut key, and then select the desired key from the shortcut key list in the Menu Editor. The key will be assigned to that function, and the shortcut key information will appear next to the menu item in the menu (see fig. 13.8). There are 75 shortcut keys that you can use.

Fig. 13.8
When a shortcut key is assigned to a menu item, the information is displayed next to the item in the menu.

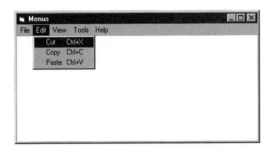

Shortcut keys are discussed further in Chapter 1, "Learning Your Way Around Visual Basic."

While you can assign any shortcut key to any function, there are a few "standard" keys that are used in most Windows programs. You should use these shortcut keys to avoid confusing your users. (Some of these keys are listed in table 1.1 in Chapter 1.)

TIP   **As with access keys, you should try to have the shortcut key** correspond to the first letter of the item name, such as Ctrl+P for print. This makes it easier for the user to remember the shortcuts.

Q&A   **When I tried to save the changes to my menu, I got the error message** Shortcut key already defined. **What happened?**

If you got this message, you have inadvertently given two or more functions the same shortcut key. You will need to look through the menu item selection area to find the duplicate definition, then assign another key to one of your items.

Adding limits to where people can go

For some of your programs, you will want to control what functions a user can access from the menu, and possibly when the functions can be accessed. For example, you probably don't want your users accessing any of the Edit functions if there is no information to edit.

Visual Basic's menus support two properties that control the availability of the menu items—Enabled and Visible. By changing the values of these properties in your program, you can control if and when a user can access a particular item.

Controlling what the user can run

The Enabled property lets you show menu items to the users but prevent the items from being accessed. When the Enabled property of a menu item is True (the default value), the menu item is shown in its normal color, usually black. This indicates to the user that the item can be chosen and its function can be run. When an item's Enabled property is set to False, the menu item is shown grayed as in figure 13.9. This indicates to the user that the function is currently unavailable.

Fig. 13.9
Disabling a menu item keeps the user from selecting it.

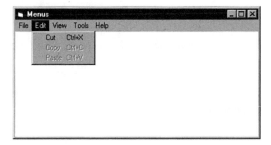

You can set the Enabled property of an item from the Menu Editor by checking or clearing the Enabled checkbox. You can also set the Enabled property from code as seen in listing 13.2.

Listing 13.2   The Enabled Property Activates and Deactivates Menus

```
If filActive Then
   mnuEdit.Enabled = True
Else
   mnuEdit.Enabled = False
End If
```

This code enables or disables the Edit menu depending on whether a file is open. The variable filActive would be set to True during a file open routine in another part of the program. When this variable is True (meaning a file is open), the Edit menu is enabled to allow the user to run Edit functions. The filActive variable could be set to False when files were closed. This would then cause the Edit menu to be disabled.

TIP **When an item is disabled or enabled, any submenus associated** with it are also disabled or enabled at the same time. This allows you to control an entire menu section at one time, as was shown with the Edit menu in the previous code example.

Q&A *Can I turn off the entire menu at once?*

No. There is no single object that controls the entire menu.

Out of sight, out of mind?

The Visible property of the menu items allows you to show or hide the items. When the Visible property for a menu item is set to True (the default value), the item is visible to the user. If the Visible property is set to False, the menu item is hidden from view. When an item is hidden, any other menu items below or to the right of the item shift to fill in the gap. There is no indication that the item is present in the menu at all.

Like the Enabled property, the Visible property can be set in the Menu Editor by checking or clearing the checkbox next to the word Visible. The Visible property can also be set in code to either True or False using an assignment statement. Also, like the Enabled property, the Visible property of an item has an effect on any submenu items associated with the item. That is, if the Visible property of an item is set to False, no submenu items will be displayed either.

How can I use this in the real world?

The most common reason for hiding menu choices is to prevent users from trying to access sensitive information. For example, if you have an employee information system that contains payroll information, you may want to hide the payroll functions from any users that should not see that information.

Enhancing your program with pop-up menus

Our discussion of menus has so far looked at the menu bar that appears along the top of the form. Visual Basic also supports pop-up menus in your programs. A pop-up menu is a small menu that appears somewhere on your form in response to a program event.

Pop-up menus are often used to handle operations or options related to a specific area of the form. An example of this type of pop-up menu would be a format pop-up for a text field that would allow you to change the font or font attributes of the field (see fig. 13.10). This type of menu is found in many of the latest generation of Windows programs.

Fig. 13.10
A pop-up menu is used to handle tasks related to a specific form or control.

When a pop-up menu is invoked, the menu appears on the screen at the current mouse location. The user would then make a selection from the menu. After the selection is processed, the menu disappears from the screen. A pop-up menu is typically selected by clicking the secondary mouse button (usually the right button).

Creating a pop-up menu

You create a pop-up menu the same way that you create the main menu for your program—from the Menu Editor. There is, however, one extra step that you need to perform. The pop-up menu needs to be hidden so that it does not appear on the menu bar. Therefore, you need to set the `Visible` property of the top level item to `False`. (Hiding the pop-up menu is not required by Visual Basic and is strictly optional.)

Now let's create a simple pop-up menu for changing the format of an item. To create this menu, follow these steps:

1 Open up the Menu Editor dialog box by clicking the Menu Editor icon.

2 Create a top level menu item by entering **Format** in the Caption field and **popFormat** in the Name field.

3 Make sure that the Visible checkbox is unchecked. (This sets the Visible property of the item to False.)

4 Create three submenu items under popFormat by entering **Bold**, **Italic**, and **Underline** in the Caption field, and **popBold**, **popItalic**, and **popUnder** in the Name field.

5 Click the OK button to accept the menu changes.

You will notice that the Format menu does not appear on the menu bar of your form. However, the menu is present.

Q&A *If I can't see the menu I created for the pop-up, how can I add code to the events?*

The code editing window has an object selection list in the upper left corner. You can use this list to select the menu item by its Name. When you have selected the item from the list, you can add code to its Click event.

Invoking the pop-up menu

To have the pop-up menu appear on your screen, you will have to invoke the menu using the PopUpMenu method.

Speaking of *PopUpMenu*

The syntax for invoking a pop-up menu is:

```
formname.PopUpMenu menuname
```

formname is the name of the form on which the menu is to be displayed. If the name is omitted, the currently active form is assumed. PopUpMenu is the name of the method itself. menuname is the name of the menu that will be shown. This is the name assigned to the menu in the Menu Editor. Any menu or submenu that has multiple items can be used as a pop-up menu.

While you can use this method from anywhere in your code, pop-up menus are most often used in response to a mouse click, usually using the right mouse button. Listing 13.3 shows how the Format menu you created in the last section would be called up by clicking the right mouse button anywhere on your form.

Listing 13.3   Invoking the Pop-up Menu

```
Private Sub Form_MouseDown(Button As Integer, Shift As
Integer,
   X As Single, Y As Single)
If Button = 2 Then
   PopUpMenu popFormat
End If
End Sub
```

To learn more about passing parameters, see Chapter 26, "Basic Building Blocks: Procedures and Functions."

The `MouseDown` event for the form is triggered when any mouse button is pressed. When the event is triggered, several parameters are passed to the event procedure which tell you which button was pressed and where the mouse cursor was located.

The variable `Button` contains a value which tells us whether the left, right, or middle button of the mouse was pressed. These values are 1, 2, and 4, respectively.

The `If` statement in the code checks to see if the right mouse button was pressed. If so, the next line of code invokes the Format pop-up menu. If any other button was pressed, the line containing the `PopUpMenu` method is skipped, and the menu is not shown.

Q&A *Can I have more than one pop-up menu on any one form?*

Yes. You could have a pop-up menu for each of the mouse buttons, or for different areas on the screen. You might also want to code pop-up menus for different controls on your screen.

Q&A *Must I remember exactly where the pop-up menu is on the screen to call it up?*

No. As the code above is written, the pop-up menu will be shown wherever you place the cursor. However, if you were to code different pop-up menus for different screen areas, the position on the screen would be important.

Summary

Menus can bring order out of chaos by providing convenient access to your program's functions. In addition, a well-designed menu which makes use of standard elements can speed the learning process for a new user by building on the familiarity with other programs.

Review questions

1 List all the ways you can create or modify a menu.

2 Which property do you use to indicate that an option has been selected?

3 How do you assign an access key for an item? A shortcut key?

4 Can you use the same access key for multiple menu items?

5 How do you prevent a user from accessing a menu item, but still allow them to see it?

6 What is the difference between a standard menu and a pop-up menu?

Exercises

1 Using the example menu you created, add a separator bar and Exit item to the File menu.

2 Add access keys and shortcut keys to the example menu.

3 Using code similar to that shown for the Enabled property, set up the menu so that the Edit menu is not visible until a file is opened.

14

Communicating with the User Through Dialog Boxes

● **In this chapter:**

- How do I tell the user about things that happen in the program?

- How to distinguish between important and trivial messages

- Can I let the user make decisions about program operations?

- Making messages into two way communications

With Visual Basic's built-in dialog boxes, communicating with your user is easy; you can have full-functioning, Windows-compatible professional dialog boxes without writing more than a single line of code. . . . . ➤

A dialog box, or dialog, is a specialized window (or form) used in Visual Basic to communicate with the user by displaying and obtaining information. A simple dialog box can be used to display a message to the user or to get a single piece of information from the user. More complex dialog boxes can be used to get multiple pieces of information, or even to set the options for an entire application. You have probably used a dialog if you have ever set up the options for your word processor or spreadsheet. You have seen a simple dialog box if you have ever tried to write over a file that already exists (see fig. 14.1).

Fig. 14.1
A simple dialog box can be used to display messages and get user decisions.

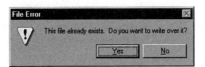

Many dialogs are in essence the visual equivalent of voice mail. These days, many companies have phone systems which present you with choices and allow you to make choices using your phone's buttons. Dialogs provide the same function for your programs.

Tell me more about dialogs

You probably noticed that the dialog looks suspiciously like a form, and you're right. A dialog is really just a specialized form. Its behavior, though, is different from the usual forms in several ways:

- A dialog box cannot be resized, so it has only a single line border and no minimize or maximize buttons.

- You must exit a dialog box by clicking one of the buttons on it. You cannot just click outside the dialog box to return to your program.

- A dialog box is designed to be used briefly, then get out of the way. It is not the main work area of your program.

Visual Basic provides several different types of dialog boxes. This chapter looks at two simple dialog boxes—the message box and the input box. Chapter 15, "Use the Common Dialog for Specialized Information," examines the Common Dialog used to get file, font, color, and printer information.

Then, in Chapter 16, "Creating Your Own Custom Dialogs," you will look at how to design and create a dialog box when the built-in ones won't do.

Giving information to the user

Often during the course of a program run, you will need to inform the user about an error that has occurred or get a decision from the user about how to proceed with the next step. You may need to prompt the user for a particular action, such as inserting a disk, or you may just want to keep the user informed about the status of the program. All of these tasks can be handled using the Windows message box like the one shown in figure 14.2. In a sense, the message box is the Windows equivalent of road signs you would see on the highway. It can be used to inform or warn the user.

Fig. 14.2
Simple communication with the user can be achieved with the message box.

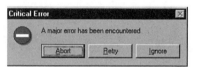

The message box is an internal Windows function (i.e., it is not specific to Visual Basic) that displays a text message, one or more command buttons, and (optionally) an **icon** in a box on the screen. The message box is automatically sized to fit the message, and is placed at the center of the screen. The only thing you have to do with the message box is tell it what you want displayed.

 Plain English, please!

An **icon** is a small picture measuring 32×32 pixels (your screen is typically 640×480 pixels or larger). An icon is often used to represent a program such as in the Program Manager, though the picture can be used for any purpose. **"**

 Q&A *Can I create my own icons, or am I limited to those provided by Visual Basic?*

You can create an icon with the Paintbrush program (provided in Windows), or with the IconWorks program that is one of the Visual Basic sample programs. There are also a number of commercial programs that create icons, as well as libraries of icons available from third-party vendors.

Why use the message box?

The message box provides you with a convenient means of displaying information. You could use a form to display messages, but you would have to set up code to handle all the little pieces such as determining the size of the text, centering the text on the form, determining the size of the form, and centering it on the screen. You would also have to determine which buttons to display and how they are positioned. As you can imagine, this would take a fair amount of code and some form design work.

The message box handles all these pieces for you and requires only a single line of code to display any message you want.

 TIP   **Chapter 16, "Creating Your Own Custom Dialogs," looks at how** to build an alternative to the message box. This alternative will provide greater flexibility than the standard message box.

What the message box can't do

Of course, the message box does have a few limitations, such as the following:

- It can only display information; it cannot accept any input.

- The message box limits you to using only specific command buttons and icons. You cannot define your own buttons.

- The message box requires that you respond to the message before your program will continue. You cannot use a message box to provide continuous monitoring of your program.

Even with these limitations, the message box is very useful for a variety of programming tasks.

How to create a simple message

The most common usage of the message box is to create a simple message to display to the user. A simple message box consists of the message text and a single command button labeled OK (see fig. 14.3). In the road sign analogy, simple message boxes are like street signs or speed limit signs. They simply provide a little information to the user.

Fig. 14.3
The simple message
box stays on the
screen until the user
clicks OK.

Simple messages, like all messages in Visual Basic, are created using the
MsgBox function. This function has one required argument and four optional
arguments. We will be covering only the required argument and the first two
optional ones in this chapter.

Specifying the message

The required argument of the MsgBox function specifies the message to
display to the user. The MsgBox function can be run in one of two ways. The
first way only displays the message box without getting a return value. The
second way returns a value to your code which can be used to process user
choices. This section looks at the first method. The second method will be
examined when we look at giving the user choices in a later section.

Speaking of *MsgBox*

The full syntax of the MsgBox function is as follows:

```
MsgBox text[, options][, title][, helpfile, context]
```

The word MsgBox is the name of the function. Placing this in the statement
starts the MsgBox function. The first argument, text, is a string containing the
message to be displayed in the message box. The string can either be a string
variable or the text of the message enclosed in double quotations (""). The text
can contain up to 1,024 characters.

The second argument, options, determines how many buttons will be placed
on the message box as well as the captions on the buttons. In addition, the
argument determines what icon is used in the box, and how the message box will
respond to the user.

The third argument, title, if included, contains a text string that is shown in
the title bar of the message box.

The last two arguments, helpfile and context, are used if the message box is
associated with any custom help files for your program.

To produce the message box shown in figure 14.3, issue the following command:

```
MsgBox "Please insert a disk in drive A"
```

The message box will automatically size itself to fit the message being displayed. If necessary, it will automatically wrap the text onto additional lines to accommodate the message.

More than just a single line

The Chr function will be discussed in more detail in Chapter 19, "Handling Strings of Data."

There may be times when you want to force the message box to break lines at a specific place and show multiple lines. This can be accomplished by placing the carriage return and line feed characters where you want the break to occur. These characters are generated using the Chr function and are Chr(13) and Chr(10), respectively.

You may want to use the multiple lines to improve the readability of your message or to add emphasis to a particular section. You can even use multiple carriage returns to produce larger spaces between lines. The following code sets off a line of text using the carriage return in the message string:

```
msgtxt = "Long messages can be broken up"
msgtxt = msgtxt & Chr(13) & Chr(10) & "by including the"
msgtxt = msgtxt & "carriage return and line feed characters."
MsgBox msgtxt
```

This code illustrates several points in handling the string for a message box. The first line of code starts setting up the message to be displayed by setting the variable msgtxt to a text string. The ampersand (&) is an operator that joins two strings. This operator is used to combine the first string, the carriage return and line feed, and the second string.

The second line of code continues the setup of the message by adding a second carriage return and line feed as well as a third line of text to the initial string.

The final line of code runs the MsgBox function, using a string variable (msgtxt) to contain the message. The results of this code are shown in figure 14.4.

Fig. 14.4
You can force the message box to break the lines of the message anywhere you want.

 TIP **To avoid typing the Chr function each time I need the carriage** return and line feed combination, I set a constant at the beginning of the program to contain the string. (See Chapter 17, "Adding Variables to Your Programs," for information on setting up constants.)

Catch the bug

You want to show the user a message that the program has finished. Why won't the following code work?

```
MsgBox Your program has finished running.
```

Answer: *The text of the message must be enclosed in quotation marks in the statement. The following is the correct code:*

```
MsgBox "Your program has finished running."
```

Information in the title

By default, the message box will use the name of your program in the title bar. You can, however, specify a different title to use when you call the message box. You can use the title to tell the user about the type of message that appears in the box, such as an error message or warning.

To add a custom title to the message box, you need to specify the optional title argument as shown in the following code:

```
MsgBox "This box has a custom title.",,"Informational
Message"
```

Notice that the title information is separated from the message by two commas. This is because you have omitted the optional argument that specifies the buttons. However, the placeholder for the argument must still be used to tell Visual Basic that you did omit the argument.

Catch the bug

This message box is supposed to show a message and a custom title, but it doesn't work. Can you determine why?

```
MsgBox "Your program crashed.", "Bombs Away"
```

Answer: *The title text was not separated from the message text by two commas. You must use the second comma as a placeholder to indicate that the options argument was omitted. The following is correct:*

```
MsgBox "Your program crashed.", , "Bombs Away"
```

Adding information with pictures

The Windows message box is capable of displaying an icon within the box in addition to the message text. There are four available icons that are available for use. These icons give the user a visual indication of the type and severity of the message being shown in the message box. Table 14.1 shows these four icons and describes the purpose of each one. These four icons are familiar to Windows users and perform a function similar to the shapes of various road signs. As you are driving, a square or rectangular sign usually indicates information. A diamond-shaped yellow or orange sign indicates a warning. Similarly, these icons give the user an idea of what the message means before they ever start reading the message text.

Table 14.1 Message Box Icons and What They Mean

Icon	Name	Purpose
⊗	Critical message	Indicates that a severe error has occurred. Often a program is shut down after this message.
⚠	Warning message	Indicates that an error has occurred in the program which requires user correction or which may lead to undesirable results.
?	Query	Indicates that the program requires additional information from the user before processing can continue.
ⓘ	Information message	Informs the user of the status of the program. Most often used to notify the user of the completion of a task.

To tell Visual Basic that you want to use an icon in the message box, you set a value for the options argument of the MsgBox function. (See the Speaking VB section earlier in the chapter for the syntax of the function.) The options argument can be set to one of four values as defined in table 14.2. You can use either the numerical value or the constant from the table.

Table 14.2   Icons and Their Options Arguments

Message type	Options value	Constant
Critical	16	vbCritical
Query	32	vbQuestion
Warning	48	vbExclamation
Information	64	vbInformation

The options argument can either specify the number or the constant directly (both shown below) or can reference a variable containing a number. (This second use will be shown in the next section, "Giving the user choices.") The following code will display an informational message with the appropriate icon. The first line of the code shows the use of the numerical value, while the second line shows the use of the constant. Both code lines will produce the same result (see fig. 14.5).

```
MsgBox "This message contains an icon.", 64, "Icon Demo"
MsgBox "This message contains an icon.", vbInformation, "Icon
Demo"
```

Fig. 14.5
An icon can be added to the message box for visual effect.

Giving the user choices

Earlier in this chapter, you looked at one syntax for the MsgBox function. That syntax displayed some message text, and optionally displayed an icon and a custom title. The message box is also capable of displaying multiple command buttons to allow the user to make choices and to return a value to indicate which button was pressed. This ability requires the use of the second syntax of the MsgBox function.

Continuing with the road signs (last time, I promise), the command buttons indicate choices which are available, sort of like a sign for a fork in the road.

What choices does the user have?

Visual Basic provides six possible sets of command buttons for use in the message box (see fig. 14.6). These choices include the following:

- OK—displays a single button with the caption "OK." This simply asks the user to acknowledge receipt of the message before continuing.

- OK, Cancel—displays two buttons in the message box, allowing the user to choose between accepting the message and requesting a cancellation of the operation.

- Abort, Retry, Ignore—displays three buttons, usually along with an error message. The user may choose to abort the operation, retry it, or ignore the error and continue with program execution.

- Yes, No, Cancel—displays three buttons, typically with a question. The user may answer yes or no to the question, or choose to cancel the operation.

- Yes, No—displays two buttons for a simple yes or no choice.

- Retry, Cancel—displays the two buttons for retry the operation or cancel it. A typical use for this would be to indicate that the printer is not responding, retry or cancel the printout?

Speaking of returning a value

The syntax used to return a value from the MsgBox function is:

```
retvalue = MsgBox(text[,options][,title][,helpfile,context])
```

The key difference between this syntax and the one described earlier is the addition of the return value (identified by retvalue) and the equal sign. The arguments of the MsgBox function are the same as were used for the other syntax.

Note also that for this syntax, the arguments of the function are enclosed within parentheses. The variable represented by retvalue contains a number which defines which button was pressed by the user to exit the message box.

Fig. 14.6
You can specify one of
six sets of command
buttons to allow the
user to make choices in
the message box.

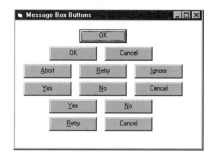

TIP **These buttons only provide the user with choices. You must write** code to implement each of the choices the user can make.

Q&A *Is there a way to create my own unique message box command buttons?*

Not with Visual Basic's built-in message box. However, you can build your own message box. This will be covered in Chapter 16, "Creating Your Own Custom Dialogs."

Specifying the buttons

To tell Visual Basic which buttons to display in the message box, you set the value of the options argument. The values and constants representing each set of buttons are shown in table 14.3.

Table 14.3   Options Arguments and Their Button Sets

Button set	Value	Constant
OK	0	vbOKOnly
OK, Cancel	1	vbOKCancel
Abort, Retry, Ignore	2	vbAbortRetryIgnore
Yes, No, Cancel	3	vbYesNoCancel
Yes, No	4	vbYesNo
Retry, Cancel	5	vbRetryCancel

The following code would display a short error message and then request the choice of Abort, Retry, or Ignore from the user. The first line of code shows the use of the numerical value and the second line shows the use of the constant:

```
retvalue = MsgBox("File does not exist", 2)
retvalue = MsgBox("File does not exist", vbAbortRetryIgnore)
```

 Q&A *Since I have to set the options argument to specify the button set and to specify an icon, how can I use both?*

The message box is set up to allow you to combine the values of the different options. For example, to add a warning icon to the previous error message, you would use the following code. The result of the code is shown in the figure.

```
optval = vbExclamation + vbAbortRetryIgnore
retvalue = MsgBox("File does not exist", optval)
```

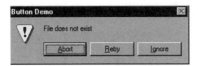

Setting a default button

The final item that can be included in the options argument is to specify which button is the default. This value can be added to the other values in the argument. There are a maximum of three possible buttons in the message box. Table 14.4 shows the possible default buttons and the values of the options argument for each choice.

Table 14.4   The Default Button Specified by the Options Argument

Default Button	Value	Constant
First	0	vbDefaultButton1
Second	256	vbDefaultButton2
Third	512	vbDefaultButton3

Catch the bug

You want to find out if the user wants to try again to print a document, or cancel the print. The code below should show a message box to do this, but it doesn't work. What's wrong?

```
usrchoice = MsgBox "Printer not responding", vbRetryCancel
```

Answer: The syntax of the MsgBox function which returns a value requires that parentheses enclose the arguments of the function. The correct code is as follows:

```
usrchoice = MsgBox("Printer not responding", vbRetryCancel)
```

Dealing with the choices

The main reason for specifying a button set for the message is to get a response from the user. Therefore, you also need a means of determining which of the buttons was pressed by the user and you need to take actions based on that choice. Visual Basic supplies you the identity of the chosen button via the value returned by the function. The values for each of the seven possible buttons are summarized in table 14.5. As usual, the constants which represent the values are also shown.

Table 14.5   Each Message Box Button Returns a Unique Value

Button	Value	Constant
OK	1	vbOK
Cancel	2	vbCancel
Abort	3	vbAbort
Retry	4	vbRetry
Ignore	5	vbIgnore
Yes	6	vbYes
No	7	vbNo

So now that you know what the value is, what do you do with it? In a typical application, you will have some code which calls the message box, then responds to the button. Let's take a look at an example where the user is being asked to confirm a file deletion. Listing 14.1 shows how to set up the message box to handle the response.

Listing 14.1   Use a Message Box to Confirm an Action

```
trgtfil = "MYDATA.TXT"
msgtxt = "Do you really want to delete file: '" & trgtfil
& "'?"
optval = vbExclamation + vbYesNo + vbDefaultButton2
ttlval = "Delete Confirmation"
retval = MsgBox(msgtxt, optval, ttlval)
If retval = vbYes Then Kill trgtfil
```

In the first line of this code, you set the variable `trgtfil` to a filename. In an actual application, you would have gotten this filename from an input field or from the Common Dialog. The next line of text builds the message that you want to place in the message box. Use the concatenation operator to include the name of the file in the message.

The third line of the code sets up the value of the options argument for the message box. For this example, you want to place the warning icon in the box using the `vbExclamation` constant. You want the user to answer either yes or no to the message, so you use the `vbYesNo` constant to specify the correct button set. Finally, you want to make sure that No is the default button, just in case the user automatically presses the Enter key. Since No is the second of the two buttons, add the `vbDefaultButton2` constant to the options value.

The next line simply specifies a custom title for the message box. The fifth line of code calls the message box function and tells it to return the value of the chosen button to the variable `retval`.

Finally, in the last line, you compare the return value from the function to the constant `vbYes`. If they are equal, indicating that the Yes button was pressed, you go ahead and delete the file using the `Kill` statement. If the user pressed No, the return value will not equal `vbYes` and the deletion is canceled.

To learn more about If and Select Case statements, see Chapters 24 and 25, respectively.

While the code above used a single If statement, you can use multiple If statements or a Select Case statement to handle actions for each possible return value.

The message box resulting from this example is shown in figure 14.7.

Fig. 14.7
This message box returns a value which determines whether the user really wants to delete a file.

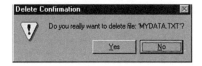

Getting information from the user

Many times in a program, you will come across a need to get a single piece of information from the user. You might need the user to enter a person's name, the name of a file, or a number for various purposes. While the message box allows your users to make choices, it does not allow them to enter information in response to the message. Therefore, you have to use some other means to get the information. Visual Basic provides a second built-in dialog for exactly this purpose—the input box.

The input box works something like a bank-by-phone system. If you have ever used one of these, you know that it uses prompts (in this case, voice commands) to tell you what information to enter. This information can be an account number, password code, or amount. After the prompt, you enter the information using the phone buttons instead of a keyboard. When you have finished entering the information, you press the # button (or some other one) to indicate that you have finished your entry, just as you click the OK button of the input box.

The input box displays a message to tell the user what to enter, a text box where the user can enter the data, and two command buttons (OK and Cancel) that can be used to either accept or abort the input data (see fig. 14.8).

Prompt

Fig. 14.8
An input box allows
the user to enter a
single piece of data in
response to a message.

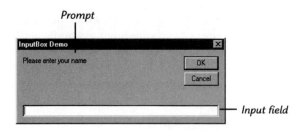

Input field

Setting up and running the input box

The input box works very much like the message box with a return value. You specify a variable to receive the information returned from the input box, then supply the message, and (optionally) a title and default value as arguments to the function.

The syntax used for the input box function is:

```
userinput = InputBox(prompt[, title][, default])
```

In this statement, the word `userinput` represents the variable which will contain the information input by the user into the input box. `InputBox` is the name of the function itself.

`prompt` represents the message that will be displayed to the user to indicate what should be entered in the box. Like the message in the message box, the prompt can be up to 1,024 characters. Word-wrapping will automatically be performed on the text in the prompt so that it will fit inside the box. Also like the message box, you can insert a carriage return or line feed character to force the prompt to show multiple lines or to separate lines for emphasis.

The `title` argument specifies the text that will be shown in the bar at the top of the input box. This is an optional argument and can be excluded.

The other optional argument of the function is the `default` argument. If this is included, it is used to specify an initial value for the text box in the input box dialog box. This value can be accepted by the user or modified, or it can be erased and a completely new value entered.

There is no option in the input box function to specify any command buttons other than the defaults of OK and Cancel.

Checking for an answer

When you use the input box, the user can enter data in the box and then choose the OK or Cancel button. If the user chooses the OK button, the input box returns whatever text is in the input field. If the user chooses the Cancel button, the input box returns an empty string, regardless of what the user typed.

Len, Val, and other string handling functions will be covered in detail in Chapter 19, "Handling Strings of Data."

In order for you to be able to use the information entered by the user, you need to determine if the data meets your needs. First, you probably want to make sure that the user actually entered some information and chose the OK button. You can do this using the Len function to determine the length of the returned string. If the length is zero, the user pressed the Cancel button or left the input field blank. If the length of the string is greater than zero, you know that the user entered something.

To learn about variable types, see Chapter 17, "Adding Variables to Your Programs."

You may also need to check the returned value to make sure it is of the proper type. If you are expecting a number, which will be compared to another number, an error message will occur if the user enters letters. To make sure that you have a numerical value with which to work, you can use the Val function to get the numerical value of the string. If the string contains only numbers, the function returns the number. If the string contains anything else, the function returns zero. Listing 14.2 illustrates the additional processing of the returned value of the input box.

Listing 14.2 Process the Information From an Input Box in Your Code

```
inptval = InputBox("Enter your age")
If Len(inptval) = 0 Then
    MsgBox "You forgot to enter your age"
Else
    If Val(inptval) = 0 And inptval <> "0" Then
        MsgBox "You did not enter a number"
    Else
        MsgBox "Congratulations for surviving this long"
    End If
End If
```

The first line of this code starts the InputBox function and asks the user to enter an age. The second line of code is a conditional statement that checks the length of the returned string to make sure that the user entered something in the input field. If not (length is zero), the program writes a message that the user forgot to enter an age. If something was entered, the program proceeds to the next conditional statement that checks the value of the user's entry.

If the value is zero, the program assumes that the user did not enter a number, but entered some other characters instead. If this is the case, the program displays a message to this effect. If the user did enter a number, the program displays a different message.

In addition to showing how to check for proper input, this example also shows the use of multiple conditional statements. This will be covered further in Chapter 24, "If I Go This Way, Where Will I End Up?"

Catch the bug

The following code is supposed to get the user's age in an input box. However, the code won't work. What is wrong with it?

```
usrinput = InputBox(,"Age Input",25)
```

Answer: *The prompt argument of the input box is not an optional argument and must be included. The example tries to exclude the prompt and just put information in the title bar of the input box. The following is the correct code:*

```
usrinput = InputBox("Enter your age","Age Input",25)
```

Summary

This chapter has shown how to use two of Visual Basic's built-in dialog boxes to display messages to the user and get single input values. While these dialogs are somewhat limited in scope, you will find them very useful for many of your user communication needs.

Review questions

1 What is the only required argument for the message box function?

2 How do you display an icon in the message box?

3 How do you know which button was pressed by the user to exit a message box?

4 How do you know which button was pressed by the user to exit an input box?

5 What are some of the limitations of the message box?

6 What are some of the limitations of the input box?

Exercises

1 Create a message box with the following information:

Message—`File too large to fit on target disk`

Title—`File copy error`

Warning icon

Retry, Cancel command buttons

2 Create an input box to get the location of a file.

3 Change the file deletion example (from fig. 14.7) to set the Yes button as the default.

15

Use the Common Dialog for Specialized Information

● **In this chapter:**

- **How the Common Dialog helps me write programs**

- **What information can I get from the Common Dialog?**

- **How to run the Common Dialog**

- **What to do with the information from the Common Dialog**

For quick and easy file, font, color, or printer information, the Common Dialog can't be beat. You can create powerful, full-functioning Windows dialog boxes in seconds . . . .➤

What is the Common Dialog?

The Common Dialog is one of the custom controls that comes with Visual Basic. It is typically loaded automatically and displayed in the toolbox when you start Visual Basic. If, for some reason, it is not loaded, you can add it to the toolbox by choosing it in the Custom Controls dialog box accessible from the Tools menu.

The Common Dialog provides you with several different dialog boxes that you can use to obtain information from the user. You can use it to get the name of a file to open or the name under which a file should be saved. You can also use it to allow your users to select fonts or colors. It also contains a printer dialog that lets your users control various portions of the print process.

These dialog boxes look like the dialog boxes used by Windows itself and by most commercial applications. This similarity helps the users, since they should already know how to perform selections. Figure 15.1 shows the Open dialog box generated by the Common Dialog.

Fig. 15.1
The dialog boxes generated by the Common Dialog look similar to the dialog boxes used by many commercial programs.

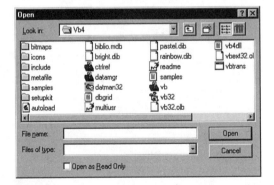

Q&A *Can't I create my own dialog boxes?*

Yes, you can. Visual Basic provides other tools such as file, folder, and drive list boxes that you could use. But unless you specifically enjoy the achievement of creating your own, why reinvent the wheel? It's like the choice of building a house yourself, or buying one that is already built. Buying one is much quicker and easier, if you can find one already built which meets your needs. In addition, the Common Dialog provides an interface that the user is probably already familiar with.

How do I use the Common Dialog in my program?

To make the Common Dialog available to your program, you have to place an **instance** of the control on your form. You do this by choosing it from the toolbox and drawing it on your form. The Common Dialog will appear as an icon on your form no matter how large you try to draw it (see fig. 15.2). This icon will not be visible on the form when your application is run. The dialog boxes only show up when you call them.

Fig. 15.2
The Common Dialog only appears as an icon in design mode.

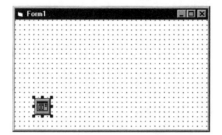

 Plain English, please!

> An **instance** is a single copy of a control or form. As you develop your programs, you use many different objects, such as forms and controls. Each different type of object is known as a **class**. So text boxes are one class, labels are another. As you use multiple copies of a class, such as text boxes, you are creating instances of the class. **99**

When you have placed the Common Dialog on your form, you should also assign it a unique name. You assign the control a name by specifying a value for the Name property. The default value of the Name property is CommonDialog1. I often assign a name which represents my most common use of the control, such as GetFile if I will be working most often with the file dialog boxes.

TIP You can create multiple copies, or instances, of the Common Dialog, but it is unnecessary and wastes system resources.

You can create custom titles for the Common Dialog

When you use one of the dialogs from the Common Dialog, the title of the dialog defaults to a description of the function, such as Open for the File Open dialog. However, you can create a custom title that is unique to your program and function if you want. You can do this by setting a value for the `DialogTitle` property. This can be done at designtime through the Properties dialog box, or at runtime using a statement such as the following:

```
GetFile.DialogTitle = "Choose a Bitmap file to open"
```

This way, your dialogs can be a little more unique, and you can provide some information to the user. Figure 15.3 shows the same Open dialog as figure 15.1, but with a custom title added.

Fig. 15.3
Custom titles enhance the quality of your dialog box.

Custom title —

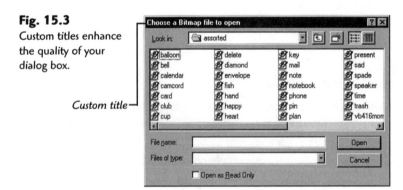

Using the Common Dialog with the file functions

One of the key uses of the Common Dialog is to obtain file names from the user. The Common Dialog can be used in either of two modes—the File Open mode and the File Save mode. The File Open mode is used to allow the user to specify a file to be retrieved and used by your program. The File Save mode is used to allow the user to specify a name for a file to be saved. This is the equivalent of the Save As dialog box for many programs.

The dialogs for the Open and Save functions are very similar. Figure 15.4 shows the dialog with the major components indicated. These components are as follows:

- Drive/Folder list—the current folder is indicated. You can move up the folder levels from this list.

- File/Folder selection—you select the file or folder to be used. The folders indicated in this area are the subdirectories of the folder in the Drive/Folder list. A folder can be selected by double-clicking it, or by highlighting it and pressing Enter. This will change the display to show the files and folders contained within the new folder. A file is selected by clicking its icon. Its name is then displayed in the filename text box.

- Filename text box—the user may enter a filename, or the name of the selected file is displayed.

- Files of type list box—the user selects the type of files to display. These types determine the extension of the file, and the available types are controlled by the `Filter` property of the Common Dialog.

- Command buttons—the buttons in the upper right corner allow the user to move up one folder level, create a new folder, or switch the file display area between the File List and File Details modes. The buttons in the lower right allow the user to process the selection or cancel the dialog.

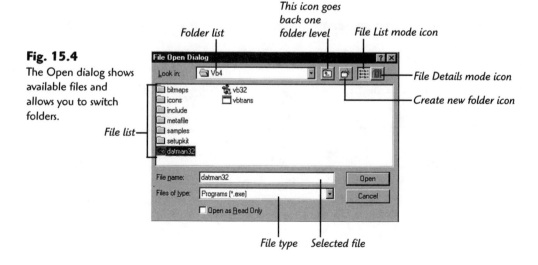

Fig. 15.4
The Open dialog shows available files and allows you to switch folders.

Opening an existing file

To open an existing file, you use the ShowOpen method of the Common Dialog. This method displays the dialog that was shown in figure 15.4.

Saving files

Running the Common Dialog to get a file name to save is essentially the same as for the open file. In this case, however, the name of the method is ShowSave. There are a few subtle differences between the dialogs shown for the Open and Save functions. Figure 15.5 shows the Save dialog and points out where it is different from the Open dialog.

Fig. 15.5
The Save dialog box has a few subtle differences from the Open dialog.

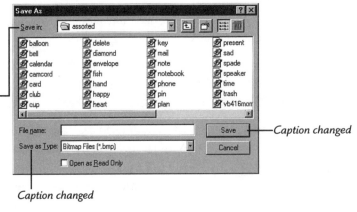

Caption changed

Caption changed

Caption changed

Speaking of *ShowOpen*

The syntax of the method to run the File Open dialog is:

```
controlname.ShowOpen
```

controlname is simply the name that you gave the Common Dialog when you created it. This statement is issued from your program whenever you want to display the Open dialog of the Common Dialog.

Making use of the filename entered by the user

When the user enters or selects a filename using the Common Dialog (either Open or Save), the dialog only gets the filename for you. It does not automatically open or save the file; you have to write the code to do that. The filename that is specified by the user is stored in the `FileName` property of the Common Dialog control. The `FileName` contains the complete **path** for the file.

 Plain English, please!

The **path** is the information about the subdirectories or folders in which a file is contained. A complete path starts with the specification of the drive on which the file resides and lists each folder that must be accessed to get to the file. Think of the path as your phone extension in an office. For other people in the office, you just need to tell them your extension. For people calling from outside the office, you need to tell them the office phone number. And for people in another area code, you need to specify your area code. Your extension is like the file being accessed, and the area code and office phone number are the path to your phone.

A typical file with the path specified might be:

C:\VB4\VB.EXE

Catch the bug

Your program tries to use the following code to get a file name from the user, but the code has an error. Where is the error?

```
GetFile.DialogTitle = "Available Document Files"
ShowOpen
opnfil = GetFile.Filename
```

Answer: The problem is in the second line of code. You must specify the name of your Common Dialog control with the `ShowOpen` *method. The correct code would have been:*

```
GetFile.ShowOpen
```

You can use the `FileName` property directly, or you can assign it to a variable, which is what I would recommend. The following code shows how the Common Dialog is used to get a file to open, then the file is opened for use. This code might be placed in the `Click` event of an `Open` menu item:

```
GetFile.ShowOpen
usrFile = GetFile.FileName
Open usrFile For Input As #1
```

The first line of code displays the Open dialog, which allows the user to choose a file. The second line assigns the file chosen by the user to a variable. You could use a text box to get the filename, but then you would have to verify that the file existed in the current folder or have the user specify the folder to search for the file. This ease of programming is what makes the Common Dialog so useful. The last line of code actually opens the file for use by your program. In this case, the user would have selected an input file from which data would be read.

Specifying file types using the *Filter* property

So far, I have only shown you how to display the file dialogs showing all files in a folder. You may, however, want to specify that only certain file types, such as text or document files, be shown. You can accomplish this with the Common Dialog as well; the file types shown in the dialog are specified using the `Filter` property.

You set the `Filter` property either in the design mode from the Properties dialog box or at runtime with an assignment statement like the following:

```
controlname.Filter = "description¦filtercond"
```

`controlname` is the assigned name of the Common Dialog control, and `Filter` is the name of the property. `description` is a text description of the type of files to be shown. Examples of the description are Text Files, Documents, and All Files. The vertical line (¦) is known as the pipe symbol. This symbol must be present. `filtercond` is the actual filter for the files. You typically express the filter as an asterisk followed by a period and the extension of the files you want to display. The filters which correspond to these descriptions are `*.txt`, `*.doc`, and `*.*`, respectively.

CAUTION   **Do not include spaces before or after the pipe symbol, or you may** not get the file list you desire.

If you specify the `Filter` property in your code (using an assignment statement), you must enclose the filter in double quotes. The quotes are omitted if you specify the filter from the Properties dialog of the design environment.

You can specify multiple `description¦filtercond` pairs within the `Filter` property. Each pair must be separated from the other pairs by the pipe symbol as shown in the following example:

```
GetFile.Filter = "All Files¦*.*¦Text Files¦*.txt"
```

Q&A   ***If I specify multiple filters, how do I tell Visual Basic which one to start out using?***

By default, the first filter condition is used when the dialog is invoked. However, if you want a different filter used on startup, you can specify the filter number using the `FilterIndex` property. Filters are numbered from left to right, starting with 1.

Catch the bug

You want to prompt the user to select a text file from the common dialog by setting the Filter property. What is wrong with the following code?

```
GetFile.DialogTitle = "Custom File Filters"
GetFile.Filter = "All Files¦*.*¦Text Files"
GetFile.FilterIndex = 2
GetFile.ShowOpen
```

Answer: *The error is in the second line. The filter condition was not specified for the* `Text Files` *portion of the* `Filter` *property. The correct code is as follows:*

```
GetFile.Filter = "All Files¦*.*¦Text Files¦*.txt"
```

Use the Common Dialog with the font functions

Back in Chapter 5, "Making Your Words Look Good," we discussed fonts and how you can use different fonts to enhance your forms. As you may recall, a font is defined by the base font, the font size, and the font attributes—bold, italic, and underline.

While most of that discussion centered on changing fonts from the Properties dialog, there was mention of changing them from a program. The big question was, "How do you let your users choose the fonts they want to see?" The answer to this question is the Font dialog that is part of the Common Dialog control.

Set up the dialog to retrieve font information

Setting up the Common Dialog to show the Font dialog is quite easy. First make sure you have an instance of the Common Dialog on your form. If you already have one set up, say for the file functions, you can use that. If you don't have one set up, you can add it to the form.

Next you will have to set a value for the Flags property. This property tells the Common Dialog the type of fonts you want to make available to the user. The Flags property can be set to one of the three constants listed in table 15.1. In addition, you can specify other constants to further control the fonts, such as displaying only TrueType fonts. These other constants are listed in the Visual Basic Help file.

Table 15.1   Fonts Chosen by the *Flags* Property

Font set	Constant	Value
Screen Fonts	cdlCFScreenFonts	1
Printer Fonts	cdlCFPrinterFonts	2
Both sets	cdlCFBoth	3

CAUTION If you do not set a value for the Flags property, you will get an error message stating that no fonts are installed.

You can also set the value of the Flags property from your program using an assignment statement. Once the Flags property has been set, you can run the Font dialog from your code using the ShowFont method. This method has the same syntax as the ShowOpen method described previously. Figure 15.6 shows the Font dialog that is presented to the user. This particular dialog contains only screen fonts.

Fig. 15.6
Sizes, fonts, and attributes can all be selected from the Font dialog box.

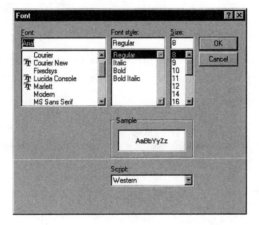

Use the font information

The information about the fonts chosen from the Common Dialog is contained in the properties of the control. Table 15.2 shows the properties of the control and the font attributes they control.

Table 15.2   Font Attributes Stored in the Control's Properties

Property	Attribute
FontName	The name of the base font
FontSize	The height of the font in points
FontBold	Whether boldface was selected
FontItalic	Whether italics was selected
FontUnderline	Whether the font is underlined
FontStrikethru	Whether the font has a line through it

The code in listing 15.1 shows how the font information would be retrieved and used to change the fonts in a text box. The form for this program is shown in figure 15.7.

Listing 15.1   Selected Values That Set the Attributes of a Text Box

```
GetFont.ShowFont
txtSample.Font.Name = GetFont.FontName
txtSample.Font.Size = GetFont.FontSize
txtSample.Font.Bold = GetFont.FontBold
txtSample.Font.Italic = GetFont.FontItalic
txtSample.Font.Underline = GetFont.FontUnderline
txtSample.Font.Strikethru = GetFont.FontStrikethru
```

Fig. 15.7
This program shows the use of the Font dialog to change the appearance of text in a text box.

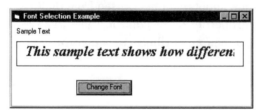

Let your users specify colors

The Color dialog of the Common Dialog allows the user to select colors that can be used for the foreground or background colors of your forms or controls (see fig. 15.8). The user has the option of choosing one of the standard colors, or creating and selecting a custom color.

Fig. 15.8
The Color dialog
lets your users choose
a color to use in
the program.

Setting up the Common Dialog for colors is basically the same as for fonts. You set the Flags property to the constant cdlCCRGBInit, and then call the ShowColor method.

When the user selects a color from the dialog, its color value is stored in the Color property of the control. The following code shows how to change a form's background color using the Color dialog:

```
GetColor.Flags = cdlCCRGBInit
GetColor.ShowColor
Myform.BackColor = GetColor.Color
```

Working with printers

The Print dialog of the Common Dialog allows the user to select which printer to use for a printout and to specify options for the print process (see fig. 15.9). These options include specifying all pages, a range of pages, or the selection to print. There is also an option to specify the number of copies to be printed and an option to print to a file.

To run the Print dialog, you only have to call the ShowPrinter method of the Common Dialog. There are no flags to set prior to the call.

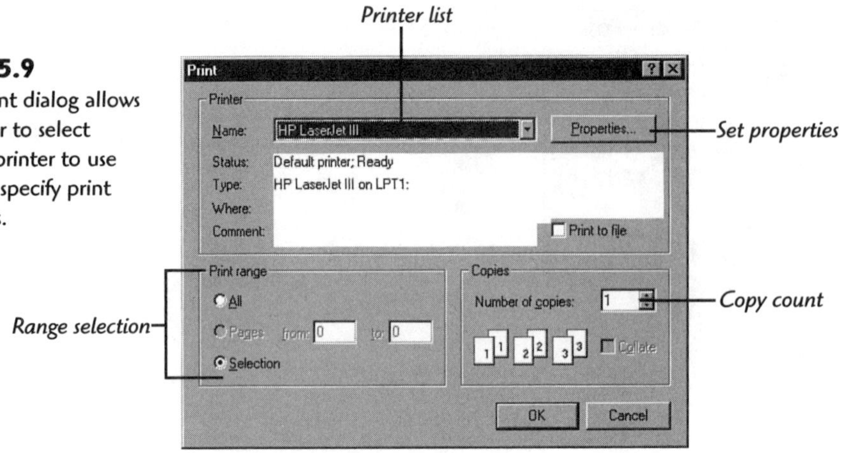

Printer list

Fig. 15.9
The Print dialog allows
the user to select
which printer to use
and to specify print
options.

—Set properties

Range selection—

—Copy count

Selecting a printer with the dialog

Once the Print dialog is displayed, the user can select the printer from the
Name list at the top of the dialog. This list contains all the printers installed
in Windows. Right below the Name list is the Status line, which tells you the
current status of the selected printer.

If the user wants to change any of the printer's parameters (such as paper
size and margins) he or she can click the Properties button on the Print
dialog. This will bring up the Properties dialog for the selected printer, as
shown in figure 15.10. This dialog lets you control all the settings of the
printer just like the Windows control panel.

Fig. 15.10
The Properties dialog
for the printer lets you
control paper size,
margins, and other
attributes of the
printer.

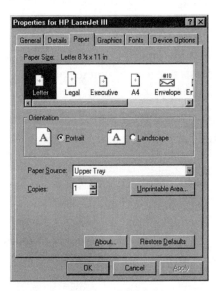

Using the information

The Print dialog returns the information from the user in its properties. The FromPage and ToPage properties tell you the starting and ending pages of the printout selected by the user. The Copies property tells you how many copies the user wants printed.

This is only provided as information. The Print dialog does not automatically set up the desired printout. Your program must do that. You will look more at controlling the printer in Chapter 32, "Printing the Results of Your Programs."

Summary

The Common Dialog provides you with a shortcut to get information from the user about files, fonts, colors, and printers. Using the Common Dialog is far easier than trying to gather this information on your own.

Review questions

1 How do you specify to the Open dialog which particular files to display?

2 What property determines which fonts will be displayed in the Font dialog?

3 How do you run the Print dialog?

4 Which property tells you the filename selected by the user?

5 What font attributes can be selected by the user?

6 How do you set up the Common Dialog to allow color selection?

Exercises

1 Change the Filter property of the example to show document files (DOC extension).

2 The Font dialog in figure 15.6 shows only the screen fonts available. Change its setup to show both screen and printer fonts.

3 Set up a Common Dialog to select colors.

4 Set up a Common Dialog to allow the user to select from various database files (extensions MDB, DBF, PDX).

16

Creating Your Own Custom Dialogs

● In this chapter:

- Why should I build my own dialog?

- I wanna add icons to my dialog

- Run, baby, run—making a custom dialog run

- What is a control array?

- Can I customize my command buttons for each dialog?

Sometimes message boxes, input boxes, and the common dialog boxes just aren't adequate. Then, you have to roll up your sleeves and build your own . . . . ➤

f you remember from our discussions of the message box and input box, there are limitations to what you can do with these dialogs. With the message box, you can only display messages, one of four icons, and a limited set of command buttons. You cannot change the captions of the command buttons or accept any user input. The input box can accept input, but is limited to one input field. Also, the input box's command button choices are limited to OK and Cancel, and you can't use any icons.

Why do you need a custom dialog?

So what do you do if your program requires more capabilities than these dialogs (the message and input boxes) provide? You build your own. Now, before you start thinking, "Those dialogs were built by professional programmers; I can't possibly build one," let me reassure you. A dialog is just a specialized form. You design a form for a dialog just like any other program form. In other words, you can build a dialog as simple or as complicated as you need using just the controls and code in Visual Basic. You don't need any special tools or development kits.

Setting up the form for the dialog

The first thing you need to do to create a custom dialog is to add another form to your project. You do this by clicking the New Form button on the toolbar or by choosing Form from the Insert menu (Alt+I, then F). This new form will appear on the screen looking just as your first form initially did. You will also see that a second form has been added to the project window of your program, as shown in figure 16.1.

Fig. 16.1
The project window is updated to show that a second form has been added to the project.

After you have added the new form, you need to change a few of the properties. First you need to give the form a unique name by setting the `Name`
property. For the dialog you are creating, let's give the form the name
`frmSuperDialog`. Next, to make the form look like a dialog when it is shown
to the user, you will need to change the `BorderStyle` property of the form to
`1` (Fixed Single). While you won't see the change in the design mode, this
will make the border of the form look like those of the message and input
boxes. Finally, to complete the dialog appearance, you will need to set both
the `MinButton` and `MaxButton` properties to `False` (their default values are
`True`). This will eliminate the minimize and maximize buttons that appear in
the top right corner of the form. Again, these changes won't appear in design
mode but will be seen by the user when the dialog is run. Figure 16.2 shows
how the border and buttons of the form will look to the user.

Fig. 16.2

Changing the border
and eliminating the
minimize and maximize
buttons makes the
form look like other
dialog boxes.

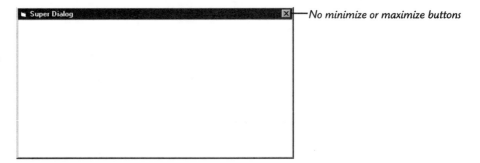

—*No minimize or maximize buttons*

Let's start simple—a label and one command button

Now that you have the form looking like a dialog, you need to make it do
something useful. To start with, just add a message and a single command
button to the form. This will give you a dialog similar to the simple message
box.

To allow your dialog to show a message, you need to add a label control to
the form. You will want to size the control so that it can take a one or two
sentence message easily. Mostly you are interested in the width of the label
control, since its height will be controlled by the message we choose to
display. After placing the label on the form, give it the name `lblMessage`.
Next you will need to set up the label to automatically change size to fit the
messages displayed. To do this, first set the `WordWrap` property to `True`, then
set the `AutoSize` property to `True`.

CAUTION **If you set the `AutoSize` property first, the control will shrink to fit the width of the current text, `Label1`, and it will be too narrow to accommodate most messages.**

To complete the simple dialog, add a command button to the form next to the label control. Change the `Name` property of the button to `cmdReturn`, and change the `Caption` property to `OK`. When you have finished, your form should look like figure 16.3.

Fig. 16.3
This form emulates the simple message box.

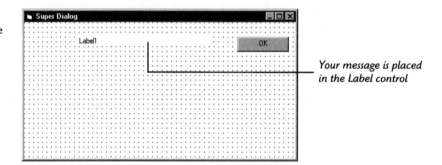

Your message is placed in the Label control

TIP **Placing the command buttons along the side of the form makes it easier to add and position other buttons later.**

Adding text boxes for user input

Now to do something the message box and input box cannot do—set up multiple input fields. For your first dialog, you are going to set up two input fields to accept a user ID and password for network access. To get the information from the user, use two text boxes.

Place two text boxes on the form below the label control and approximately the same width as the label. Set the `Text` property of each text box to a blank string. Next, set the `Name` property of the top text box to `txtUser` and the `Name` property of the other text box to `txtPassWord`. Your form should now look like figure 16.4.

Fig. 16.4
Your dialog box can now do something neither the message nor input box can do—accept two pieces of input.

Running the dialog you created

The dialog has been built; all that is left is to run it. Running a custom dialog is a little different than running one of Visual Basic's built-in dialogs. To run the custom dialog, follow these steps:

1 Load the form into memory.

2 Set the properties of the form and its controls.

3 Show the form to the user as a **modal** form.

66 *Plain English, please!*

In Visual Basic, forms can be shown in one of two ways, **modal** or **modeless**. Modal simply means that the user must take some action on the current form before work can continue on other forms. All Visual Basic dialogs are modal. 99

Speaking of *Load*

To load a form into memory, you use the Load statement as follows:

    Load formname

formname is the name of the form to be loaded. The name is contained in the form's Name property.

After the form is loaded and the properties are set, you can show the form using the Show method as follows:

```
formname.Show [style]
```

Again, formname is the name of the form to be shown to the user. Show is the name of the method which causes Visual Basic to display the form. style is an optional property which determines whether the form is shown as modal or modeless. If style is set to 1, the form is shown modal. If style is set to 0 or omitted, the form is shown modeless.

If a form has not been loaded (see the Load statement) prior to using the Show method, Show will automatically load the form, then display it. It is only necessary to load the form before issuing the Show method if you need to set properties of the form or its controls from your code prior to displaying the form.

Setting it up and presenting it to the user

The code in listing 16.1 sets up your user ID and password dialog and displays it to the user.

Listing 16.1 This Code Runs the Custom Dialog

```
crlf$ = Chr(10) & Chr(13)
Load frmSuperDialog
frmSuperDialog.Caption = "Password Authorization"
msgtxt = "Enter your user ID and password in the boxes below"
msgtxt = msgtxt & crlf$ & crlf$ & "Press OK when finished"
frmSuperDialog.lblMessage.Caption = msgtxt
lbltop = frmSuperDialog.lblMessage.Top
lblhigh = frmSuperDialog.lblMessage.Height
frmSuperDialog.txtUser.Top = lbltop + lblhigh + 200
lbltop = frmSuperDialog.txtUser.Top
lblhigh = frmSuperDialog.txtUser.Height
frmSuperDialog.txtPassWord.Top = lbltop + lblhigh + 200
lbltop = frmSuperDialog.txtPassWord.Top
lblhigh = frmSuperDialog.txtPassWord.Height
frmSuperDialog.Height = lbltop + lblhigh + 500
frmSuperDialog.Show 1
```

 The first line of code simply sets the value of a variable containing the carriage return and line feed characters. This variable will be used to put separation lines in the message. The second line of code uses the Load statement to place your dialog in memory. Next, you set the caption of the dialog to an appropriate title, in this case, Password Authorization.

The next three lines of code create the message to be displayed in your dialog box and then set the Caption property of the label to the requested message. Note that in assigning the label's Caption property, you have to specify the form on which the label appears. This is because the label is on a form other than the one which is active. (A form only becomes active when it is shown.)

The next two lines set variables to the values of the Top and Height properties of the label. Use these properties to set the relative position of the text boxes. Top tells you where the top of the label occurs, and Height tells you how tall the label is after the message is entered. By using these values, you can set the top of the first text box 200 twips below the bottom of the label, no matter what message you put in the label. This avoids having too much space between the label and the text box, or worse, having the label cover part of the text box.

This routine is repeated to set the position of the second text box. Finally, the Top and Height of the second text box are used to set the height of the form. You add 500 twips to the position of the bottom of the text box to account for the fact that you have a title bar on the form.

The last line of code displays the dialog to the user as a modal form. The result of this code is shown in figure 16.5.

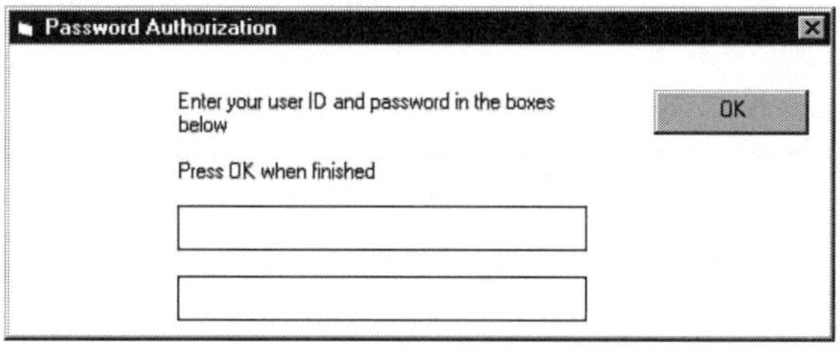

Fig. 16.5
Your custom dialog can display a message and multiple input entry fields.

To run this dialog, place the code of listing 16.1 in the `Click` event of a command button on your main form (not on the `frmSuperDialog` form). When you run the program and click the command button, the dialog will be shown.

How do I remove it from the screen?

You have gotten the dialog to display a message and text boxes on the screen. But you also need a way to get the dialog off the screen. There are two commands which will remove a form from the screen—the `Hide` method and the `Unload` statement.

The `Hide` method removes the form from the screen but leaves it in memory. This way the properties of the form and its controls can still be accessed. The `Unload` statement removes the form from the screen and removes it from memory.

 TIP **If you will be showing a form again, hide the form instead of unloading it.** The display of the form is much faster if it has only been hidden instead of unloaded.

For your example dialog, you can remove the form from the screen by placing the following code in the `Click` event of the `cmdReturn` command button on the dialog:

```
Unload frmSuperDialog
```

Speaking of *Hide* and *Unload*

The `Hide` method uses a syntax similar to the `Show` method:

```
formname.Hide
```

`formname` is, of course, the name of the form you want to remove from the screen. `Hide` tells the program the action to be taken. There are no optional parts of the `Hide` method.

The `Unload` statement works exactly like the `Load` statement:

```
Unload formname
```

I want pictures

Just like the message box, your dialog can have pictures. These pictures can give the user a clue to the message, and provide visible impact for your dialog. Unlike the message box, your dialog can use any picture you desire, instead of being limited to the four major icons.

Including space for an icon

The easiest way to add an icon to your dialog is to add an Image control to the form. Figure 16.6 shows your super dialog with this control added. The Image control is a better choice than the Picture control for this purpose since it will automatically adjust to the size of the picture being displayed, and it uses fewer resources than the Picture control.

Fig. 16.6
The Image control is represented by a dotted outline on the form.

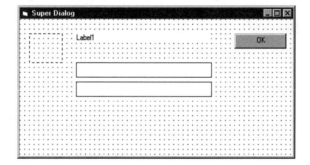

To add the picture to the Image control when you call your dialog, you can use the `LoadPicture` function to call up a picture from a file.

For more information on the `LoadPicture` function and the capabilities of the Image control, see Chapter 7, "Adding Pictures to Convey More Information."

Use control arrays to store icon choices

The problem with loading pictures from a file is that you must distribute the picture files with your application. You must also make sure that the path you are specifying for the location of the files is correct. If the `LoadPicture` function cannot find the requested file, an error will occur.

A better way to make the pictures available for your dialog is to store them in an array of Image controls on the dialog form itself. This **control array** can have its `Visible` property set to `False` so these Image controls are not seen by the user.

66 *Plain English, please!*

A **control array** is a group of controls of the same type with the same name, but with a different index number. The index number is like the page number of a report. You have probably created a report where you indicated "Page 1 of 5," "Page 2 of 5," and so on. The page number could also be called the page index, and your report could be considered an array of pages.

In a control array, all the controls must be of the same type. You cannot mix text boxes and image controls. You can only use one or the other.

By using a control array, a picture may be accessed easily by specifying the index of the array. This index can be one of the arguments passed to the dialog. 99

To create the image control array, follow these steps:

1 Draw the Image control on the form, give it a unique name, and set its `Visible` property to `False`.

2 Press the Ctrl+C key combination (or choose Copy from the Edit menu) to copy the button to the Clipboard.

3 Press the Ctrl+V key combination (or choose Paste from the Edit menu) to make a second copy of the button on the form. The first time you paste a copy of the button, you will be shown a message box like the one in figure 16.7, asking if you want to create a control array. Answer Yes to this question.

Fig. 16.7

A message box is used to confirm that you want to create a control array when you try to place a copy of a control on the form.

4 The new copy of the button will be placed in the upper left corner of the form. Click it with the mouse and drag it to its desired location.

5 Repeat steps 3 and 4 until you have the number of Image controls that you need.

TIP These steps will work to create any kind of control array.

After you have created the array, you can store a different icon in each of the controls. These controls will be used as the source for your dialog icon. Figure 16.8 shows how the dialog form looks with an array of icons ready for use.

Fig. 16.8
A control array of Image controls stores the icons needed for the dialog.

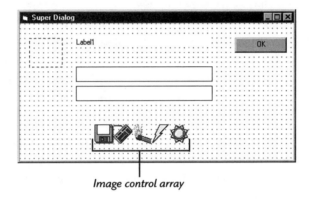

Image control array

Adding custom icons

The other advantage of working with the Image control array is that you can use the index number of the array to select the image to show in the dialog. Index numbers for a control array start with 0 and continue to one less than the total number of controls (i.e., a five-element control array would use index numbers 0 through 4). The following code shows how to display the desired icon in the dialog:

```
frmSuperDialog.imgDialog.Picture =
frmSuperDialog.imgIcons(0).Picture
```

This code would be added to listing 16.1 right before the Show method was used.

Give me better buttons

Another advantage I stated for creating your own dialog was that you could have as many buttons as you want. Also, the buttons on your dialog could have more descriptive captions than OK, Cancel, Retry, or Abort.

Handling the changing number of buttons

Let's look first at how you add buttons to the dialog. Obviously, you could just add more buttons in the design mode, but that would still limit your dialog to the number initially set up. The idea of the custom dialog is for it to be called from multiple places in your program to serve multiple purposes. A better way to provide the multiple buttons is to again use a control array.

Since you already have a command button on the form, you can change it from a single button to a one-element control array. You do this by setting the Index property of the command button to 0 (previously the Index property was blank). You have now created a control array. What does this gain you? With a control array, you have the unique ability to add array elements at runtime. This means that you can add more command buttons from within your code.

Adding another element of a control array is done with the Load statement. Once you have added the new elements, you must also set their Visible property to True to have them displayed. Listing 16.2 shows how this would be used in a program.

Listing 16.2   The *Load* Statement Adds Elements to a Control Array

```
Load frmSuperDialog.cmdReturn(1)
Load frmSuperDialog.cmdReturn(2)
lbltop = frmSuperDialog.cmdReturn(0).Top
lblhigh = frmSuperDialog.cmdReturn(0).Height
cmdLeft = frmSuperDialog.cmdReturn(0).Left
frmSuperDialog.cmdReturn(1).Left = cmdLeft
frmSuperDialog.cmdReturn(1).Top = lbltop + lblhigh + 200
frmSuperDialog.cmdReturn(2).Left = cmdLeft
frmSuperDialog.cmdReturn(2).Top = lbltop + 2 * (lblhigh + 200)
frmSuperDialog.cmdReturn(0).Caption = "Continue Copy"
frmSuperDialog.cmdReturn(1).Caption = "Abort the Copy"
frmSuperDialog.cmdReturn(2).Caption = "Different Drive"
frmSuperDialog.cmdReturn(1).Visible = True
frmSuperDialog.cmdReturn(2).Visible = True
```

The first two statements of the code load two additional elements of the command button array. (Remember, the first element is already on the form.) Be aware that the new buttons will be the same width as the original button. Therefore, you need to make sure that the original size will accommodate any text you want to use for the button captions.

The next seven statements set the Left and Top properties of each of the new buttons to establish their positions on the form. This is the same thing you did in listing 16.1 to position the text boxes. The next three lines of code set the Caption property of each of the command buttons. Finally, the last two lines set the Visible property of the command buttons to True so they can be seen.

The code in listing 16.2 was combined with the code from listing 16.1 to produce the dialog box shown in figure 16.9. (Obviously, a few captions were changed as well.)

Fig. 16.9

New command buttons can be added at runtime using a control array.

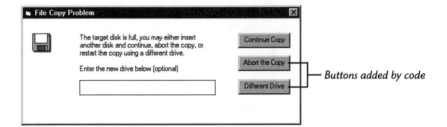

Buttons added by code

Captions you design

In listing 16.2, you saw how the captions on the command buttons were changed to give users better information about their choices. Since you have complete control over the properties of the controls on your form, this means you can make the captions anything you want.

I think you'll agree that the captions shown in the example are much better than Abort, Retry, or Cancel.

Getting the user's responses

For a custom dialog, you will also need a way to get the responses from the user. For the text boxes, you know that anything the user types is stored in the Text property. Therefore, you can check that property for the user's answers.

How, though, do you figure out which command button was pressed by the user? Well, fortunately (or slyly), an array of command buttons was used. This means that when one of the buttons is pressed, Visual Basic passes the Index of the button to the Click event procedure. So Visual Basic tells you which button is pressed. All you have to do is pass the information back to the calling program of our dialog. The easiest way to do this is to use the

`Caption` property of the command button itself to store the index value. Listing 16.3 shows the `Click` event procedure that achieves this.

Listing 16.3   The *Caption* Property of the First Button Stores the *Chosen* Button

```
Private Sub cmdReturn_Click(Index As Integer)
frmSuperDialog.Hide
cmdReturn(0).Caption = Index
End Sub
```

The first line of the listing shows the start of the procedure. Notice the argument `Index` that is passed to the event procedure. This is the index of the button which was pressed. The second line of the listing assigns the `Index` value to the `Caption` property of the first command button. You use the first button because it is the only one guaranteed to be present. Next, you remove the dialog from the screen using the `Hide` method. The last line just indicates the end of the procedure.

Summary

While you would not want to use custom dialogs for every purpose, hopefully you have seen how they can be used when Visual Basic's built-in dialogs are insufficient for the task. I hope you have also seen that while they are not simple to build, custom dialogs are not all that hard, either.

Review questions

1 What is the advantage of using a custom dialog?

2 What are the three steps involved in displaying the dialog to the user?

3 What is a control array?

4 Why is a control array useful for the command buttons?

Exercises

1 Modify the dialog created for listing 16.1 to add another text box. Remember to include code to handle the positioning of the text box.

2 Working from listing 16.2, add additional command buttons to the dialog.

3 Create a new and unique dialog based on the concepts shown in this chapter.

17

Adding Variables to Your Programs

● **In this chapter:**

- **The difference between a variable and a constant**

- **How are variables used in a program?**

- **Data in a variety of flavors**

- **Does a variable hold the data I put in it forever?**

- **You are not limited to just the constants defined by Visual Basic**

Sometimes you may have variables, or information that changes frequently. Visual Basic lets you create a generic variable, or pseudonym, to represent these changing numbers throughout your programs, to save you from having to repeatedly change them on your own. . . . . ❯

You have already worked a little bit with variables. In several of the code listings in earlier chapters, variables were used to hold a piece of data. But what exactly is a variable? In simplest terms, a variable is something that can change, like the variable rate for some types of mortgages. The technical definition of a variable is the name you give to a location in your computer's memory. This memory location stores a single piece of data temporarily while your program is running. In more simple terms, you can think of a variable as sort of a Post-It note for your program. You jot down the information, put it where you can find it, then throw it away when you are finished with it.

The value of a variable can be changed while your program is running, hence the name. There are two kinds of variables that you will be working with in Visual Basic programs—variables that you define yourself and the properties of Visual Basic controls and forms. Yes, properties are a kind of variable in that the properties may be changed from your program while it is running.

Why store data in variables?

Variables store data in the computer's memory, but how do you tell it what to store and where to store it? The "where" part of the question is easy. You don't have to tell the computer anything about where the information should be stored; Visual Basic does that for us. All you have to do is assign the variable a name.

What's in a name?

You can assign a variable any name within the following restrictions:

- The name must start with a letter, not a number or other character.

- The name cannot contain a period.

- The name must be unique.

- The name can be no longer than 255 characters.

Within these restrictions, you have a lot of flexibility. You can use a simple, one-character variable name like I, or a long descriptive name like `TotalofAllGradesforSpanishClassinRoom211`.

TIP **Make your variable names descriptive of the task to make your** code easy to read, but also keep them short to make it easy to type.

Telling the variable what to store

To store a piece of information in a variable, you assign it a value using an assignment statement. Assigning the value "writes" the value to memory, like you would write a value down on a piece of paper.

The following lines of code show several examples of assignment statements using either variables or properties:

```
Let ClassName = "Spanish"
NumberofStudents = 45
AverageAge = 21.75
txtStudent.Text = "Mike"
```

 Plain English, please!

> A **keyword** (used in the "Speaking of assigning a value" section) is a word used by Visual Basic as part of the programming language. Keywords are used to identify a command, a property, an event, or a method. These words are also referred to as reserved words. You cannot use a keyword as a variable name, or an error will occur. A list of keywords can be found in the Visual Basic help file.

Speaking of assigning a value

The syntax of an assignment statement is as follows:

```
[Let] variablename = value
```

This is a simple statement that you have seen used previously. The **keyword** Let is optional in the statement and is most often omitted. variablename represents the name of the variable (as defined previously) or the name of the property of a control. The equal sign must be included in the statement. Also, there must be at least one space between the variable name and the equal sign, and between the equal sign and the value. value represents the information you want to assign to the variable.

As you can see from the code examples, the assignment statement works for both variables and for properties of controls. Let's look a little more closely at the use of variables by creating a simple program. This program will get input from the user and calculate the average value of the input numbers. In the program, statements such as those shown previously will be used to set the values of variables and properties. You will also see how variables are used to calculate values, and as arguments for functions.

To start, place a label control, a text box, and a command button on a form. Change the name of the text box to txtAverage; change the Caption of the form to Variable Demonstration; change the Caption of the label to Average; and change the Caption of the command button to Enter Numbers. When you have done this, your form should look like the one in figure 17.1.

Fig. 17.1
Variables store the count and the sum of the numbers you enter.

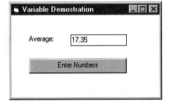

Now for the meat of the program. Place the code in listing 17.1 in the Click event of the command button. This code will use the input box to get numbers from the user. Then when the user enters -1, the code will calculate the average of the numbers entered.

Listing 17.1   Variables Calculate the Average of the Numbers Entered

```
avgval = 0
numval = 0
inptval = 0
Do While Not inptval = -1
    inptmsg = "Input a positive integer or -1 to calculate
    the average"
    inptval = InputBox(inptmsg, "Input Values")
    If Val(inptval) > 0 Then
        avgval = avgval + inptval
        numval = numval + 1
    End If
Loop
txtAverage.Text = avgval / numval
```

The first three lines of code set up three variables—avgval, numval, and inptval. The assignment statements set these variables to a particular value (in this case, 0) for the beginning of the program. This is known as initializing the variables.

Program loops of this type are discussed in Chapter 22, "Conditional Loops: Keep Going Until I Tell You to Stop."

The next line of code, starting with the word Do, begins a program loop. This loop will continue until the value of the variable inptval is equal to -1. The end of the program loop is indicated by the word Loop.

To learn more about the InputBox function, see Chapter 14, "Communicating with the User Through Dialog Boxes."

The next line sets up a variable (inptmsg) which contains the prompt to be used for the input box. The following line actually calls the InputBox function and sets the output of the function to the variable inptval. The function uses the variable inptmsg as one of its arguments.

After the user enters a number, a conditional statement checks to make sure that a number was entered and that the number was greater than zero. If so, the number is added to the avgval variable, and one is added to the numval variable to indicate that another number is to be included in the average.

When the user finally enters -1, the loop stops and the average of the numbers is calculated. This average is then displayed in the text box by using an assignment statement to set the Text property of the box to the calculated average. Note how the variables avgval and numval appear on the right side of the equal sign in the assignment statement.

What type of information can a variable hold?

Listing 17.1 showed how variables are used to contain numbers and text. However, variables are not limited to these two data types. Variables can hold a number of different types of data. They can contain text, integer numbers, decimal numbers, dates, times, logical values, and even OLE objects (such as pictures).

How can I use this in the real world?

Variables are used in most programs to get input from the user, to set up control properties, and to store intermediate results of calculations. One example is shown in listing 17.1, where a program is used to get a series of numbers from the user, and then calculate the average value of the numbers.

Table 17.1 shows the different types of variables that are available in Visual Basic. The table also shows the range of values that the variable can hold and the amount of memory required to store the information in the variable. The memory requirements are important in optimizing your code. Variables with smaller memory requirements should be used wherever possible to conserve system resources.

Table 17.1 Variables Available in Visual Basic

Type	Stores	Memory requirement	Range of values
Integer	Whole numbers	2 bytes	–32,768 to 32,767
Long	Whole numbers	4 bytes	Approximately +/– 2 billion
Single	Decimal numbers	4 bytes	+/– 1E-45 to 3E38
Double	Decimal numbers	8 bytes	+/– 5E-324 to 1.8E308
Currency	Numbers with up to 15 digits left of the decimal and 4 digits right of the decimal	8 bytes	+/– 9E14
String	Text information	1 byte per character	Up to 65,000 characters
Byte	Whole numbers	1 byte	0 to 255
Boolean	Logical values	2 bytes	True or False
Date	Date and time information	8 bytes	1/1/100 to 12/31/9999
Object	Pictures, OLE objects	4 bytes	N/A
Variant	Any of the other data types	16 bytes + 1 byte per character	N/A

❝ *Plain English, please!*

E (in the previous table) is shorthand for exponential and stands for powers of 10. Using exponential notation for large numbers lets you write the number in a compact format. For example, one of the ranges included 1.8E308. This is the numbers 1 and 8 followed by 307 zeros. It would take about 6 lines on a page to write this number out. Negative exponents represent fractions. Here are a couple of examples. One million is written out as 1,000,000 or 1E6 in exponential notation. The fraction 1/1000 can be written as 0.001 or 1E-3. **❞**

You must tell the program what the variable can hold

You know what a variable can hold, and you know what type of information you want to store. But how do you tell the program what you want to store? Well, first of all, you don't have to tell the program anything. As you have seen in listing 17.1 and in other examples in the book, you can just assign a value to a variable and let the program figure out what it is.

When you do this, Visual Basic automatically uses the variant data type. (We will look more closely at the variant type in a minute.) The problem with using a variant for every variable in your program is that it wastes space. For example, to represent the number 100 in a variant requires 19 bytes, compared to only 2 bytes if you specify the variable as an integer. Do this a lot, and you will use up your available memory much more quickly.

To tell Visual Basic what type of variable to use, you must declare the variable. There are two ways to do this—**explicit declaration** and **implicit declaration**.

Explicit declaration

Explicit declaration means that you use a statement to define the type of a variable. These statements do not assign a value to the variable but merely tell Visual Basic what the variable can contain.

The following code shows the use of declaration statements for actual variables:

```
Private numval As Integer
Private avgval As Integer, inptval As Variant
Static clcAverage As Single
Dim inptmsg As String
```

TIP   **Unless otherwise specified, the default variable type is variant. See** the section "Changing the default variable type" later in this chapter to see the use of other types.

Implicit declaration

You can also specify the type of data in a variable using an implicit declaration. With this type of declaration, a special character is used at the end of the variable name when the variable is first assigned a value. The characters for each variable type are shown in the following table.

Speaking of explicit declarations

The following statement can be used to explicitly declare a variable's type:

```
Dim varname [As vartype][, varname2 [As vartype2]]
```

Dim is a Visual Basic keyword that defines how and where the variable can be used. Private, Static, and Public are also keywords that can be used in the place of Dim. (These terms are covered in detail in Chapter 26, "Basic Building Blocks: Procedures and Functions.") varname and varname2 represent the names of the variables that you want to declare. As indicated in the syntax, you can specify multiple variables in the same statement, as long as you separate the variables by commas. (Note that the syntax only shows two variables, but you can specify any number.)

vartype and vartype2 represent the type definition of the respective variables. The type must be one of the ones specified in table 17.1. As indicated, the variable type is an optional property. If you include the variable type, you must include the keyword As. If you do not include a variable type, the default type is used.

Variable type	Character
Integer	%
Long	&
Single	!
Double	#
Currency	@
String	$
Byte	None
Boolean	None
Date	None
Object	None
Variant	None

Looking back at the examples in the previous code, the following statements would have the same effect in setting the type for the variables:

```
numval% = 0
avgval% = 1
inptval = 5
clcAverage! = 10.1
inptmsg$ = "Mike"
```

Notice on the variable `inptval` that a declaration character wasn't used. This means that `inptval` will be of the variant type.

Special strings

Both the implicit and explicit declarations previously shown for strings created what is known as a variable length string. This type of string changes size to fit the data stored within it.

There is a second type of string that is in Visual Basic. This string type is a **fixed-length string**. As the name implies, a fixed-length string remains the same size, regardless of the information assigned to it. If a fixed-length string variable is assigned an expression shorter than the length, the remaining length of the variable is filled with the space character. If the expression is longer than the variable, only the characters that fit in the variable are stored; the rest are truncated. This is like the forms you fill out that specify the number of spaces available for your name. If your name is longer than the number of blanks, you just don't write in all the letters.

Changing the variable type

As was stated, Visual Basic assumes that if you don't specifically declare a variable, it will be of the variant type. But suppose you need to use a lot of integer variables. Do you have to declare every single one of them? No. Visual Basic provides you with a means of changing the default variable type for a range of variable names.

The variable types and their definition keywords are defined in the following table.

Speaking of fixed-length strings

A fixed-length string variable may only be declared using an explicit declaration of the form, as follows:

```
Dim varname As String*strlength
```

You can use the `Private`, `Public`, or `Static` keywords for the declaration as well as the `Dim` keyword. `varname` is the name of the variable you want to create. The keyword `String` identifies the variable as a string. The asterisk (*) tells Visual Basic that the string will be of a fixed length. `strlength` tells the program how many characters the variable can contain.

Variable type	Keyword
Integer	DefInt
Long	DefLng
Single	DefSng
Double	DefDbl
Currency	DefCur
String	DefStr
Byte	DefByte
Boolean	DefBool
Date	DefDate
Object	DefObj
Variant	DefVar

Speaking of changing the default variable type

The following statement allows you to specify that a range of variable names be of a specific data type:

```
Defvartype range1[, range2]
```

In this statement, the word Defvartype represents one of the definition keywords for the variable type. range1 and range2 represent the letter ranges that will use the variable type. The range can be a single letter, such as A, or a range of letters, such as M through P. You can have one or more ranges in a Deftype statement. After a Deftype statement is issued, all variables that start with the letter in the letter range will be defined as that variable type unless they are explicitly or implicitly declared as shown here.

In the following code, `numval` is automatically set up as an integer, `msgtxt` as a string, and `decAverage` as a single:

```
DefInt N-P
DefStr M
DefSng A-F
numval = 5
msgtxt = "This is a string"
decAverage = 15.3
```

You can assign values using literals

In the preceding pages, you have seen values assigned to variables using other variables or actual values. For string and date variable types, these actual values are called **literals** and must be input in a specific manner.

For string variables, the information you want to store in the variable must be enclosed within double quotation marks (" "). If a word is not enclosed in quotes, Visual Basic assumes that it is the name of another variable and will generate an error if that variable does not exist. If you try to assign a number to a string variable without enclosing it in quotes, an error will be generated. These concepts are illustrated in the following code.

The following is the right way:

```
msgtxt$ = "This is a message"
strnum$ = "1000"
```

This is the wrong way (an error will occur):

```
msgtxt$ = This is a message
strnum$ = 1000
```

For dates, a literal date must be enclosed between two pound, or number, signs (#). Otherwise, a date like 3/4/1995 will be assumed to be a mathematical operation (three divided by four, divided by 1995), and an error may occur. At best, you will get a date, but not the one you want.

The following is the right way:

```
Dim ThisDay As Date
ThisDay = #3/4/1995#
```

This is the wrong way:

```
Dim ThisDay As Date
ThisDay = 3/4/1995
```

You can also use the variant variable

The variant data type can handle any type of information—text, numbers, dates, objects, etc. This flexibility means that you don't have to worry about errors occurring when you assign a value to a variant type variable. You do still have to worry about errors when you compare a variant to another variable or to a literal value. For instance, the following code would generate an error if it was run:

```
Dim ThisData As Variant
ThisData = 5
ThisData = "Enter your name"
If ThisData > 5 Then MsgBox "The variable is greater than 5"
```

The first line of code defines the variable `ThisData` as a variant data type. This means that you can assign any information to the variable. The second and third lines of code show how different data types (a number and a string) can be assigned to the variable. In the last line, we try to compare the variable to the number 5. Since the last value stored in `ThisData` is `"Enter your name"`, a string, the two pieces of data are not the same type, and an error message, `Type mismatch`, will be displayed.

Fortunately, Visual Basic provides functions that allow you to determine what type of information is in a variant variable. For the case just presented, you could use the `IsNumeric` function to test the data type before you compare the variable to 5.

Speaking of *IsNumeric*

The `IsNumeric` function returns either a `True` or `False` value telling you whether the variable you pass to the function was a number (`True`) or not (`False`). You can assign the returned value of the function to a variable, or use it directly in a conditional statement. The syntax for the function is:

```
IsNumeric(varname)
```

`varname` represents the name of a variable or a literal string that you need to know about.

In the following example, the `IsNumeric` function would return `True`:

```
ThisData = 5
retvalue = IsNumeric(ThisData)
retvalue = IsNumeric("15.375")
```

The following lines would return a `False` value:

```
ThisData = "Enter your Name"
retvalue = IsNumeric(ThisData)
retvalue = IsNumeric("Mike")
```

You can now use this function to modify your previous example to avoid the `Type mismatch` error as follows:

```
Dim ThisData As Variant
ThisData = 5
ThisData = "Enter your name"
If IsNumeric(ThisData) Then
    If ThisData > 5 Then MsgBox "The variable is greater
    than 5"
End If
```

Catch the bug

This code should calculate the average of some numbers, but it doesn't work. Can you find the problem(s)?

```
Dim Astr As String, Inumber As Integer
NewAvg! = 0.0
Astr = "The average is:"
TotScores = 5075
Inumber = "Five"
NewAvg! = TotScores / Inumber
ShowStr$ = Astr + NewAvg!
```

Answer: This code contains two errors. The first error is trying to assign the text "Five" to an integer variable. The second error is trying to combine the string Astr with the number NewAvg! to assign to another string, ShowStr$. Also, if Inumber did contain a string, trying to use it in the calculation of NewAvg! would also create an error. The following code is correct:

```
Dim Astr As String, Inumber As Integer
NewAvg! = 0.0
Astr = "The average is:"
TotScores = 5075
Inumber = 5
NewAvg! = TotScores / Inumber
```

Constants—some things never change

We have talked through most of this chapter about things that change, or variables. Now for the things that don't change. Variables provide you with a means to temporarily store something in memory. But what if you want to make sure that the value you store does not change during the course of the program? Then you need to use a **constant**.

To illustrate the difference between constants and variables, think of your drive to work. As long as you drive along the same route every day, the distance to work never changes. This is a constant. However, the time it takes you to make the drive can change, depending on the traffic, the time of day, weather conditions, and how many red lights you hit (usually, all of them, in my case). The driving time then is a variable.

Constants in a program are treated a special way. Once you define them (or they are defined for you by Visual Basic), you cannot change them later in the program using an assignment statement. If you try, Visual Basic will generate an error when you run your program.

Why use a constant instead of the value it represents?

Constants are most often used to replace a value that is hard to remember, such as the color value for the Windows title bar. It is easier to remember the constant `vbActiveTitleBar` than the value $-2,147,483,646$. You can also use a constant to avoid typing long strings if they are used in a number of places. For example, you could set a constant such as `FileFoundError` containing the string, `The requested file was not found`.

Constants are also used a lot for conversion factors, such as 12 inches per foot or 3.3 feet per meter. The following code example shows how constants and variables are used:

```
Const MetersToFeet = 3.3
inpmeters = InputBox("Enter a distance in meters")
distfeet = inpmeters * MetersToFeet
MsgBox "The distance in feet is: " & Str(distfeet)
```

The first line of this code declares a constant, `MetersToFeet`, and assigns it a value of `3.3`. The second line uses the input box to prompt the user to enter a distance in meters, then get the input value. The third line converts the distance to feet using the constant that was defined. Finally, the distance in feet is displayed using the message box. The function `Str` is used to convert numbers to strings. This function will be covered in more detail in Chapter 19, "Handling Strings of Data."

Constants supplied by Visual Basic

Visual Basic supplies a number of constants that you can use in your programs. You saw an example of these constants in the discussion on message boxes. There were constants that were used to define the icon and button set used in the message box.

Visual Basic supplies a number of sets of constants for various activities. Among others, there are color definition constants, data access constants, keycode constants, and shape constants.

The constants that you need for most functions are defined in the Help topic for the function. If you want to know the value of a particular constant, you can use the Object Browser dialog box shown in figure 17.2. The Object Browser is accessed by clicking its icon in the Visual Basic toolbar. You can use the list to find the constant you want. Then when you select it, its value and function are displayed in the text area at the bottom of the dialog.

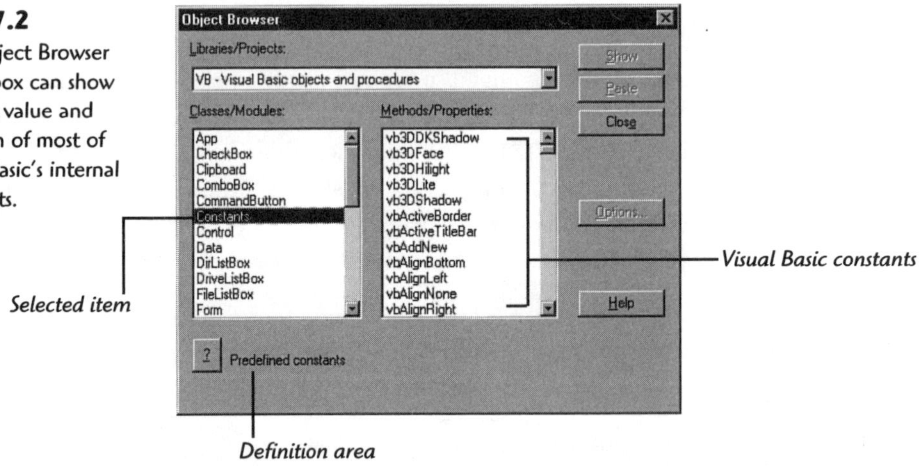

Fig. 17.2
The Object Browser dialog box can show you the value and function of most of Visual Basic's internal constants.

Selected item

Visual Basic constants

Definition area

Creating your own constants

While Visual Basic provides you with a number of constants that can be used in your programs, you may want to define some of your own. You may want a constant to contain the value of a conversion factor or perhaps a color constant that isn't defined by Visual Basic. To define your own constants, you need to use the `Const` statement.

TIP **While you can use the** `Const` **statement anywhere in a procedure,** it is best to define all the necessary constants at the beginning of the procedure.

To set up a constant, you use the `Const` statement as follows:

```
Const constantname [As constanttype] = value
```

The `Const` keyword tells Visual Basic that this statement defines a constant, instead of just assigning a value to a variable. `constantname` represents the name of the constant. A constant is named the same way as a variable with all the same restrictions. The As clause is an optional part of the statement that allows you to define the type of data that the constant will hold. The types for a constant are the same as those for a variable.

Finally, to define a constant, you must include the equal sign and the value to be assigned. If you are defining a string constant or date constant, remember to enclose the value in either quotes or pound signs, respectively.

Catch the bug

This program will generate an error when you try to run it. Can you find where the error will occur and what causes it?

```
Const MetersToFeet = 3.3
distmeters = 7.5
distfeet = distmeters * MetersToFeet
MetersToFeet = 5.9
```

Answer: *The problem is in the last line when you try to assign a new value to a constant. If you need to change the value of* `MetersToFeet`, *don't make it a constant. The correct first line is as follows:*

```
MetersToFeet = 3.3
```

Summary

Variables are used to hold bits of information for processing in your code. Variables allow you to pass information between parts of your program and to manipulate data. Constants provide you with an easy way to set up definitions of things that don't change. Using constants makes your code easier to read and to maintain. Without variables and constants, your programs wouldn't be able to do much.

Review questions

1 What type of data can a variant type variable store?

2 What are the two types of declarations you can use to create a variable?

3 Do you have to declare a variable before you use it?

4 What is the difference between a variable and a constant?

5 How do you create a constant for your program?

6 Why does Visual Basic provide you with built-in constants?

Exercises

1 Change the code in the average value example (from listing 17.1) to display a running average (i.e., calculate the average after each number).

2 Change the unit conversion (meters to feet) code to convert feet to inches. This will involve defining a new constant.

3 Using the appropriate constants (that you define), write a program to convert length measurement from English to metric units.

18

Power Up Your Visual Basic Programs with Some Basic Math

● **In this chapter:**

- **How do I perform basic math in a program?**

- **You can also perform math operations on dates**

- **How built-in functions help you with trigonometry and other math**

One of the real beauties of Visual Basic is that it hides most of the math from you, allowing you to create valuable programs without writing any more math statements than you choose

● ➤

Math is the subject that most people love to hate when they are in school. But when you think about it, you use math every day. You use it to determine how much change you should get back when you make a purchase. You also use it to determine how much longer it will take to get to your destination if you keep driving at 65 miles per hour.

In fact, without math, we wouldn't be able to do a lot of things in our daily lives. You couldn't balance your checkbook. You couldn't determine if you had enough money to buy gas and still eat out tonight.

Introduction to math operators

So now that you realize what math does for you, let's review a little of the stuff from school and introduce you to how it works on a computer. Afterwards, we'll look at some more complex math functions that Visual Basic performs for you and look at how you use all this in a program.

Addition and subtraction

The simplest form of math is addition and subtraction. As you well know, these are the operations that you use in keeping up your checkbook. You add in the deposits and subtract out the checks and ATM withdrawals (I always forget these). If you're like me, you use a calculator for these functions just to avoid mistakes.

Since you know how to use a calculator, you will find that addition and subtraction is equally easy to write into your computer programs. You are already familiar with all the symbols you need to use. With a program, though, you have greater flexibility in the operations you can perform. Your programs are not limited to only working with literal numbers (that is, 1, 15, 37.63, –105.2). Your program can add or subtract two or more literal numbers, numeric variables, or any functions that return a numeric value.

While the order does not matter in addition, in subtraction the number to the right of the minus sign is subtracted from the number to the left of the sign. If you have multiple numbers, the second number is subtracted from the first, then the third number is subtracted from that result, and so on, moving from left to right. For example, enter the equation:

```
result = 15 - 6 - 3
```

The computer first subtracts 6 from 15 to yield 9. It then subtracts 3 from 9 to yield 6, which is the final answer stored in the variable `result`.

You can use addition and subtraction operations either alone or in combination with one another. The following code lines show a few valid math operations.

```
val1 = 1.25 + 3.17
val2 = 3.21 - 1
val3 = val2 + val1
val4 = val3 + 3.75 - 2.1 + 12 - 3
val4 = val4 + 1
```

Speaking of addition and subtraction

The operator for addition in Visual Basic is the very familiar plus sign. It is used as follows:

```
result = number1 + number2 [+ number3]
```

`result` is a variable (or control property) that contains the sum of the numbers. The equal sign indicates the assignment of a value to the variable. `number1`, `number2`, and `number3` are the literal numbers, numeric variables, or functions that are to be added together. You can add as many numbers together as you like, but each number pair must be separated by a +.

The operator for subtraction is the minus sign. The syntax is basically the same as for addition:

```
result = number1 - number2 [- number3]
```

Wait a minute! What was that last line? How can something equal itself plus another number? Visual Basic allows you to enter code like this. What the code is telling the computer to do is take the current value of the variable (val4), add 1 to it, and then store the new value back in val4. While it may look funny at first, this is a perfectly valid and quite useful statement. Of course, val4 must have a value (either assigned or calculated) before you can use it in this manner.

Multiplication and division

The next two big math topics are multiplication and division. These operations are what you use to calculate how much paint you need for a room or how many miles per gallon your car got on that last tank.

Multiplication in Visual Basic is very straightforward. You simply use the multiplication operator to multiply two or more numbers.

To illustrate the use of multiplication and division operators, consider the following cost-estimating program for a painter. This program contains a form that lets the painter enter the length and width of the room, the height of the ceiling, and the coverage and cost of a single can of paint. The program can then calculate the number of gallons of paint required and the cost of the paint. The data-entry form for the cost-estimating program is shown in figure 18.1, and the code required to make it work is shown in listing 18.1.

Speaking of multiplication

The multiplication operator in Visual Basic is the asterisk operator. It is used in a similar manner to the addition and subtraction operators:

```
result = number1 * number2 [* number3]
```

Again, result is the variable used to contain the product of the numbers being multiplied, and number1, number2, and number3 are the literal numbers, numeric variables, or functions.

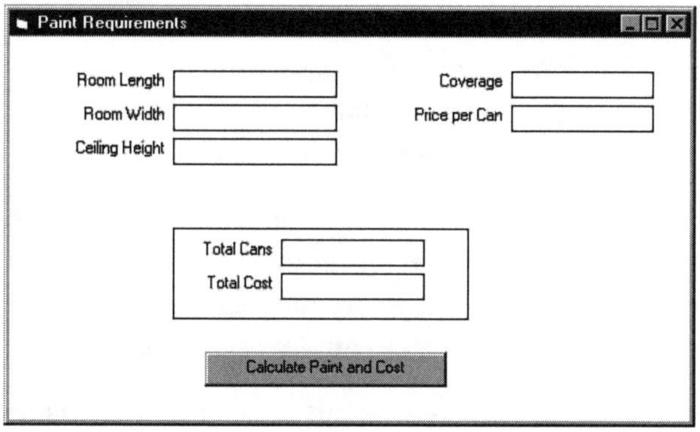

Fig. 18.1
A cost-estimating program is a simple but useful demonstration of multiplication and division.

Listing 18.1   The Cost-Estimating Program

```
rmLength = txtLength.Text
rmWidth = txtWidth.Text
rmHeight = txtHeight.Text
canCoverage = txtCoverage.Text
canCost = txtCost.Text
rmPerimeter = 2 * rmLength + 2 * rmWidth
wallArea = rmPerimeter * rmHeight
numGallons = wallArea / canCoverage
projCost = numGallons * canCost
txtGallons.Text = numGallons
txtTotalCost.Text = projCost
```

The first five lines of the code retrieve input values from the text boxes on the form. The sixth line calculates the perimeter dimension of the room by adding twice the length of the room to twice the width. This gives you the total wall length around the room. Next, the total surface area to be painted is calculated by multiplying the perimeter by the height of the walls.

Once the area of the walls is known, the number of cans of paint required can be calculated by dividing the total surface area by the area covered by a single can of paint. Finally, the cost of the paint can be calculated by multiplying the number of cans by the cost per can.

The last two lines of code assign the results of the calculations to text boxes for display on the form.

Division in Visual Basic is a little more complicated than multiplication. In listing 18.1, you saw one type of division used. This is the division that you are most familiar with and that you find on your calculator. This type of division returns a number with its decimal portion if one is present.

However, Visual Basic supports three different ways to divide numbers. These are known as **floating-point division** (this is the normal division that you're familiar with where numbers include a decimal portion), **integer division**, and **modulus**, or **remainder**, **division**.

To show the difference between these types of division, let's create a simple program. Place five text boxes and one command button on the form. For simplicity, use the default names for all the controls. You can also place labels on the form to identify each text box. Then place the following code in the `Click` event of the command button.

Speaking of division

Floating-point division is the typical division you learned in school. You divide one number by another and the result is a decimal number. The floating-point division operator is the forward slash (/).

```
result = number1 / number2 [/ number3]
```

Integer division divides one number into another one, and returns only the integer portion of the result. The operator for integer division is the backward slash (\).

```
result = number1 \ number2 [\ number3]
```

Modulus, or remainder, division divides one number into another, and returns what is left over after you have obtained the largest integer quotient possible. The modulus operator is the keyword mod.

```
result = number1 mod number2 [mod number3]
```

As with the case of addition, subtraction, and multiplication, if you divide more than two numbers, each number pair must be separated by a division operator. Also, like the other operations, multiple operators are handled by reading the equation from left to right.

```
inpt1 = Text1.Text
inpt2 = Text2.Text
Text3.Text = inpt1 / inpt2
Text4.Text = inpt1 \ inpt2
Text5.Text = inpt1 Mod inpt2
```

After you have set up the form, run the program and enter **5** in the first text box and **3** in the second text box; then click the command button. Your form should look like figure 18.2.

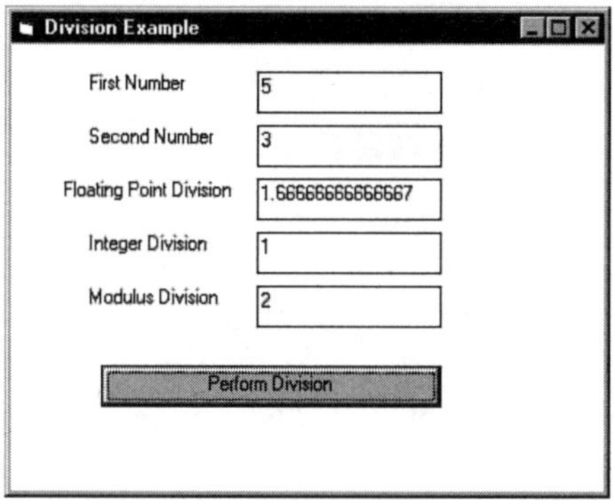

Fig. 18.2

Visual Basic supports three types of division operators.

As you can see, floating-point division gives you the result you normally expect in division (`5/3 = 1.6666667`). The integer division performs a floating-point division but only gives you the whole number portion of the answer (`5\3 = 1`). Finally, modulus division gives you what is left over if you take the integer division answer, multiply it by your dividing number, and then subtract it from the original number (`5 mod 3 = 2`). Try it with some other numbers and see what happens.

Exponents

Exponents are also known as powers of a number. For example, 2^3 is equivalent to $2 \times 2 \times 2$, or 8. Exponents are used quite a lot in computer operations, where many things are represented as powers of 2. Exponents are also used extensively in scientific and engineering work where many things are represented as powers of 10 or as natural logarithms. Simpler exponents are used in statistics where many calculations depend on the squares and the square roots of numbers.

As an example of using exponents, consider the following equations. This is the square of the number:

```
3 ^ 2 = 9
```

The following is the square root of the number.

```
9 ^ 0.5 = 3
```

A fraction is obtained by using a negative exponent, like the following:

```
2 ^ -2 = 0.25
```

Order of operations

When a number of operators are used in a single equation, operators are processed in a specific order. For all operators of the same type, they are processed from the left of the equation to the right. For mixed operators, the operations are processed in this order: exponentiation first, followed by multiplication and division, integer division, modulus division, and finally addition and subtraction.

Let's look at a complex equation to see how this works. This equation is shown in the following code:

```
ClearAsMud = 3 * 4 + 4 / 6 ^ 2 * 5 - 2
```

Speaking of exponents

To raise a number to a power, you use the exponential operator, which is a caret (^). Exponents greater than 1 indicate a number raised to a power. Fractional exponents indicate a root. And negative exponents indicate a fraction. The syntax for using the exponential operator is:

```
result = number1 ^ exponent
```

result is the variable containing the result of the operation. number1 is the number to be raised, and exponent is the number of powers of the base number.

To clear up the results of the equation, let's break it down by the order of operation. First, you handle the exponential operator portion 6^2. Solving this operation changes the equation to:

```
ClearAsMud = 3 * 4 + 4 / 36 * 5 - 2
```

Next, you handle all multiplication and division since they have the same precedence. You evaluate the first multiplication, 3*4, to get 12. Then in the second set, 4/36*5, you evaluate the operators from left to right since multiplication and division have the same precedence. Therefore, you handle the division first since it is the leftmost operator. This gives you 0.111111*5, or 0.555555. This changes the equation to the following:

```
ClearAsMud = 12 + 0.555555 - 2
```

Finally you handle the addition and subtraction, again working from left to right within the equation, to give you the final answer of:

```
ClearAsMud = 10.555555
```

Using parentheses to ensure order

The equation above does work if you group everything correctly, but it is extremely confusing. Visual Basic gives you a way to force the order of operations and make the code more readable. You can group operators and numbers using parentheses. When this is done, all groups in parentheses are evaluated first, as if they were individual equations. Then all other operators are handled. You can use multiple levels of parentheses for groupings, but you must make sure that the parentheses appear in pairs (a right one for every left).

What difference does this grouping make? Take look at a simple equation:

```
result = 9 / 3 * 3
```

You know that the operators in this equation evaluate from left to right giving you 9/3*3 = 3*3 = 9. This is equivalent to grouping the equation as follows:

```
result = (9 / 3) * 3
```

Now, what if you move the parentheses to change the grouping as follows:

```
result = 9 / (3 * 3)
```

This new grouping gives you $9/(3*3) = 9/9 = 1$. This is an entirely different result. You can also use intermediate results stored in variables to achieve the same result as using parentheses. This is shown in the following code lines:

```
intrslt = 3 * 3
result = 9 / intrslt
```

 TIP For very complex equations, using intermediate results makes the code much easier to read and, therefore, to maintain.

Catch the bug

The following code is intended to perform a series of calculations but results in an error. Can you find the improper statement?

```
intrslt1 = 257 * 398
intrslt2 = intrslt1 / 22
intrslt3 = (intrslt1 * intrslt2) (16 / 2.75)
result = intrslt3 ^ 2
```

Answer: *In the third line, there is no math operator between the two parenthetical groups. While it is permissible to write equations this way in algebra class, it doesn't work on the computer.*

Variable types are important when performing math

The math operators you have learned about work on any type of variable that contains a number. This includes integer, long, single, double, currency, and variant variable types. You can even perform some math operations on dates as you will shortly see. You cannot perform math on strings or objects.

Something you should be aware of, though, in working with math and math functions, is the type of variable you are using to store the answer. Believe it or not, the variable type actually affects the answer that Visual Basic returns for a given equation.

The main concern is when you assign the results of an equation to an integer or long variable. Because these variable types cannot handle the decimal portions of a number, any equation that results in a decimal is **rounded** to the nearest whole number.

 Plain English, please!

Rounding is a process where a number that has a decimal portion (for example, 1.25) is changed to make it an integer. If the decimal portion is less than .5, the number is rounded down to the next lower integer (1.25 becomes 1). If the decimal portion is .5 or above, the number is rounded up to the next higher integer (2.51 becomes 3).

You can learn about text boxes in Chapter 4, "Letting the User Enter Text," and about command buttons in Chapter 12, "Other Controls You Should Know About."

You can see the results of rounding in an example program. Place four text boxes on the screen, along with a command button. Next, place the following code in the Click event of the command button. Then run the program and type a number in each of the first two text boxes. When you click the command button, you see the difference between rounded values (caused by assigning the result to an integer variable) and unrounded values.

```
num1 = Text1.Text
num2 = Text2.Text
rslt1% = num1 / num2
rslt2 = num1 / num2
Text3.Text = rslt1%
Text4.Text = rslt2
```

The first two lines of code retrieve the numbers you entered from the text boxes.

The third line divides the first number by the second number and stores the result in an integer variable. (Note the declaration character %.) Using an integer variable for the result forces Visual Basic to round the answer.

For more information on variable types, see Chapter 17, "Adding Variables to Your Programs."

The fourth line of code performs the same division but stores the result in a variant variable. Because a variant variable can handle decimal numbers, no rounding of the answer is performed.

The last two lines of code assign the results of the two divisions to text boxes for display.

 Q&A *Doesn't rounding produce the same result as integer division?*

Not always. Integer division always returns the next lower number, even if the decimal portion of the number is above .5. To see for yourself, change the fourth line of the previous code to the following:

```
rslt2 = num1 \ num2
```

Rerun the code and try out some different values.

How to use math in your programs

Now that you know the basics of math operations, what can you do with it? Let's apply the math operations to a real world application.

If you have ever taken a trip by car, you have probably calculated how long the trip would take and how many times you would need to fill your gas tank. The code example in listing 18.2 creates a trip calculator which does the math for you.

To create the trip calculator, you need to create seven text boxes on a form. For these to work with the following code, you need to name the text boxes txtMiles, txtSpeed, txtMPG, txtCapacity, txtHours, txtMinutes, and txtStops. You also need to place labels and a command button on your form. When you finish, it should look like figure 18.3.

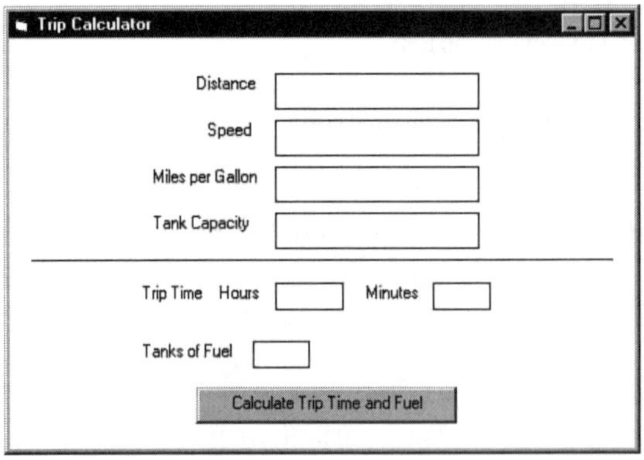

Fig 18.3
A trip calculator shows you how long a trip will take and how many gas stops you will need to make.

After you have created the form, place the code in listing 18.2 in the Click event of the command button.

Listing 18.2 The Trip Calculator Uses Many Math Operations

```
miles% = txtMiles.Text
speed% = txtSpeed.Text
mpg% = txtMPG.Text
flcap% = txtCapacity.Text
drvhours = miles% \ speed%
```

```
drvminutes = (miles% Mod speed%) / speed% * 60
drvrange = mpg% * flcap%
flstops = miles% / drvrange
txtHours.Text = drvhours
txtMinutes.Text = drvminutes
txtStops.Text = flstops
```

The first four lines of the code retrieve the input values from the text boxes for distance, speed, miles per gallon for your car, and the capacity of your fuel tank. The next line of code uses integer division to determine how many hours the trip will take based on the distance and the speed. This value is stored in the drvhours variable.

Next you calculate the minutes portion of the trip time using the modulus operator. The modulus operator, inside the parentheses, gives you the number of miles left after you have driven drvhours. This distance divided by the speed gives you the fractional hours left in the trip. Multiplying by 60 then gives you the minutes. This is stored in the drvminutes variable.

Next you determine the range that the car can go on a tank of gas. This is simply the miles-per-gallon value multiplied by the fuel capacity. You then store the value in the drvrange variable. Finally, you determine the number of tanks of gas needed by dividing the trip's distance by the range per tank and store it in the flstops variable.

In the last three lines of the code, you assign the results of the calculation to the text boxes that display the output.

Manipulate dates and times with math

While most math operators and functions are designed for use with numbers and numeric variables, you can also perform some calculations on dates and times using some of the math operators. For example, you can add or subtract a specific number of days from a date to get a new date (that is, adding seven to a date moves the date one week). If you use integer numbers, you can change the date by entire days; the time is not affected. If you use fractional numbers, you change the date and time.

Addition and subtraction are the only operators you can use with a date, and you can only use them to add or subtract days and hours. These operators cannot be used to determine the number of days between two dates. For that, you need to use a special function as described in the next section, "Determining the number of days between dates."

To add or subtract days from a date, you use the following syntax:

```
newdate = datevar + numdays
```

In this syntax, newdate is a date variable that stores the date resulting from the equation. datevar can be a date variable, a literal date (for example, #3/10/95#), or a function that returns a date. The + operator tells the program to perform an addition. numdays is a number, numeric variable, or numeric function that specifies the number of days to be added. The integer portion of the number adds days to the date, while the decimal or fractional portion of the number adds hours and minutes to the time portion of the date.

The subtraction operator uses exactly the same syntax except that – is used instead of +.

Determining the number of days between dates

While you can add and subtract days from a date using math operators, you cannot determine the number of days between two dates with these operators. Visual Basic, however, does provide a function that handles this for you—the DateDiff function. This function not only tells you the number of days between two dates but also the number of weeks, months, years, hours, or minutes between the two dates.

Speaking of *DateDiff*

The syntax of the DateDiff function is:

```
result = DateDiff(interval, firstdate, seconddate)
```

firstdate and seconddate are date variables that contain the two dates you want to determine the difference between. If firstdate specifies a later date than seconddate, the result of the function is a negative number. Otherwise, the returned value is positive.

interval is a literal string or string variable that determines which time interval is returned (that is, hours, days, weeks).

`DateDiff` uses a literal string or string variable. The string can have any of the settings defined in the following table. For a literal string, the setting must be enclosed in quotes.

Setting	Period of Time
yyyy	Years
q	Quarters
m	Months
w	Weekdays of the same day
d	Days
h	Hours
n	Minutes
s	Seconds

Another function related to the `DateDiff` function is the `DateAdd` function. This function allows you to add or subtract a period of time from a date. This function gives you more flexibility than using the math operators for this purpose.

Speaking of *DateAdd*

The `DateAdd` function is used as follows:

```
newdate = DateAdd(interval, numintervals, olddate)
```

`newdate` and `olddate` represent date variables in the equation. `olddate` can also be a literal date or a function that returns a date. `interval` is again a string expression defining the type of time period to be applied. `numintervals` specifies the number of time periods added to or subtracted from `olddate`. If `numintervals` is positive, the time intervals are added to the `olddate`. If `numintervals` is negative, the time intervals are subtracted from `olddate`. The same values are used for `DateAdd` as were used for `DateDiff`.

Q&A ***Can you mix time periods within the function to get, for example, days and hours?***

No. The `DateDiff` and `DateAdd` functions can only work with a single time period.

Other date and time functions

There are several other date functions that return a date or a time. These functions can be used to store a value in a date variable, or they can be used directly in the `DateDiff` and `DateAdd` functions described previously.

Each of these date functions has the same syntax, as follows:

```
result = functionname
```

`result` is a date variable that stores the output of the function. `functionname` is the actual function to be used as defined in the following table.

Function name	Returns
Date	The current date from your computer
Time	The current time from your computer
Now	The current date and time

Catch the bug

You want a program that tells you how many days and weeks it is until Christmas. You enter the following code but it doesn't work. What is wrong with it?

```
daysTilChristmas = 12/25/95 - Date
weeksTilChristmas = daysTilChristmas / 7
```

Answer: *There are two errors in this code, both occurring in the first line. First, a literal date must be enclosed between # signs (#12/25/95#). Second, you cannot use a math operator to get the days between dates, you must use the* DateDiff *function.*

Using more advanced math functions

In addition to the operators used to set up math equations, Visual Basic also contains a number of math functions for specific calculations. Each of the math functions takes a single argument and returns a value. You can use these functions anywhere that you use a variable, except on the results side of an equation. You can, therefore, use functions as part of an equation or in conditional statements. For more information on how functions work in general, see Chapter 26, "Basic Building Blocks: Procedures and Functions."

General math functions

Each of the functions in table 18.1 uses the syntax shown in the "Speaking of math functions" section. The table shows the function keyword, a description of the function, any restrictions on the numbers for the argument, and a sample input and result from the function.

Table 18.1   Math Functions Simplify Certain Tasks

Keyword	Description	Restrictions	Input	Result
Abs	For a positive number, returns the number; for a negative number, returns the number without the negative sign.	None	2, –3	2, 3

continues

Speaking of math functions

Each of the math functions uses the same syntax:

```
result = functionname(argument)
```

The `result` is, of course, the variable that stores the output of the function for further use. `functionname` is the keyword for the individual function. These keywords and their associated functions are summarized in tables 18.1 and 18.2. `argument` can be any numeric variable or a number that the function operates on. Certain functions may restrict the range of numbers that can be used. Be aware that the parentheses around the argument are required.

Table 18.1 Continued

Keyword	Description	Restrictions	Input	Result
Exp	Returns e (natural log base = 2.718) raised to the power of the argument.	None	2	7.389
Int	Returns the next lowest integer for the number.	None	7.35, -6.16	7, -7
Log	Returns the natural log (base e) of a number. The inverse of the Exp function.	Argument must be greater than 0	10	2.3025
Rnd	Returns a random value between 0 and 1.	No restrictions on the argument, but the argument is optional	1	0.705
Sgn	Returns −1 if the number is negative, 1 if it is positive, and 0 if the number is 0.	No restrictions	125, -37	1, −1
Sqr	Returns the square root of a number	Argument must be greater than or equal to 0	4, 0.25	2, 0.5

Trigonometry

Trigonometric functions deal with the relationship between the angles and the sides of a triangle. They are used quite often for engineering and scientific calculations. I won't go into the details of how trigonometry works here; instead, I'll just summarize the available functions from Visual Basic. Each function takes a single number as an argument. The number can be any numeric value. These functions are summarized in table 18.2.

Table 18.2 Visual Basic Supports These Trigonometric Functions

Keyword	Function name
Atn	Arc tangent
Cos	Cosine
Sin	Sine
Tan	Tangent

Summary

The math that you studied in school is used throughout many computer programs. You have operators to perform the simple math, functions for some of the more complex functions, and even a few ways to get dates into the act. A good grasp of these concepts serves you well as you write your programs.

Review questions

1 What items do the numeric expressions in an equation include?

2 What are the three types of division supported by Visual Basic?

3 What is the order of preference of math operations?

4 What are two means of ensuring that a complicated equation produces the desired results?

5 Which math operators can be used for date calculations?

Exercises

1 Write the code to determine the number of days between now and Christmas. (Refer to the second "Catch the bug" example).

2 Using listing 18.1, add a piece of code that subtracts the space occupied by doors and windows from the total wall area.

3 Again using listing 18.1, change the calculation of the number of cans to return an integer number. If a fractional can is calculated, the number should be rounded up to the next whole number.

19

Handling Strings of Data

● In this chapter:

- How to see if a word is in a string of text

- Can I pull pieces of a string out of a larger string?

- Use numbers and strings together

- What tells me how long a string is?

- How are upper- and lowercase letters handled?

Much of the data you'll input into your programs, whether from disk or from a user, will be in the form of strings of numbers or letters (such as names, addresses, and data). Visual Basic has built-in functions that manipulate this data for you without programming it . . . . ▶

f you're new to programming, you probably think of a string as something you use to bind packages, or to keep a child's kite from flying away. However, in programming, a string is a type of variable that contains text. If the application you are designing gathers, manipulates, and displays text, you are working with strings.

For more on using the text box to enter and display text, see Chapter 4, "Letting the User Enter Text."

Variable declarations are discussed in Chapter 17, "Adding Variables to Your Programs."

For most applications, a string of text is input by the user through the TextBox control. The text box is also one of the primary display methods for strings. In fact, the Text property of the TextBox control is very similar to a string variable.

There are two kinds of strings that can be handled by Visual Basic—**variable length** and **fixed length**. Variable length strings can contain any amount of text up to about 65,000 characters. As the name suggests, a variable length string changes length with the contents of the string. This type of string is the default type created with either an implicit or an explicit declaration statement. Fixed length strings are initially declared, using an explicit declaration, to contain a certain number of characters. This length does not change, no matter what the string contains, and represents the maximum number of characters that can be stored in the variable. Fixed length strings are most often used in conjunction with a database, where the length of the data stored in the file is specified.

Tying strings together

One great thing about strings is that you can combine two or more strings to create a third string. This allows you to take information from different sources and put it together for display or printing. You saw an example of this in Chapter 12 when you combined several strings to create the message to be displayed in the message box.

The way you combine strings in Visual Basic is by using the concatenation operator. This operator is the ampersand symbol (&). When you combine two strings with the concatenation operator, the second string is added directly to the end of the first string. The result is a longer string containing the full contents of both source strings. This is like tying the ends of two ropes together. The result is a "new" rope that is equal in length to the sum of the two pieces (minus the knot).

The concatenation operator is used in an assignment statement as follows:

```
newstring = stringexpr1 & stringexpr2 [& stringexpr3]
```

In this syntax, `newstring` represents the variable that contains the result of the concatenation operation. `stringexpr1`, `stringexpr2`, and `stringexpr3` all represent string expressions. These can be any valid strings including string variables, literal expressions (enclosed in quotes), or functions that return a string. The & between a pair of string expressions tells Visual Basic to concatenate the two expressions. The & must be preceded and followed by a space. The syntax shows an optional second & and third string expression. You can combine any number of strings with a single statement. Just remember to separate each pair of expressions with a &.

 TIP   **Previous versions of Visual Basic and older BASIC languages also** used a + operator to combine strings. Visual Basic still supports this, in case it is present in older code that you are modifying. However, it is recommended that you use the & for any work you do to avoid confusion with the mathematical addition operation.

Let's build a mailing label generator. Because you may not want to print the created labels, you will print the labels in a picture box on the form. When you finish, the application will look like the one shown in figure 19.1.

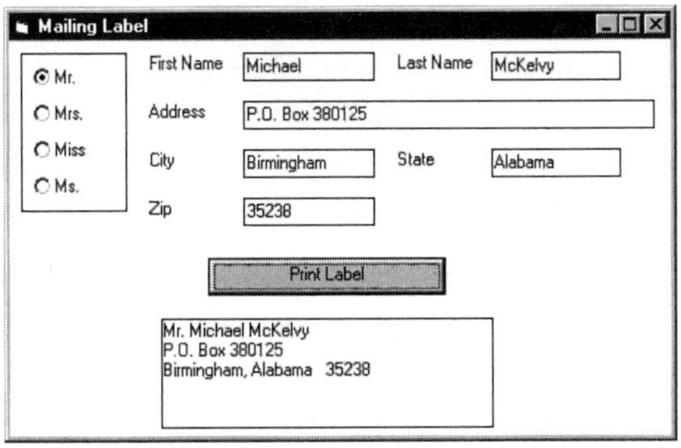

Fig. 19.1
The Mailing Label application shows how strings are combined for display or printing.

To create the application, start by placing four option buttons on the form. Make the captions of the buttons `Mr.`, `Mrs.`, `Miss`, and `Ms.`. Name the option buttons `optTitle1` through `optTitle4`. Next place six text boxes on the form and name them `txtFirst`, `txtLast`, `txtAddress`, `txtCity`, `txtState`, and `txtZip`. You might also want to go ahead and delete the text in the `Text` property of each box so that they appear blank. Next, add a picture box to the form and name it `picOutput`. Lastly, place a command button on the form with the `Caption` property set to `"Print Label"`, and name the button `cmdPrint`. To complete the application as shown in figure 19.1, you need to add the appropriate labels to the form.

After you have added all the necessary controls to the form, you need to add the code in listing 19.1 to the `Click` event of the command button to make the application work.

Listing 19.1   Produce Mailing Labels Using String Operatons

```
strFirst$ = txtFirst.Text
strLast$ = txtLast.Text
strAddr$ = txtAddress.Text
strCity$ = txtCity.Text
strState$ = txtState.Text
strZip$ = Format(txtZip.Text,"00000")
If optTitle1.Value Then strTitle$ = "Mr. "
If optTitle2.Value Then strTitle$ = "Mrs. "
If optTitle3.Value Then strTitle$ = "Miss "
If optTitle4.Value Then strTitle$ = "Ms. "
strLine1$ = strTitle$ & strFirst$ & " " & strLast$
strLine3$ = strCity$ & ", " & strState$ & "  " & strZip$
picOutput.Print strLine1$
picOutput.Print strAddr$
picOutput.Print strLine3$
```

 In the first five lines of the code, you are retrieving the values entered in the text boxes for the person's name, address, city, and state. In the next line, you are retrieving the zip code information; but because the zip code may be treated as a number, you use the `Format` function to ensure that you get a string variable and that any leading zeros are included.

The next four lines of code check the option buttons to see which one was chosen by the user. The `strTitle` variable is then set to the appropriate value. Only one of the option buttons can have a `Value` property set to `True`, so only one of the assignment statements is performed.

In the next two lines, you create the name line and city/state/zip line of the mailing label. To create the name line, you combine the person's title with the first name and last name. Notice that you also include a literal string containing a space so the first and last names don't run together. The concatenation operator is used to combine these strings. The city/state/zip line is created the same way by concatenating the three strings. Again, you use literal strings to create the appropriate separators for the different parts of the line.

Finally, in the last three lines, you use the `Print` method to display the lines of the mailing label in the picture box. If you want to print this label, you can change the object of the `Print` method from `picOutput` to `Printer` (for example, `Printer.Print`). This tells Visual Basic to direct the output to the printer.

Run the application and enter your personal information.

How can I use this in the real world?

One frequent use of concatenation of strings is in the processing of mailing labels. For personnel information, you often have separate fields for a person's first and last names. Typically, you also have separate fields for the city, state, and zip code of the address. These all appear on the same line of the mailing label. To create the label, use the concatenation operator to combine fields that appear on the same line. The figure shows the result.

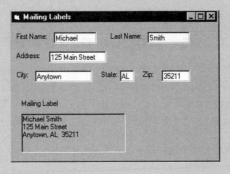

Changing the appearance of text in a string

For information on changing fonts and text size, see Chapter 5, "Making Your Words Look Good."

You have probably had some experience with a word processor and know a little bit about changing the appearance of text. You can change the fonts and font attributes of text in your documents, and you can do the same in the text boxes of Visual Basic programs.

There are other things that change the appearance of text that can be accomplished through some of the string manipulation functions. The case (whether or not the letters are capitalized) of the letters in the text changes how the text looks. The case of the text is not something that can be changed using the properties of a control. It can only be changed by the user as he enters or edits text, or through the use of the case functions. Figure 19.2 shows the appearance of text using two different case methods.

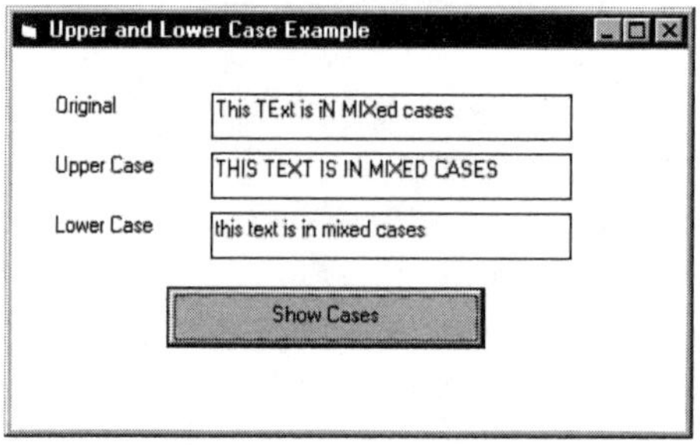

Fig. 19.2
The case of the letters in the text can be changed using string functions.

In either case—upper or lower

There are two functions that can modify the case of letters in a string. These are the UCase and LCase functions. The UCase function returns a string with all the letters converted to uppercase or capital letters. The LCase function does just the opposite. The syntax for the UCase function is:

```
UpperString = UCase(inputstring)
```

UpperString represents the variable that holds the return value of the function. This can be any variable that is declared a string either through an implicit or explicit declaration. UCase is the name of the function. inputstring can be any string variable or literal string. The two following lines of code are equally valid uses of the UCase function:

```
OutputStr$ = UCase(InputStr$)
OutputStr$ = UCase("This is a literal string.")
```

Whether you use a variable or a literal, the parentheses are required for the function. If you use a literal, the text must be enclosed in double quotes.

The syntax for the LCase function is basically the same as for the UCase function:

```
LowerString = LCase(inputstring)
```

These two functions were used to create the form shown in figure 19.2. To create this form, place three text boxes and a command button on the form. Name the text boxes txtInput, txtUpper, and txtLower. Then place the following code in the Click event of the command button:

```
InputStr$ = txtInput.Text
UpperStr$ = UCase(InputStr$)
LowerStr$ = LCase(InputStr$)
txtUpper.Text = UpperStr$
txtLower.Text = LowerStr$
```

Run the program, type any text using upper- and lowercase letters, and then click the command button to see the effect of these two functions.

Justifying the text

Two other functions that can change the appearance of text are the LSet and RSet functions. These functions justify the text within the string by placing spaces either in front of (RSet) or after (LSet) the text in the string. Neither of these functions change the length of the string. These two functions produce the same effect as the Alignment property of the text box (and other controls), but actually modify the string itself. These functions can be used to align text with either the right or left margin of a control.

To try out these functions, go back to the last example and substitute the following code in the Click event of the command button:

```
Dim LeftStr As String * 20, RightStr As String * 20
InputStr$ = txtInput.Text
LSet LeftStr = InputStr$
RSet RightStr = InputStr$
txtUpper.Text = LeftStr
txtLower.Text = RightStr
```

Run this and try typing in different length strings to see how the LSet and RSet functions work.

Getting pieces of a string

The most important aspect of manipulating strings is the ability to add, remove, or change single characters, words, or sections of a string. Visual Basic provides you with a number of functions that are designed for this purpose:

- Three functions remove spaces

- Three functions remove a section of a string

- One function determines the length of a string

- One function performs a search

- One function exchanges one piece of a string for another string

This section looks at each of these functions in detail. Then, later in the chapter, you will write a program that uses many of these functions and the UCase function to capitalize the first letter of the first word in each sentence of a string.

Speaking of *LSet* and *RSet*

The LSet and RSet functions have the same syntax, with the exception of the name of the function:

    LSet *stringvar* = *stringexpr*

    or

    RSet *stringvar* = *stringexpr*

stringvar is a fixed length string that contains the result of the function. stringexpr is a string expression, either a string variable or a literal string. If the string expression is shorter than the length of the variable, spaces are placed before or after the expression to make up the rest of the length. If the expression is longer than the variable, the leftmost characters in the expression are copied to the variable, and the remaining characters are truncated.

Determining what is in the string

Being able to determine whether a particular word or group of words is in a string allows you to perform word searches of text. This can be used to perform a global replacement of a string, like replacing the word *text* with the word *string* throughout a word processing document. A word search can also be used to find out whether a string in a database pertains to your particular query.

The function that allows you to search a string for the occurrence of a character, word, or group of words is the InStr function.

The code in listing 19.2 performs a search of a string and tells you how many times your item of interest occurs. For example, how many times did the word "the" occur in the last paragraph? Figure 19.3 shows how this program would look.

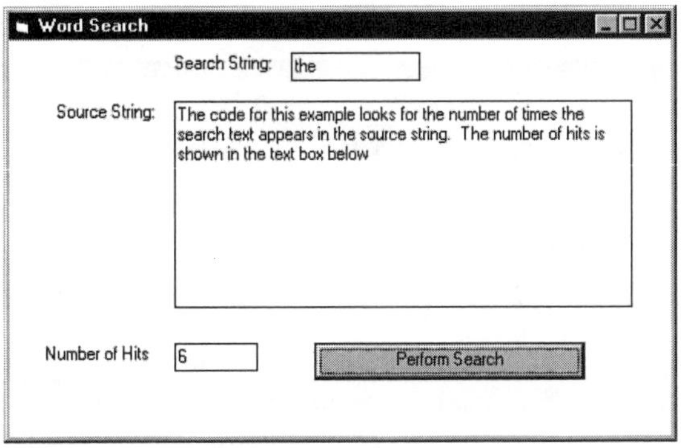

Fig. 19.3
The *InStr* function works like the find function of your word processor.

How can I use this in the real world?

The ability to search for a word or phrase within a string of text is important to many businesses. For instance, you may have a database that contains regulations that control your industry. You can use a text search to determine which regulations pertain to a particular topic. In this way, you could find every regulation that mentions carbon dioxide. The search would also tell you where in the regulation the text occurred. Then you could go back and examine each regulation to see if it applied to your situation.

Listing 19.2   The *InStr* Function Tells You If One String Is Contained in Another String

```
tgtText = txtSource.Text
srchText = txtSearch.Text
numHits = 0
stPoint = 1
fnPoint = 1
Do While fnPoint > 0
    fnPoint = InStr(stPoint, tgtText, srchText, 1)
    If fnPoint > 0 Then
        numHits = numHits + 1
        stPoint = fnPoint + 1
    Else
        stPoint = 0
    End If
Loop
txtHits.Text = numHits
```

SPEAKING VB

Speaking of *InStr*

The syntax of the InStr function is:

> *result* = InStr(*[startpos,]sourcestr, searchstr[, compare])*

result is the variable that contains the returned value of the function. The function returns a Null value if either the sourcestr or searchstr strings are Null, and returns a numeric value otherwise.

startpos is an optional argument that specifies the character position in the sourcestr where the search begins. If this argument is omitted, the search begins with the first character in the string. startpos is a numeric argument. sourcestr is the string that is being searched. searchstr is the string that you want to find.

compare is an optional, numeric argument. If compare is set to 0 (the default value), a case sensitive search is performed (for example, the words *CASE* and *case* are not the same). If compare is set to 1, a case insensitive search is performed. If you omit the compare argument, its value is assumed to be 0.

If searchstr is found in sourcestr, the position at which searchstr starts is returned by the function. If searchstr is not found, a zero is returned.

 The first two lines of code retrieve the search string and the string to be searched from text boxes. The next two lines initialize the variables `numHits`, which counts the number of times the search string is found, and `stPoint`, which indicates at which character the search should start each time.

The next section of code is a conditional loop that continues running until the search string is no longer found. When the `InStr` function fails to find the search string, it returns a zero, and the loop terminates. The end of the loop's range is indicated by the `Loop` statement.

The line containing the `InStr` function is called each time the loop is run. The function starts at the point specified by the variable `stPoint` and searches for the occurrence of the search string in the target string. The 1 as the last argument tells the function to perform a case insensitive search. Therefore the function treats all possible combinations of case the same (that is, *The, THE,* and *the* all count as hits).

If the function finds the search string, it returns the position of the string, which will be greater than zero. The `If` statement tests for this condition and increments the number of hits (finds) each time it occurs. Also, if a find occurs, the starting point for the next search is set to one character past the position of the last find. If the search string was not found, the `stPoint` variable is set to zero to terminate the loop.

Catch the bug

Even though the word "the" exists in the phrase below, `InStr` is returning 0. What is wrong with the code?

```
txt1 = "the"
txt2 = "The quick brown fox jumped over the lazy dog"
txtFind = InStr(txt1, txt2)
```

Answer: *While there is not a syntax error in the code, the search and source strings were probably reversed. If the search string is longer than the source, `InStr` returns 0. The following is the correct code:*

```
txtFind = InStr(txt2, txt1)
```

Determining the length of the string

For many operations, you need to know how many characters are in a string. You might need this to know whether the string with which you are working will fit in a fixed length database field. Or if you are working with big strings, you may want to make sure that the combined size of the two strings does not exceed the capacity of the string variable. In any case, to determine the length of any string, you use the Len function.

The Len function returns the number of characters in a string variable or expression:

```
result = Len(inputstr)
```

inputstr represents any valid string variable, literal string expression, or variant variable. If the variable is a variant, the number of characters is returned even if the variant contains a number or date.

Q&A ***Can I use the Len function to determine whether or not a string will fit in a text box or on a line of print?***

The TextWidth and TextHeight methods are covered in Chapter 32, "Printing the Results of Your Programs."

No. The Len function only tells you how many characters are in a string. The display size on a form or on a printer is dependent on the font type, size, and other font attributes. The Len function does not give you this information. You need to use the TextWidth and TextHeight methods for this.

Getting rid of spaces

Whenever you work with strings, you may end up with spaces that you don't want. These spaces can occur when the user accidentally types a space at the beginning of a text field. They also show up when you are using a fixed length string, the contents of which are shorter than the available number of characters.

Most of the time, spaces don't do any harm, except take up a little memory. However, when you combine strings or try to print strings, unwanted spaces can cause you all kinds of problems. Consider the mailing label example in listing 19.1. If the user accidentally enters spaces in front of the names, your label could look like this—Mr. John   Smith—instead of the way it should look—Mr. John Smith.

To get rid of those unsightly spaces, you can use one of three functions: LTrim, RTrim, or Trim. These functions remove spaces from various places in a string.

Q&A ***Is there a function that removes excess spaces from the middle of a string, like where a user typed two spaces between words?***

No. There is no specific function for that purpose. However, you can selectively remove characters from a string using the Mid statement described in the section "Replacing characters in a string" later in this chapter.

Carving out certain characters

You've looked at how to locate items in a string, and how to remove spaces from the ends; but what about pulling a piece of a string out to work with it? Being able to get parts of a string is essential for performing cut, copy, and paste type operations on string variables. Performing these functions on the string is like moving pieces of a report around in a word processor.

Speaking of *Trim, LTrim,* and *RTrim*

The Trim, LTrim, and RTrim functions all use the same syntax:

```
result = LTrim(inputstr)
```

or

```
result = RTrim(inputstr)
```

or

```
result = Trim(inputstr)
```

inputstr represents any valid string variable or literal string expression. The LTrim function removes spaces that are at the front of a string (that is, the left end). The RTrim function removes spaces from the end of a string. The Trim function removes spaces from both ends of the string.

Visual Basic provides three functions that allow you to take different pieces out of a string. These are the `Left`, `Right`, and `Mid` functions.

The `Left` function is used to take a specified number of characters out of a string, starting at the beginning. The syntax of the `Left` function is as follows:

```
newstr = Left(sourcestr, numchars)
```

`newstr` represents the variable that contains the string returned by the function. `sourcestr` is the string that contains the information you want to retrieve. This string can be a literal string, a string variable, or another function that returns a string. `numchars` specifies the number of characters from the `sourcestr` that you want to retrieve. `numchars` must be an integer number greater than or equal to zero. If `numchars` is zero, a zero length string is returned by the function. If `numchars` is greater than the length of the source string, the entire string is returned. For any other value of `numchars`, the function returns the number of characters specified starting at the beginning of the string.

The `Right` function works the same way as the `Left` function, except the `Right` function starts from the end of the string. Its syntax is:

```
newstr = Right(sourcestr, numchars)
```

For both the `Left` and `Right` functions, both arguments must be specified. There are no optional arguments.

To retrieve first and last names from a field where both are entered, see listing 19.3. This is a good example of the use of the `Left` and `Right` functions.

Listing 19.3   Retrieve First and Last Names Using the *Left* and *Right* Functions

```
namestr = Trim(txtName.Text)
howlong = Len(namestr)
firstlen = InStr(namestr, " ")
lastlen = howlong - firstlen
firstname = Trim(Left(namestr, firstlen))
lastname = Trim(Right(namestr, lastlen))
```

 For the example, you are using a text box to input a person's name. The first line of code retrieves the full name from the text box. For a data import function, you would have read the name from a file. When you retrieve the

name, you use the `Trim` function to eliminate any spaces at the beginning or end of the name.

Next, you determine the length of the name that was entered. This length will be used to help determine the number of characters to take from the right of the string to get the last name. You then determine the number of characters in the first name by using the `InStr` function to look for the space between the names. The function returns the position of the first space, which you can use with the `Left` function to retrieve the first name. The remaining length of the string, which contains the last name, is then equal to the total length minus the length of the first name.

Finally, you use the `Left` and `Right` functions, along with the lengths you obtained, to retrieve the first and last names respectively. You also use the `Trim` function in these statements to ensure that there are no extra spaces at the ends of the names. These statements also show how the argument of one function can be another function.

The other function used to retrieve parts of strings, the `Mid` function, works in a similar manner to the `Left` and `Right` functions, but it has one additional argument. The `Mid` function is what you would use to retrieve a letter, word, or phrase from the middle of a string.

The `Mid` function contains two required and one optional argument as shown in the syntax:

```
newstr = Mid(sourcestr, startpos[, numchars])
```

Most of the parts of this function are the same as the `Left` and `Right` functions. `startpos` represents the character position where the retrieved string begins. If `startpos` is greater than the length of the string, a zero length string is returned. The optional argument `numchars` represents how many characters are returned from the `sourcestr`. If `numchars` is omitted, the function returns all characters in the `sourcestr` from the starting position to the end.

Replacing characters in a string

Now to add a little confusion to your life. You just saw how the `Mid` function retrieves a piece of a string from the middle of a source string. The same keyword, `Mid`, is used to replace a part of a string. However, the syntax is quite different. When used to replace characters in a string, it is referred to as the `Mid` statement.

Catch the bug

The following code is supposed to extract part of one string and combine it with another. Can you see why it won't work?

```
inptStr = "This string can be anything you want"
newstr = Left(inptstr)
newstr2 = "The new string is: " & newstr
```

Answer: *You must include the number of characters to retrieve in the* Right *and* Left *functions. The correct code follows:*

```
newstr = Left(inptstr, 15)
```

The Mid statement replaces part of one string with another string. The syntax for the Mid statement is:

```
Mid(sourcestr, startpos[, numchars]) = replstr
```

The sourcestr in this case is the string that receives the replacement characters. sourcestr must be a string variable; it can't be a literal string or string function. startpos is the character position where the replacement starts. This must be an integer number greater than zero. numchars is an optional argument that specifies the number of characters from the replacement string that is used by the function. replstr represents the string containing the replacement characters. This string can be a string variable, a literal string, or a string function.

The Mid statement preserves the length of the original string. In other words, if the space remaining between the starting position and the end of the string is less than the length of the replacement string, only the leftmost characters from the replacement string are used.

The example from the "How can I use this in the real world?" section is done for a single sentence in listing 19.4. Figure 19.4 shows the results of this program.

How can I use this in the real world?

One of the uses of the Mid statement is to verify the capitalization of sentences in a paragraph. The function can be used to replace the first letter of each sentence with the uppercase version of the letter.

> **Listing 19.4   Capitalize the First Letter of a Sentence**
>
> ```
> inptstr = Trim(txtInput.Text)
> frstLtr = UCase(Left(inptstr,1))
> Mid(inptstr, 1) = frstLtr
> txtOutput.Text = inptstr
> ```

Fig. 19.4

Use the *Mid* statement to capitalize your text.

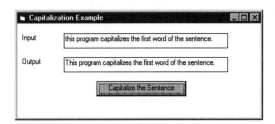

 First, the input string is retrieved from the text box and any extra spaces are removed. Next, the UCase and Left functions are used to retrieve the first letter of the sentence and make it uppercase. In the third line, the Mid statement is used to replace the first letter of the sentence with the upper-case letter. Finally, the revised sentence is displayed in an output text box.

Combining strings and numbers

One final topic I need to cover is the relationship between strings and numbers. You may know that some numbers are often treated as character strings. Zip codes and phone numbers are examples of these. However, there are times when you need to convert a number to a string variable to use it in a string function, or to print it in combination with another string. (An example of this was shown in the mailing label example in listing 19.1.) Likewise, there are times when you need to use numbers contained in a string variable in a mathematical equation or a numeric function.

Visual Basic provides the Cstr function to convert a number to a string and the Cint, Clng, Csng, and Cdbl functions to convert a string to a number.

 TIP   **Use a variant variable type with the Val function to be sure that** the variable can handle any number.

Summary

Being able to manipulate strings allows you to accomplish many tasks, such as modifying documents, creating mailing labels, and retrieving pieces of information from larger strings.

Review questions

1 Can you use the + operator to join two strings?

2 Which function strips spaces from the end of a string?

3 How do you replace characters in a string?

4 Which functions allow strings and numbers to be used together?

Speaking of *Cstr*

To convert a number to a string, you use the Cstr function as shown:

        numstr = Cstr(*inptnum*)

numstr represents a string variable that contains the output of the function. inptnum represents the number to be converted. This can be a number, numeric variable, or numeric function.

To convert a string to a number, you use the Cint, Clng, Csng, or Cdbl functions. Which function you use depends on the type of number that results from the string. Cint is used for integers, Clng for long integers, Csng for single type numbers, and Cdbl for double type numbers. If you are unsure of the data type of the result, you may use the Val function. Each function uses the same syntax as shown in the following for Cint:

        numvar = Cint(*inptstr*)

numvar represents a numeric variable that stores the output of the function. inptstr can be a literal string, string variable, or string function. The Cint function first strips out any spaces from the string, then starts reading the numbers in the string. If the first character in the string is not a number, Cint returns 0. Otherwise, Cint reads the string until it encounters a non-numeric character. At this point, it stops reading, and converts the digits it has read into a number.

Exercises

1 Change the code in listing 19.1 to include the Trim function to eliminate any spaces that might be typed in.

2 Change listing 19.3 to handle a first, middle, and last name.

3 Set up the capitalization program of listing 19.4, and then modify it so it works for every sentence in a paragraph.

20

Making Decisions Based Upon Data Comparisons

● In this chapter:

- How do you compare numbers?

- What is a logical condition?

- Comparing strings

- There's more than one condition to test

Logic is not something used only by Star Trek characters. Programs use it to determine a course of action . . . . ➤

f you're like me, your first exposure to "logical thinking" came while watching Mr. Spock work out problems on *Star Trek*. This type of logic uses reasoning based on facts, not emotion or intuition, to arrive at a conclusion. Logic used in a computer program is similar. A program uses logical comparisons based on the values of variables (the facts) to make decisions. These decisions then determine the course of the computer program and the outcome (conclusion) arrived at by the program.

Comparisons are logical operations

You can learn more about conditional loops in Chapter 22, "Conditional Loops— Keep Going until I Tell You To Stop."

For more information about decision statements, see Chapter 24, "If I Go This Way, Where Will I End Up?"

If all of this sounds a little high tech, just remember that the purpose of logical operators is to determine whether a statement is True or False. The logical operations in a computer program can compare numbers, strings, or dates. Information of different data types cannot be compared to each other. You can only compare numbers to numbers and strings to strings.

The predominate use of logical operations in a program is in conditional statements. These statements are used in decision (If) statements and in conditional loops (Do statements). Conditional statements are what you concentrate on in this chapter.

You can compare numbers

Comparisons of numbers are probably the easiest for most people to understand. You compare numbers all the time. If you comparison shop for the best price, you are doing a numerical comparison. Does store A have a lower price than store B, or is the sales tax lower in the next town?

These types of comparisons are used all the time in computer programs. The only difference is that your program usually compares two numeric variables to each other or compares a variable to a literal number. For most cases, you can also use a numeric function in place of a numeric variable. Comparing numeric values in the computer is straightforward. In all cases, 3 is greater than 2, 2 is greater than 1, and so on.

Are these values equal?

One of the numeric comparisons is determining whether two numeric expressions are equal—known as the **equivalence comparison**. This comparison uses the = operator. This should not be confused with the assignment statement that you have often used to set the values of variables or properties. In the assignment statement, the expression stands by itself as shown in the following statement:

```
newval = 7 * 3
```

In a comparison statement, the equation is always part of another statement, such as the following If statement:

```
If newval = 7 * 3 Then MsgBox "The values are equal"
```

Used in this manner, the comparison statement is commonly called a **condition**. Another difference between the assignment statement and the comparison statement is that a literal number or equation can be used on either side of the comparison. This is not so for the assignment. For the comparison, the previous statement could just as easily have been written as the following:

```
If 7 * 3 = newval Then MsgBox "The values are equal"
```

Visual Basic also has an inverse of the equivalent comparison, the **not-equal comparison**. The operator for this comparison is <>. This comparison uses the same syntax as the equivalence comparison but substitutes <> for the = operator.

Speaking of equivalence comparison

The equivalence comparison uses the following syntax. Note that this statement cannot stand on its own but must be part of a conditional statement:

```
numexpr1 = numexpr2
```

numexpr1 and numexpr2 represent numeric expressions. These expressions can be numeric functions, numeric variables, or literal numbers. If the expressions are equal, the comparison returns True. Otherwise, the comparison returns False.

The not-equal comparison returns a value of `True` if the two numeric expressions are different. It returns `False` if the numeric expressions are equal.

Which one is bigger?

In addition to determining whether two expressions are equal, you may need to know which of the two expressions is larger. This is the type of comparison that you do when you are price shopping.

The four comparison operators, their descriptions, and results are summarized in table 20.1. To illustrate the results, table 20.1 uses the following variable assignments:

```
A = 5      C = 5
B = 10     D = 7
```

Table 20.1 The Comparison Operators

Operator	Description	True examples	False examples
>	Greater than	B > A	D > B
>=	Greater than or equal to	B >= A, C >= A	C >= D
<	Less than	C < D	B < A
<=	Less than or equal to	C <= A, C <= D	B <= D

Speaking of comparison statements

To determine which expression is larger, your comparison statement takes the following form:

```
numexpr1 comparison numexpr2
```

numexpr1 and numexpr2 are again any valid numeric expressions. comparison represents the comparison operator. There are four comparison operators that are used for determining which numeric expression is larger.

You can compare strings

You can find the complete ASCII chart in the Visual Basic help file.

String comparisons are a little more complex than numeric comparisons because of the way Visual Basic considers string comparisons. For example, you and I probably say that the words "The" and "the" are the same. However, the computer doesn't see it that way. Visual Basic compares strings based on the order of the characters in the **ASCII** chart. While I won't repeat the whole chart here, I will illustrate this example further. The ASCII value for a capital T is 84, while the ASCII value for the lowercase t is 116. Therefore, according to the computer "T" is less than "t," and it follows that "The" is less than "the." You can change the behavior of the string comparisons using the `Option Compare` statement described later in this chapter.

 Plain English, please!

ASCII stands for **American Standard Code for Information Interchange**. It is a set of 128 numbers that represent the characters and keys found on the standard keyboard and many printed characters. All letters (both upper- and lowercase) and all digits are represented.

Do these strings match?

A string equivalence comparison is very similar in form to the numeric equivalence comparison. Also, like the numeric comparison, there is a not-equal comparison available for strings.

Speaking of string equivalence comparison

The string equivalence comparison takes the following form:

```
strexpr1 = strexpr2
```

strexpr1 and strexpr2 are string expressions, which can be a literal string, a string variable, or a function that returns a string. The not-equal comparison is basically the same:

```
strexpr1 <> strexpr2
```

When you're trying to determine if two strings are equal, the comparison makes sure that both strings are the same length and contain exactly the same characters in exactly the same positions. If all these conditions are true, an equivalence comparison of the strings returns a True value; otherwise, the comparison returns False.

The not-equal comparison is just the opposite. If the two expressions are an exact match, the comparison returns a False value; otherwise, it returns True.

Which string comes first?

Determining which string is the greater of two strings is a little more complex than determining equality or inequality. The comparison has to consider the length of each string, the letters in the string, and the case of each letter.

With the exception of the case of the letters, this comparison is exactly like placing people's names in alphabetical order. Remember in school when seating was assigned by the order of your name? Your class was sorted by last name with names beginning with A coming first. If two people had the same last name, they would be sorted by their first name. Also, if one name was shorter than another but had the same characters in the beginning, the shorter name was first. Hence, Green comes before Greene.

The only difference between a person comparing names and the computer comparing names is that the computer puts all capital letters before any lowercase letters. This causes a name like Zurn to be placed ahead of a name like deLoach.

The string comparison operators are the same as those for the numeric operators. These operators are shown in table 20.1.

How can I use this in the real world?

String comparisons, such as the comparison of names, are the basis for indexes in database systems. They are also used in sorting routines in a program and conditional statements. An often-used function is to sort people by name. This is used in personnel programs, library programs that sort by author, or membership tracking programs.

*For more informa-
tion about creating
a control array, see
Chapter 16,
"Creating Your Own
Custom Dialogs."*

To illustrate the way Visual Basic compares strings, you need to build a simple sort routine. Start out by placing a five-element control array of text boxes on your form along with a command button. Figure 20.1 shows how this should look. After placing the controls on the form, place the code from listing 20.1 in the `Click` event of the command button.

Fig. 20.1
Prior to a sort, the
names are in a random
order.

Listing 20.1 How to Sort a Group of Names

```
For I = 0 To 4
    For J = I + 1 To 4
        If Text1(I).Text > Text1(J).Text Then
            temp$ = Text1(I).Text
            Text1(I).Text = Text1(J).Text
            Text1(J).Text = temp$
        End If
    Next J
Next I
```

This listing contains a simple sort routine. It consists of two counter loops. The first loop looks at each text box in the array. Each time the first loop looks at an element, the second loop looks at all the elements after the current one. Inside the second loop, a conditional statement compares the strings in the two text boxes. If the string with the larger index is greater than the string with the smaller index, the contents of the two text boxes are swapped.

To run this sort, type a name in each text box and click the command button. Figure 20.1 shows a sample set of names, while figure 20.2 shows the same set after the sort.

Fig. 20.2
After the sort is run,
the names appear in
alphabetical order,
with one exception.

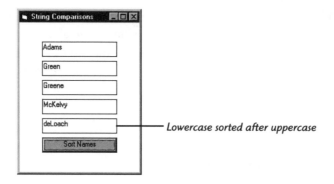

Lowercase sorted after uppercase

TIP For people who have some programming experience, the sort
shown is not the fastest or most efficient way to sort information. However,
it does provide a simple way to look at string comparisons.

Sorting upper- and lowercase letters together

You saw in the example shown in figures 20.1 and 20.2 that lowercase letters
get sorted after uppercase letters. As stated earlier, the ASCII character set
determines the order of characters. The problem is most people want names
and other strings sorted alphabetically whether the letters are upper- or
lowercase. This type of sorting is referred to as **case-insensitive**.

*The UCase and
LCase functions
are covered in
detail in chapter
19, "Handling
Strings of Data."*

There are two ways to change the way the comparisons are performed in the
sorting function (or for any other string comparison). The first way is to use
the UCase or LCase functions to make all the letters in the string the same
case. Listing 20.2 shows how this is implemented for the sort in listing 20.1.

Listing 20.2 A Modified String Comparison

```
For I = 0 To 4
    For J = I + 1 To 4
        If UCase(Text1(I).Text) > UCase(Text1(J).Text) Then
            temp$ = Text1(I).Text
            Text1(I).Text = Text1(J).Text
            Text1(J).Text = temp$
        End If
    Next J
Next I
```

The key line of code in this listing is the If statement. For this comparison, the UCase function converts the text strings to all uppercase letters prior to the comparison being performed.

The second way of accomplishing this task is to use the Option Compare statement.

Figure 20.3 shows how the sort order changes using either of the two methods for case-insensitive comparisons.

Fig. 20.3
Using the *UCase* function or the *Option Compare* statement results in a case-insensitive string comparison.

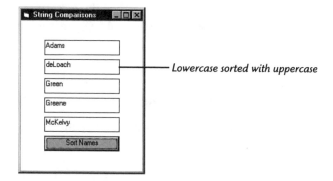

— *Lowercase sorted with uppercase*

Speaking of *Option Compare*

The Option Compare statement is placed in the declarations section of your form, outside of any procedures. Its syntax is as follows:

```
Option Compare comparetype
```

comparetype is replaced by either the word Binary or Text. If Binary is used, any string comparisons are based on the ASCII values of the letters. This is the comparison in listing 20.1. If Text is used, the comparisons are case-insensitive, meaning that upper- and lowercase letters are treated as equal.

Checking a string to see if it fits a pattern

There are times when you want to know if a string fits a certain pattern (that is, if a person's last name start with "S", or if a book title contains the word "Star"). You can also create more complex comparisons, such as, "Is the string a five-letter word starting with 'M' and ending with 'H'?" Visual Basic uses the LIKE operator for this type of comparison.

When creating a pattern, some of the wildcards and character lists may be combined, allowing greater flexibility in the pattern definition. The pattern can be a literal string or a string variable. Character lists, when used, must meet three criteria:

- The list must be enclosed in square brackets.

- The first and last characters must be separated by a hyphen.

- The range of the characters must be defined in ascending order (that is, a–z, not z–a).

In addition to using a character list to match a character in the list, you may precede the list with an exclamation point to indicate that you want to exclude the characters in the list.

SPEAKING VB

Speaking of *LIKE*

The LIKE comparison operator is used exclusively for string comparisons. The format of the LIKE operator is the following:

    expression LIKE *pattern*

expression is the string expression being compared. This can be a literal string, a string variable, or a string function. pattern is the grouping of letters and characters that the string is being compared to. The patterns defined for the LIKE operator make use of wildcard matching and character-range lists.

Table 20.2 shows the type of pattern matching that can be used with the LIKE operator.

Table 20.2   The *LIKE* Operator Uses a Variety of Pattern Matching

Wildcard	Used To Match	Example Pattern	Example Results
*	Multiple characters	S*	Smith, Sims, sheep
?	Single character	an?	and, ant, any
#	Single digit	3524#	35242, 35243
[list]	Single character in list	[c-f]	d, e, f
[!list]	Single character not in list	[!c-f]	a, b, g, h
combination	Specific to pattern	a?t*	art, antique, artist

How can I use this in the real world?

The best example I've seen of using pattern matching with the LIKE operator is in electronic card catalogs for a library. Using a pattern, you can look for titles of books that contain a particular word or phrase.

I've also seen pattern matching used for electronic phone directories, where you can enter a person's name or just part of the name. For instance, if you know my name starts with "McK" but don't know the rest of the spelling, you can look for the name using the pattern McK*.

Catch the bug

The following code is used to determine if a book title contains the word "Basic." However, the code doesn't work. Can you find the problem?

```
If booktitle Like *Basic* Then
    txtTitle.Text = booktitle
Else
    MsgBox "No matching titles were found"
End If
```

Answer: *The pattern in the condition must be enclosed in quotes since it is a literal string. The following is the correct code line:*

```
If booktitle Like "*Basic*" Then
```

You can even compare conditions!

What do you do when your conditional statement needs to evaluate two or more conditions? You know, "If we can get a sitter, *and* if we can get reservations, we'll go to that new restaurant." Visual Basic provides several logical operators that allow you to combine multiple comparison statements. There is no limit to the number of comparisons you can string together with these operators.

How do I use the *And* operator?

One of the operators used to combine comparison statements is the And operator. This is the operator you used in the previous dinner example. The And operator returns a True value only if both conditions are True. Otherwise, it returns a False value.

How do I use the *Or* operator?

The Or operator is used in a situation where only one of the conditions needs to be True for the statement to be True. For example, "If your car has a full tank *or* my car has a full tank, we can go for a drive."

The Or operator returns a True value if either or both of the comparisons is True. It only returns a False value if both of the conditions are False. The Or operator uses the same syntax as the And operator.

What is *Xor*?

The Xor operator is somewhat similar to the Or operator, but Xor *requires* that only one of the comparisons be True. If both comparisons are True or both are False, the Xor statement returns a False value. If one, and only one, of the comparisons is True (it can be either comparison), the Xor statement returns a True value. The Xor statement has the same syntax as the Or and And statements.

What are parenthetical groups for?

To see how these compare to math operators, refer to Chapter 18, "Power Up Your Visual Basic Programs with Some Basic Math."

In describing the previous operators, we only talked about combining two comparisons or conditions. However, you can combine multiple conditions with these operators. As with math operators, there is an order of precedence with the logical operators. For multiple conditions of the same type (that is, condition1 Or condition2 Or condition3), the operators are evaluated from left to right. If you use operators of different types, the operators are processed based on the following precedence:

1 Not

2 And

3 Or

4 Xor

Speaking of *And*

The And operator is placed between two comparison statements that you want to combine:

```
comparison1 And comparison2
```

comparison1 and comparison2 can be any valid comparison statements. In fact, one can be a numeric comparison and the other a string comparison. As with the simple comparisons, this combined statement cannot be placed on a line of code by itself; it must be part of another statement that supports a condition, such as the If or Do statements. The following code shows an example of using the And operator to determine if a student is to be accepted into a school:

```
If SATScore > 1200 And HSGPA > 3.0 Then MsgBox "Student
is accepted"
```

As with the math operators, you can ensure the order of processing by grouping the conditions with parentheses. The following code shows you an example:

```
Age = 58
ServiceYears = 18
If Age > 65 Or (Age > 55 And ServiceYears > 15) Then
    MsgBox "Eligible for retirement"
Else
    MsgBox "Keep working"
End If
```

The key statement in this code is the If statement. What the condition tells the code is to look first at Age. If Age is over 65, the statement is True. If Age is less than 65, the code looks at the parenthetical conditions. If Age is greater than 55 and the years of service (ServiceYears) is greater than 15, this condition is True. Based on the assigned values of the variables, the parenthetical condition is True; therefore, the entire condition is True.

Can I make sure something is *False*?

One final operator to take a look at is the Not operator. This operator is not a comparison in and of itself, nor is it used to join multiple conditions. Rather, the Not operator is used to invert the value of a condition. That is, it makes a True condition False, or a False condition True.

Speaking of *Not*

The Not operator is always placed immediately in front of the condition it is to modify:

```
Not comparison
```

comparison can be any type of comparison. It can be a numeric or string comparison. You can even place the Not operator in front of a parenthetical group.

The following code lines show several examples of the Not operator.

```
If Not Age < 18 Then MsgBox "You can vote"
If Not YourName = "Mike" Then MsgBox "Our names are not
the same"
If Not (Age > 65 Or ServiceYears > 15) Then MsgBox "You
cannot retire"
```

Summary

Comparison operators are used in conditional statements such as Do loops and If statements throughout most programs. Learning the ins and outs of these comparisons allows you to set up your program to handle all kinds of decisions.

Review questions

1 Can you compare a number to a string?

2 Are "computer" and "Computer" equal in a string comparison?

3 Which logical operator requires that both conditions be True to return a True value?

4 How is Xor different from Or?

How can I use this in the real world?

There are other functions that return either a True or False value. For example, there is a function that tells you if you have reached the end of an input file or database file.

Reading files is one situation where the Not operator is used. You can set up a loop to continue to read data from a database file while you have Not reach the end of the file.

These functions will be covered in the chapters on using files and databases.

Exercises

1 Change the code in listing 20.1 to have the names sorted in descending (Z–A) order instead of ascending (A–Z).

2 Create a program that sorts people by both the first and last names.

3 Create a program to count the number of people whose names fall in the range of A to M.

21

How Can I Manage Lots of Data? Use Arrays!

● **In this chapter:**

- The difference between an array and a variable

- What kind of data can be stored in an array?

- Accessing a specific value in an array

- How do I set up an array and use it in a program?

- What are dimensions?

Arrays are just like variables, except they're much larger, more powerful, and much more complex! Actually, arrays work very similar to variables and give you a lot more power. . . . . . ▶

By now, you've seen a number of examples of how variables are used to store information in a program. Variables can be used to store numbers, text strings, dates, even pictures and objects. Using variables is so important in programming that, without them, it would be impossible to write any but the simplest programs.

How is an array different from a simple variable?

To learn more about how variables work, see Chapter 17, "Adding Variables to Your Programs."

However, as useful and flexible as variables are, they do have limitations. The main limitation is that all variables must be specified in the design of the program. This means that you cannot create additional variables while the program is running. So if a user needs to enter more data than you have variables for, they (and you) are out of luck.

The second limitation is that a simple variable can only store a single piece of data. Using just simple variables, you have to define a variable name for each piece of data you need to store. For example, if you wanted to store the prices of ten retail items, you have to have a separate variable for each item as shown in listing 21.1. If you had fewer than ten items, space is wasted. If you had more than ten items, your program couldn't handle it.

Listing 21.1   Simple Variables Can Limit the Flexibility of Your Program

```
item1 = InputBox("Enter a price")
item2 = InputBox("Enter a price")
item3 = InputBox("Enter a price")
item4 = InputBox("Enter a price")
item5 = InputBox("Enter a price")
item6 = InputBox("Enter a price")
item7 = InputBox("Enter a price")
item8 = InputBox("Enter a price")
item9 = InputBox("Enter a price")
item10 = InputBox("Enter a price")
total = item1 + item2 + item3 + item4 + item5
total = total + item6 + item7 + item8 + item9 + item10
```

Fortunately for you, Visual Basic provides another vehicle for storing information in a program—the **variable array** (usually just called an **array**). An array is very similar to a simple variable in that it can store the same types of data and it uses the same naming conventions and the same type declarations. The difference is that an array is made up of **elements**, each of which can contain a piece of data. The different elements in the array are identified by their **index**. An array is like a row of motel rooms. All of the rooms are exactly alike but are identified by unique room numbers. Figure 21.1 illustrates the concept of an array.

66 *Plain English, please!*

An **element** is a single piece of data in an array. If you work with spreadsheets, the element is like a cell in a spreadsheet. Each cell can contain a single piece of data, yet it is part of the total sheet.

An **index** is a numeric value used to reference a specific element in an array. Expanding on the spreadsheet example, the index is like the row and column identifiers in the spreadsheet. You refer to a specific cell as R3C5 or row 3, column 5. 99

Fig. 21.1
An array is made up of elements that are identified by their index.

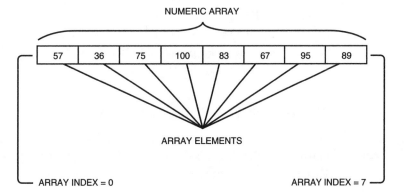

Another difference between an array and a simple variable is that the size of an array can be changed while a program is running, as you will see later in this chapter. Arrays can also simplify some of your programming. For example, listing 21.2 performs the same function as listing 21.1 but uses an array to gather the data. This code is more efficient and easier to maintain than the code in listing 21.1.

Listing 21.2 Arrays That Make Your Programming Simpler

```
Dim Items(1 To 10)
total = 0
For I = 1 To 10
    Items(I) = InputBox("Enter a Price")
    total = total + Items(I)
Next I
```

Arrays are usually used to contain related data, such as customers per day or sales per month. In such an array, each day is represented by one element of the array, and the value of the element is the number of customers served.

Start with a simple array

The simplest array contains a single **dimension**. You might think of this type of array as a line in a bank. Each person in line is like an element of the array. If there are nine people in front of you, then you are the tenth element in the line.

> ❝ *Plain English, please!*
>
> You may normally think of **dimensions** in terms of real objects. Three-dimensional objects have height, width, and depth. The dimensions of an array are similar. You can use a three-dimensional array to represent total sales by region, month, and year. (You use this example later in the chapter.) You can then add a fourth dimension to show sales by item. In fact, you can have up to 60 dimensions in an array. (I've rarely seen more than five or six used at a time.) ❞

How do I set up an array?

To see how the Public, Private, and Static statements are used to declare arrays, see Chapter 26, "Basic Building Blocks: Procedures and Functions."

To set up an array in your program, you have to use a declaration statement like the ones you used for defining variable types in Chapter 17 "Adding Variables to Your Programs." The one most often used is the Dim statement.

When you set up an array, the indexes for the array typically start with 0, so the size of the array is one more than the largest index number (that is, a subscript value of 9 indicates a ten-element array). This is also known as the **upper bound** of the array. If you are specifying multiple dimensions, you must include a separate expression for each dimension and separate the dimensions by commas. The subscripts for an array must all be integers.

You can also set up multiple arrays in a single Dim statement. To do this, just separate the variable definitions by commas as shown in the following example:

```
Dim firstarray(10) As Integer, secondarray(20),
thirdarray(10,10)
```

TIP **You can leave out the subscripts in the Dim statement. Doing this** creates a dynamic array that can be resized later in your program using the ReDim statement.

How do I get to the elements of the array?

Once you have set up the array, you can use it in code almost like a simple variable. You can assign information to an element of an array, use it in an equation, or use it in a function. The only difference in using an array is that you must tell your program which element of the array to use. This is done by specifying the index of the array. This is much like calling a hotel and asking to be transferred to a certain room number. The following statement assigns a value to the fifth element of a simple array:

```
NewArray(5) = 25
```

The index must be enclosed in parentheses, and it must be within the range of indexes specified in the Dim statement. The index can be specified as an actual number, as previously shown, or you can use a variable as you'll see in several example programs.

Speaking of *Dim*

To use the Dim statement to create an array, you use the following syntax:

```
Dim varname(subscripts) [As vartype]
```

This syntax is similar to that used in Chapter 17 to declare a variable. However, the parentheses and the subscripts argument are added to tell the program that the variable is actually an array and to define the size of the array. varname is the name of the array. Array names follow the same naming conventions as simple variables.

The subscripts argument contains one or more numbers that represent the largest index number for each dimension of the array.

The As vartype clause is optional and is used to define the type of information that is contained in the array. vartype specifies the type of data. The valid types are summarized in table 17.1. As with simple variables, if a type is not explicitly declared, the variant data type is used.

Catch the bug

This program is set up to calculate a grade average. What is wrong with the `Dim` statement?

```
numstd = 5
Dim Grades(numstd) As Integer
For I = 1 to numstd
  totgrd = totgrd + Grades(I)
Next I
avggrd = totgrd / numstd
```

Answer: *You cannot use a variable for the index of an array in a Dim statement. You can however use a constant to set the size of the array. The following code lines are correct:*

```
Const numstd = 5
Dim Grades(numstd) As Integer
```

One of the uses of arrays is to sort information and segregate it into groups. This can be used in demographics information (that is, the number of people in an area in different age groups, in different income groups, or with particular interests). Figure 21.2 shows one such use. The form in the figure uses the grades in a class to show how an array can be used to determine the maximum and minimum scores and to group the scores according to grade ranges. The listing for the example is in listing 21.3.

Fig. 21.2

Arrays can be used to store related data for further processing.

Grade Distribution		
Maximum Score	95	A's 1
Minimum Score	50	B's 1
Average Score	74.66666	C's 2
		D's 1
		F's 1
	Input Scores	

Listing 21.3 The Grade Distribution Code Uses Arrays

```
Dim numstd As Integer, maxscr As Integer, minscr As Integer
Dim totscr As Integer, grdidx As Integer
numstd = 9
Dim inpGrades(9) As Integer, GradeDist(4) As Integer
For I = 0 To numstd
    inpGrades(I) = InputBox("Enter a grade")
Next I
maxscr = 0
minscr = 100
totscr = 0
For J = 0 To 4
GradeDist(J) = 0
Next J
For I = 0 To numstd
    If inpGrades(I) > maxscr Then maxscr = inpGrades(I)
    If inpGrades(I) < minscr Then minscr = inpGrades(I)
    totscr = totscr + inpGrades(I)
    grdidx = inpGrades(I) \ 10 - 5
    If grdidx < 0 Then grdidx = 0
    If grdidx > 4 Then grdidx = 4
    GradeDist(grdidx) = GradeDist(grdidx) + 1
Next I
For J = 0 To 4
    txtGrade(J).Text = GradeDist(J)
Next J
txtMaxScore.Text = maxscr
txtMinScore.Text = minscr
txtAvgScore.Text = totscr / (numstd + 1)
```

 In the first two lines of the code, you use the Dim statement to declare the type of each of your variables. Then in the next statement, you assign numstd a value. In the next line, you use the Dim statement to declare two arrays. The first array stores the actual grades as they are input. This array has an upper bound that matches the value of the numstd variable. (Using the numstd variable in the code becomes important later when you look at changing an array's size.) The second array holds the number of students who got grades in a certain range (As, Bs, and so on).

Next you use a counter loop to input each of the grades. You use the input box to prompt the user for the grade and then store the grade in the inpGrades array. Notice that the loop runs from 0 to the value of numstd, the index numbers of the array.

In the next section of code, you initialize the values of the maxscr, minscr, and totscr variables, and the GradeDist array. For the array, you have to

For information about the input box (and other dialog boxes), see Chapter 14, "Communicating with the User through Dialog Boxes."

specifically assign a value to each element of the array. This is again done with a counter loop.

TIP **Counter loops perform a series of commands a specific number of** times. You will find that arrays and counter loops are used together quite often. Counter loops are covered in Chapter 23, "Counter Loops: How Many Times Will This Occur?"

In the next loop, you start determining the distribution of grades as well as the high, low, and average scores. First, you check the current score against the maximum score. If it is higher than the maximum score, you change the value of the maximum score to that of the current score. Next you compare the current score to the minimum score. Then you add the current score to the total score. The total score is what you use to determine the average.

You could also group the grades using a `Select` *statement. You can find out about the* `Select` *statement in Chapter 25, "Select Case: The Right Tool for Making Major Decisions."*

Next you use a little trick to determine which grade range the score belongs in. The scores are grouped in ranges of 10 with 90 and above being an A and below 60 being an F. To find the group that the score belongs in, you divide the score by 10 using integer division. This gives you a number between 0 and 10. From this result, you subtract 5, so that the numbers are between –5 and 5. Next you check for a value less than 0, and set the value to 0 if it is less. Then, in the same way, you check for values greater than 4. The final value of `grdidx` is a number between 0 and 4, which is the index range of the `GradeDist` array. You use the value of `grdidx` to determine to which element of the `GradeDist` array the score should be added.

Finally, you assign the grade distribution and the minimum, maximum, and average scores to text boxes for display on the form. Notice that you use a control array to hold the grade distribution. This makes it easy to assign all the distribution numbers in a loop.

Where does the array start?

As previously stated, unless otherwise told to do so, an array's index starts with 0. This can lead to some confusion when you are programming (that is, you put a value of nine in the array subscript for a ten-element array). To avoid this confusion, you can change the starting index of an array using either of two methods—the `Option Base` statement or the `To` clause of the `Dim` statement.

Option Base

The Option Base statement allows you to set the starting index of arrays to either 0 (the default) or 1. The starting index is known as the **lower bound** of the array. This statement must be placed in the declarations section of your form (or module). This statement affects all the arrays in the form.

 CAUTION To make your code easier to maintain, it is better to not use the Option Base statement and explicitly specify the range of index values. This way you always know what the range is, just by looking at the Dim statement.

 Q&A *I used the Option Base statement but got the error* Invalid inside procedure *when I tried to run my code. What happened?*

This error occurs when the Option Base statement is placed in procedure code. Remember, the statement can only be used in the declarations section of your form.

Speaking of *Option Base*

The Option Base statement is used as follows:

```
Option Base 0
```

or

```
Option Base 1
```

If you set the base to 1, the indexes of your arrays start with one, and the upper bound index is the size of the array. If the base is set to 0, the indexes start at zero, and the upper bound is one less than the size of the array. The following two code segments each define a ten-element array.

```
Option Base 0
Dim ThisArray(9)

Option Base 1
Dim ThatArray(10)
```

To keyword

The other way to change the lower bound index of an array is to define it explicitly. This is done by including the `To` clause in the `Dim` statement. This method is more flexible than the `Option Base` statement because you can set the lower bound to any number you want.

The `To` clause is included in the `Dim` statement as follows:

```
Dim varname(lower To upper) [As vartype]
```

This statement is essentially the same as the `Dim` statement you looked at earlier, except that `subscripts` has been replaced by the clause `lower To upper`. In this syntax, `lower` represents the lowest index number for the array, and `upper` represents the highest index number. The size of the array is obtained by subtracting the value of lower from the value of upper and adding one. As with `subscripts` argument, both `lower` and `upper` must be integers. Though you only show one dimension in the syntax, you can specify multiple dimensions using multiple `lower To upper` clauses separated by commas.

Use the *To* clause in defining all arrays. This way you always know the bounds of the array, and your code *is* self-documenting.

Q&A ***Do I have to specify each dimension the same way, or can I mix the To clauses with single dimensions?***

You can mix the two methods of defining dimensions. The following statement is valid for defining a 10 by 5 array:

```
Dim ThisArray(1 To 10, 5)
```

However, you need to remember the setting of the `Option Base` to make sure your array is sized correctly.

Catch the bug

What is wrong with the Dim statement in the following code?

```
Dim NewArray( To 10)
For I = 1 To 10
    NewArray(I) = 0
Next I
```

Answer: If you include the To keyword in the Dim statement, you must specify both a lower and upper bound index. The following declaration works:

```
Dim NewArray(1 To 10)
```

Or, assuming that Option Base is set to 1, the following statement also works:

```
Dim NewArray(10)
```

Most real–world arrays are multidimensional

As useful as a one-dimensional array is, many of the programs you work with require **multiple dimensions**. Using multiple dimensions allows you to explore multiple dependencies of data. Two- or three-dimensional arrays are often visualized in terms of real-world objects. A two-dimensional array, for example, is like theater seating (that is, you're in seat 7, row 23). Similarly, a three-dimensional array can be compared to your parking space in a multi-level parking garage (that is, space 12, row 6, level 5).

One use of a two-dimensional array is to analyze your company's monthly sales by region (see fig. 21.3). The rows can be sales regions and the columns can be the months. Many people use a spreadsheet to accomplish this purpose. In fact, the two-dimensional array can be thought of as a spreadsheet.

Fig. 21.3
A two-dimensional array works very much like a spreadsheet.

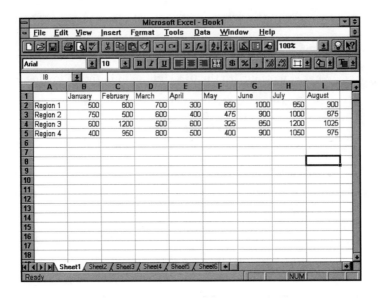

	A	B	C	D	E	F	G	H	I
1		January	February	March	April	May	June	July	August
2	Region 1	500	800	700	300	650	1000	850	900
3	Region 2	750	500	600	400	475	900	1000	875
4	Region 3	600	1200	500	600	325	850	1200	1025
5	Region 4	400	950	800	500	400	900	1050	975

But how do you represent this in an array, and what can you do with it? Listing 21.4 shows the code used to enter data into a two-dimensional array and then total the information by region and month. Figure 21.4 shows the form used to enter and process this information. To enter the data, the user enters the number for the sales region, the number for the month, and the sales figure. The region and month numbers are used as the indexes for the array. When the information is processed, you use loops to total the sales by region and total them by month.

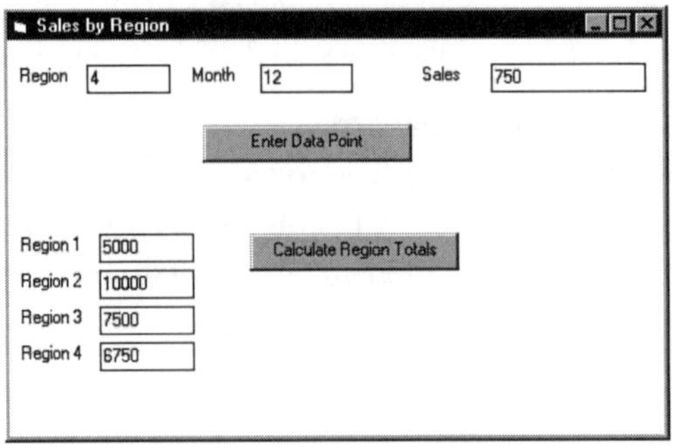

Fig. 21.4
A two-dimensional array can be used like a spreadsheet for data analysis.

Listing 21.4   Loops Used To Process the Information in a Two-Dimensional Array

```
Dim RegSales(1 To 4, 1 To 12) As Single

Private Sub cmdDataEntry_Click()
regid% = CInt(txtRegionID.Text)
monid% = CInt(txtMonth.Text)
RegSales(regid%, monid%) = CInt(txtSales.Text)
End Sub

Private Sub cmdCalculate_Click()
Dim TotSales(1 To 4)
For I = 1 To 4
    TotSales(I) = 0
    For J = 1 To 12
        TotSales(I) = TotSales(I) + RegSales(I, J)
    Next J
Next I
txtRegion1 = TotSales(1)
txtRegion2 = TotSales(2)
txtRegion3 = TotSales(3)
txtRegion4 = TotSales(4)
End Sub
```

The first statement of the code creates the array that will contain the sales data. This statement is placed in the declarations section of the form so that it is available to all the procedures.

The next section of the code shows the Click event procedure for the data entry command button. The code gets the region ID and month ID from the text boxes. It then uses these numbers to determine where to place the sales data in the array.

To learn about nested loop and decision statements, see Chapter 23, "Counter Loops: How Many Times Will This Occur?"

The third section of the code performs the calculation that totals the sales figures by region. The code sets up an array to hold the totals for each region. Using an array allows you to use the nested loop structure to simplify the code for summing up all the elements. After all the totals are calculated, they are assigned to the appropriate text boxes for display.

I didn't make the array big enough!

At the beginning of the chapter, one of the advantages I mentioned for using arrays is that you can change the size of the array from inside the program. This allows you to adapt the array to different tasks in the program and even to allow the array to be resized to respond to user input.

Changing the size of the array

To change the size of an array, you use the ReDim statement. This statement allows you to specify new dimensions for an existing dynamic array. You can also use the ReDim statement in place of the Dim statement to initially set up an array.

The syntax of the ReDim statement is similar to that of the Dim statement. The ReDim statement is used as follows:

```
ReDim [Preserve] varname(subscripts) [As vartype]
```

varname is the name of the array as was the case with the Dim statement. Also, like the Dim statement, the As vartype clause is an optional clause that allows you to specify the type of data that can be in the array.

The subscripts argument for the ReDim statement is a little different than for the Dim statement. First, you must include the subscripts in the ReDim statement. Second, you can use a variable as the lower bound, upper bound, or both ends of the array range. This allows you to size the array based on conditions within your program or based on user input.

 CAUTION   **You cannot change the type of data in an array after it has been** initially declared. Therefore, if you include the As vartype, the type must be the same as the original.

The optional argument, Preserve, allows the values of the array to be retained when the size is changed. If this argument is left out, the array is reinitialized and all data in it is lost. If you include Preserve, your data is carried over to the new array size.

Q&A *When I tried to run my program, I got the error* `Array already dimensioned`*. What caused this?*

You get this error when you try to resize an array that was initially defined with a `Dim` statement that included `subscripts`. If you know you need to change the size of your array in your program, you should either use the `Dim` statement without the `subscripts` or use the `ReDim` statement to set up your array.

Change the array's size with variables

In the description of the `ReDim` statement, I said that a variable can be used as one or both of the bounds for an array's dimension. You may wonder, "How do I use this?" Look back at the grade distribution example in listing 21.3. This code works only for a class with ten people in it, but suppose you wanted to make it generic so that any teacher could use it regardless of the class size. First you make a slight change to the form itself to allow the user to enter the number of grades. This change is shown in figure 21.5. You also change the code to use the `ReDim` statement to allow us to have a resizable array for collecting data as shown in listing 21.5.

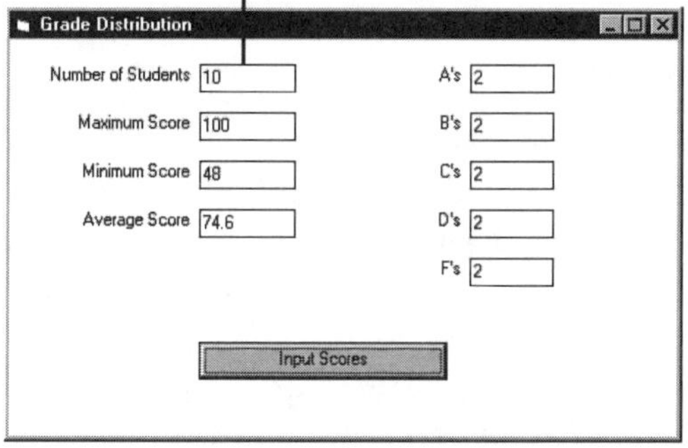

Fig. 21.5
By adding the ability to enter the number of grades to be processed, the grade program becomes more useful.

Input for number of students added

Grade Distribution	
Number of Students	10
Maximum Score	100
Minimum Score	48
Average Score	74.6

A's	2
B's	2
C's	2
D's	2
F's	2

Input Scores

Listing 21.5   Using the *ReDim* Statement Makes the Program More Generic

```
Dim numstd As Integer
numstd = Val(txtNumStudents.Text)
ReDim inpGrades(1 To numstd) As Integer, GradeDist(4) As
Integer
```

continues

Listing 21.5   Continued

```
For I = 1 To numstd
    inpGrades(I) = InputBox("Enter a grade")
Next I
maxscr = 0
minscr = 100
totscr = 0
For J = 0 To 4
GradeDist(J) = 0
Next J
For I = 1 To numstd
    If inpGrades(I) > maxscr Then maxscr = inpGrades(I)
    If inpGrades(I) < minscr Then minscr = inpGrades(I)
    totscr = totscr + inpGrades(I)
    grdidx = inpGrades(I) \ 10 - 5
    If grdidx < 0 Then grdidx = 0
    If grdidx > 4 Then grdidx = 4
    GradeDist(grdidx) = GradeDist(grdidx) + 1
Next I
For J = 0 To 4
    txtGrade(J).Text = GradeDist(J)
Next J
txtMaxScore.Text = maxscr
txtMinScore.Text = minscr
txtAvgScore.Text = totscr / numstd
```

While all the code was shown again for completeness, you only look at the parts that changed.

In the second line of the modified code, the variable numstd is set to the number of students entered in the text box txtNumStudents. In the next line, numstd is used as the upper bound of the array inpGrades. In this listing, you use the ReDim statement to allow the array size to change as needed. Also note that you specified a lower bound for the array. This is so the size of the array is equal to the value of the numstd variable. Since you changed the lower bound of the array, you also had to change the starting point of the two loops that handle the input and processing of the grades.

All other code in the listing is the same as in listing 21.3.

Catch the bug

Why does an error occur when the size of the array is changed in the following code?

```
Dim ThisArray(1 To 10) As Integer
For I = 1 To 10
    ThisArray(I) = 0
Next I
ReDim ThisArray(1 to 20) As Single
```

Answer: There are actually two errors in this listing, both involving the ReDim statement. First, you cannot resize an array that was originally set up with the Dim statement with a specified size. Second, you cannot change the type of data for an array using the ReDim statement. Use the following correct code:

```
ReDim ThisArray(1 To 10) As Integer
For I = 1 To 10
    ThisArray(I) = 0
Next I
ReDim ThisArray(1 to 20)
```

Regaining your memory

After you have used a dynamic array, you want to recover the memory used by the array. This is done using the `Erase` statement. To use the `Erase` statement, you specify the `Erase` keyword and any arrays that you want to eliminate. Each array name must be separated by commas. The following code line erases two arrays, `MemNames` and `MemScores`.

```
Erase MemNames, MemScores
```

If you need to use an array after it has been erased, you need to use the `ReDim` statement to reinitialize the array.

Summary

As you have seen, arrays behave in many ways like simple variables. However, arrays are more versatile than simple variables in that the size of an array can be changed during program execution. Also, because the elements of an array are accessed by an index, arrays are easily processed with loops, making for simpler programming.

Review questions

1 What kind of data can be stored in an array?

2 What tells the program which element of an array to use?

3 How many dimensions can an array have?

4 How do you create a simple array?

5 How do you change the size of an array?

6 What can the ReDim statement do that the Dim statement cannot?

Exercises

1 Change listing 21.2 to handle a variable number of items.

2 Add code to listing 21.4 to calculate monthly totals.

3 Change the code in listing 21.2 to use only a single number to specify the dimension.

4 Starting from listing 21.4, add the capability of specifying sales by item number and totaling on items.

22

Conditional Loops: Keep Going Until I Tell You to Stop

● **In this chapter:**

- **I need to do a repetitive task**

- **How does the loop know when to quit?**

- **The different types of loops in Visual Basic**

- **How do I handle other Windows operations when the program is in a long loop?**

- **Hey! My loop won't stop!**

Although you probably get bored doing the same task over and over again, computers don't—computers were designed to dutifully perform the same operation over and over without complaint. . . . . **>**

You've heard it said, "You only go around once in life." For people, this may be true. Most people don't like to keep repeating the same tasks over and over. Fortunately for us, computers don't have this problem. Computers are excellent at performing repetitive tasks. A computer repeats a task as many times as you tell it to. In fact, if you're not careful in your programming, a computer repeats a task indefinitely, even after you want it to stop. (This, of course, has never happened to me. Yeah, right!)

The way you get a computer to repeat operations is with the use of a **loop**. There are two basic types of loops that you can use in Visual Basic—the **conditional loop** and the **counter loop**. This chapter addresses the conditional loop, while Chapter 23, "Counter Loops: How Many Times Will This Occur?" discusses the counter loop.

 Plain English, please!

A **loop** is simply a group of commands that is repeated a specified number of times or for a specific length of time. Consider posting checks to your checkbook. For each check in a stack, you enter the date, the payee for the check, the amount, and possibly the purpose of the check. Next you subtract the amount of the check from the balance in your account. After you have finished one check, you look to see if you have any more. If so, you repeat the process for the next check. That's how a loop works. **99**

To learn more about the logical conditions that can be used in a conditional loop, see Chapter 20, "Making Decisions Based Upon Data Comparisons."

The key feature of a conditional loop is, of course, the condition. The condition is any expression that can return either a True or a False value. This can be a function, such as EOF; the value of a property, such as the Value property of an option button; or an expression, such as numval < 15. The various forms of the conditional loop use the condition in different ways (as you'll see), but the one thing they have in common is that the condition must always be present.

Keep looping while you wait

Conditional loops are often called Do loops because the word Do is the keyword that starts the set of commands in the loop. It also happens that Loop is the keyword that ends the set of commands in the loop. The first type of conditional loop you'll examine is the Do While loop.

The keyword `While` in the statement tells the program that the loop is repeated while the condition expression is `True`. You can think of this like sitting in traffic at a traffic light. You continue to sit at the light while the light is red. When the light is no longer red, you move on. A `Do While` loop executes while the condition is `True`. Then when the condition becomes `False`, the program moves on to the next statement after the `Loop` statement.

There are two forms of the `Do While` loop. The difference between the two is the placement of the condition. The condition can be placed either at the beginning or the end of the loop, as you'll see in a following section "I want to always run the loop at least once."

How can I check the condition?

The first form of the `Do While` loop places the condition at the beginning of the loop.

Speaking of *Do While*

To use this form of the Do While loop, you use the following syntax:

```
Do While condition
    repetitivestatement#1
    repetitivestatement#2...
    repetitivestatement#n
Loop
nextstatement
```

The loop starts with the Do statement. In this form, you use the While keyword to indicate that you want to run the loop while the condition is True. By placing the While condition clause in the Do statement, you tell the program that you want to evaluate the condition before you run any statements inside the loop. If the condition is True, the repetitive statements between the Do statement and the Loop statement run. Then the program returns to the Do statement to evaluate the condition again. As soon as the condition is False, the program moves to the statement following the Loop statement, indicated above by nextstatement.

Both the Do and the Loop statements must be present.

With this form of the loop, the statements inside the loop may never be run. If the condition is `False` before the loop is run the first time, the program just proceeds to the statements after the loop. The program flow of this type of loop is shown in figure 22.1.

Fig. 22.1
Placing the condition in the *Do* statement checks the condition before the loop is run each time.

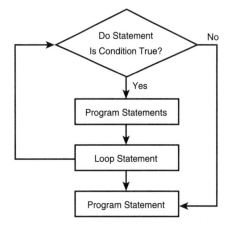

One use of this type of loop is in the allocation of parts to a client's order. Parts are often required to be traced by material lots, and each lot has a set number of pieces in it. If one lot is insufficient to completely fill the order, part of another lot is used. This continues until the entire order is filled. Listing 22.1 shows the code for this type of processing. The listing assumes that a database contains information about the lot numbers and pieces in each lot.

How can I use this in the real world?

One place you might use a loop is in the processing of measurement data. For example, if you had to write a program to handle weather data, you would use a loop to check the temperature every five minutes on a continuous basis. The loop could run for a 24-hour period, then print out the minimum, maximum, and average temperature for the day.

Listing 22.1   A Do While Loop Can Be Used in Order Processing

```
Dim OldDb As Database, OldWs As Workspace, OldTbl As
Recordset
Set OldWs = Workspaces(0)
Set OldDb = OldWs.OpenDatabase("C:\PARTS.MDB")
Set OldTbl = OldDb.OpenRecordset("Instock", dbOpenTable)
ordquant = Val(txtOrder.Text)
OldTbl.MoveFirst
Do While ordquant > 0
    If OldTbl("Pieces") > ordquant Then
        Print OldTbl("LotID"), ordquant
        ordquant = 0
    Else
        Print OldTbl("LotID"), OldTbl("Pieces")
        ordquant = ordquant - OldTbl("Pieces")
        OldTbl.movenext
    End If
Loop
OldTbl.Close
OldDb.Close
```

 The first section of the code sets up the database that you are taking inventory parts from. In the fifth line of the code, you get the quantity of parts needed to fill the order. Next you move to the first record of the recordset and check the number of pieces it contains. If the first record contains enough parts to fill the order, you print out the lot ID and the order quantity. You then set the order quantity to zero to terminate the loop.

If the lot doesn't contain enough pieces to completely fill the order, you print out the quantity in the lot, reduce the order quantity by the number of pieces in the lot, and then move to the next record and repeat the entire process.

I want to always run the loop at least once

The second form of the Do While loop places the condition in the Loop statement. This tells the program that you want the loop to run at least once and then evaluate the condition to determine whether to repeat the loop. The flow for this form of the loop is shown in figure 22.2.

Fig. 22.2
Placing the condition
in the *Loop* statement
causes the loop to be
run at least once.

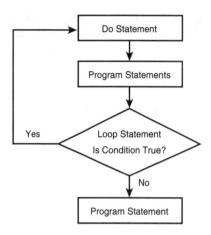

Speaking of *Do While*

The second form of the Do While loop uses this syntax:

```
Do
    repetitivestatement#1
    repetitivestatement#2...
    repetitivestatement#n
Loop While condition
nextstatement
```

As before, the loop starts with the Do statement. However, in this form, the repetitive statements are processed as soon as the loop starts running. By placing the While condition clause in the loop statement, you tell the program that you want to evaluate the condition after you run any statements inside the loop.

When you reach the Loop statement, if the condition is True, the program returns to the Do statement and the repetitive statements between the Do statement and the Loop statement run again. As soon as the condition is False, the program moves to the statement following the Loop statement, indicated by nextstatement.

Again, both the Do and the Loop statements must be present.

CAUTION **Do not put the** `While` **condition clause in both the** `Do` **and the** `Loop` statements, as this causes an error when you try to run your program.

You may be working on code that was developed by someone else and find a loop that starts with a `While` statement and ends with a `Wend` statement.

This type of loop works the same as a `Do While` loop with the `While` clause in the Do statement. Visual Basic still supports a `While…Wend` loop, but it is recommended that you use the `Do While` type of loop because it is more flexible. Look at the following code:

```
'********
'This code
'********
Ichk = 0
While Ichk < 10
    Ichk = Ichk + 1
Wend
'***********************
'Is the same as this code
'***********************
Ichk = 0
Do While Ichk < 10
    Ichk = Ichk + 1
Loop
```

Catch the bug

What is wrong with the following Do statement?

```
OldTbl.MoveFirst
Do OldTbl.EOF
    Print OldTbl("Author")
    OldTbl.MoveNext
Loop
```

Answer: *The Do statement does not include the* `While` *keyword. The correct code line is as follows:*

```
Do While Not OldTbl.EOF
```

Keep looping until it's time

Have you ever sat in front of your TV changing channels trying to find something worth watching? Then you understand the concept of a Do Until loop. When you're "channel surfing," you keep changing the channel until you see something that looks interesting. (In other words, your response to "Is this interesting?" is True.) The Do Until loop works the same way. The loop repeats the operations inside the loop until the condition statement becomes True (that is, while the condition is False). This is in contrast to the Do While statement, which performs operations while the condition is True. Figure 22.3 shows the program flow for a Do Until loop.

Fig. 22.3
A *Do Until* loop runs until the condition expression returns a *True* value.

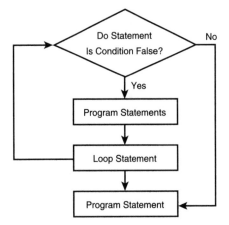

You can use the Do Until statement to read and process data files. A loop starts with the first record of the file and processes each record until the loop reaches the end of file. Listing 22.2 uses a loop to load all the authors from the BIBLIO.MDB sample database into a list box. Figure 22.4 shows the results of the program.

Listing 22.2   A Loop with a Data File

```
Private Sub cmdListAuthors_Click()
Dim OldDb As Database, OldWs As Workspace, OldTbl As
Recordset
Set OldWs = Workspaces(0)
Set OldDb = OldWs.OpenDatabase("C:\VB4\BIBLIO.MDB")
Set OldTbl = OldDb.OpenRecordset("Authors", dbOpenTable)
OldTbl.MoveFirst
```

```
Do Until OldTbl.EOF
    lstAuthors.AddItem OldTbl("Author")
    OldTbl.MoveNext
Loop
OldTbl.Close
OldDb.Close
End Sub
```

Speaking of *Do Until*

Like the Do While loop, the Do Until loop can take one of two forms. The loop condition can be placed in the Do statement at the beginning of the loop, or it can be placed in the Loop statement at the end of the loop. The syntax for the Do Until loop is essentially the same as the Do While loop except for the difference in the keywords. The syntax for the first form is:

```
Do Until condition
    repetitivestatement#1
    repetitivestatement#2...
    repetitivestatement#n
Loop
nextstatement
```

As with the Do While loop, the condition is evaluated before the statements inside the loop are processed. If the condition is False, the loop runs. If the condition is True, the loop terminates. The second form's syntax is:

```
Do
    repetitivestatement#1
    repetitivestatement#2...
    repetitivestatement#n
Loop Until condition
nextstatement
```

Again, the loop runs at least once before the condition is evaluated. When the condition is checked, if it is False, the loop runs again; otherwise, the loop terminates.

Fig. 22.4
The list was set up
using a *Do Until* loop.

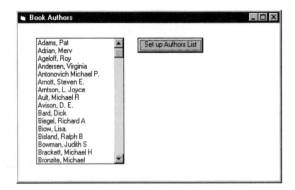

The listing starts with the Sub statement, identifying the beginning of the procedure and showing the name of the control and event. The next line uses the Dim statement to declare three variables as workspace, database, and recordset objects.

You'll look at data access objects in greater detail in Chapter 29, "Accessing Databases."

The next three lines use the set statements to assign a workspace, database name, and table name to the data access variables. The database file is the BIBLIO.MDB file found in your Visual Basic subdirectory. Depending on where you installed Visual Basic, you may need to change the drive or directory designation for the file.

Next, you use the MoveFirst method to access the first record in the table.

In the next line, you start setting up the Do Until loop. For the condition, you use the EOF property of the recordset. When you have processed the last record in the recordset, the EOF property is set to True. Until then, the property is False. Since you want to continue the processing of records as long as the property is False, you use the Until clause instead of the While clause.

The next line uses the AddItem method to add each author's name to the selection list. After you have processed one author, you use the MoveNext method to access the next record in the recordset. The Loop statement then tells the program to go back to the Do statement, where the condition is evaluated again. Once the end of the file is reached, the loop terminates.

The last two statements close the recordset and the database.

TIP **Indenting your code inside a loop or other structure (such as an If** statement) makes the code easier to read.

CAUTION　**I've mentioned the differences between the Do While and the Do** Until loops already, but let me state them once more very clearly. A Do While loop executes as long as the condition is True. A Do Until loop executes as long as the condition is False.

Which type of loop should I use?

Since the Do While and the Do Until loops are so similar, which of the two should you use, and where should you put the condition? For many cases, you can use either type of loop. In fact, with a properly stated condition, you can perform the same function with either loop. Consider the code in listing 22.3.

Listing 22.3　*Do While* and *Do Until* Loops Perform the Same Function

```
'*******************
'The "Do While" loop
'*******************
Ichk = 0
Do While Ichk <= 10
    Ichk = Ichk + 1
Loop
'*******************
'The "Do Until" loop
'*******************
Ichk = 0
Do Until Ichk > 10
    Ichk = Ichk + 1
Loop
```

In the first loop, the condition ("Is Ichk less than or equal to 10?") initially evaluates to True (0 is less than 10). Therefore, the loop executes. This continues until the value of Ichk reaches 11, which makes the condition False (11 is not less than or equal to 10) and terminates the loop.

In the second loop, the condition ("Is Ichk greater than 10?") initially evaluates to False (0 is not greater than 10). Again, the loop executes. When the value of Ichk reaches 11, the condition becomes True, and the loop terminates.

In both of the loops in listing 22.3, the statement inside the loop is executed 11 times.

So, if you can perform the same function with either loop, which do you use? For comparisons, such as the one in listing 22.3, it doesn't matter. If, however, you are using a function or variable that contains either a True or False value, you should use Do While if you want the loop to execute when the value is True. And, you should use Do Until if you want the loop to execute when the value is False.

As for whether you put the condition in the Do statement or in the Loop statement, that's easy. If you need to make sure the loop runs at least once, place the condition in the Loop statement. Otherwise, place the condition in the Do statement.

Can I quit a loop early?

Most of the time when you use a loop, either Do While or Do Until, you want the loop to run until it has completed its task. For some programming, however, you want to have a way to terminate the loop early. To stop a loop early, Visual Basic provides the Exit Do statement.

If you are searching for a particular author in the BIBLIO.MDB database, you can set up a loop as shown in listing 22.4. As each record is accessed, it is compared to the search name. If the names match, the name is displayed in a text box, and the loop terminates. If a match is not found, this message appears in the text box (see fig. 22.5).

Speaking of *Exit Do*

The statement to terminate a Do loop early is:

```
Exit Do
```

This statement tells the program to immediately stop processing statements inside the loop and go to the first statement following the loop.

Listing 22.4   An *Exit Do* Statement Used To Terminate a Loop Early

```
Private Sub cmdSearch_Click()
Dim OldDb As Database, OldWs As Workspace, OldTbl As
Recordset
Dim findstr As String
Set OldWs = Workspaces(0)
Set OldDb = OldWs.OpenDatabase("C:\VB4\BIBLIO.MDB")
Set OldTbl = OldDb.OpenRecordset("Authors", dbOpenTable)
OldTbl.MoveFirst
findstr = Trim(txtSearch.Text)
txtResults.Text = "No match was found."
Do Until OldTbl.EOF
    iloc = InStr(1, OldTbl("Author"), findstr, 1)
    If iloc > 0 Then
        txtResults.Text = OldTbl("Author")
        Exit Do
    End If
    OldTbl.MoveNext
Loop
OldTbl.Close
OldDb.Close
End Sub
```

Fig. 22.5

This search program uses the *Exit Do* statement to terminate the loop after a match is found.

 As with the code in listing 22.4, the first few lines declare the database variables and set up the database for use. In this listing, you also declare a string variable to hold the value of your search string. The seventh line of the listing moves to the first record in the database. The eighth line gets the value of the search string from the text box. Notice that the `Trim` function eliminates any blank spaces at the beginning and end of the string.

The next line sets an initial value of the `Text` property in the `txtResults` text box. You set the `Text` property to `"No match was found."` This message appears if the search fails to produce a match after looking at every record.

Next you set up the loop that searches through the database records. This loop uses the end-of-file condition to terminate the loop just like listing 22.2. Inside the loop, you first use the `InStr` function to determine whether the search string is contained in the current author's name. If the search string is found, `InStr` returns a number greater than zero.

After the `InStr` function returns a value, you check whether it is greater than zero. If so, you assign the author's name to the `txtResults` text box and use the `Exit Do` statement to terminate the loop. If the value from the `InStr` function is zero, you go on to process the next record.

After the loop is finished (either from the `Exit Do` or because all the records were processed), you close the table and database. At this point, the `txtResults` text box contains either the matching author's name or the `No match was found.` message.

Catch the bug

This code is set up to find a particular author. What is wrong with the code?

```
Do Until OldTbl.EOF
    iloc = InStr(1, OldTbl("Author"), findstr, 1)
    If iloc > 0 Then
        txtResults.Text = OldTbl("Author")
        Exit
    End If
    OldTbl.MoveNext
Loop
```

Answer: *The Exit statement must have a Do after it, like the following:*

```
Exit Do
```

How to avoid getting stuck in an endless loop

One of the worst things that can happen in a computer program is to get stuck in an **infinite loop**. An infinite loop is simply a Do loop that never meets its exit condition. Imagine yourself driving around a city on a highway with no exits. You would just keep going and going until your car ran out of gas.

In an infinite loop, though, your computer does not run out of gas. It just keeps going. In design mode, you can exit an infinite loop by pressing Ctrl+Break to pause the program. If, however, the infinite loop makes its way into your executable program, the only way to exit an infinite loop is to use the Ctrl+Alt+Delete combination to terminate the program. This, of course, is an undesirable way to get out of a program because all your work done in the program is lost and your data files may get corrupted. And what may be even worse, if your program is written for others, your users will be *very* unhappy with the program.

What causes an infinite loop?

The most common cause of an infinite loop (for me at least) is forgetting to put a statement in that changes part of the loop condition. To explain, look at the code in listing 22.4. The condition that exits the loop is the end-of-file condition. To get to the end of the file, you must at some point in the loop move from one record to the next. This is accomplished by the `MoveNext` method in the loop. If you leave out the `MoveNext` statement, you have an infinite loop. (To tell you how easy this is to do, I did exactly this when I first wrote the sample code in listing 22.4.) This "flawed" listing is shown in listing 22.5.

Listing 22.5 An Infinite Loop

```
Private Sub cmdSearch_Click()
Dim OldDb As Database, OldWs As Workspace, OldTbl As
Recordset
Dim findstr As String
Set OldWs = Workspaces(0)
Set OldDb = OldWs.OpenDatabase("C:\VB4\BIBLIO.MDB")
Set OldTbl = OldDb.OpenRecordset("Authors", dbOpenTable)
OldTbl.MoveFirst
findstr = Trim(txtSearch.Text)
txtResults.Text = "No match was found."
Do Until OldTbl.EOF
    iloc = InStr(1, OldTbl("Author"), findstr, 1)
    If iloc > 0 Then
        txtResults.Text = OldTbl("Author")
        Exit Do
    End If
```

continues

Listing 22.5   Continued

```
Loop
OldTbl.Close
OldDb.Close
End Sub
```

 TIP **To avoid errors in setting up Do loops, it is good practice to write** the Do statement, Loop statement, and the statement that changes the loop condition before setting up the rest of the loop.

Another way that you can generate an infinite loop is by placing the condition change statement inside an If statement. For example, the following code (derived from listing 22.5) causes an infinite loop:

```
Do Until OldTbl.EOF
    iloc = InStr(1, OldTbl("Author"), findstr, 1)
    If iloc > 0 Then
        txtResults.Text = OldTbl("Author")
        OldTbl.MoveNext
    End If
Loop
```

 In this loop, the only time that the record pointer is moved to the next record is when the search string is contained in Author. As soon as the search finds a record that does not contain the search string, the loop no longer moves and becomes infinite.

The best advice on placing loop condition statements inside an If statement is, *don't.*

Finally, let's look at one more simple mistake that can cause an infinite loop. The big problem here is the subtlety of the error. Can you see what's wrong with the following code?

```
Icond = 1
Do Until Icond = 12
    ThisArray(Icond) = InputBox("Enter a name")
    Icond = Icond + 2
Loop
```

The problem with this loop is that the variable Icond nevers equal 12, which is the exit condition. Since Icond starts out as one and has two added to it each time, it eventually reaches 11 and then 13 but never 12. In this case the proper comparison is Icond >= 12.

Catch the bug

This code creates an infinite loop. Can you find the reason?

```
Iexit = 1
Do While Iexit < 15
    Iexit = 1
    ThisArray(Iexit) = OldTbl("Author")
    Iexit = Iexit + 1
    OldTbl.MoveNext
Loop
```

Answer: *The first line inside the* `Do` *loop resets the value of* `Iexit` *every time the loop runs. Therefore, the value of* `Iexit` *never gets above two, and the loop is infinite. To correct the code, eliminate the line* `Iexit = 1` *after the* `Do` *statement.*

Be careful that your loops don't keep Windows (3.1) waiting

Sometimes you will have a very long loop, one running a number of calculations thousands or even millions of times. While this loop is not infinite, it will tie up the computer for a fairly long period of time.

What happens in a long loop?

The problem with a long loop is that the user cannot perform other tasks while the loop is running. While this may be acceptable for a loop that runs ten seconds or less, a program or loop that can tie up the computer for several minutes or longer can be frustrating to a user.

To see the effect of a long loop, place the following code in the `Click` event of a command button on a form. After you click the command button, try to access another Windows program. You won't be able to do so until the loop finishes. (Caution: This loop takes about 20 seconds on a 486/66 machine.)

```
Dim Icond As Long
Icond = 1
Do While Icond < 5000000
    Icond = Icond + 1
Loop
MsgBox "Finished"
```

Let other applications have some time

To avoid having the computer tied up for a long period of time, Visual Basic has a function that tells the computer to stop processing the current program and attend to any other user requests. This statement is the DoEvents function. This statement is mainly needed in Windows 3.1 programs, since Windows 95 and Windows NT support preemptive multitasking.

It is a good idea to place this statement in any long loop. The following code modifies the previous code to include the DoEvents function:

```
Dim Icond As Long
Icond = 1
Do While Icond < 5000000
    Icond = Icond + 1
    If Icond Mod 1000 = 0 Then
        junk = DoEvents
    End If
Loop
MsgBox "Finished"
```

In this loop, you added the DoEvents function to allow other things to occur while the loop is running. To avoid interrupting the program too often, a condition has been set up that only executes the DoEvents function on every 1000th iteration of the loop. This condition is in the If statement of the code.

Speaking of *DoEvents*

To include the DoEvents function, simply enter it on a line of code as follows:

```
DoEvents
```

DoEvents pauses the program, checks for other Windows events to be processed, and then returns control to the current program.

Summary

Computers are great at handling repetitive tasks, and loops are the way to perform the repetitions. You can set up loops to execute any number of times or not at all depending on the conditions you use. Loops are very powerful programming tools, but remember to watch out for the "gotchas" of infinite loops.

Review questions

1 Which type of loop executes as long as the condition is True?

2 Where do you place a loop condition to make sure the loop is executed at least once?

3 Explain the difference between a Do While and a Do Until loop.

4 What statement can you use to terminate a Do loop early?

5 Name two things that can cause a loop to become an infinite loop.

6 How do you let the computer handle other tasks while a long loop is running?

Exercises

1 Change the code in listing 22.4 so that it counts the number of records that contain the search string.

2 Change the code in listing 22.3 so that it only lists the first 10 authors in the database.

3 Write a program to retrieve temperature information and find the minimum, maximum, and average temperature for a day.

23

Counter Loops: How Many Times Will This Occur?

● **In this chapter:**

- How is a counter loop different from a conditional loop?

- How do you tell the loop how many times to repeat?

- Counting backwards through the loop

- Use variables to define the ends of the loop

- Multiple loops and conditional statements

A counter loop is like running a track race—when you finish the required number of laps, you can stop. . . . . ●

n the last chapter, I talked about using conditional loops to make your computer perform repetitive tasks while a certain condition prevails. While conditional loops are the most flexible way of performing repetitive tasks, there is another way: the counter loop.

You use a **counter loop** when you want the computer to perform a task a specific number of times. This is similar to swimming laps in a pool in a race. For any given distance, you will swim a set number of laps (for example, a 500 meter race requires 10 laps of a 50 meter pool). While swimming, you count the number of laps completed, and when you have completed the required number, you stop.

What's different about counter loops?

You can also think of a counter loop as a very specialized conditional loop. The counter loop runs as long as the value of the count variable is less than or equal to the maximum value. Listing 23.1 shows how to use a counter loop and a conditional loop to get 10 input values. The two loops are identical in function.

Listing 23.1   Equivalent Counter and Conditional Loops

```
'*******************************************************
 'This For Loop executes a set of instructions 10 times
 '*******************************************************
For Icnt = 1 To 10
   ThisArray(Icnt) = InputBox("Enter a value")
Next Icnt
'*******************************************************
'This Do Loop also executes the instructions 10 times
'*******************************************************
Icnt = 1
Do While Icnt <= 10
   ThisArray(Icnt) = InputBox("Enter a value")
   Icnt = Icnt + 1
Loop
```

The basic *For* loop

A counter loop is also known as a For loop, or a For/Next loop. This is because the ends of the loop are defined by the For statement and the Next statement. The program flow for a For loop is shown in figure 23.1. Compare this figure to figure 22.1 to see the similarities between the For loop and the Do While loop.

Fig. 23.1
A *For* loop runs until its maximum value is reached.

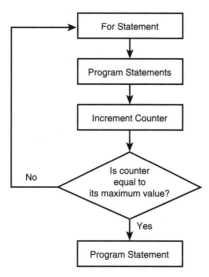

How the *For* loop works

At the beginning of a For loop, you define a counter variable and the beginning and end points of the variable's value. The first time the loop is run, the counter variable is set to the value of the beginning point. Then, each time the program runs through the loop, the value of the counter is checked against the value of the end point. If the counter is larger than the end point, the program skips to the first statement following the loop.

CAUTION  **If the beginning value of the loop is greater than the ending** value, the loop will not execute at all. The exception to this is if you set up the loop to count backwards (which you'll learn to do later in this chapter).

The counter variable changes each time the loop reaches the Next statement. Unless otherwise specified, the counter increases by one for each loop.

A For loop requires two statements: the For statement at the beginning of the loop and the Next statement at the end of the loop. The syntax of the For loop is as follows:

```
For varname = start To end
Statements to be repeated
Next [varname]
```

The For statement at the beginning of the loop defines the variable that will count the number of times the loop repeats. This variable is represented by the varname argument. The counter variable must be either a numeric variable or a variant variable. It cannot be a string or an element of an array.

start represents the initial value to be used for the counter. This can be a number, a numeric variable, or a function which returns a number. You can use any value for start including negative numbers and decimal numbers.

end represents the value of the loop counter that will cause the loop to terminate. The loop ends when the counter is greater than the value of end. For example, if end is set to 10, the loop will execute when the counter reaches 10, but will terminate when the next increment is added. The same types and ranges of numbers can be used for end as were used for start.

The word To in the For statement is a required keyword and must be included.

After the For statement, you place any statements that you want to repeat. There is no limit to the number or type of statements that may be present in the loop.

At the end of the loop, you must place a Next statement. This statement tells the program to increment the loop counter and return to the top of the loop. The varname argument in the Next statement is optional, but if you include it, the variable name must match the one used in the For statement.

TIP For ease of reading your program, it's good practice to include the variable name in the Next statement. This is especially important in nested loops.

CAUTION While you can use any numeric variable for the counter, you need to be aware of the limits of variable types. For example, trying to run a loop 40,000 times using an integer variable will cause an error during execution because an integer has a maximum value of 32,767.

For the limits of variable types, see Chapter 17, "Adding Variables to Your Programs."

To illustrate the For loop example shown in the "How can I use this in the real world?," section figure 23.2 shows a potential setup screen to be used for placing bottles in cases.

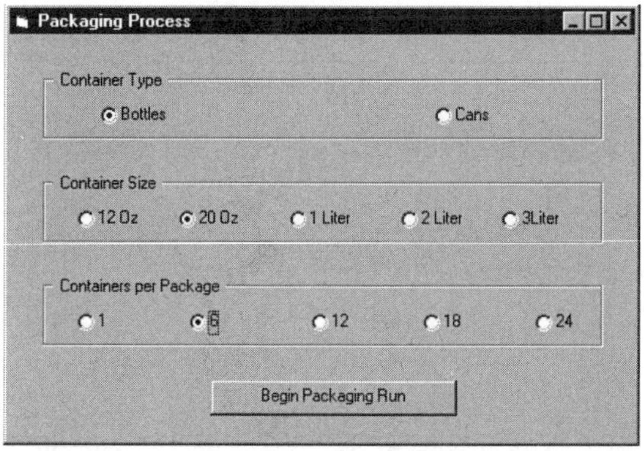

Fig. 23.2
You could use a *For* loop to load bottles into a case.

```
┌─ Packaging Process ──────────────────────[_][□][X]┐
│ ┌─ Container Type ──────────────────────────────┐ │
│ │   ⊙ Bottles                      ○ Cans        │ │
│ └───────────────────────────────────────────────┘ │
│ ┌─ Container Size ──────────────────────────────┐ │
│ │   ○ 12 Oz  ⊙ 20 Oz  ○ 1 Liter  ○ 2 Liter  ○ 3 Liter │ │
│ └───────────────────────────────────────────────┘ │
│ ┌─ Containers per Package ──────────────────────┐ │
│ │   ○ 1      ⊙ 6      ○ 12      ○ 18     ○ 24    │ │
│ └───────────────────────────────────────────────┘ │
│              [ Begin Packaging Run ]               │
└───────────────────────────────────────────────────┘
```

How can I use this in the real world?

A manufacturing plant uses a For loop to fill packages for shipping. If you've ever visited a bottling plant, you have probably seen the bottles placed in an empty case, then the case is moved down the conveyor for wrapping and further processing. Each case contains a specific number of bottles. Each bottle is counted as it is placed in the case, and when the required number of bottles is in the case, processing is finished for the case.

The following listing does not contain actual program commands, but task statements. The listing uses a variable, `MaxBottles`, to determine how many times the loop should be executed. This variable is set in code which responds to the option buttons on the screen.

```
For Bottles = 1 To MaxBottles
    Print Label
    Fill Bottle
    Cap Bottle
    Load Bottle
Next Bottles
```

The loop for this process would use the number of bottles per case from the input screen to set up the number of times the loop would be executed. Commands for the loop might include printing a label on the bottle, filling the bottle, capping the bottle, then placing the bottle in the case.

Catch the bug

What is wrong with the `For` loop shown in this code?

```
Dim inpNumber(1 To 10)
For I = 10
    inpNumber(I) = 0
Next
```

Answer: *In the* `For` *statement, you must include both the starting and ending points of the loop along with the keyword* `To`*. Also, while not an error, it is good practice to include the counter variable in the* `Next` *statement. The following shows the correct code:*

```
For I = 1 To 10
```

What not to do inside the loop

Infinite loops were discussed in Chapter 22, "Conditional Loops: Keep Going Until I Tell You to Stop," in regard to conditional (`Do`) loops. While an infinite loop is very unlikely in a `For` loop, it is still possible. The main thing that you have to avoid is changing the value of the counter variable inside the loop. The following code shows an example where changing the value would cause an infinite loop:

```
Dim inpPrice(9)
For I = 1 To 10
    msgtxt = "Enter the price of item " & Str(I)
    getPrice = InputBox(msgtxt)
    I = I - 1
    inpPrice(I) = getPrice
Next I
```

 The first line of the code sets up a 10-element array with index values running from 0 to 9. This array is used to store price information.

The next line of the code starts the For loop. The code is intended to gather price information for ten items and store the values in the array. The loop is set to run from 1 to 10. The next two lines set up the message to be displayed in the input box, and then get the price for the current item using the input box.

After the price is retrieved from the input box, it must be stored in the array. Because the array index starts at zero and the loop index starts at one, the next line subtracts one from the loop counter to use the number as the array index. Because the Next statement will add one to the loop counter, this line creates a vicious cycle of subtracting and adding one to the loop counter—which means that the loop counter is always the same when the loop condition is checked. The loop counter's value will always be one and will never reach ten, which is required to exit the loop.

CAUTION **Don't ever reset the value of the loop counter inside the loop** unless you enjoy tracking down hard-to-find errors.

Exiting the loop

Like the Do loops shown in Chapter 22, the For loop can be terminated early. This is accomplished using the Exit For statement.

One use of the Exit For statement is in a search loop. The loop will continue until the counter reaches the end point or until the search criteria is met. This is similar to the example for the Exit Do statement shown in listing 22.4.

Listing 23.2 shows how the For loop would be used to search an array of names for a particular name. The array could have been entered by the user or read in from a file.

Listing 23.2 Ending a Search Using the *Exit For* Statement

```
Private Sub cmdSearch_Click()
txtResults.Text = "No match was found."
For Icnt = 1 To 30
    iloc = InStr(1, NameArray(Icnt), findstr, 1)
    If iloc > 0 Then
        txtResults.Text = NameArray(Icnt)
        Exit For
    End If
Next Icnt
End Sub
```

This loop is very similar to the Do loop in listing 22.4. For this example, the size of the array, NameArray, is assumed to be 30.

The For statement of the code sets up the loop by defining a counter variable and defining 1 and 30 as the end points of the counter value. The maximum value of 30 corresponds to the size of the array.

For more information on arrays, see Chapter 21, "How Can I Manage Lots of Data? Use Arrays!"

In the next line of the code, check to see if the search string is contained in the NameArray element. If so, print out the name and terminate the For loop using the Exit For statement.

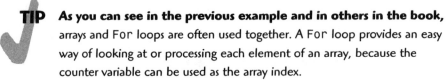

TIP **As you can see in the previous example and in others in the book,** arrays and For loops are often used together. A For loop provides an easy way of looking at or processing each element of an array, because the counter variable can be used as the array index.

Can I change the step size?

While the default change in the loop counter is one, you can specify a different value for the change. This value is known as the step size. Referring back to the swimming race analogy, changing the step size would be equivalent to swimming the same distance in a different size pool. The race that required ten laps in a 50 meter pool would require 20 laps in a 25 meter pool. In other words, the step size of the race changed.

To change the step size of the For loop, use the same basic syntax as the simple loop. However, you need to add one additional argument:

```
For varname = start To end Step stepsize
Statements to be repeated
Next [varname]
```

When you specify the size steps for the loop to use, you must include the Step keyword in the For loop. stepsize represents a numeric expression that can be a number, a numeric variable, or a numeric function. You can use any number for the stepsize, including decimal numbers and negative numbers.

How can I use this in the real world?

If you look back to the bottling plant example, you can see a use of the Step parameter for the For loop. Suppose a new machine was brought in that could process two bottles at a time instead of just one. The same program that was used previously can be used to handle the new machine—but now the processes only need to be performed half as many times. Instead of changing the end point of the counter, just change the step size by specifying two. The following code illustrates this.

```
For Bottles = 1 To 24 Step 2
    Print Label
    Fill Bottle
    Cap Bottle
    Load Bottle
Next Bottles
```

Can I count down in a loop?

Most people have seen a shuttle launch. The seconds are counted down and then the engines fire up and the shuttle takes off. If you haven't seen this, you have probably at least watched your microwave as its timer counts down. You can make your For loop do the same thing. It can count from a large number backward to a smaller number.

When you want a loop to count backwards, you simply set the step size to a negative number. You also need to make sure that the starting value of the counter is larger than the ending value. If the starting value is smaller than the ending value, the loop will not run.

The code for setting up a loop to count backwards, like in the following "How can I use this in the real world?" example, is shown in listing 23.3. The form for the program is in figure 23.3.

Fig. 23.3
Use a backward counting loop to find the most recent book on a subject.

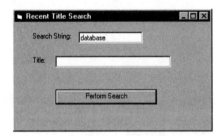

Catch the bug

This loop is designed to run backwards from 10 to 5. Why won't it work?

```
For J = 10 To 5 -1
    lstAuthors.AddItem Names(J)
Next J
```

Answer: If you specify the step size, you must include the keyword Step. In the For statement above, the program interprets 5 -1 as an equation that evaluates to 4. The program then considers the endpoint to be 4 and uses the default step size of 1. The loop would not run because 10 is greater than 4. The correct code follows:

```
For J = 10 To 5 Step -1
```

Listing 23.3   Finding the Most Recent Date Uses a Backwards Loop

```
Dim OldDb As Database, OldWs As Workspace, OldTbl As Recordset
Dim findstr As String
Set OldWs = Workspaces(0)
Set OldDb = OldWs.OpenDatabase("C:\VB4\BIBLIO.MDB")
SqlQry = "Select * From Titles Order By Year"
Set OldTbl = OldDb.OpenRecordset(SqlQry, dbOpenDynaset)
OldTbl.MoveLast
MaxBooks = OldTbl.RecordCount
ReDim TitleArray(1 To MaxBooks)
OldTbl.MoveFirst
'************************
'Load Titles into an array
'************************
For BookCnt = 1 To MaxBooks
    TitleArray(BookCnt) = OldTbl("Title")
    OldTbl.MoveNext
Next BookCnt
OldTbl.Close
OldDb.Close
'*************
'Perform Search
'*************
findstr = Trim(txtSearch.Text)
txtResults.Text = "No match was found."
For SrchCnt = MaxBooks To 1 Step -1
    iloc = InStr(1, TitleArray(SrchCnt), findstr, 1)
    If iloc > 0 Then
        txtResults.Text = TitleArray(SrchCnt)
        Exit For
    End If
Next SrchCnt
```

How can I use this in the real world?

One situation in which you would want the loop to count backward is in processing date information. Say that some books are processed in a database. The `recordset` sorts the books in the order in which they are published—from oldest date to the most recent date. This is so the list can print in date order. However, when a you search for a particular subject, you want to find the most recent book that covers the subject. Therefore, you work backwards through the list by setting up the loop to count backwards.

The first section of the code sets up the database for use by the loops. This code makes use of an SQL statement to set an order for the records in the recordset. After you create the recordset, the book titles are in date order from earliest to latest.

SQL statements are covered in Chapter 31, "Working with More Than One Table: Using SQL and the Data Control."

The next section of code creates an array to hold all the book titles, and uses a For loop to copy the titles from the database to the array. The RecordCount property of the recordset determines how many titles were in the database.

Finally, in the last section of the code, a For loop searches for particular text in the title of the books. Because the search should start with the latest book, which is the last one in the array, set up the loop to count backwards from the last title to the first.

Catch the bug

This loop never executes the Print statement. Can you see why?

```
For K = 1 To 10 Step -1
    Form1.Print BookTitle(K)
Next K
```

Answer: *While no error code would generate for this loop, the loop would not run because 1 is less than 10. Remember, for a backward counting loop, the starting point must be greater than the end point. The following is the correct code:*

```
For K = 10 To 1 Step -1
```

Loops can be flexible

You have seen how to use For loops for a variety of purposes. However, you won't always know what the bounds of the loop should be. For example, in listing 23.3, you don't know how many books are in the database. Visual Basic lets you handle this situation by allowing you to specify a variable for the starting and ending points of the loop or the step size. This was done in listing 23.3 with a variable that held the count of the number of books.

Look one more time at the bottling plant example. The previous listings assume that a case holds 24 bottles and that the packing machine can handle either one or two bottles at a time. However, in a real plant, there are multiple case or pack sizes that have to be handled. Using variables in the For loop, you can make the code generic enough to handle any case size and either packing machine. Listing 23.4 shows how to handle this.

Listing 23.4   Using a Variable for the End Point and Step Size

```
CaseSize = Val(txtCase.Text)
If optMachine1 Then
    AtATime = 1
Else
    AtATime = 2
For Bottles = 1 To CaseSize Step AtATime
    Print Label
    Fill Bottle
    Cap Bottle
    Load Bottle
Next Bottles
```

You can create multiple combinations of loops

Sometimes in your program, a single loop is not sufficient to handle the task at hand. When this happens, you need to use multiple loops inside one another. This programming structure is known as a **nested loop**. Nested loops are like the stacking barrels that kids play with. Each barrel contains a smaller barrel that also contains a smaller barrel. With the toy barrels, there are usually about eight different barrels.

In programming, each barrel is considered a level. The largest barrel, or outermost loop, is the first level, the next largest is the second level, and so on.

Nesting *For* loops

For loops are nested by placing one loop inside another. The following listing shows a nested loop that counts to 1,000 and displays its progress every 100 steps:

```
K = 0
For I = 1 To 10
    For J = 1 To 100
        K = K + 1
    Next J
    Form1.Print K
Next I
```

What these loops accomplish is that the inner loop (with J as the counter) runs 100 times for each time the outer loop (I as the counter) runs. Because the outer loop runs ten times, the statement inside the inner loop executes 1,000 times.

You often use For loops in conjunction with arrays because the counter makes a convenient index for the array. One use of nested For loops is to process multidimensional arrays. For example, if you have a two-dimensional array that contains sales data by month and region, you can use the following nested loops to provide the total sales:

```
Dim Sales(1 To 10, 1 To 12)
TotSales = 0.0
For iRegion = 1 To 10
    For iMonth = 1 To 12
        TotSales = TotSales + Sales(iRegion,iMonth)
    Next iMonth
Next iRegion
Form1.Print TotSales
```

The first line of the code shows how the array would be dimensioned. To add up all the entries, it assumes that the array has the sales figures input prior to the nested loops.

The first loop makes sure that each sales region is included. The second loop tells the program that for each region, the 12 monthly sales figures should be added together.

Q&A *Is there any limit to the number of levels of nesting?*

There is not a definite limit, but like many things, you might be limited by the amount of memory on your system.

Nesting other loops and decisions

For loops are not the only programming structures that can be nested. You can use multiple Do loops, multilevel If blocks, and multilevel Select statements in your programs. If statements are often used to surround other programming structures (such as loops) so that the commands are only executed for specific conditions.

One example of using nested Do loops is in printing out related records from a database. Using the BIBLIO.MDB database that comes with Visual Basic, the code in listing 23.5 prints each publisher's name and then prints all the books published by the company. Figure 23.4 shows part of the list generated by the program.

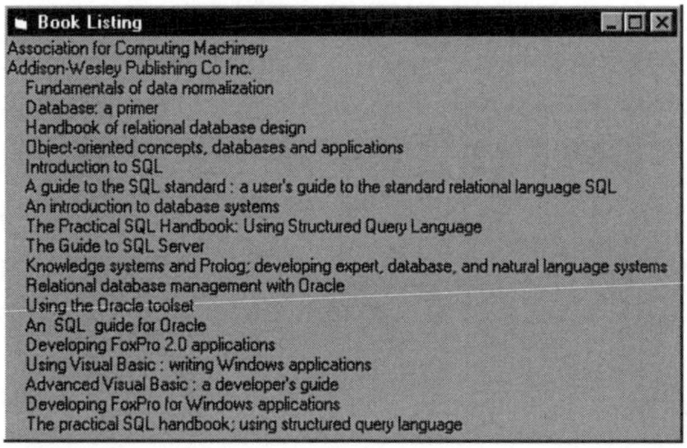

Fig. 23.4

This book list was created using nested Do loops.

Listing 23.5   Using Nested Loops to Print the Books by Publisher

```
Dim OldWs As Workspace, OldDb As Database, PubTbl As Recordset
Dim TitTbl As Recordset
Set OldWs = DBEngine.Workspaces(0)
Set OldDb = OldWs.OpenDatabase("C:\VB4\BIBLIO.MDB")
Set PubTbl = OldDb.OpenRecordset("Publishers", dbOpenTable)
Set TitTbl = OldDb.OpenRecordset("Titles", dbOpenDynaset)
PubTbl.MoveFirst
Do Until PubTbl.EOF
    Form1.Print PubTbl("Company Name")
    pubno = PubTbl("PubID")
    TitTbl.FindFirst "PubID = " & pubno
    Do Until TitTbl.NoMatch
        Form1.Print "    " & TitTbl("Title")
        TitTbl.FindNext "PubID = " & pubno
    Loop
    PubTbl.MoveNext
Loop
```

The first five lines of the code set up the database and the tables that will be used for the program. The example assumes that the database is in the VB4 subdirectory. You might have to use a different directory name if you enter this code.

The next line moves the record pointer of the Publishers table to the first record. The outer Do loop then starts. This loop will move through the Publishers table and will print out the company name then each book published for each publisher. The loop terminates when it reaches the end of the file. The line after the Print statement retrieves the publisher ID for the current publisher. This ID is used to determine which books to include in the publisher's list.

The second (inner) loop starts by finding the first book that was published by the current publisher. This loop will continue as long as the FindNext command continues to find books by the same publisher. For each book, the title is printed out, then the program attempts to find another book.

After the second loop terminates for the current publisher, the outer loop moves to the next publisher record. This process continues until the last publisher has been printed out. The outer loop then terminates.

You are not limited to nesting loops or decisions of the same type. You can also nest If statements inside of Do loops, For loops inside of Select blocks, or any combination.

Improper nesting

The main thing to be careful of in nesting loops and decisions of different types is to make sure you are nesting them properly. To put it simply, if you start a loop or a decision inside another structure, you must complete it within the same structure. Listing 23.6 illustrates this point. The first code segment is improperly nested; the second is correctly nested.

Listing 23.6   Right and Wrong Ways of Nesting Loops

```
'************************
'This is improperly nested
'************************
If chkvar < 25 Then
   For J = 1 To 10
      K = J * 2
```

```
      End If
   Next J
   '***********************
   'This is correctly nested
   '***********************
   If chkvar < 25 Then
      For J = 1 To 10
         K = J * 2
      Next J
End If
```

 TIP **One way to help avoid nesting problems is to enter the start and** end statements of a structure at the same time, and then go back and place the desired code within the statements.

Summary

While a Do loop can be programmed to do anything a For loop can do, a For loop provides a more convenient means of programming repetitive tasks when you know how many times the task must be performed, or when you can let the user specify the number of repetitions.

Review questions

1 Which two statements are part of every counter loop?

2 What is the default step size of the loop?

3 What kinds of numbers can be used as the end points of the loop?

4 Can an infinite loop result from a counter loop?

5 How do you exit a loop early?

6 How do you change the step size of the loop?

7 How can you make a loop count backwards?

8 What is a good use of nested For loops?

9 What types of programming structures can be nested?

Exercises

1 Change listing 23.1 to handle any size array.

2 Change listing 23.3 to look for the oldest book containing the search string in the title.

3 Rewrite listing 23.3 to use Do loops instead of For loops.

24

If I Go This Way, Where Will I End Up?

● **In this chapter:**

● **If the condition is** True**, run this code**

● **Can I handle both** True **and** False **conditions?**

● **What do I do about multiple conditions?**

● **Is there an easy way to assign a value to a variable based on a condition?**

If statements enable you to make decisions in your program and handle changing conditions while your program is running. . . . . >

We have to make hundreds of decisions every day of our lives. Many are little decisions like what to have for breakfast or what to wear to work. Others are big decisions like "Where am I going for vacation?" or "Should I take that job on the other coast?" You have to make decisions in your programs, too.

When your program makes decisions, it is deciding whether to process a statement or set of statements. This chapter describes how most decisions in a program are handled using the various forms of the If statement. You also see how a related function, the IIF function, can be used to assign a value based on a condition. The other method of handling decisions in a program, the Select Case statement, will be covered in the next chapter.

I only care if the results are *True*

For many decisions, you will want to execute a statement (or group of statements) only if a condition is True. You make this type of decision when you check the weather every morning; for example, "If it is going to rain, I will take my umbrella."

There are two forms of the If statement for handling True conditions—the **single line** If statement and the **multiline** If statement. Each form uses the If statement to check a condition. If the condition is True, the program will run the commands associated with the If statement. If the condition is False, the commands will be skipped. This logic is shown in figure 24.1.

Fig. 24.1
An *If* statement executes commands when the condition is *True*.

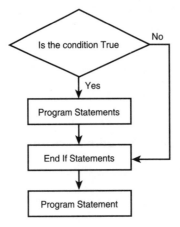

How to use a single line *If* statement

For more information on the use of procedures, see Chapter 26, "Basic Building Blocks: Procedures and Functions."

The single line If statement is used to perform a single task when the condition in the statement is True. The task can be a single command, or you can perform multiple commands by calling a procedure.

The single line If statement uses the following syntax:

```
If condition Then command
```

The argument condition represents any type of **logical condition**, which can be any of the following:

- Comparison of a variable to a literal, another variable, or a function.

- A variable or database field that contains a True or False value.

- Any function that returns a True or False value.

For more on logical conditions, look at Chapter 20, "Making Decisions Based Upon Data Comparisons."

The argument command represents the task to be performed if the condition is True. This can be any valid Visual Basic statement, including a procedure call.

The If and Then keywords must be included in the statement or an error occurs.

The code for the If statement example discussed in the "How can I use this in the real world" section is shown in listing 24.1. The listing is part of the program shown in figure 24.2.

How can I use this in the real world?

You have already used the If statement in a number of programming examples in previous chapters. One use of the single line If statement would be to print a name that matches a search criteria as a database is scanned. Another use would be to keep track of the total taxable items in a customer's order.

Fig. 24.2

An order entry program can use an *If* statement to keep up with taxable items.

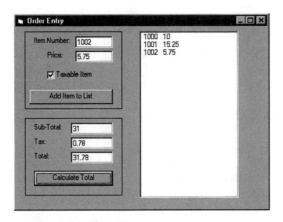

Listing 24.1 Taxable Items Separated Using an *If* Statement

```
Dim TaxTotal As Single, TotalCost As Single

Private Sub Form_Activate()
TaxTotal = 0#
TotalCost = 0#
End Sub

Private Sub cmdEnterItem_Click()
itmcost = Val(txtPrice.Text)
taxable = chkTax.Value
itmlist = Str(txtItem.Text) & "   " & Str(itmcost)
lstOrder.AddItem itmlist
TotalCost = TotalCost + itmcost
If taxable Then TaxTotal = TaxTotal + itmcost
End Sub

Private Sub cmdTotal_Click()
txtSubtot.Text = TotalCost
taxes = TaxTotal * 0.05
taxes = Int(taxes * 100) / 100#
txtTax.Text = taxes
txtTotal.Text = TotalCost + taxes
End Sub
```

The first line of the code defines two variables—TaxTotal (which contains the total amount that is taxable) and TotalCost (which is the total of the prices of all items). The Dim statement is placed in the Declarations section of the form so that the variables are available to all the event procedures.

The next section initializes the two variables as the form is activated. The `Activate` event occurs just after the form is loaded and just before the form starts accepting input.

The next section of the code processes the individual items as they are entered. As each item is entered, its price is retrieved from the `txtPrice` text box and a variable is set that determines whether the item is taxable, based on the value of the checkbox. The item and its price are then added to the list box to show all the items that have been entered.

After adding the item to the list box, the price is added to the total cost for the order. Then if the item is taxable, its price is also added to the total taxable amount. The task of determining whether to include the item is accomplished in the single line `If` statement.

The final section of the code processes the total amount due for the order. The code first displays the subtotal, the total of all prices. It then calculates the taxes due for the taxable items. The `Int` function rounds off the taxes to two decimal places. The taxes are then displayed in a second text box. Finally, the subtotal and the taxes are added together to yield the total amount due, which is displayed in the last text box.

How to use multiple commands for a condition

If you need to execute more than one command in response to a condition, you can use the multiple line form of the `If` statement. This is also known as a **block `If` statement**. This form bounds a range of statements between the `If` statement and an `End If` statements. If the condition in the `If` statement is `True`, all the commands between the `If` and `End If` statements are run. If the condition is `False`, the program skips to the first line after the `End If` statement.

To execute multiple commands for a condition, use the following syntax of the `If` statement:

```
If condition Then
commands to be executed
End If
```

As with the single line `If` statement, the condition can be any logical expression that produces either a `True` or `False` value. The `If` and the `Then` keywords must be present in the `If` statement. You may place any number of commands between the `If` and the `End If` statements.

If you use the block `If` statement, you cannot place a command to be executed after the `Then` keyword in the `If` statement itself.

TIP **If you have a lot of commands between the `If` and `End If`** statements, you may want to repeat the condition as a comment in the `End If` statement. This makes your code easier to read.

TIP **As with the loop statements, it makes your code easier to read if** you indent the commands between the `If` and `End If` statements.

Catch the bug

What is wrong with the `If` statement in the following code?

```
inpt = InputBox("Enter a score")
If Val(inpt) >= 90 Then grd$ = "A"
    MsgBox "Congratulations, you got an " & grd$
End If
```

Answer: With a block `If` statement, you cannot place a command after the `Then` keyword in the first line. The following is the correct code:

```
If Val(inpt) >= 90 Then
    grd$ = "A"
    MsgBox "Congratulations, you got an " & grd$
End If
```

What if the results are not *True*?

Of course, if a condition can be `True`, it can also be `False`, and there may be times when you want code to execute only on a `False` condition. There may be other times when you want to take one action if a condition is `True` and another action if the condition is `False`. This section looks at handling the `False` side of a condition.

How to use the *Not* operator

If you are only concerned with executing code when a condition is False, you can use either the single line If statement or the block If statement discussed in the section "I only care if the results are True." You say, "But that only works if the condition is True." You're right, but you can use a little trick to create a True condition from a False one.

By using the Not operator as part of the condition, you can use an If statement to run code for a False condition. For example, suppose you have a membership roster that contains members' names, addresses, and so on, and has a logical field for marital status. The field is True for married people and False for singles. From this database, you can create a mailing list to announce an upcoming singles event. Listing 24.2 would accomplish that task.

Listing 24.2   The *Not* Operator Used to Process *False* Conditions

```
MbrRec.MoveFirst
Do Until MbrRec.EOF
    If Not MbrRec("Married") Then
        Form1.Print MbrRec("Name")
        Form1.Print MbrRec("Address1")
        Form1.Print MbrRec("Address2")
    End If
    MbrRec.MoveNext
Loop
```

 This code prints out the name and address of any single members. The code assumes that a database containing this information has previously been accessed.

The first line of the code moves the pointer to the first record of the recordset. The next line starts a loop, which continues to search records until the end of the file is reached.

The If statement inside the Do loop looks at the value of the "Married" field of the database. This field contains either a True or a False value. If the value of the field is False, the Not operator will cause the condition to be True, and the address information for the member will be printed. If the field is True, the Not operator will cause the condition to be False, and the statements inside the block If will be skipped.

After the block If statement is executed for each record, the MoveNext method causes the record pointer to proceed to the next record in the database.

How to handle *True* and *False* conditions

The other way of handling False conditions enables you to process different sets of instructions for the True or False condition. Think about baking a cake. At a certain point, you pull the cake out to see if it is done. If it is done (True), you set it aside to cool. If it is not done (False), you stick it back in the oven for a little more time.

You can handle this choice in Visual Basic with the Else part of the If statement. This logic is shown in figure 24.3.

Fig. 24.3
An *If-Else-End If* statement handles both *True* and *False* conditions.

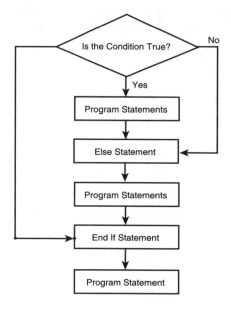

To handle both the True and False conditions, you start with the block If statement and add the Else statement as follows:

```
If condition Then
statements to process if condition is True
Else
statements to process if condition is False
End If
```

The If and End If statements of this block are the same as before. The condition is still any logical expression or variable that yields a True or False value. The key element of this set of statements is the Else statement. This statement is placed after the last statement to be executed if the condition is True and before the first statement to be executed if the condition is False. For a True condition, the program processes the statements up to the Else statement, and then skips to the first statement after the End If. If the condition is False, the program skips the statements prior to the Else statement and starts processing with the first statement after the Else.

It is not required that any commands be placed between the If and the Else statements.

Listing 24.3 illustrates the code used in the example from the following section, "How can I use this in the real world?".

Listing 24.3 *True* and *False* Conditions Used in the Handicap Program

```
If slope = 1 Then
    avgdif! = totdif! / bstscr
    hcidx! = Int(avgdif! * 0.96 * 10) / 10
    hcp% = Int(hcidx! + 0.5)
Else
    hcidx! = 0!
    avgdif! = Int(totdif! / bstscr * 100) / 10
    hcp% = 0
    Call Hcpchrt(avgdif!, hcp%)
End If
' Get member record
Get #1, pnt, mmbr
' Set maximum handicap for gender
If mmbr.gendr = "M" Then
    If hcp% > 36 Then hcp% = 36
Else
    If hcp% > 40 Then hcp% = 40
End If
```

The first If statement checks the type of scoring system used by the club. The system is indicated by the value of the variable slope. If slope is equal to 1, the next three lines of code are run to calculate the handicap. After the three lines, the Else statement is reached and the program skips to the line after the End If statement.

For more on using procedures, see Chapter 26, "Basic Building Blocks: Procedures and Functions."

If `slope` is not equal to 1, the program immediately skips to the line following the `Else` statement and calculates the handicap based on a table of values. The first three statements in this part of the block are familiar assignment statements. The fourth statement calls a procedure to perform the actual table lookup.

For more on file processing, see Chapter 27, "Storing Your Information in Files."

After the handicap is first calculated, the member's personal records are accessed to get the gender of the member. This is done with the `Get` statement to read the data from a file.

In the next block `If` statement, the maximum handicap is determined. This value is different for men and women. The first `If` statement checks the gender of the member. If gender is equal to `M`, the member is a man; otherwise, the member is a woman. In each case, a single line `If` is used to determine whether the calculated handicap exceeds the maximum allowable. If so, the handicap is set to the maximum value.

You can set up a loop to evaluate many conditions

In the previous sections, you have seen the simple block `If` statements, which evaluate one condition and can execute commands for either a `True` or `False` condition. You can also evaluate multiple conditions with an additional statement in the block `If`. The `ElseIf` statement enables you to specify another condition to evaluate if the first condition is `False`. Using the `ElseIf` statement, you can evaluate any number of conditions. The logic for the `ElseIf` statement is shown in figure 24.4.

How can I use this in the real world?

As an example of code handling the `True` and `False` conditions, consider code that calculates the handicap of a golfer. The handicap calculation is different for men than for women. It is also different for clubs that use different scoring systems. The code checks the scoring system of the club and the gender of the player, and runs the applicable portion of the code.

Fig. 24.4
The *ElseIf* statement lets you evaluate multiple conditions.

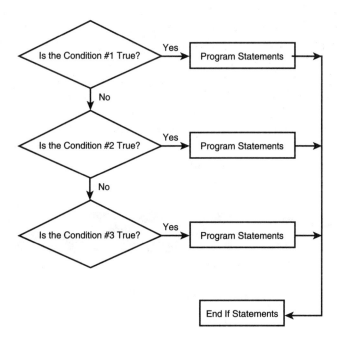

The `ElseIf` statement is used inside the block `If` as follows:

```
If condition1 Then
statement group 1
ElseIf condition2 Then
statement group 2
ElseIf condition3 Then
statement group 3
Else
statement group 4
End If
```

Each of the conditions (represented by `condition1`, `condition2`, and `condition3`) can be any valid logical condition. As before, these can be comparisons, logical variables, or functions. In both the `If` and the `ElseIf` statements, the word `Then` must be included.

The setup works by evaluating the condition in the `If` statement. If the condition is `True`, `statement group 1` is executed, then the program skips to the first statement after the `End If` statement.

If `condition1` is `False`, the program skips to the first `ElseIf` statement and evaluates `condition2`. If `condition2` is `True`, `statement group 2` is executed, and then control passes to the statement after the `End If`. This process continues for as many `ElseIf` statements as there are in the block.

If all the conditions are `False`, the program skips to the `Else` statement and processes the commands between the `Else` and the `End If` statements. You are not required to have an `Else` statement in the code. It is only needed if code should be run for all conditions being `False`.

In Chapter 19, there was a "How can I use this in the real world?" example that determined the distribution of grades. In that instance, I used a trick to determine where the grade fell. A more easily programmed and more readable method of handling the distribution is with the `If-ElseIf-Else-End If` block statement. This revised program is shown in listing 24.4.

Listing 24.4   Programming a Distribution Using the *ElseIf* Statements

```
For I = 0 To numstd
    If inpGrades(I) >= 90 Then
        GradeDist(4) = GradeDist(4) + 1
    ElseIf inpGrades(I) >= 80 Then
        GradeDist(3) = GradeDist(3) + 1
    ElseIf inpGrades(I) >= 70 Then
        GradeDist(2) = GradeDist(2) + 1
    ElseIf inpGrades(I) >= 60 Then
        GradeDist(1) = GradeDist(1) + 1
    Else
        GradeDist(0) = GradeDist(0) + 1
    End If
Next I
```

For each grade in the `inpGrades` array, the score is evaluated to determine whether it is an A, B, C, D, or F. The first `If` statement checks for scores equal to or above 90. If the score meets this condition, the A grade range is incremented by one. The program then skips to the `Next` statement to process additional grades.

If the score is below 90, the program skips to the first `ElseIf` statement. This statement checks to see if the score is equal to or above 80. If so, the B grade range is incremented by one. If the score is below 80, the program proceeds to the second `ElseIf` statement. This continues for other scores.

Finally, if the score is below 60, the program skips to the `Else` statement and the lowest grade range is incremented.

Catch the bug

What is wrong with the condition statements in the following code?

```
inpt = Val(InputBox("Enter a number between 1 an 10"))
If inpt < 2 Then
    numGroup = 1
ElseIf inpt < 4 Then
    numGroup = 2
Else
    numGroup = 5
ElseIf inpt < 6 Then
    numGroup = 3
ElseIf inpt < 8 Then
    numGroup = 4
End If
```

Answer: *There are two errors in this decision block. The first is that the* `Else` *statement must follow all* `ElseIf` *statements in the block. Second, the last* `ElseIf` *statement does not include the Then keyword. The correct code is as follows:*

```
If inpt < 2 Then
    numGroup = 1
ElseIf inpt < 4 Then
    numGroup = 2
ElseIf inpt < 6 Then
    numGroup = 3
ElseIf inpt < 8 Then
    numGroup = 4
Else
    numGroup = 5
End If
```

How do I handle conditional values?

In some parts of your program, you merely need to assign a value to a variable based on a given condition. You could use a block `If` statement to do this as follows:

```
If J > 5 Then
    I = 1
Else
    I = 2
End If
```

However, Visual Basic provides a function that performs this same task with a single line of code. The function is the `IIF` function.

The `IIF` function can be used to assign a value to a variable or anywhere else a function can be used. To assign a value, the following syntax is used:

```
result = IIF(condition, truevalue, falsevalue)
```

Just as with the conditions for `If` statements, the condition can be any valid logical expression. If the condition is `True`, the function will return the value contained in the `truevalue` argument. If the condition is `False`, the function will return the value contained in the `falsevalue` argument.

The arguments `truevalue` and `falsevalue` can be literal expressions, variables, or even other functions. All arguments must be specified for the function. None of them are optional.

CAUTION **The `truevalue` and `falsevalue` arguments must both contain the** same type of data, and the results variable must be capable of receiving that data type.

To illustrate how the `IIF` function can be used, let's look back at two examples shown earlier in this chapter. In listing 24.4, you looked at the grade distribution task. Suppose the only thing that someone needed to know was whether the grade was a pass or a fail. The following code shows how the `IIF` function could be used to assign the appropriate string to a text box:

```
inptGrade = Val(InputBox("Enter the test score"))
txtStatus.Text = IIF(inptGrade > 70, "Passed", "Failed")
```

Second, consider the membership list in listing 24.2. This time instead of printing only the single members, you want to print all the members along with their marital status. This example is shown in the following code and illustrates how the `IIF` function can be used in a statement other than an assignment statement:

```
MbrRec.MoveFirst
Do Until MbrRec.EOF
    Form1.Print MbrRec("Name")
    Form1.Print MbrRec("Address1")
    Form1.Print MbrRec("Address2")
    Form1.Print IIF(MbrRec("Married"),"Married","Single")
     MbrRec.MoveNext
Loop
```

Summary

As you can see, there are many ways to evaluate conditions in your program and have the program respond accordingly. The decisions can be used to handle simple tasks such as assigning values to variables, or complex tasks such as directing the flow of the program in any number of directions. You will find that the decision statements are some of the most powerful programming tools available to you.

Review questions

1 What must be included in every If statement?

2 How do you handle multiple commands based on a condition?

3 What are two ways to execute commands when a condition is False?

4 How can you cope with multiple conditions?

5 How does the IIF statement work?

Exercises

1 Modify listing 24.1 to calculate a total of taxable items and a total of non-taxable items.

2 Change listing 24.3 to use an IIF statement for the maximum handicap calculation.

3 Using multiple conditions (remember the And and Or operators), rewrite listing 24.4 to use a series of single line If statements.

25

Select Case: The Right Tool for Making Major Decisions

● **In this chapter:**

- I have twenty possible choices, what do I do?

- The value is somewhere in this range

- Comparing the different ways of making choices

The Select Case statement makes quick work of handling multiple outcomes . . . . ▸

n Chapter 24, you looked at the various forms of the `If` statement. You saw that the `If` statement can be used to handle `True` conditions, `True` or `False` decisions, and even handle multiple possibilities. But is the `If` statement necessarily the best tool for all types of decisions?

If you are looking at a series of unrelated conditions, the `If` statement is the best way to go. If, however, you are evaluating a variable against a range of conditions, the `Select Case` statement provides a much easier and more flexible way to handle the decision.

What do I mean by comparing something to a range of conditions? An unpopular but illustrative example is in calculating your income taxes. After you have gone through all the intricate calculations to arrive at your taxable income, you then look up your income number in a table to determine the actual tax. In a program, this table is represented by a `Select Case` statement. You compare your income (the variable in `Select Case`) against ranges of values (the income ranges in each line of the table).

Making a selection

While the `Select Case` statement is very flexible and can handle a wide variety of decisions, it is also relatively easy to set up. You use a `Case` statement to specify the condition for which a code segment is to be run.

CAUTION **The `testvalue` and value expressions must represent the same** data type. For example, if the `testvalue` is a number, the values in the `Case` statements must also be numbers.

As the `Select Case` is processed, the program will run the code segment associated with the first `Case` statement that meets the specified condition. The program runs the commands between this `Case` statement and the next `Case` statement or the `End Select` statement. If the `testvalue` is not equal to the value expression, the program proceeds to the next `Case` statement.

Only one case in the `Select Case` block runs for a given value of `testvalue`. This is true even if the code being executed changes the value of `testvalue`.

All I need is a simple comparison

Listing 25.1 shows how you would use a Select Case statement to process the payroll example discussed in the "How can I use this in the real world?" section. Figure 25.1 shows a form that can be used to calculate pay for hourly employees with various job classifications.

Speaking of *Select Case*

The basic syntax of the Select Case statement is

```
Select Case testvalue
Case value1
statementgroup1
Case value2
statementgroup2
Case Else
statementgroup3
End Select
```

The first statement of the Select Case block is the Select Case statement itself. This statement identifies the value to be tested against possible results. This value, represented by the testvalue argument, can be any valid numeric or string expression, including literals, variables, or functions.

Each conditional group of commands (those that run if the condition is met) is started by a Case statement. The Case statement identifies the expression that the testvalue is compared to. If the testvalue is equal to the expression, the commands after the Case statement are run.

The End Select statement identifies the end of the Select Case block.

How can I use this in the real world?

The simplest form of the Select Case block uses only a single value for the comparison expression. You might use this type of statement to handle a payroll calculation where you have a single pay for each job grade. The program would use the pay grade to determine the hourly wage to be paid for the worker. It could then multiply this value by the hours worked to obtain the gross pay.

Fig. 25.1
A payroll calculator can use a *Select Case* statement to handle different wages for different classes of employees.

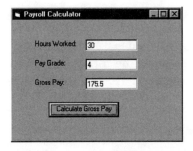

Listing 25.1 The *Select Case* Statement Uses Numeric Classifications To Calculate Pay

```
totpay = 0.0
paygrd = Val(txtGrade.Text)
payhrs = Val(txtHours.Text)
Select Case paygrd
    Case 1
        totpay = payhrs * 4.35
    Case 2
        totpay = payhrs * 4.85
    Case 3
        totpay = payhrs * 5.35
    Case 4
        totpay = payhrs * 5.85
End Select
txtPay.Text = totpay
```

The first two lines set the values of the variables `paygrd` and `payhrs` using the information from the text boxes on the form. The `Val` function is used to make sure that a number is returned.

Next, a `Select Case` block is set up to determine the actual pay for the employee. The `Select Case` statement defines the variable that is evaluated, in this case, `paygrd`. If `paygrd` is equal to 1, then the pay is `4.35` times the number of hours worked. After the pay is calculated, the program skips to the statement following the `End Select` statement. If `paygrd` is not equal to 1, the next `Case` statement is evaluated, and so on, until a `Case` statement is found that matches the value of `paygrd` or the program runs out of `Cases` to evaluate. If `paygrd` does not match any of the `Case` statements, no calculation is performed.

The final statement assigns the value of the `totpay` variable to the `txtPay` text box for display.

Listing 25.1 showed how to check a value against a series of numbers. You can perform the same payroll task using strings as the comparison (see listing 25.2).

Listing 25.2   Use String Comparisons to Handle Pay Grades

```
totpay = 0#
paygrd = txtGrade.Text
payhrs = Val(txtHours.Text)
Select Case paygrd
    Case "Waitress"
        totpay = payhrs * 4.35
    Case "Busboy"
        totpay = payhrs * 4.85
    Case "Dishwasher"
        totpay = payhrs * 5.35
    Case "Cook"
        totpay = payhrs * 5.85
End Select
txtPay.Text = totpay
```

How can I do more?

What happens if your test expression doesn't match any of the comparison expressions in the Case statements? Well, for what I have shown so far, nothing. If none of the Case comparisons match, the Select block does not execute any commands, it just skips to the first statement after the End Select statement.

However, if you want to have your code do something for all other possible values of the test expression, you can add a Case Else statement to your program. The Case Else statement follows the last command of the last Case statement in the block. You then place the commands you want executed between the Case Else and the End Select statements.

You can use the Case Else statement to perform calculations for values not specifically called out in the Case statements. Or you can use the Case Else statement to let the user know that they entered an invalid value. Listing 25.3 shows how you add just such an error notification to the payroll program from listing 25.1

Listing 25.3   The *Case Else* Statement Handles Invalid Values

```
totpay = 0#
paygrd = Val(txtGrade.Text)
payhrs = Val(txtHours.Text)
Select Case paygrd
    Case 1
        totpay = payhrs * 4.35
    Case 2
        totpay = payhrs * 4.85
    Case 3
        totpay = payhrs * 5.35
    Case 4
        totpay = payhrs * 5.85
    Case Else
        MsgBox Str(paygrd) & " is an invalid pay code."
End Select
txtPay.Text = totpay
```

Catch the bug

What is wrong with the following `Select Case` block?

```
Select Case paygrd
    Case 1
        totpay = payhrs * 5
    Case Else
        totpay = payhrs * 4.35
    Case 2
        totpay = payhrs * 5.50
End Select
```

Answer: *The* `Case Else` *statement must follow all the other* `Case` *statements that contain a value. The correct code is as follows:*

```
Select Case paygrd
    Case 1
        totpay = payhrs * 5
Case 2
        totpay = payhrs * 5.50
Case Else
        totpay = payhrs * 4.35
End Select
```

For real power, try multiple comparisons

As useful as the Select Case block is using single values for the comparisons, its real power comes through when you place multiple comparison values in each Case statement. This allows you to handle multiple cases in a single statement.

There are two ways to handle multiple values. First, you can input multiple, discrete values in a single Case statement. Second, you can use a value range for the comparison.

You can use specific values

To input multiple discrete values in a Case statement, you simply list all the desired values for the Case. The values are separated by commas. Using the multiple values has the same effect as multiple If comparisons using the Or operator. For example, the following two code segments in listing 25.4 perform the same task.

Listing 25.4 Multiple Test Values May Be Used

```
'****************************************************************
'This case statement increments a counter if inptNum = 1, 3,
'or 5
'****************************************************************
Select Case inptNum
   Case 1, 3, 5
      OddNums = OddNums + 1
End Select
'****************************************************************
'This If block also increments a counter if inptNum = 1, 3,
'or 5
'****************************************************************
If inptNum = 1 Or inptNum = 3 Or inptNum = 5 Then
   OddNums = OddNums + 1
End If
```

 TIP **This type of comparison is looking at exact matches of the test** expression to one of the values in the Case statement. If you are comparing strings, the strings must be identical, including the case (upper or lower) of each letter.

You can use ranges of values

For more information about the comparison operators, see Chapter 20, "Making Decisions Based Upon Data Comparisons."

There are two ways for you to input a range of values to be evaluated in the Case statement. You can use the To keyword to input both ends of a range (that is, numbers between 1 and 10). Or if you prefer, you can use the Is keyword and any of the comparison operators (<, <=, >, >=, or <>) to input an open-ended range (that is, numbers greater than 100).

Between here and there

The To keyword allows you to input a range of values in each Case statement that can be compared to your test expression. In using the To keyword, the smaller value of the range must appear to the left of the word To, and the larger value must appear to the right.

Speaking of *To* and *Is*

You can input a single range or multiple ranges using the To or Is keywords:

```
Case range1[, range2]
```

Each range can use either the To keyword to specify a value between two endpoints or the Is keyword to use the comparison operators. For example:

```
Case 5 To 10

Case Is > 15
```

These two methods of specifying ranges are described further in the following sections.

How can I use this in the real world?

Looking back at the payroll example, many companies have multiple job classifications that have the same pay scale. For example, in one company, analysts and engineers have the same pay scales. The difference between the jobs is the education needed and the tasks performed. In this situation, you could include multiple classification values in a single Case statement to calculate the pay.

Listing 25.5 shows the use of two `Select Case` blocks that use ranges of weights and distances to calculate the shipping charges for a package as described in the next "How can I use this in the real world?" section. The form for this program is shown in figure 25.2.

Fig. 25.2

Shipping charges are based on weight and distance ranges.

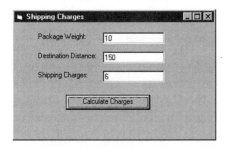

Listing 25.5   Two *Select Case* Blocks Are Used To Calculate Shipping Cost

```
dist = Val(txtDistance.Text)
wght = Val(txtWeight.Text)
'*******************************
'Determine rate based on distance
'*******************************
Select Case dist
    Case 0 To 100
        chgrate = 1#
    Case 101 To 250
        chgrate = 2#
    Case 251 To 500
        chgrate = 3#
    Case 501 To 1000
        chgrate = 4#
    Case Else
        chgrate = 7.5
End Select
'*****************************************
'Determine charge based on rate and weight
'*****************************************
Select Case wght
    Case 0 To 2
        chrg = chgrate
    Case 2.1 To 10
        chrg = chgrate * 3
    Case 10.1 To 20
        chrg = chgrate * 5
```

continues

Listing 25.5   Continued

```
    Case 20.1 To 50
        chrg = chgrate * 10
    Case Else
        MsgBox "Cannot accept package"
End Select
txtCharge.Text = chrg
```

The first two statements get the weight and the distance to the destination from the text boxes on the form. The program then calculates the shipping charge rate based on the distance between the origination and destination points. The distances are divided into ranges. Each range is specified in a Case statement using the To keyword as shown in the "Speaking of To and Is" section. If the distance is greater than 1000 miles, the rate is set in the Case Else block.

Once the charge rate is determined based on distance, the total charge is determined based on the package weight. This is the subject of the second Select Case block. As with the distance, the weight is divided into ranges. Again, a Case Else statement is used to handle any values that are outside the specified ranges. In this case, a message is displayed that tells the user not to accept the package.

From here to eternity

The other way to input a range of values is with the Is keyword and a comparison operator. The Is keyword allows you to use any of the logical comparison operators (<, <=, >, >=, or <>) to determine if a variable falls within the range.

How can I use this in the real world?

When you ship a package using one of the express services, the charges that you pay depend on two things—the weight of the package and the distance between you and the destination. Since both the weight and the distance are grouped in ranges, you can use Select Case statements to calculate the shipping charges.

TIP **Use of the not-equal comparison operator (<>) has essentially the** same effect as the Case Else statement.

I hate to beat a dead horse, but to show the use of comparison operators in establishing a range, you're going to look one more time at the grade example shown in Chapter 24, "If I Go This Way, Where Will I End Up?" This time, instead of using the If ElseIf series of statements, you use a Select Case block. This final rewrite of the example is shown in listing 25.6.

Listing 25.6   Use Comparison Operators To Check Ranges

```
For I = 0 To numstd
    Select Case inpGrades(I)
    Case Is >= 90
        GradeDist(4) = GradeDist(4) + 1
    Case Is >= 80
        GradeDist(3) = GradeDist(3) + 1
    Case Is >= 70
        GradeDist(2) = GradeDist(2) + 1
    Case Is >= 60
        GradeDist(1) = GradeDist(1) + 1
    Case Else
        GradeDist(0) = GradeDist(0) + 1
    End Select
Next I
```

Q&A *Does it matter which order I place the Case state-ments in?*

Absolutely. The Select Case looks for the first condition that matches the test value. It doesn't look for the best match. When you are using discrete values, this does not have any effect, but when you are working with ranges, it can give the wrong answer. Consider the grade example. If you put the statement Case Is > 60 as the first statement, all grades above 60 are lumped into the D group, even if they should be a different grade.

Q&A *Can I use variables for the values or ranges in the Case statements?*

Yes, you can substitute a variable or a function that returns the proper data type for any literal expression that you have seen in the examples.

Catch the bug

What is wrong with the range definitions in the following `Case` statements?

```
Select Case Distance
    Case 0 - 100
        chgrate = 1#
    Case 101 - 150
        chgrate = 2#
End Select
```

Answer: *To include a range of values, you must use the* To *keyword. In each of the* Case *statements above, the hyphen is evaluated as a minus sign and the second number is subtracted from the first, leaving you a single negative value for each* Case. *The following code is correct:*

```
Select Case Distance
    Case 0 To 100
        chgrate = 1#
    Case 101 To 150
        chgrate = 2#
End Select
```

Try using different conditions in the same block

You might be wondering if you can use different types of conditions in the same `Select Case` block. The answer is "Yes, you can."

Visual Basic lets you not only combine different comparisons in the `Select Case` block, but also combine comparisons in the same `Case` statement. For example, you can have a single value, a range using the `To` keyword, and a range using the `Is` keyword all in the same statement. The only catch is that each value or range must be separated from the others by commas. A sample statement follows:

```
Case 1, 3 To 10, Is > 25
```

Listing 25.7 shows a portion of the code that is used in the tax calculation described in the next "How can I use this in the real world?" section (see fig. 25.3). Obviously, the entire tax table has not been input here.

Fig. 25.3

Tax tables can be set up using a *Select Case* statement.

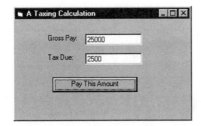

Listing 25.7   Several Comparison Methods Used in Tax Calculations

```
GrossPay = Val(txtGross.Text)
Select Case GrossPay
    Case Is < 10000
        yourtax = 0#
    Case 10001 To 20000
        yourtax = 1000#
    Case 20001 To 30000
        yourtax = 2500#
    Case Is >= 30001
        yourtax = 0.28 * GrossPay
End Select
txtTaxes.Text = yourtax
```

The first line of the code gets the gross pay from the text box on the form. Next, a `Select Case` statement is set up to determine the amount of tax due, based on the gross pay entered. The first case checks for a value less than $10,000. If the gross pay is less than this, no tax is due. The `Case` statement uses the `Is` keyword and comparison operator to set the range.

The next two `Case` statements use the `To` keyword to set other ranges and specify a tax due amount.

How can I use this in the real world?

The perfect example of using different types of comparisons is the tax table analogy mentioned at the beginning of the chapter. If you look carefully at the tax tables, you will see that the ranges only go up to a certain income, after which you must use equations to calculate the tax.

The final `Case` statement again uses the `Is` keyword to handle any pay amounts above $30,001. In this case, the tax is calculated as a percentage of the gross pay.

Should I use *Select Case* or *If/Then/ElseIf?*

As I showed you with the grade example in listing 25.5, the `Select Case` is very similar to the `If/Then/ElseIf` block of statements. The two types of statements can be used in similar situations. So which one is better?

If your comparison is not based on the value of a single variable, your only choice is the `If/Then/ElseIf`. For example, the following code cannot be duplicated easily with a `Select Case` block:

```
If X < Y Then
    X = X + 1
ElseIf X = Y Then
    Y = Y + 1
ElseIf Y > 0 Then
    X = X + Y
End If
```

But what about the situations where either one can be used? For comparison to a single value (that is, each condition is one value, not a range), it's a matter of personal choice. Both the `If/Then/ElseIf` and the `Select Case` work equally well and are equally easy to use. My personal preference is to use the `Select Case`.

However, for multiple values or ranges, the `Select Case` is much easier to use. Consider the following two code segments:

```
'********************************
'If/Then/ElseIf is harder to write
'********************************
If X = 1 Or X = 3 Then
    taxes = 25
ElseIf X > 3 And X <= 10 Then
    taxes = 50
ElseIf (X > 10 And X <= 50) Or X = 60 Then
    taxes = 100
End If

'*****************************
'than this Select Case statement
'*****************************
Select Case X
    Case 1, 3
```

```
        taxes = 25
    Case 4 To 10
        taxes = 50
    Case 11 To 50, 60
        taxes = 100
End Select
```

As you can see, the `Select Case` statement is much easier to write and easier to read. Again, either structure works equally well, but part of programming is designing the programs to make your job easier, both in initial development and in maintenance.

Finally, speed is always a consideration. So which method is faster? I have programmed several tests that run through thousands of iterations to determine whether the `If/Then/ElseIf` is faster than the `Select Case` or vice versa. In all my test runs, I have found no appreciable difference between the two methods.

Summary

While similar in function to the `If` statement, the `Select Case` statements can be easier to use for evaluating multiple possible values of a variable.

Review questions

1 How does a `Select Case` statement work?

2 What do you use to handle nonspecific values of the test expression?

3 Name the two methods to specify a range of values.

4 In what situation must you use an `If/Then/ElseIf` statement instead of a `Select Case`?

Exercises

1 Modify the code in listing 25.1 to handle multiple job classifications with the same pay.

2 Change the code of listing 25.3 to have the `Case Else` commands assign minimum wage to the employee.

3 Change the code of listing 25.4 to use the `Is` keyword to define ranges instead of the `To` keyword.

➤

26

Basic Building Blocks: Procedures and Functions

● **In this chapter:**

- **What are procedures?**

- **Passing information to a procedure**

- **Running a procedure**

- **Procedures can be reused in other programs**

- **How does a function work?**

- **Differences between functions and procedures**

The most efficient manufacturing model is the assembly line; each part of a product is built separately and then assembled at the end. As a programmer, you can learn something from this model. Bulding your program in modular blocks saves time and effort and makes maintenance much easier. . . . . . . ⊘

I f you have ever seen a car being built, you know that the famous assembly line does not build each piece of the car. Rather, it takes pieces that were built elsewhere in the factory or at other factories and puts them all together to make the final product. Each of the pieces of the car, such as the radio and the engine, is built and tested (or inspected) as a piece before it is sent to the assembly line. This makes the overall production operation more efficient.

Modular construction

Well-written programs use the same principal of modular construction that is used in building a car. Most of a program is written in components known as **procedures** or **functions**. These are pieces of program code that perform a specific task. When the task needs to be performed, the procedure is called by another part of the program.

You have already been exposed to working with procedures even if you didn't know it. Each time you entered code to be executed by a command button (or other control) in response to an event, you were building a procedure. These procedures are called automatically by the program when an event is triggered. You can build other procedures that you can specifically call from your program for other tasks. The procedures that you build are referred to as Sub procedures to distinguish them from event procedures. These **Sub procedures**, along with functions, are the subject of this chapter. Many of the development principles also apply to event procedures (those specifically associated with a Visual Basic event).

Why use a procedure?

There are several advantages to programming using procedures rather than trying to write all the code in one large program. Some of these advantages include the following:

To learn about finding errors in your code (debugging), see Chapter 34, "Finding Bugs in Your Programs."

- You can test each task individually. The smaller amount of code in a procedure makes it easier to debug.

- You can eliminate redundant code by calling a procedure each time a task needs to be performed, instead of repeating the program code.

- You can create a library of procedures that can be used in more than one program, saving yourself development time in many of your projects.

How does a procedure work?

A Sub procedure works exactly like the event procedures you've been reading about so far. Once called, the procedure executes commands (such as assignment statements), runs loops, and makes decisions. All of the programming commands discussed in this book can be used in a procedure.

How can I use this in the real world?

One of the most frequent uses of procedures is to contain the code needed for menu options. This is especially useful when a toolbar button or command button on a form performs the same task as the menu item. By using the procedure, you only have to write the code to accomplish the task one time. Then you can call the code from any number of places. The figure shows the main form for a program that makes use of this capability.

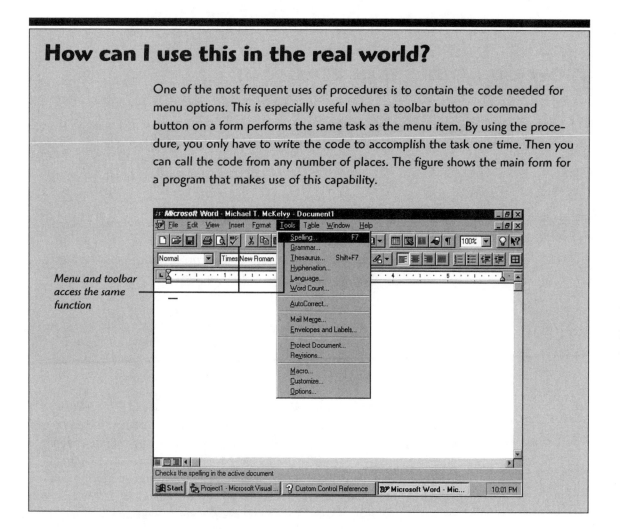

Menu and toolbar access the same function

Once the procedure has completed its task, it returns control of the program back to the statement that called it. The program then moves to the next statement in the calling program and continues processing. This program flow is illustrated in figure 26.1.

Fig. 26.1
When a procedure is called, it does its work and then returns control of the program to the next statement of the calling program.

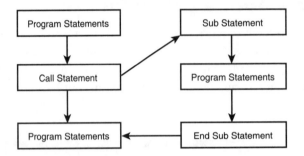

How do I build a procedure?

Okay. I'm sure by now that you are convinced of the merits of writing a program using procedures and are chomping at the bit to get started. But before you go off building a procedure, you should think about the task you want performed by the procedure and the data that is required. A procedure is like a miniature program and, as such, requires some thought about its design.

Starting construction

Once you have thought out the design of your procedure, you are ready to start building. There are two methods to start the construction of a procedure: use the Sub statement or use the Insert Procedure dialog box.

To create a procedure, you start in the code editing window of Visual Basic (see fig. 26.2). In the code editing window, choose (`General`) in the Object drop-down list and (`declarations`) from the Proc drop-down list. This places the cursor in an area that is not already part of a procedure.

You then start the new procedure by entering the keyword **Sub** and the procedure name at the cursor location. Procedures are named the same way that variables are named. (These naming conventions were summarized in Chapter 17.) When you enter the Sub keyword and the procedure name, three things happen—a set of parentheses is added to the end of the Sub statement, an End Sub statement is placed in the code window, and the current object in the Proc drop-down list of the code editing window becomes your new procedure name. This is shown in figure 26.3 for a procedure named NewProc.

Fig. 26.2

Move to the *(General)* area of the code editing window to start a new procedure using the *Sub* statement.

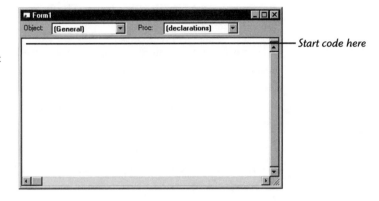

Start code here

The Proc drop-down list changes to the new procedure name

Fig. 26.3

The *End Sub* statement is automatically added when you define a new procedure.

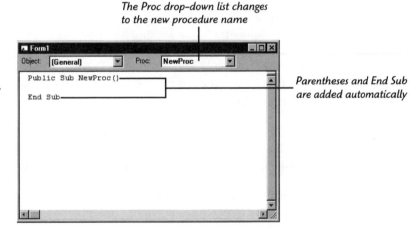

Parentheses and End Sub are added automatically

You are now ready to enter any commands that you want to run when the procedure is called.

The full syntax of a Sub procedure includes the Sub statement, the End Sub statement, and the procedure commands:

```
[Public ¦ Private] [Static] Sub procname([arguments])
statements_to_be_run
End Sub
```

The **Public**, **Private**, and **Static** keywords in the Sub statement are optional parameters that affect the location that procedure may be called from.

Plain English, please!

> **Public** variables are ones that are available to all procedures and functions in your program. They can be used to store information that needs to be used by multiple procedures.
>
> **Private** variables are used only within the procedure or function where they are defined. When the procedure ends, the memory used by the variables is released and the information is no longer accessible. Variables that are not specifically declared as Public or Static are Private by default.
>
> A **Static** variable works essentially the same as a Private variable except that its value is preserved for subsequent use in other calls to the procedure.

procname represent the name of the procedure. Like variable names, procedure names must be unique. The procedure name must begin with a letter and follow the same naming conventions as a variable.

arguments represents optional values that are sent to the procedure for processing. These arguments are variable names that may be used in the procedure code.

Inside the procedure, the statements_to_be_run can include any number of statements of any type. This can include assignment statements, decision statements, loops, and even calls to other procedures.

The End Sub statement is a required part of the procedure and indicates the last line of the procedure. When the program reaches this statement, processing is returned to the calling program.

The other method of creating a procedure is to choose Insert, Procedure. This displays the Insert Procedure dialog box (see fig. 26.4).

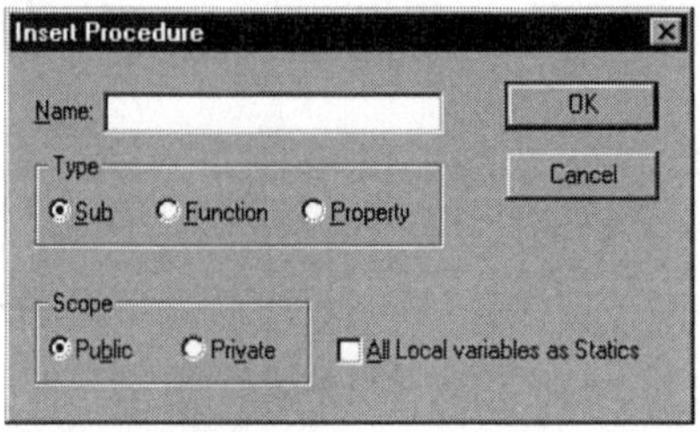

Fig. 26.4
You can create a procedure using the Insert Procedure dialog box.

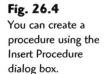

In the Insert Procedure dialog box, you perform the following steps:

1 Enter the name of the procedure in the <u>N</u>ame text box.

2 Choose the type of procedure (<u>S</u>ub, <u>F</u>unction, or <u>P</u>roperty).

3 Choose whether the procedure is Pu<u>b</u>lic or Pri<u>v</u>ate.

4 Choose whether to treat <u>A</u>ll Local Variables as Statics.

Choosing <u>S</u>ub creates a Sub procedure. Choosing <u>F</u>unction creates a function like the ones described later in this chapter. The `Property` procedure is beyond the scope of this book. Also, the Pu<u>b</u>lic, Pri<u>v</u>ate, and <u>A</u>ll Local Variables as Statics options are covered in later sections.

Once you have entered the necessary information, choose OK. Visual Basic then creates the framework of a procedure in your code window.

If you choose to use parameters in your procedure, you need to include them in the `Sub` statement at the beginning of the procedure.

Q&A ***When I click the Insert menu, the Procedure option is grayed out and I can't access it.***

This occurs if you do not have the code editing window open when you access the menu.

Running the procedure

Once a procedure has been developed, you need a way to run it from other parts of your program. There are two methods for running a procedure: use just the procedure name or use the `Call` statement. With either method, you simply specify the procedure name and any arguments that are required by the procedure. (The arguments are the ones specified in the `Sub` statement when you defined the procedure.) The syntax for running a procedure is:

```
Call procname([arguments])
```

or

```
procname arguments
```

In either syntax, `procname` refers to the name of the procedure. This is the name that is specified in the `Sub` statement that defined the procedure.

arguments refers to the parameters passed to the procedure. In the calling statement, the arguments can be literal values, variables, or functions that return the proper data type. This is different from the Sub statement where all the arguments have to be variable names. All parameters have to be separated by commas. This is shown in the following example code:

```
Sub TestGame (New As String, Option As Integer)
    MyAppID = Shell(New, Option)
    AppActivate MyAppID
End Sub
```

The following statement calls the procedure TestGame and passes to it the variables New and Option.

```
Call TestGame (New, Option)
```

 CAUTION **You must include the same number of parameters in the calling** statement as are present in the definition of the procedure. Also, the parameters in the calling statement must be the same data type as defined in the procedure. Violating either of these conditions results in an error when you run your program.

Finally, as you can see, the Call keyword can either be included or omitted in running the procedure. However, the Call keyword and parentheses go together. If you use the Call keyword, you must include the parameters in a set of parentheses. If you omit the Call keyword, you must also omit the parentheses around the parameters list.

 TIP **Including the Call keyword in all your procedure calls makes your** code easier to read since it immediately identifies a procedure.

Passing data to the procedure

There are two ways to get information into a procedure for processing—you can define the variables as public variables that are available everywhere in your program, or you can pass the variables directly to the procedure in the calling statement.

If you are going to be using the variables in a number of procedures and the procedure is specific to the current program, it is better to set up the variables as public variables. However, if the variables are local in scope, or if the procedure will be used in various places in the program or in multiple programs, you should define the parameters to be passed to the procedure in the Sub statement and pass the parameters in the calling statement.

Catch the bug

What is wrong with the following Call statement for running a procedure?

```
Call MMFileOpen filnam, alias
```

Answer: *If you use the Call keyword, you must enclose the arguments in parentheses. Either of the following lines work:*

```
Call MMFileOpen(filnam, alias)

MMFileOpen filnam, alias
```

The parameters used by a procedure provide two-way communication between the procedure and the calling program. The procedure can use information in the parameters to perform a calculation and then pass the results back to the calling program in another parameter.

For example, the following procedure gets the height and width of a rectangle from the parameters list and then calculates the area and perimeter of the rectangle. These values are returned through the parameters list:

```
Sub CalcRectangle(rcWidth, rcHeight, rcArea, rcPerimeter)
    rcArea = rcWidth * rcHeight
    rcPerimeter = 2 * (rcWidth + rcHeight)
End Sub
```

The procedure can be called by either of the following code segments in listing 26.1.

Listing 26.1   Two Ways of Calling a Procedure

```
'*******************************
'This code can call the procedure
'*******************************
sqWid = 5
sqHgt = 5
```

continues

Listing 26.1 Continued

```
sqArea = 0
sqPerm = 0
Call CalcRectangle(sqWid, sqHgt, sqArea, sqPerm)
'************************************
'This code can also call the procedure
'************************************
newArea = 0
newPerm = 0
CalcRectangle 4, 10, newArea, newPerm
```

In the procedure portion of the preceding listing, the procedure code uses the variables defined in the Sub statement to get data from the calling program and to pass data back to the program. The variables rcWidth and rcHeight are used as input, while rcArea and rcPerimeter are used as output.

In the calling portion of the listing, values were defined for each of the parameters prior to the Call statement. Then the procedure was called and the information was passed to it. Notice that the names of the variables in the Call statement are not the same as those defined in the procedure. In fact, in the second call example, variables are not used for the input values.

Working with passed arrays

Passing an array to a procedure is a little different than passing standard variables. The procedure has to be set up to handle any size array since typically the procedure doesn't know how big the array is beforehand. This is accomplished by setting up a dynamic array in the procedure's argument list.

To set up a dynamic array, you simply specify an array name followed by a set of parentheses in the argument list of the Sub statement. This is shown in the following code line:

```
Sub ArraySort(InptArray(), ardim)
```

Once the procedure is set up, it can be called like any other procedure, using the name of a valid array as one of the arguments in the argument list. When you call the procedure, you only specify the name of the array to be passed. You do not include any dimensions or parentheses in the procedure call.

Procedures can be used to handle a variety of array processing tasks. One such task is to sort the contents of an array. A procedure to accomplish this is shown in listing 26.2. The calling program for the procedure generates an array of random letters, then prints the original order of the array and the sorted order (see fig. 26.5).

Fig. 26.5
The original and sorted orders of the array are shown on the form.

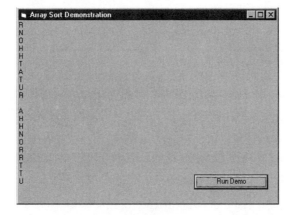

Listing 26.2   Array Sorting Is One Use of a Procedure

```
Public Sub ArraySort(InptArray(), ardim)
    For I = 1 To ardim
        For J = I To ardim
            If InptArray(I) > InptArray(J) Then
                temp = InptArray(I)
                InptArray(I) = InptArray(J)
                InptArray(J) = temp
            End If
        Next J
    Next I
End Sub


'*********************************************************************
'The following statements set up the initial array and do the
printing
'*********************************************************************
Dim ThisArray(1 To 10)
For I = 1 To 10
    J = Int(Rnd() * 25 + 1)
    ThisArray(I) = Chr$(64 + J)
Next I
```

continues

Listing 26.2   Continued

```
For I = 1 To 10
    Form1.Print ThisArray(I)
Next I
ArraySort ThisArray, 10

For I = 1 To 10
    Form1.Print ThisArray(I)
Next I
```

The procedure starts with the Sub statement as do all procedures. The argument list defines the array that is used in the procedure and a variable that contains the number of elements in the passed array.

The actual code inside the procedure uses a set of nested For loops to check the value of each element in the array and place them in the proper order. When the sort is completed, the program returns to the calling statement.

The routine that calls the procedure first defines an array and then stores random letters to the elements of the array. After the array is loaded, the initial order of the array is printed out. Then the sort procedure is called. After the sort procedure does its work, the array is again printed out, showing the new order.

Exiting a procedure early

Like the conditional and counter loops discussed in earlier chapters, there may be times when you don't need to execute all the commands in the procedure. If you need to exit the procedure before all the commands have run, you can use the Exit Sub statement.

You can learn more about data validation in Chapter 35, "Error Handling: Anticipating Mistakes that Users Will Make."

One way that I often use the Exit Sub statement is in the beginning of the procedure in a routine that checks parameters for proper values. If any of the parameters passed to procedure are the wrong type or have values that could cause a problem for the procedure, I use the Exit Sub to terminate the procedure before the error occurs. This is part of **data validation**. The following code modifies the previous area calculation code to perform this check:

```
Sub CalcRectangle(rcWidth, rcHeight, rcArea, rcPerimeter)
    If rcWidth <= 0 Or rcHeight <= 0 Then
      Exit Sub
    End If
```

```
        rcArea = rcWidth * rcHeight
        rcPerimeter = 2 * (rcWidth + rcHeight)
   End Sub
```

Where do I put a procedure?

You can create a procedure in either of two places—a form or a module. Where you place the procedure depends upon where you need to use it and what its purpose is. If the procedure is specific to a form or modifies the properties of the form or its associated controls, you should probably place the procedure in the form itself.

If, on the other hand, you are using the procedure with multiple forms in your program or have a generic procedure used by multiple programs, you should place it in a **module**. The storage location of your procedure is determined by where you create it. If you want, you can move a procedure from a form to a module or vice versa using cut and paste editing.

 Plain English, please!

A **module** is simply a file that contains procedures for use in a program. The module can have any name you want. Your project file keeps track of the names and locations of any module files used by your program. Module files are stored with the file extension of BAS.

Storing a procedure in a form file

To create a procedure in a form file, you just need to choose the form from the project window and then access the code for the form. This is done by either double-clicking on the form itself (or any control) or choosing the View Code button in the Project window (see fig. 26.6). Once the code editing window appears, you create a procedure as described in the section "Starting construction."

Fig. 26.6
You can select a form for your procedure from the Project window.

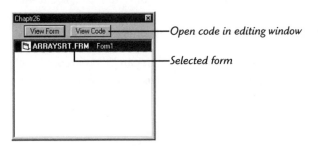

Chaptr26

View Form　View Code ——————*Open code in editing window*

ARRAYSRT.FRM　Form1

——————*Selected form*

Using a module file for procedures

If you already have a module file in your project, you can create a new procedure by selecting the file, opening the code window, and then using the previously listed steps to build the procedure.

 TIP   **Double-clicking the module name in the project window auto-** matically opens the code editing window for the module.

If you don't have a module file in your project, or if you want to use a new module, you can create a module by choosing Insert, Module. You can also create a new module by clicking the Module button in the toolbar. Either way, a new module is created and the code editing window appears for you to begin editing. When you save your project or exit Visual Basic, you are asked for a filename for the module file.

What does a function do?

Procedures provide one method of creating reusable pieces in your Visual Basic programs. Functions provide another method of creating these pieces. In many ways, functions and procedures are similar to one another. Both are typically designed to perform a very specific task and then return control to the main program. Both can perform very simple or very complex tasks. The key difference between the two is the way that you request them to perform their tasks.

A procedure is like a worker on an assembly line—when the product gets to employee's station, the worker performs the task and the product moves on to the next station. A function, on the other hand, is like a parts supplier. The factory sends a request to the supplier and the supplier returns the requested parts. Like a supplier, a function returns something to the program that called it. In the case of a function, the item returned is a value.

Creating a function

As with a procedure, a function can be created either with the Insert Procedure dialog box or the Function statement. As with procedures, a function can be public or private and can be stored in a form or in a separate module file. The syntax for a function is almost identical to that of a procedure.

Calling a function

Unlike a procedure, a function cannot stand alone in a statement. It must be assigned to a variable or used in another type of statement. This is true of both the functions you create and Visual Basic's internal functions. To illustrate this, listing 26.3 defines a simple function and shows two uses of the function in statements.

Listing 26.3   This Function Averages Two Numbers

```
'******************
'Define the function
'******************
Public Function VarAverage(varavg1,varavg2)
   VarAverage = (varavg1 + varavg2) / 2
End Function
'*********************************************
'Call the function in an assignment statement
'*********************************************
newavg = VarAverage(25,15)
'*********************************************
'Call the function from a decision statement
'*********************************************
If VarAverage(num1,num2) > 25 Then
   NumSum = num1 + num2
End If
```

 The function `VarAverage` performs a simple arithmetic average of two numbers passed to it. The function takes the two numbers, adds them, and then divides the result by two. This value is assigned to the function name to be returned to the calling statement.

The first calling statement simply assigns the return value of the function to a variable. This is one use of a function. The result of the statement is that the variable `newavg` contains the value of 20.

In the second calling statement, the function is used in an `If` statement as part of the condition. If the average of the two numbers determined by the function is less than 25, the condition is `True` and the statement inside the `If` block executes.

Catch the bug

There is a problem with either the function definition or the calling statement. Can you find the error?

```
'*******************
'Define the function
'*******************
Function VarProduct(num1, num2)
VarProduct = num1 * num2
End Function
'******************
'Call the function
'******************
newnum = VarProduct 25, 75
```

Answer: *When a function is called, the arguments must be enclosed in parentheses, like in the following:*

```
newnum = VarProduct(25, 75)
```

Useful functions you can create

While Visual Basic contains a number of internal functions, there are some that you have to develop for yourself. In the following listings are a few functions that I have found very useful. Hopefully, you will too.

String functions

String functions are designed to return a text string to the calling program. These functions can be used anywhere a string variable or literal can be used.

Proper names

The purpose of this function is to capitalize the first letter of the string that is passed to the function:

```
Public Function Proper(inptstr As String)
    Dim wrkstr As String, fstltr As String
    wrkstr = Trim(inptstr)
    fstltr = Left(wrkstr, 1)
    Mid(wrkstr, 1, 1) = UCase(fstltr)
    Proper = wrkstr
End Function
```

This function works by first using the `Trim` function to remove any spaces from the beginning and end of the input string. Next the function retrieves the first letter of the string using the `Left` function. Then the first letter of the string is replaced with the uppercase equivalent of the letter. The `UCase` function only affects alphabetic characters. Any other characters remain unchanged. Finally, the modified string is assigned to the function as the return value.

Speaking of *Function*

The full syntax of a function includes the `Function` statement, the `End Function` statement, and the function commands. It also includes a statement that assigns the value to the function. The syntax for a function is as follows:

```
[Public ¦ Private] [Static] Function funcname([arguments])
statements_to_be_run
funcname = expression
End Function
```

The `Public`, `Private`, and `Static` keywords in the `Function` statement are optional parameters that affect the location that the function may be called from.

`funcname` represents the name of the function. Like variable names, function names must be unique. The function name must begin with a letter and follow the same naming conventions as a variable.

`arguments` represents optional values that are sent to the function for processing. These arguments are variable names that may be used in the function code. Most functions have at least one variable in the argument list.

The statement `funcname = expression` must be included in a function. `funcname` is the name of the function that is defined in the `Function` statement. The equal sign is required in the statement. `expression` represents the value to be returned by the function. This expression can be a literal value, a variable, an equation, or even another function. The expression must be of the same type as the function itself.

The `End Function` statement is a required part of the function and indicates the last line of the function. When the program reaches this statement, processing is returned to the calling program.

Pad a string with spaces (or other characters)

This function is useful for creating a string of a specified length with a specific character occupying the empty space. This is useful in a check writing program to add asterisks at the end of a check amount to make sure the line is filled. Listing 26.4 shows the code for this function.

Listing 26.4   Add Characters to a String with *FillStr*

```
Public Function FillStr(inptstr, newlen, filltype, fillchar)
wrkstr = Trim(inptstr)
oldlen = Len(wrkstr)
If Len(fillchar) = 0 Then
    fillchr = " "
Else
    fillchr = Left(fillchar, 1)
End If
If oldlen > newlen Then
    FillStr = wrkstr
    Exit Function
End If
Select Case UCase(filltype)
    Case "L"
        inschr = newlen - oldlen
        For I = 1 To inschr
           wrkstr = fillchr + wrkstr
        Next I
    Case "R"
        inschr = newlen - oldlen
        For I = 1 To inschr
           wrkstr = wrkstr + fillchr
        Next I
    Case "C"
        inschr = newlen - oldlen
        frntchr = Int(inschr / 2)
        backchr = inschr - frntchr
        For I = 1 To frntchr
           wrkstr = fillchr + wrkstr
        Next I
        For I = 1 To backchr
           wrkstr = wrkstr + fillchr
        Next I
    Case Else
        FillStr = wrkstr
End Select
FillStr = wrkstr
End Function
```

This function requires four parameters to be passed to it. These parameters are the initial string, the length of the desired string, the position of the "pad" characters (right, left, or centered), and the pad character itself.

The function first eliminates any blank spaces at the beginning or end of the input string and determines the length of the trimmed string. It then makes sure that a pad character has been passed to the function. If not, the default pad character of a space is used. The function then checks to see if the input string is longer than the desired output string. If so, the function just returns the original string trimmed of any spaces.

If the new length is greater than the original length, the function proceeds to add pad characters to the requested location of the string. If the calling program specifies `"L"`, pad characters are added to the left side of the string. `"R"` causes characters to be added to the right side of the string, and `"C"` causes characters to be added to both ends. In all cases, pad characters are added until the desired new length of the string is reached.

Backwards in a string

The purpose of this function is to complement the `InStr` function that is internal to Visual Basic. This function starts at the right hand end of a string and searches backwards to find the search character. This only works with a single character as the search criteria. If the character is found, the character's distance from the right end of the string is returned. If the character is not found, zero is returned. Listing 24.5 shows the code for the function.

Listing 26.5 Finds the Last Occurrence of a Character in a String

```
Public Function RinStr(inptstr, srchstr)
    wrkstr = UCase(Trim(inptstr))
    findstr = UCase(srchstr)
    srchlen = Len(wrkstr)
    For I = srchlen To 1 Step -1
        If Mid(wrkstr, I, 1) = findstr Then
            RinStr = srchlen - I + 1
            Exit Function
        End If
    Next I
    RinStr = 0
End Function
```

Math functions

For more on Visual Basic's built-in math functions, see Chapter 18, "Power Up Your Visual Basic Programs with Some Basic Math."

Math functions are used to return a number based on the input numbers. Visual Basic has several built-in math functions such as square root and absolute values. The following are a few others that can be useful.

Square of a number

This function simply calculates the square of a number and returns its value:

```
Public Function Square(inptnum)
    Square = Val(inptnum) ^ 2
End Function
```

Maximum and minimum of numbers

These two functions in listing 26.6 evaluate the two numbers passed to them and return either the minimum (`Min` function) or maximum (`Max` function) of the two.

Listing 26.6 Finding Minimum and Maximum Values

```
Public Function Max(inptnum1, inptnum2)
    If inptnum1 > inptnum2 Then
        Max = inptnum1
    Else
        Max = inptnum2
    End If
End Function

Public Function Min(inptnum1, inptnum2)
    If inptnum1 < inptnum2 Then
        Min = inptnum1
    Else
        Min = inptnum2
    End If
End Function
```

Array functions

Like procedures, functions can also be used to process arrays. The function in listing 26.7 searches for a string among the elements of an input array. The arguments passed to the function are the array itself, the size of the array, and the search string. The function returns the index of the first element containing the search string. If the search string is not in any of the elements, -1 is returned.

Listing 26.7   Finds a Specific Item in an Array

```
Public Function ArraySrch(InptArray(), ardim, srchstr)
For I = 1 To ardim
    fndstr = InStr(InptArray(I), srchstr)
    If fndstr > 0 Then
        ArraySrch = I
        Exit Function
    End If
Next I
ArraySrch = -1
End Function
```

Does my procedure work throughout the whole program?

When you create a procedure, it may be limited in where it can be used. The limitations are determined by where the procedure is stored and whether you include the Public, Private, or Static keywords in the definition of the procedure. Where a procedure can be used is referred to as the **scope** of the procedure.

Like procedures, variables also have a scope. They can be local to a specific procedure, available to an entire form, or available to the entire program. Again, the scope depends on where the variable is defined and which keyword is used in its declaration.

To give you a better idea of the concept of the scope of variables and procedures, think about how your telephone works. If you dial the number for a friend of yours in town, your call goes through with no problem. However, if you go to another area code and dial the same seven digits (without dialing the area code), you either get a message that tells you that the number cannot be dialed, or you might get another person that happens to have the same number in the other area code. A local procedure or variable works the same way.

If you add the area code to the number, you can call your friend from anywhere in the country. The phone number with the area code works like a form or module level variable. Even with the area code, though, you still have trouble calling your friend from overseas. To accomplish this, you need the international prefix code. This is similar to the public or global procedure or variable.

Scope of procedures

Procedures can be defined in either of two ways—Public procedures or Private procedures. Which of these keywords you use in the Sub statement determines which other procedures or programs have access to your procedure.

Procedures that can be used anywhere

Using the Public keyword in the definition of the procedure allows the procedure to be accessed from anywhere in your program. This means that a procedure defined in one form or module can be called from another form or module. It also means that you have to be more careful with the names of your procedures because each Public procedure must have a unique name.

If you omit the keywords Public and Private from the Sub statement, the procedure is set up as a Public procedure by default.

Procedures for a specific form

Using the Private keyword in the Sub statement allows the procedure to only be accessed from the form or module that it is defined in. There are, of course, advantages and disadvantages to this approach. The advantage is that you can have private procedures of the same name in separate modules. The disadvantage is that the procedure isn't accessible from other modules.

One thing you may have noticed in working with event procedures in other chapters is that they are by default Private procedures. This is because, typically, controls are not accessed outside of the form where they reside.

Scope of variables

You have more choices for the scope of variables than for the scope of procedures. The scope is dependent not only on the keyword used to declare the variable but also on the location of the declaration statement.

Variables everybody can use

In most programs, you will find that you need to have some variables available to all parts of the program. Often these global variables are used as flags that indicate various conditions in the program such as open files or data modifications.

The use of declaration statements in defining variables is covered in Chapter 17, "Adding Variables to Your Programs."

To create a variable that can be used anywhere in your program, you need to use the `Public` keyword in the declaration statement. This statement can be placed anywhere in your code.

 TIP **It is good practice to place all your `Public` variable declarations** in one place, typically in the `(General)` area of your module file or primary form.

Doing business locally

When you don't need global access to your variables, but you need them in more than one procedure, you can create a module level variable. These variables are created by using the `Dim`, `ReDim`, or `Private` statement to declare the variable. These declarations must be placed in the `(General)` area of the module or form where the variables are used.

Keeping it private

The same declaration statements used to create module level variables are also used to create private variables inside a procedure. (The keywords are `Dim`, `ReDim`, and `Private`.) The difference between procedure level variables and module level variables is where they are declared. To keep a variable private to a specific procedure, the variable must be declared in that procedure.

In addition to the declaration of variables, any variables that are defined by an assignment statement are also considered private.

Private variables only exist while the procedure is running. When the procedure terminates, the memory used for the variable is released and the value of the variable is lost.

What is a *Static* variable?

In both the declaration of procedures and the declaration of variables, the keyword `Static` can be used. When present, `Static` tells the program to preserve the value of variables after a procedure has terminated.

When `Static` is used in a variable declaration, only the variables included in the `Static` statement are preserved. If you use the `Static` keyword in the procedure declaration, all the variables in the procedure are preserved.

Summary

Writing programs in small pieces makes it easier to develop and test the different elements of your program. It also makes you more efficient by allowing you to develop a specific routine once and then use it over and over in your program or in multiple programs.

Review questions

1 How do you create a new procedure in a program?

2 What are the two ways to run a procedure?

3 How do you get information from one part of your program to the procedure?

4 Where are procedures stored?

5 What is the difference between a public and a private procedure?

Exercises

1 Modify the procedure in listing 26.1 so that the array is sorted in reverse order.

2 Modify the RinStr function so that it finds more than the first occurrence of the character.

3 Create a function that finds the average value of numbers in an array, the maximum value, and the minimum value.

4 Create a procedure that calculates the area of a circle, given the radius.

27

Storing Your Information in Files

● **In this chapter:**

● **How is information stored in a file?**

● **Sequential and random access files—what they are and how they work**

● **Getting out what you put into a file**

● **How do I store information in a file?**

● **Manage your files with Visual Basic commands**

Forever is a long time, but you can save your data that long by storing it in a file . . . . ●>

Files on a computer are a repository for all the information that you need to have available for more than the current session of your program. The computer's files serve the same function as the paper files in your office. You can also consider the files to be like a library where books of information are stored. (If you use many CD-ROMs, you practically have a library sitting on your desk.)

File dialog boxes are available as part of the Common Dialog box discussed in Chapter 15, "Use the Common Dialog for Specialized Information."

You probably have some idea already about using files in programs. Any documents you write with a word processor or spreadsheets you create with a spreadsheet program store information in files. When you need to use this information, you just select the file name from the most recently used (MRU) list or from a File dialog box (see fig. 27.1). After you select the file, the program does the rest of the work, reading the information and displaying it in the proper form. The figure actually shows the Open Project dialog for Visual Basic, but an open file dialog works exactly the same.

Fig. 27.1

Most programs use a File dialog box that let you select the file you want to work with.

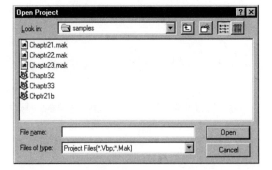

When you work with files in Visual Basic, though, you have to do all the work of getting the information from the file and displaying it on the screen. This chapter covers the basics of how to get information from files and place new information into files.

The first thing you need to know about files is that there are two basic file types, as defined by their access methods: **sequential files** and **random access files**. All the files that you use are accessed with one of these two methods.

 Plain English, please!

Sequential files work like the cassettes you use in your car stereo. As the cassette plays, each song is played in sequence as it is recorded on the cassette. Even if you have the feature that allows you to skip to the next song, the cassette deck is still "reading" each consecutive piece of the cassette to find the break between songs. In a sequential file, each piece of information is read or written in order.

Random access files on the other hand work like your CD player. You can program your CD player to play any of the songs you want in any order. Information on the CD tells the player the exact location of each song so that the player can go directly to it. A random access file performs the same function with your data. You tell the program the location of the piece of data you want to read, and the program reads it directly from the file. **⁹⁹**

 TIP **Database files are a special type of random access file that are not** normally accessed using the commands presented in this chapter. The creation and use of database files is covered in chapters 28 through 31.

I'll present information about both types of file access. Since some of the commands are the same for both types, some commands are repeated in both sections but with the syntax specific to the current file type.

How does sequential file access work?

Sequential data files are used to store information in ASCII text format. This means that these files can also be read and written to by any text editor. You can use sequential files to store text, numbers, or any other type of data that can be represented by the ASCII character set. You cannot use sequential files to store information such as bitmaps because these files work only with binary data.

There are three basic tasks that you must be able to accomplish to work with data in sequential files:

- Open the file to gain access to its contents.

- Read information from the storage media (disk or CD) to get it into your program.

- Write information to the storage media to be able to keep it permanently.

How do I open the file?

Before you can perform any other tasks with a file, the file must be opened—you have to open a book before reading its contents or open a notebook before writing in it.

In Visual Basic, you have to tell the program what task you want to perform when you open a file. There are several ways to open files for use. If you are going to read data from the file, you must open it in input mode. If you are going to write to a file, you must open it in the append or output mode. If you try to write to an input file or read from an output file, you get an error.

Opening a file requires that you issue the Open statement. This statement has the following syntax:

```
Open filename [For mode] As [#]filenum
```

In this syntax, all words with an initial capital letter are keywords.

filename is the full path of the file that you want to open. You can specify the file as a literal string (enclosed in quotes) or as a variable that has a valid file name assigned to it.

The For mode clause tells the program how to set up the file. While this is indicated as an optional property, if you exclude it, Visual Basic automatically places the For Random clause in the command statement. This assumes that the requested file is a random access file. For sequential files, you need to specify one of the following as the mode:

- Input—Tells the program that the file is used to read data into the program.

- Output—Tells the program that the file has information written to it, starting at the beginning of the file. Any information currently in the file is erased.

- Append—Tells the program that the file has information written to it starting at the end of the file. Current information in the file is preserved.

The As clause is used to specify the file handle or number that is used by input and output statements to identify the file. This number can be any integer between 1 and 511. You can specify the filenum argument with either a literal number or a variable. The # symbol is optionally used with the file number. It may be omitted.

How do I read the file's contents?

Once you have the file open, there are three ways to read information from the file. Which method you use depends on the task you need to accomplish.

You can read it a line at a time

You can read a single line of information from a file at a time using the Line Input statement. This statement retrieves all text from the current pointer position to the next line feed or carriage return character.

The Line Input statement uses the following syntax:

```
Line Input #filenum, varname
```

filenum is the number or handle of the open file that you are using for input. This is the same number that you specified in the Open statement for the file. As with the Open statement, it can either be a literal number or a numeric variable. The # symbol just tells the program that a numeric expression follows.

For more on variable types and naming conventions, see Chapter 17, "Adding Variables to Your Programs."

varname is the name of a variable that is used to store the information in the line of the file. The variable must be either a string or variant type.

One use of the Line Input command is to read information from a configuration or **initialization file**. Initialization (**INI**) files are used by many windows programs to specify conditions that the program uses while executing. This may be a directory for storing files or a default font. These options are stored in the form of

```
option = value
```

Line Input allows you to read each line and process the *option*s. The code in listing 27.1 reads the entire contents of a file to get the default font information. The font is then assigned to a text field for use in editing.

Listing 27.1   Read a File One Line at a Time

```
Open "A:\TEST1.TXT" For Input As #1
Do While Not EOF(1)
    Line Input #1, fstlin
    eqpos = InStr(fstlin, "=")
    optparm = Trim(UCase(Left(fstlin, eqpos - 1)))
    strlen = Len(fstlin)
    optval = Right(fstlin, strlen - eqpos - 1)
    If optparm = "DEFONT" Then
        txtTest.Font.Name = Trim(optval)
    End If
Loop
Close #1
```

The first line of the code opens the file for input. The next line starts a Do loop that continues until the end of the file is reached.

Each time the loop is executed, the Line Input command reads a line of text from the file. The InStr function is then used to determine where in the line the equal sign is located. The program then uses the Left and Right functions to get the name of the option (Left) and the value of the option (Right) from the input line. The name of the option is converted to upper-case and trimmed of spaces so that extra spaces or mixed case don't affect the comparison in the If statement.

The program then evaluates the option name. If the option name is DEFONT, the program assigns the value of the option to the Font Name property of the text box. In a program used to process a number of options, you can use a Select statement to look for each of the option names you needed to process.

You can read a specific number of characters

If you want to read a specific number of characters from a file or even the entire file at once, you can use the Input function to retrieve the characters from the file. The Input function starts at the current position in the file (after the last read) and reads the number of characters you specify from the file. The Input function reads and stores in the variable all characters that it encounters including line feeds, carriage returns, spaces, and so on.

To read an entire file, you need to use the LOF function to determine the number of characters in the file.

The LOF function determines the number of characters or bytes in a file. The function is used as follows

```
resultvar = LOF(filenum)
```

resultvar represents the variable that contains the return value of the function. filenum is the number of a file opened by the Open statement.

The code in listing 27.2 reads the entire contents of a file into a text box for editing. The user can specify the file name using the other text box on the form. The form is shown in figure 27.2. The code is placed in the Click event of the command button on the form.

Listing 27.2 *LOF* Determines the Size of a File

```
Dim numchars As Long
filnam = txtFileName.Text
Open filnam For Input As #1
numchars = LOF(1)
If numchars > 32000 Then
    MsgBox "File is too long for this program"
```

continues

Speaking of *Input*

The syntax of the Input function is:

```
varname = Input(numchars, [#]filenum)
```

As with the Line Input statement, filenum refers to the handle of the open file that you are reading information from. As before, this can be a literal number or a numeric variable. The # symbol is optional, but is usually included by most programmers.

varname is the name of a string or variant type variable that contains the results of the input operation.

numchars represents the number of characters that are to be read from the input file. This is any integer number from 1 to the length of the input file. numchars can be a literal number or a numeric variable.

```
        Exit Sub
    End If
    txtFileContent.Text = Input(numchars, #1)
Close #1
```

This code gets the name of the file from a text box on a form. The file is then opened, using the Open statement, to allow its contents to be read. Next, the LOF function is used to determine whether the file's contents will fit in the text box. If not, an error message is displayed. Otherwise, the entire file is read in, using the Input statement.

Fig. 27.2
This form functions like the Notepad application in Windows.

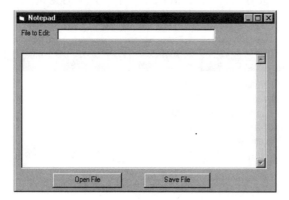

You can read multiple variables

Visual Basic also allows you to read data into multiple variables in a single statement. The command for this is the Input # statement. This statement is also the only way for you to read numbers and other information directly into your program. The other input methods, Line Input and the Input function, only read information into a string variable.

The data in a file that is to be read by the Input # statement must be separated by commas or appear on separate lines. Data set up in this manner is known as **comma-delimited data** (see fig. 27.3).

Fig. 27.3
All data items are separated by commas; string items are enclosed in quotes.

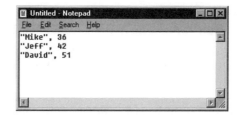

 Q&A *Is there any way that I can read data from a file into an array?*

Yes. While you cannot specify an array in an Input statement, you can specify an array element. Therefore, the following code can be used to read in an array:

```
Dim ThisArray(1 To 10)
For I = 1 To 10
    Input #1, ThisArray(I)
Next I
```

How can I add new information to be stored in a file?

Usually, if you need to read information from a file, you also have a need to write information as well. Visual Basic gives you two statements that can write information to a file—the Write and Print statements. The difference

Speaking of *Input #*

The Input # statement allows you to read multiple variables. It is used as follows:

```
Input #filenum, varlist
```

Again, filenum is the number of the file that was opened for input.

varlist represents the list of variables that are to be read in from the file. This can be any number of variables of any type. However, the variables cannot be arrays. The order and type of data in the varlist must match the order and type of data in the file. For example, if you try to read a string and an integer using the Input # statement, but your data file contains two strings, an error is generated telling you that your program tried to read the wrong type of data.

between these two statements is that the Print statement allows you greater control over the formatting of the information. The Write statement, on the other hand, is better for files that will later be read using the Input # statement because it automatically separates the output fields with commas and encloses strings in quotation marks.

Before you can use either the Write or Print statement to send output to a file, you have to open the file in one of the two output modes described previously.

The Write statement is used to set up data in a file that can later be read with the Input # statement. The Write statement automatically places quotation marks around string data and separates data items with commas:

```
Write #filenum, [outputlist]
```

filenum is the number of the file that has been opened to accept the output of the commands. outputlist is a list of variables or literal expressions that you want stored in a file. This can include a single data item or multiple data items. For multiple data items, the items must be separated by commas, spaces, or semicolons. When the Write statement reaches the end of the list, a carriage return character is written to the file. This causes the next Write statement to begin on a new line.

If desired, you can issue the Write statement without any expressions in the outputlist. This causes a blank line to be written to the file.

The Print statement allows you some control over where the information is printed on a line. The syntax of the Print statement is similar to that of the Write statement:

```
Print #filenum, printlist
```

How can I use this in the real world?

One of the most frequent uses for comma-delimited data is to transfer information between programs or to store a set of values for later use. For example, a manufacturing control program might print out a list of items used, along with the quantity consumed for a particular process, to a comma-delimited file. This file is then turned over to other groups in the company, such as marketing or finance, to load into their computer systems for further processing.

filenum is the number of a file open in either the output or append access mode.

printlist is the list of information that you want printed on a line. This information can include variables, literals, or function values. In addition, you can specify one of two special functions in the Print # statement. The first function is the Spc function. This allows you to insert a number of spaces between two other fields. The function requires an integer number as the argument. This function is shown in the following line of code:

```
Print #2, var1; Spc(5); var2
```

The other special function is the Tab function. This allows you to specify a particular column location for the next item to be printed. The Tab function is used as follows:

```
Print #2, var1; Tab(10); var2
```

In the Print statement, each of the data items needs to be separated by field separators—either a comma or a semicolon. If a semicolon separates the data items, the first character of the second item is printed in the next space following the last character of the first item. If a comma is used as the separator, the second item is printed at the beginning of the next **print zone**. A print zone is 14 characters long.

Catch the bug

This code attempts to print information to a file. What is wrong with the code?

```
Open "A:\TEST.INI" For Input As # 1
Do Until EOF(1)
    Line Input #1, fstlin
Loop
Print #1, "Defsize = 15"
Close #1
```

Answer: *Everything in the code works fine until the* Print # *statement is encountered. Since the file was not opened for output, an error occurs when you try to write to the file. The correct code is as follows:*

```
Open "A:\TEST.INI" For Append As # 1
Print #1, "Defsize = 15"
Close #1
```

How does random file access work?

Sequential files work well if you're going to read in an entire file or large blocks of data that are stored together. However, a sequential file is very inefficient for retrieving a single piece of information from a file or for retrieving multiple pieces of data from various locations in a file. For this task, a random access file is much more useful.

Random access files are handled a little differently in Visual Basic than are sequential files. With a sequential file, you only have to specify a variable to store the contents of the data items. You don't have to worry about how many characters are in the item. On the other hand, a random access file stores data in a series of equal length records. Therefore, the variable that you use to get the data must be the same length as the record being retrieved.

Defining the record variable

The first step in retrieving information from a random access file is defining the variable that contains the data. This is not done with the `Dim` statement as you define a typical variable. Instead, you use the `Type` statement to define all the information that is contained in the record. You must then define the variable as that `Type`.

To create a user-defined data type, you begin with the `Type` statement and end the declaration with the `End Type` statement:

```
Type typename
    elementname As vartype
    elementname As vartype
End Type
```

How can I use this in the real world?

Earlier, I spoke of using the `Line Input` statement to read the contents of an INI file. Many programs also create or write to an INI file to store configuration information. Configuration information can be used to allow a user to customize a program to his/her liking. You may even have a different configuration file for each user. If you need to write this type of information, you use the `Print` statement.

typename is the name that you want to give to this user-defined data type. This name follows the same naming conventions as a variable name.

Within the Type block, you define the elements of the record. Each of these is represented by an elementname. As with the typename, elementname follows the naming conventions for variables. vartype defines the type of data in the element. These are the standard variable types covered in Chapter 17. One caveat should be noted—Type declarations cannot include variable length strings. Therefore, any string in a Type statement must use the syntax that specifies the length of the string.

Once the user-defined type has been declared, variables may be set up as that data type using a Dim statement as shown:

```
Dim varname As typename
```

CAUTION **A dimension statement that references a user-defined type must** follow the Type declaration in code.

Catch the bug

The following code attempts to declare a variable as a user defined type. What is wrong with the code?

```
Dim newvar As Customer
Type Customer
    LastName As String * 30
    FirstName As String * 30
    PurchaseAmount As Single
End Type
```

Answer: *The Dim statement appears before the Type statement that declared the user-defined type. The correct code follows:*

```
Type Customer
    LastName As String * 30
    FirstName As String * 30
    PurchaseAmount As Single
End Type
Dim newvar As Customer
```

Opening a random access file

Gaining access to a random access file uses the Open statement just like opening any other file. However, the syntax of the command is just a little different.

To open a random access file, use the following syntax for Open:

```
Open filename For Random As #filenum Len = reclen
```

In this syntax, filename and filenum have the same meaning as in the syntax used for sequential files. The access mode for the file must be specified as random. The new clause that must be included is the Len clause. This clause specifies the size of a single record in the file. The size is determined by the value of the reclen argument. This argument is a numeric expression that must represent an integer greater than zero. Also, reclen must be equal to the length of the user-defined variable that is used to read information from the file.

TIP **Use the Len function to determine the length of the user-defined** variable. Then use this value as the reclen for a random access file.

How can I use this in the real world?

There are many applications that you use random access files for and one might be to store membership information. The following code defines a simple data type for a membership application:

```
Type member
    Lastname As String * 30
    Firstname As String * 30
    BirthDate As Date
    Income As Single
End Type
```

A membership application allows you to quickly access information about individual members, or prepare mailing lists for newsletters or special event notices. It can also help you keep track of club usage and whether dues have been paid.

Reading and writing information in a record

Once you have defined the data type that is used to access the information in a random access file, you can read or write data to the file. You start by looking at writing to the file because you need a method of getting information in before you can get information out.

To prepare to write data to a random access file, you must do three things:

1 Define the data type for the record.

2 Open the file as a random file.

3 Assign the information to be written to a variable.

You've already covered the first two steps in this chapter. Assigning information to a variable for a random access file is similar to assigning information to a normal variable in that you use an assignment statement. However, a single assignment statement doesn't suffice. You have to assign a value to each element of the variable that you want to write out. The elements are accessed using the **dot operator**.

The dot operator tells the program that the name following the dot is an element of the object before the dot. Information is assigned to an element of a user-defined type as follows:

```
varname.elementname = value
```

varname is the name of the variable that was declared as the user-defined type. This is the name that was in the Dim statement.

elementname is the name of the element from the Type statement. This name must be the same as the name used in the Type statement.

value is the information you want assigned to the element. This must be of the same variable type as was defined in the Type declaration for the element. value can represent a literal, variable, function, or equation.

After you have defined the variable type, opened the file, and assigned information to the variable, you are ready to write information to the file. To write information to a random access file, you use the Put statement.

Close it when you're finished

When you have finished working with a file, you need to close it. This allows the program to clear any information out of the data buffers and release the file handle that was used. Closing a file is accomplished using the `Close` statement.

File management

In addition to reading and writing data from files, Visual Basic includes commands that allow you to perform file management from within your program. File management commands include the following tasks:

- Renaming a file
- Copying a file

Speaking of *Put*

The Put statement not only tells the program what file to write to and what information to write but also defines the location in the file where the information is to be written:

```
Put #filenum, recnum, varname
```

filenum is the file number that was defined for the file with the Open statement. varname is the variable that contains the information to be written to the file.

recnum specifies the record number where the information is to be written. This number must be an integer greater than 0. This recnum is typically determined by your program. Usually in writing a program to use a random access file, you have some type of sorted list that contains a key value and a record number. You can then reference the list to determine the record number of the information.

To read information from a random access file uses almost the same syntax as writing the information. The information can be the data you just wrote to the file, or any other data the file contains:

```
Get #filenum, recnum, varname.
```

- Deleting a file

The Name statement is used to rename a file, such as the following:

```
Name oldfilename As newfilename
```

oldfilename and newfilename are string expressions that specify the current name of the file and the desired name of the file, respectively. These expressions can be any valid filenames and can include the drive and folder designations.

To copy a file, use the FileCopy statement as follows:

```
FileCopy sourcefile, targetfile
```

sourcefile and targetfile are string expressions containing valid filenames.

To delete a file, use the Kill statement.

```
Kill filename
```

filename is a string expression containing the name of the file to be deleted.

The following code uses the Kill and FileCopy commands to make a daily backup of a database file.

```
Kill "Daily.MDB"
FileCopy "Clients.MDB", "Daily.MDB"
```

Speaking of *Close*

To close a file, simply issue the following command:

```
Close [filelist]
```

filelist is a list of the file numbers to be closed. The file numbers are the ones you defined for the files with the Open statement. If you close more than one file, the numbers must be separated by commas. If you omit the optional filelist, all open files are closed.

Summary

Visual Basic provides you with a number of tools to read, write, and manage files. These commands allow you to store data from your program, pass data back and forth between programs, and even control the configuration of your program.

Review questions

1 What type of file stores data in ASCII text?

2 What access mode is used to write data to a file without deleting the current contents?

3 What input statement is used to handle comma-delimited data? What output statement?

4 What is a user-defined data type used for?

5 How do you close all the open files in a program?

Exercises

1 Write a short program to display the contents of an INI file in a text box.

2 Write a program to create an INI file.

3 Write a program to read and write member information from a random access file.

28

Creating a Database

- ● In this chapter:

  - ● What is a database?

  - ● Databases that Visual Basic can access

  - ● Organizing your data

  - ● How do I create a database with Visual Basic?

Databases allow you to organize your data and view it in different ways; most Visual Basic programmers use it to create or manage databases . . . . ➤

Before we talk much about how to organize and build a database, it is probably a good idea to tell you what one is. In the simplest terms, a database is a collection of information, usually organized in a particular order. An example of a database that is familiar to most of us is a Rolodex. A Rolodex is a collection of names, addresses, and phone numbers, typically arranged in alphabetical order.

A Rolodex is a very useful tool for organizing information, but it is limited in its usefulness. Suppose, for example, that you only want to send a business flyer to the people in your city, not your worldwide contacts. With the Rolodex, you would have to look at each card and determine whether the person was local. This would be a very time consuming process. Also, after you found all the names, someone would have to type or write all the addresses.

What is a computer database?

Even storing your data on a computer does not necessarily give you all the advantages of using a database. For example, the Cardfile application in Windows allows you to search for a particular entry but does not allow you to rearrange the entire list (see fig. 28.1).

Fig. 28.1
The Cardfile application is an example of a simple database.

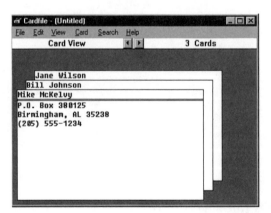

Visual Basic allows you to store information in a **Relational Database Management System (RDBMS)**. An RDBMS allows the computer to store information in a way that is easily retrieved and, more importantly, allows the users to look at multiple views of the data. For example, an address list could be sorted in alphabetical order by company or by person. The list could also be arranged by address or phone number, or if the information was available, by a person's age or special interests. The RDBMS even allows you to work with small pieces of the database to make your processing faster and more efficient.

In this chapter and the three that follow, I will be discussing the creation and use of databases in Visual Basic. These chapters, will be making use of a number of terms that refer to different pieces of a database. These terms are summarized in table 28.1.

Table 28.1   The Elements of a Database Management System

Element	Description
Database	A group of data tables that contain related information. Note that a database may consist of only a single table.
Table	A group of data records each containing the same type of information. In the example of the Rolodex, the entire Rolodex would be a data table.
Record	A single entry in a table consisting of a number of data fields. For a Rolodex, this would be one of the cards.
Field	A specific item of data contained in a record. In the Rolodex, fields would be last name, first name, address, and phone number.
Index	A special type of table which contains the values of a key field(s) (defined by the user) and pointers to the location of the actual record. These values and pointers are stored in a specific order (again defined by the user) and may be used to present the data in the database in that order. For the Rolodex example, one index may be used to sort the information by last name and first name, while another index may be used to sort the information by street address. If you so desired, you could also create an index to sort the information by phone number.
Query	A SQL command designed to retrieve a certain group of records from one or more tables, or to perform an operation on a table.
Filter	A filter is not actually a part of the database, but it is used in conjunction with indexes and sort orders to determine what data is displayed or processed. A filter is a condition imposed on the data, such as "Last name starts with 'M'."
View	A view of the data consists of the number of records seen (or processed), and the order in which they are displayed (or processed). A view is typically controlled by filters and indexes. Examples of a view of the Rolodex data are: 1) an alphabetical listing of all people who live on Main Street, 2) the first ten people whose last names start with 'S'.

To help illustrate the concepts of database design, creation, and management, we will create a simple inventory database. This database will track information about products in a warehouse, their prices, the current quantity on hand, and information about the suppliers of items.

How does Visual Basic work with databases?

Visual Basic uses the Microsoft Jet database engine to connect to databases and access the information in them. The Jet engine is the same database engine used by Microsoft Access. The Jet engine allows the user to work with data in the native Jet databases (files with the MDB extension) as well as databases from other systems such as dBase, FoxPro, Paradox, BTrieve, and SQL Server. You can even access Excel and text file data with the Jet engine.

Database access from Visual Basic is accomplished through the use of the data control and bound controls (covered in Chapter 29) or the data access objects. The Jet engine, Data control, and bound controls make it easy to handle data entry and retrieval. In addition, Visual Basic provides two add-ins, the Data Manager and the Form Designer, that make it easy to create databases and create data access forms.

Q&A **Is the Jet engine the only way I can work with databases in Visual Basic?**

No. In addition to the Jet engine, you can use Open Database Connectivity (ODBC) drivers to access other databases. There is also a variety of third-party database engines that can be used with Visual Basic.

How can I use this in the real world?

One frequent use of a database is in inventory control. The database would house information about the items carried by a store. This information could include a description of the item, its wholesale and retail prices, the quantity of the item on hand, and the supplier of the item. The database could also record transactions such as receipt of items from the supplier and sales of items to customers to maintain the inventory information on a real-time basis.

What kind of data can I store?

To refresh your memory on variable types, refer back to Chapter 17, "Adding Variables to Your Programs."

The data types supported in a database depend upon the database engine and the file format. For this book, I will be discussing only the Jet engine and the native Jet (MDB) databases. The data types supported by Jet databases are summarized in table 28.2. You will notice that many of these data types are the same as the variable types used by Visual Basic.

Table 28.2   Data Types Available with the Jet Engine

Name	Information stored	Size or range
Text	Character strings	255 characters max
Memo	Long character strings	Up to 1.2 GB
Byte	Integer Numeric data	0 to 255
Integer	Integer Numeric data	-32,768 to 32,767
Long	Integer Numeric data	-2,147,483,648 to 2,147,483,647
Counter	Long integer, automatically incremented	
Single	Real numeric data	-3.4×10^{38} to 3.4×10^{38}
Double	Real numeric data	-1.8×10^{308} to 1.8×10^{308}
Yes/No	Logical/Boolean	
Date	Date values	
Binary	Binary data	Up to 1.2 GB
OLE	OLE objects	Up to 1.2 GB

What else can a Jet database do?

One of the key functions of a database application is to assure, as much as possible, the accuracy of the data in the database. Data accuracy refers not only to making sure that the individual data items are correct, but also to making sure that relationships between data tables are properly maintained. These two functions are referred to, respectively, as data validation and data integrity. These functions can be handled by the database engine, by your application, or by a combination of the two.

The most effective way to handle validation and integrity is through the database engine itself. If the information is stored in the database, the rules are enforced any time any application accesses the database. For the Jet database engine, this means that any Visual Basic application will follow the rules, as well as any Access application or database access from Excel or other products.

The Jet databases and the Jet engine support two types of data integrity monitoring and two forms of data validation. These features are defined as follows:

- Primary key integrity, which ensures that each record in a table is uniquely identified by a field or combination of fields.

- Referential integrity, which ensures that the relationships between tables are properly maintained.

- Field level validation, which ensures that the information in a field is within a certain range of values. This is handled using simple expressions such as comparing the field contents to a constant.

- Record level validation, which is responsible for checking the information in a field against data in other fields of the record, or checking the results of a combination of fields against a criterion.

You can implement each of these functions when you initially set up your database. The validation and integrity rules then are stored as part of the database and applied whenever the database is accessed, whether by your program or by another program.

Planning is required

In order to create a successful database application, you need to begin with a plan. For database applications, you not only have to plan the program tasks, but you also need to plan how the data will be organized and how various pieces of data will relate to each other.

Creating a good database design involves seven key activities:

- Modeling the application

- Determining the data required for the application

- Organizing the data into tables

- Establishing the relationships between tables

- Setting index and validation requirements for the data

- Creating and storing any necessary queries for the application

- Reviewing the design

What data do I need?

When you are developing an application for your own use, it is fairly easy to determine what data you need. You just sit down and think about the information that you want to be able to get out of the database. This is the same information that will have to be put in and stored at some point. For instance, in the example of the Rolodex, do you want to keep just the work phone of each person or do you also need the home phone as well? Do you also want to keep up with the name of a person's spouse and/or children? Knowing what information you need allows you to determine how the information should be stored in the database.

Organizing the data into tables

After determining what data is needed in the database, the data must be organized into tables. Most databases have multiple tables in them, though a database can contain only a single table. The objective of assigning data to tables is to store the information as efficiently as possible with as little wasted space as possible.

Tables as topics

A **table** is a collection of information related to a particular topic. By thinking of a key topic for the table, you can determine if a particular piece of data fits into the table. For example, if you are a store owner and you want to track information about both your customers and your employees, you might be tempted to put both in the same table because both groups refer to people.

While both groups require information about a person's name and address, and possibly phone number, the employee group also requires information about the person's social security number, job category, payroll, and tax status. If you were to create just one table, many of the entries would be blank for your customers. You would also have to add a **field** to distinguish between a customer and an employee.

Plain English, please!

A **field** is the smallest unit of information in a data record. Using a phone book as an example, each line (or record) could contain several fields of data such as a person's last name, first name, address, and phone number. **99**

Clearly, this technique would result in a lot of wasted space. It could result in slower processing of employee transactions or customer transactions because the program would have to skip a number of records in the table. Figure 28.2 shows the table with the two groups combined. Figure 28.3 then shows the reduction in the number of fields in a customer table.

Fig. 28.2

Combining the Employee and Customer tables creates wasted space.

lname	fname	address	city	state	zip	SocSec	JobCat	Paycode
Jones	John	45 W 3rd	Metropolis	AL	33332			
Adams	Bill	23 E 1st	Metropolis	AL	33332			
deLugas	Gail	15 Airport	Weston	AL	33343			
Smith	Arnie	12 Airport	Weston	AL	33343			
Barnes	Josh	35 Easter	Shelby	AL	35555			
Davis	Mike	365 Berkly	Shelby	AL	35554			
Johnson	Michele	132 Clark	Pelham	AL	35555	123456789	Clerk	3

Record: 7 of 7

Wasted space

Fig. 28.3

Using a separate Customer table with only required fields is more efficient.

lname	fname	address	city	state	zip
Jones	John	45 W 3rd	Metropolis	AL	33332
Adams	Bill	23 E 1st	Metropolis	AL	33332
deLugas	Gail	15 Airport	Weston	AL	33343
Smith	Arnie	12 Airport	Weston	AL	33343
Barnes	Josh	35 Easter	Shelby	AL	35555
Davis	Mike	365 Berkly	Shelby	AL	35554

Record: 1 of 6

By thinking of the topic that a table relates to, it is easier to determine if a particular piece of information belongs in the table or not. If it results in wasted space for many records, it belongs in a different table.

Data normalization

Data normalization is the process of eliminating redundant data within the database. Taking data normalization to its fullest extent results in each piece of information in a database appearing only once.

Consider an inventory control system. Such a system needs to track information about the items you keep in inventory, inventory transactions, and vendor information for each item. If you listed all the information about each item, including the information about the vendor, in a single table, the result would be a large table with a lot of duplicate information. This table might look like the one in figure 28.4.

Fig. 28.4

Non-normalized data produces a large, inefficient data table.

	ItemDesc	ItemCost	Quantity	Name	Address	City	
▶	Cable Fasteners	1.25	500	Acme Steel Fasteners	Route 1	Santa Fe	NM
	Lag Bolts	0.75	1000	Acme Steel Fasteners	Route 1	Santa Fe	NM
	#8 Wood Screws	0.05	5000	Acme Steel Fasteners	Route 1	Santa Fe	NM
	White Paint Base	4	100	Big Drip Paint Suppliers	25 West 52nd	Painted Desert	AZ
	Caulk	2.25	50	Big Drip Paint Suppliers	25 West 52nd	Painted Desert	AZ
	2 x 4	1.35	100	Termite Proof	Main	Pine Bark	AL
	4 x 4	2.15	75	Termite Proof	Main	Pine Bark	AL
	2 x 6	2.05	75	Termite Proof	Main	Pine Bark	AL
*							

Duplicated data in several records ──────

As you can see, much of the data in the table is repeated over and over. This introduces two problems. The first problem is wasted space because you have repeated information such as the vendor name, address, and phone number several times over. The second problem is one of data accuracy or currency. If, for example, one of the vendors changed phone numbers, you would have to change it for all of the records that apply to that vendor, and there is always the possibility that you could miss one of the entries.

A better solution for handling the data is to put the vendor information in one table, and the item information in another table. You would assign each vendor a unique ID, and just include that ID in the item table to identify the vendor. This would yield two tables with a data structure as shown in figure 28.5.

Fig. 28.5

Normalized vendor and item tables eliminate data redundancy.

Items : Table

	Itemno	ItemDesc	ItemCost	Quantity
▶	1	Cable Fasteners	1.25	500
	2	Lag Bolts	0.75	1000
	3	#8 Wood Screws	0.05	5000
	4	White Paint Base	4	100
	5	Caulk	2.25	50
	6	2 x 4	1.35	100
	7	4 x 4	2.15	75
	8	2 x 6	2.05	75
*	:oNumber)		0	0

Record: |◄| ◄ | 1 | ► | ►I | ►* | of 8

Vendors : Table

	Name	Address	City	State
▶	Acme Steel Fastener	Route 1	Santa Fe	NM
	Big Drip Paint Suppli	25 West 52nd	Painted Desert	AZ
	Termite Proof	Main	Pine Bark	AL

Record: |◄| ◄ | 1 | ► | ►I | ►* | of 3

With this type of arrangement, the vendor information only appears in one place. Now, if a vendor changes phone numbers, you only have to change one record.

When information is moved out of one table and into another, you must have a way of keeping track of the relationships between the tables. This is done through the use of data keys. This topic will be discussed later in this chapter.

Rules for defining tables

While there are no absolute rules for defining what data goes into which tables, there are some general guidelines to follow for efficient database design:

- Determine a topic for each table, and make sure that all data in the table relates to the topic.

- If a number of the records in a table have fields that are intentionally left blank, the table should be split into two similar tables. (Refer to the earlier example of the employee and customer tables in the "Tables as topics" section.)

- If information is repeated in a number of records, that information should be moved to another table, and a relationship between the tables should be set.

- Repeating fields indicate the need for a child table. For example, if you have Item1, Item2, Item3, and so on in a table, you should move the items to a child table related back to the parent.

- Use lookup tables to reduce data volume and increase the accuracy of data entry.

- Do not store information in a table if it can be calculated from data in other tables.

How can I use this in the real world?

Data normalization is often used in programs that store membership information on families and individuals. The main table would keep the information that is common to all family members, such as their last name, address, home phone, and type of membership. A second, related table would keep all the information that is specific to an individual, such as the person's first name, gender, birthdate, and the last time he or she used the facility.

Establishing the relationships between tables

As stated previously, when data is normalized and information is moved from one table to another, a method must exist to relate the two tables. The method of relating tables is through the use of data keys. This section discusses the two types of table relationships and how the data keys are established.

Data keys are usually referred to as either primary keys or foreign keys. A primary key is the one that uniquely identifies a record in a table. In the case of the inventory tables shown earlier, the vendor ID in the Vendor table is the primary key. A foreign key is one used to relate a record back to a primary key in another table. Again, in the inventory, the vendor key in the Items table is a foreign key, pointing to a specific record in the Vendor table.

Key fields

Tables are related to each other through key fields. A **key field** is one that uniquely identifies a record. A key field may be one that has meaningful data in it, or it may be a created field that serves the sole purpose of providing a unique identifier for the record. The main criteria for the key field is that it must be unique. Figure 28.6 shows the vendor table with a key field added to provide a unique ID for each record.

Fig. 28.6
Table showing added key field to assure unique record IDs.

VndrCode	Name	Address	City	State
1	Acme Steel Fastener	Route 1	Santa Fe	NM
2	Big Drip Paint Suppli	25 West 52nd	Painted Desert	AZ
3	Termite Proof	Main	Pine Bark	AL

The key field is present in both databases of the relationship. For your inventory application, you would assign a unique identifier to each vendor record. You would then include that same identifier in each of the item records for the items supplied by that vendor.

If you are developing an employee database, it would be possible to have several people with the same name. One possible unique identifier is the social security number. However, because this nine digit number must also be stored in every related record, it might be desirable to create a unique employee ID that is smaller. If you knew that there would never be more than 9,999 employees, a four-digit ID number could be used, saving you five digits in every related record. Depending on the number of related records, the space savings could be significant.

One way to assure unique IDs is to use a counter field for the primary key. A counter field is an integer number field that is automatically incremented by the database engine when a new record is added. This takes the responsibility of creating unique keys off the user and places it on the database engine. The only drawback in using a counter field is that the ID has no intrinsic meaning to the user.

One-to-many relationships

A one-to-many relationship occurs when a record in one table is related to one or more records in the second table, but each record in the second table is related to only one record in the first table. One-to-many relationships comprise the majority of the table relations in a database system.

In the inventory control application, a vendor may supply many items, but each item has only one vendor (see fig. 28.7).

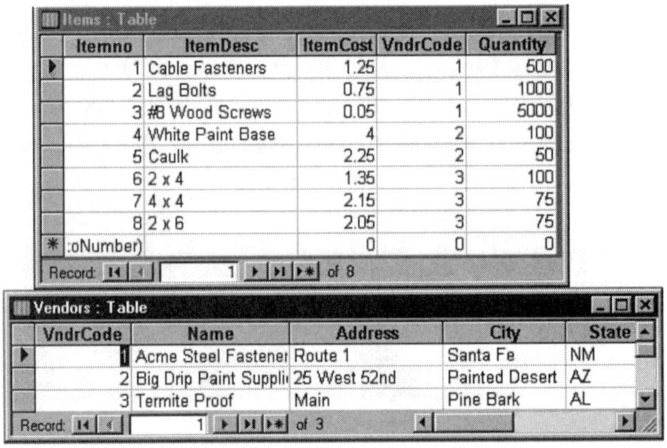

Fig. 28.7
A one-to-many relationship between tables shows the use of key fields.

Items : Table

	Itemno	ItemDesc	ItemCost	VndrCode	Quantity
▶	1	Cable Fasteners	1.25	1	500
	2	Lag Bolts	0.75	1	1000
	3	#8 Wood Screws	0.05	1	5000
	4	White Paint Base	4	2	100
	5	Caulk	2.25	2	50
	6	2 x 4	1.35	3	100
	7	4 x 4	2.15	3	75
	8	2 x 6	2.05	3	75
*	:oNumber)		0	0	0

Record: ◄◄ ◄ 1 ► ►◄ ►* of 8

Vendors : Table

	VndrCode	Name	Address	City	State
▶	1	Acme Steel Fastener	Route 1	Santa Fe	NM
	2	Big Drip Paint Suppli	25 West 52nd	Painted Desert	AZ
	3	Termite Proof	Main	Pine Bark	AL

Record: ◄◄ ◄ 1 ► ►◄ ►* of 3

Many-to-many relationships

Many-to-many relationships occur when each record from the first table can be related to multiple records in the second table, and vice versa. When this occurs, an intermediate table is usually introduced which provides a one-to-many relationship with each of the other two tables. Handling many-to-many relationships is an advanced database concept outside the scope of this book.

Tables for the inventory application

The inventory application mentioned earlier would require three tables. The first table would contain information about the date an item was used, the item number, and the quantity used. The second table would contain the item number, item description, quantity on hand, and the vendor ID of the item's supplier. The third table would contain the supplier information including the vendor ID, the vendor name, vendor address, and contact person.

The usage table (containing the quantities consumed) would be related to the item inventory table by the item ID. The item inventory table would then be related to the vendor table by the vendor ID.

Time to build your own database

Now that you have all the data defined for your database and have the data organized into tables, it is time to actually build the database. To build a Jet database, you have three choices of methods. They are as follows:

- Using the Data Manager application provided with Visual Basic

- Using the data access objects with a program to create the database

- Using Microsoft Access

Using the Data Manager application

If you do not have a copy of Microsoft Access, the Data Manager application that comes with Visual Basic provides the easiest way for a Visual Basic developer to create a Jet database. The Data Manager provides you with an interactive way of creating and modifying Jet databases. You start the Data Manager by choosing <u>D</u>ata Manager from the <u>A</u>dd-Ins menu in Visual Basic.

 TIP **There are several versions of the Jet engine. The Data Manager** will only create databases for version 3.0 of the Jet engine. If you need to create databases that are compatible with Access 2.0 or older versions of the Jet engine, you will need to use one of the other creation methods. The Data Manager is, however, capable of editing databases from older versions of the Jet engine.

After the application is active, select the <u>N</u>ew Database option under the <u>F</u>ile menu to create a new Access database. You will be presented with a file dialog box, as shown in figure 28.8, so that you can name your database and select the location for it. Enter a valid filename and click Save to enter the design mode shown in figure 28.9.

Fig. 28.8
The file dialog box
allows you to specify
the name of your new
database.

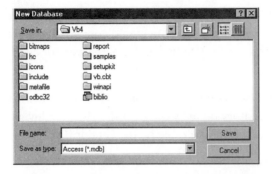

Fig. 28.9
The Data Manager
design window
provides access to the
design functions for
tables, fields, indexes,
and relations.

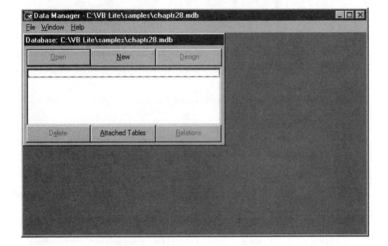

Adding a new table

The database design window gives you the choice of creating a new table,
opening an existing table to "browse" the data, changing the design of a
table, deleting a table, attaching an external table, or creating table relations.
To create a new table, click New. You will be presented with the Add Table
design area (see fig. 28.10).

Fig. 28.10
The Add Table design
window allows you to
specify a name for and
add fields to a new
table.

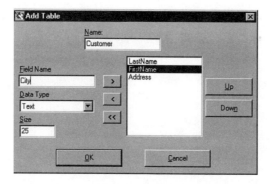

This design window allows you to specify the table name, and enter the
names, types, and sizes of each field in the table. To add a field to the table,
follow these steps:

1 Enter the name of the field.

2 Select the field type from the Data Type list.

3 Enter the size of the field (if necessary).

4 Click the > button to add the field to the table.

If you want to remove a field from the list, you can highlight the field then
click the < button. Clicking the << button removes all fields from the list.
When you are satisfied with the fields in the table, click OK to create the
table.

Making changes to the fields in your table

After you have created a new table, you will be returned to the main design
window. If you want to set any optional properties for the fields in your
table, you will need to highlight the table name and click Design to enter the
Table Editor window. This design window is shown in figure 28.11. This
window allows you to add new fields, edit existing fields, delete fields, add/
delete indexes, and process key fields.

Fig. 28.11

You can add, edit, and delete fields, or add indexes from the table design window.

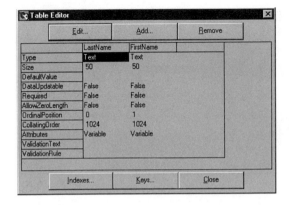

To add a new field, click Add. You will be presented with the Add Field dialog box shown in figure 28.12. This screen allows you to enter the field name, type, and size (if necessary), and set optional properties such as validation rules, default values, and required entry flag. When you have finished entering the data for the field, click OK to add the field to the table.

Fig. 28.12

You can specify the name and properties of a field using the field dialog.

To edit a field, highlight the field you want to change, then choose Edit. (These actions are performed in the Table Editor window.) You will then be presented with the Edit Field dialog box. This dialog box is exactly like the Add Field dialog box in figure 28.12 except for the dialog title. In the Edit Field dialog box, you can make changes to the field and then click OK to save the changes.

CAUTION **If you change the properties of a field that contains data, the data** in that field will be lost. The Data Manager does not preserve the data.

To delete a field from a table, highlight the field in the Table Editor window, then click Remove. This will delete the field and all of its associated data.

CAUTION You will not be asked to confirm any deletions, so be very careful when removing fields.

TIP Visual Basic will not allow you to edit or delete any field that is part of an index expression or a relation. If it is necessary to delete such a field, you must delete the index or relation containing the field, and then make the changes to the field.

Adding an index to the table

To work with the indexes for a table, click Indexes in the Table Editor and the Indexes dialog box appears (see fig. 28.13).

Fig. 28.13
You can add, edit, or delete indexes for a table from the index editor.

To add a new index, click Add. You are presented with the dialog box shown in figure 28.14. In this dialog box, you should first enter an index name. Next, select the fields to be included in the index by highlighting the field choice in the Fields in table list, then choosing either the Add(ASC) or Add(DEC) button (depending on whether you want an ascending or descending sequence) to add the field to the Fields in index list. To remove a field from the Fields in index list, highlight it, and then click Remove.

After you have defined the fields for the index, you may require the index to be unique or to be a primary index by choosing the appropriate checkbox in the window. When the index is completed to your liking, save it by clicking OK. The index you have just created will be added to the index list on the Index Editor window. To delete an index, simply highlight it in the index editor window and click Remove.

When you have finished with all of your indexes, click Close in the index editor window to return to the table design window.

Fig. 28.14
The Add Index panel
provides a visual means
of creating the indexes
for a table.

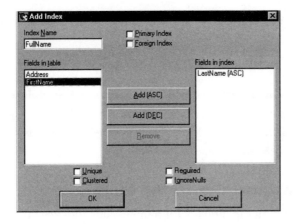

Returning to the main window

When you have finished editing a table, you can return to the Data Manager
main window by clicking Close in the Table Editor.

Creating relationships

You can also establish the relationship between two tables with the Data
Manager. To set a relationship, choose Relations from the main design
window; the Relationships window appears (see fig. 28.15). In this window,
you can choose the Primary Table and Related Table from drop-down lists.
After you have chosen the Primary Table, you will see a list of available
primary fields in the fields text block. Choose one of the fields in this block
as the primary relation key, then choose the matching field for the Related
Table from the drop-down list.

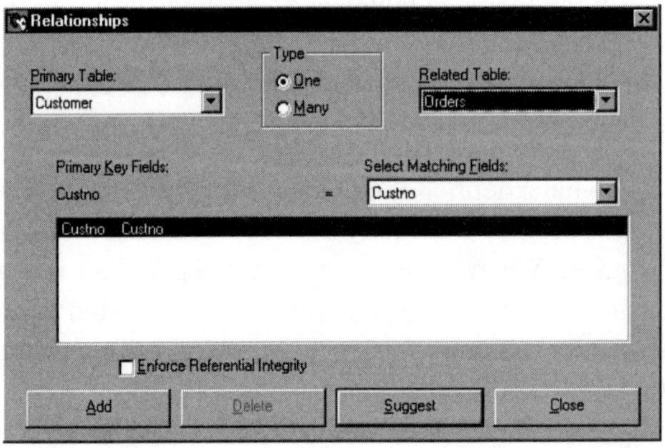

Fig. 28.15
You can create or
delete relations
between tables in the
Relationships window.

The Relationships window also allows you to choose the type of relation (one-to-one or one-to-many), and whether or not to enforce referential integrity. When you have entered all the information for the relation, you can add it to the database by choosing <u>A</u>dd. Choosing <u>C</u>lose will return you to the Database Design window.

Editing an existing database

As stated previously, the Data Manager is capable of editing any Jet database (3.0 or earlier), as well as some other databases. To edit an existing database, simply choose the <u>O</u>pen Database option from the <u>F</u>ile menu. This presents an open file dialog from which you can choose the file to edit. After you have selected the file, it is loaded, and you can edit tables and relations just as you did for a new database.

Returning to the Visual Basic design screen

Closing the Data Manager window or choosing Exit from the File menu takes you back to the Visual Basic main design screen. To manipulate databases without having to start Visual Basic every time, I have found it useful to make the Data Manager application a program item in my Visual Basic group.

Using the Data Access Objects

Visual Basic also allows you to create databases and tables using program commands. While we will not cover these in detail, I wanted to show how they can be used to create a Jet database for an earlier version of the Jet engine. The following code creates the database, then closes the file. The code does not add any fields or tables to the database. However, after the database is created, you can edit it with the Data Manager, and the information will still be readable by older versions of the Jet engine:

```
Dim OldWs As Workspace, NewDb As Database
Set OldWs = DBEngine.Workspaces(0)
Set NewDb = OldWs.CreateDatabase("A:\INVENTRY.MDB",
dbLangGeneral, dbVersion20)
NewDb.Close
```

The first line of the code defines the variables OldWs and NewDb as workspace and database objects, respectively. These objects are two of the Data Access Objects (DAOs) that can be used by Visual Basic. The second line tells the database engine to open a workspace for use by the program and assign it to the OldWs object.

The third line actually creates the database. The `CreateDatabase` method is used to create a new database file. The filename is specified as the first argument inside the parentheses. This can be any valid filename with an MDB extension. The constant `dbLangGeneral` defines the language to use in creating the database. This constant specifies the English language. Finally, the constant `dbVersion20` tells the program that the database should be created as a Jet 2.0 database. If this constant were omitted, the database would be created as a Jet 3.0 database.

The fourth line of the code closes the database file.

Q&A **Is Visual Basic the only way to use the databases I create?**

No. Visual Basic shares the Jet engine with Microsoft Access, allowing you to use that product to work with your database as well. Also, many other database and spreadsheet programs allow you to import the data from an Access database.

Summary

Database applications require even more thought than other applications. This is because you are not only defining the tasks to be performed by the program but trying to determine the most efficient way to store the data. Careful planning will lead you to successful programs.

Review questions

1 What does Visual Basic use to access databases?

2 What is a table?

3 Why do you need to normalize data?

4 What is the easiest method to create a database from Visual Basic?

5 Which method should you use to create a database that needs to be shared with older applications?

Exercises

1 Using the Data Manager, create the tables for the inventory application.

2 Design and build a table for your Rolodex.

29

Accessing Databases

● **In this chapter:**

● **Is there an easy way to work with the data in a database?**

● **The types of databases that Visual Basic can access**

● **Am I limited to working with one table at a time?**

● **Display and edit the information in a database**

Accessing databases has always been tedious. With Visual Basic's Data control, much of the grunt work of accessing databases has been eliminated. . . . .

It has been said that as many as 75% of all programs written today access databases in one form or another. Databases are everywhere. Large corporations use them to track employees, customers, product inventory, and other information. Your doctor may use a database to keep up with information about you and other patients. That information can include your insurance coverage and past medical history as well as your name and address. Even your local pizza restaurant may have a database program for processing orders and keeping up with sales.

What is needed to access a database?

For more information on creating new databases, see Chapter 28, "Creating a Database."

With all these databases out there, you will probably need to access the information in several of them as you write various programs. As you work with databases even more, you will probably even need to design and build new databases.

Whether you create your own database or tap into one that already exists, you will need tools to open the database files and display the information contained in the fields. You will probably also want to be able to modify the data and add new records. Visual Basic provides you with a variety of tools to make programming database applications as easy as possible.

Making it easy

The ease of programming database applications comes through the use of the Data control and Visual Basic's bound controls. The Data control gives you a means to quickly and easily open a database file, access information in one or more of its tables, and move from record to record in the table without having to program any of these functions. Using the Data control, you only have to set its properties to gain access to any of a number of database types. (These types will be discussed in a later section.) The bound controls allow you to easily connect a text box or other control to a particular field in a database.

 TIP In addition to the Data control, Visual Basic provides Data Access Objects (DAOs). These objects are used in program code to provide you with the maximum possible flexibility in accessing and manipulating data in a database. DAOs are briefly discussed in Chapter 28, "Creating a Database."

Figure 29.1 shows a form with the Data control and several bound controls on it. This form displays the book title information in the `BIBLIO.MDB` database. As you can see, the Data control consists of a caption (usually describing the data to which it is connected) and four buttons. These buttons look similar to the controls on your VCR.

Fig. 29.1

The Data control provides easy access to information in databases.

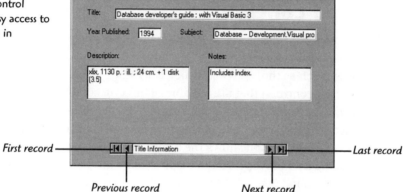

First record — Previous record — Next record — Last record

The buttons on the Data control allow the user to move between records in the **recordset**. The far left button will move the record **pointer** to the first record. The far right button will move the pointer to the last record. The near left button moves to the record immediately prior to the current one, and the near right button moves to the record immediately following the current one. As the user clicks these buttons, the bound controls on the form are updated to reflect the contents of the "new" record.

❝❝ Plain English, please!

A **recordset** is a collection of data records from one or more tables in a database (or from multiple databases). If you think of a phone book, the recordset could be the entire book, listing the names, addresses, and phone numbers of everyone in your city. A recordset could also be a subset of the entire book, such as a neighborhood phone book.

A **pointer** is an internal variable that tells Visual Basic where the information in a database is located. For example, if you look up a business in the Yellow Pages, the business is not physically located in the book. The only thing in the book is information about where to find the business (its address and phone number). The Yellow Pages listing is therefore a pointer to the business. Moving to another record in a database in essence changes the pointer to the next line of the book.

You could also think of pointers like the index at the back of this book. The index entries tell you where to find the information you need. **99**

Bound controls

For more information on third-party controls, see Chapter 37, "The Search for More Help Continues."

When previously discussing the Data control, I also mentioned bound controls. The bound controls are a group of the standard Visual Basic controls (such as the TextBox, Label, CheckBox, PictureBox, ListBox, and ComboBox controls) that are capable of directly accessing information in a database. The term "bound" comes from the fact that the controls are assigned to a particular field of the recordset in a particular Data control. The bound control then shows the information in that field, and only that field, as the user moves through records using the Data control. There are a number of bound controls that come with Visual Basic. Many of these will be discussed in the section, "Setting up the bound controls." In addition, many third-party controls may also be bound to the Data control.

How do I use the Data control?

Using the Data control is basically the same as using any other control in Visual Basic. You select the control from the toolbox and draw it on your form in the size and shape you want. You then need to set the properties of the control to make it access the desired database information. As with other controls, you can set the properties of the Data control either during the design mode or at runtime. Also, remember to set the Name property to a unique name, preferably one that indicates something about the data you are accessing. And you should set the Caption property to a value that indicates to the user the contents of the data. Figure 29.2 shows a Data control drawn on a form.

Fig. 29.2
The Data control can connect to many types of databases.

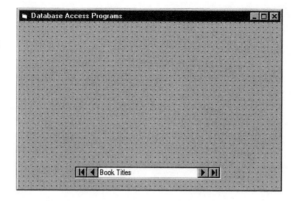

A simple database setup

After you have drawn a Data control on your form and set the Name and Caption properties, you are ready to start actually setting it up for use with a database. There are seven properties that determine what information is accessed by the Data control and how it is accessed. However, for a simple database setup, you only need to worry about setting two properties of the Data control—the DatabaseName property and RecordSource property. Using just these two properties, you can access the information in any Access (Jet) database. As previously stated, you can set the properties at either designtime or runtime.

Using the Properties dialog box

To set the properties while you are in the design mode, you use the Properties dialog. To set the DatabaseName property, select it from the dialog. When you select the property, an ellipsis button appears at the right edge of the property field as shown in figure 29.3. After you have selected the DatabaseName property, you can either enter the name of a database file or click the ellipsis button to be presented with the DatabaseName dialog shown in figure 29.4.

Fig. 29.3
Database names should include the full path name of the file.

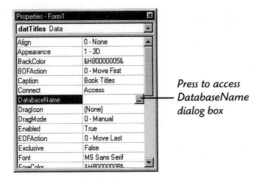

Press to access DatabaseName dialog box

Fig. 29.4
The DatabaseName dialog box lets you choose a database with which to work.

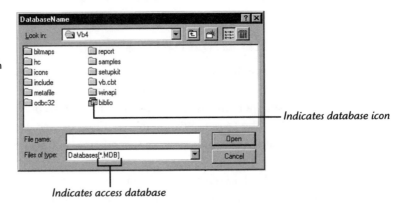

Indicates database icon

Indicates access database

Notice that the dialog presents you with a list of files using the MDB extension. This is the default extension of the Access databases. (Access databases are the native databases for Visual Basic.) When you select a file from the dialog, the name appears in the DatabaseName property field in the Properties dialog. As shown in figure 29.3, note that the name contains the complete path to the file, not just the name of the file itself.

CAUTION If you are distributing applications to others, remember that their directory structure may not be the same as yours. Therefore, the path that is shown in the DatabaseName field may be invalid.

TIP If you store your program and your database file in the same directory, you can eliminate the path information in the DatabaseName property. This will make it easier to distribute your application without having to worry about directory structures.

*For more informa-
tion on SQL state-
ments, see Chapter
31, "Working with
More Than One
Table: Using SQL
and the Data
Control."*

After you have set the `DatabaseName` property, you have created a link to a
database on your computer. However, this is only half of the link required to
get to the information in the database. You must also tell the Data control
which table in the database you want to use. This is accomplished using the
`RecordSource` property. The `RecordSource` property can be used to access
information from a single table just by entering the table name. You can also
use it to access data from multiple tables using Structured Query Language
(SQL) statements.

As with the `DatabaseName` property, you set the `RecordSource` property by
selecting it from the Properties dialog and entering a value for it. If you are
working with a single table, you can either enter the name yourself, or select
it from a list by clicking the arrow button to the right of the field. Clicking
the button presents you with a list of all tables and **queries** in the database
defined by the `DatabaseName` property (see fig. 29.5).

Fig. 29.5
You can select a table
for the *RecordSource*
property from a list of
tables in the database.

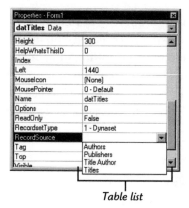

Table list

66 *Plain English, please!*

A **query** is a question that you ask your database. The answer to a query is
a recordset. Internally, a query is a predefined SQL statement that is stored
in the database. A query gives you easy access to related data in multiple
tables. 99

After you have selected or entered the value for the `RecordSource` property,
you are connected to the data in the database. At this point, you can start
adding controls to your form to allow you to display and edit the information. These bound controls are discussed in the section, "Setting up the
bound controls."

Setting the properties at runtime

As stated earlier, you can also set the properties of the Data control at runtime. This is done using assignment statements like you would use for the properties of other controls. The following statements show how you would connect the Data control to the Titles table of the BIBLIO database that comes with Visual Basic. You can use code like this in the Load or Activate events of a form, or in the Click event of a command button:

```
datTitles.DatabaseName = "C:\VB4\BIBLIO.MDB"
datTitles.RecordSource = "Titles"
```

The main reason to set the DatabaseName and RecordSource properties at runtime is to avoid locking your users into a particular directory structure. You can let the user choose the directory where the file is located or read the information from a configuration file. Then you can assign the correct file to the Data control.

Another reason to assign the properties at runtime is to allow the user to choose between multiple files. For example, you might store the 1994 sales figures in one database and the 1995 information in another database. You can then allow the user to choose which set of information to access and set up the Data control appropriately. Or, you could use two data controls on the same form to allow the user to access both databases.

Catch the bug

The following code is used to set up a Data control. Can you find what is wrong with the code?

```
datAuthors.Name = "C:\VB4\BIBLIO.MDB"
datAuthors.RecordSource = "Authors"
```

Answer: *In this listing, the database to be opened was assigned to the* Name *property of the Data control, not the* DatabaseName *property as it should have been. The following code shows this:*

```
datAuthors.DatabaseName = "C:\VB4\BIBLIO.MDB"
```

Advanced Data control options

Using just the `DatabaseName` and `RecordSource` properties allows you to open and use an Access database and gives you the capability to view and modify any of the information in the specified recordset. But, what if you want to use databases other than Access databases or restrict what your user can do with the information in the database? The Data control has some properties that you can optionally set to gain access to other databases and to give you more control over how the information is used.

Getting to other databases

The Data control allows you to connect not only to Access databases, but also to data contained in BTrieve, dBase, Excel, FoxPro, Paradox, and text files as well. To set up the Data control for one of these other file formats, you must specify a value of the `Connect` property of the Data control. The `Connect` property provides information to the Jet engine to identify the type of database being accessed. You can set the `Connect` property by selecting it from a list in the Properties dialog box (see fig. 29.6).

Fig. 29.6
The setting of the
Connect property
determines the
database format that
the Data control will
access.

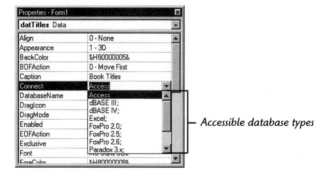

Accessible database types

After you have set the `Connect` property, you can then set the `DatabaseName` and `RecordSource` properties. You will notice that if you use the DatabaseName dialog to select the database, the default file extension is the correct one for the type of database being accessed (for example, MDB for Access, DBF for FoxPro, and so on).

TIP **For some types of databases (FoxPro and dBase, for example), the** `DatabaseName` property contains the name of the directory where the files are located, and the `RecordSource` property contains the actual filename. If you use the DatabaseName dialog to select the file, this is handled for you automatically.

Controlling what the user can do

Typically, when you open a recordset for use, you (or the user of your application) can read information from the recordset as well as modify the information and add new records. In addition, other users can access the information in the database at the same time. There may be times, however, when you want to deviate from this typical behavior. The Data control has two properties that control how the user of your application and other users can access the information in the database. These properties are the Exclusive property and the ReadOnly property.

The ReadOnly property can be set when you want to restrict your user from modifying the data in the recordset. To do this, simply set the ReadOnly property to True.

The Exclusive property is used to keep others from accessing the information in the database at the same time as your application. This is typically only done when you will be making a large number of updates with a program or are changing the structure of the database itself. To prevent others from using the data, set the Exclusive property to True.

 CAUTION Setting the Exclusive **property to** True **prevents other users from** accessing any of the data in any tables used to create the recordset. This option should be used with extreme care.

Types of recordsets

By default, when you use the Data control to access information in a database, it creates a recordset of the dynaset type. This type of recordset is really a set of pointers to the information. And while a dynaset is very

How can I use this in the real world?

One use of the ReadOnly property would be to set up an application where a user can view information that is maintained by another department in the company. For example, in the utility industry, planning departments need to have information available about the cost of producing power from various plants. However, because they are not responsible for maintaining that cost information, they should not be allowed to modify the data. Therefore, the view application can have the ReadOnly property set to True.

flexible, there are some limitations to it that will require you to use a different type of recordset for some applications. The primary limitation is that a dynaset does not support any indexes that you may have created for your data tables. This means that you cannot dynamically change the presentation order of the records in a dynaset. A dynaset must be recreated to set a different order.

Also, in a multi-user environment, a dynaset only shows the records that were present when the recordset was created. This means that any additions or deletions made by others are not reflected in the recordset. However, changes made by others to existing records will be reflected in the dynaset.

Fortunately, the Data control allows you to choose the type of recordset you want created to access your data. The three types of recordsets available are the table, dynaset, and snapshot types. You control which of these types is created by specifying the `RecordsetType` property of the Data control. The values of the `RecordsetType` property are 0, 1, and 2 for the table, dynaset, and snapshot types, respectively. Table 29.1 summarizes the advantages and disadvantages of each of these types.

Table 29.1   The Pros and Cons of the Different Recordset Types

Recordset Type	Advantages	Disadvantages
Table	Can use an index to specify the presentation order. Updates by others are shown immediately.	Can only access one table and must work with the entire table.
Dynaset	Can work with all or part of single or multiple tables.	Cannot use an index. Additions or deletions by others are not immediately shown.
Snapshot	Fast, because it works with a copy of the data.	Cannot be updated. May use a lot of memory resources.

Setting up the bound controls

As I said earlier, the Data control by itself only gives you access to the information in a database. In order to do anything with the data, you must also use the bound controls. Visual Basic comes with a variety of bound controls to handle all types of data and to make your user interfaces easy to program and use. You will look at a number of the bound controls in order of difficulty of use.

The one thing that all the bound controls have in common is that they are tied (bound) to at least one Data control. The Data control provides the link between the control and the data in the database. Which Data control is used by the bound control is determined by the `DataSource` property of the control. To bind a control to a Data control, you just set the `DataSource` property of the control to the `Name` property of the Data control. If you have more than one Data control on a form, you can select the Data control to use from a list, as shown in figure 29.7.

Fig. 29.7
The Data control
determines where the
information for the
bound control is
located.

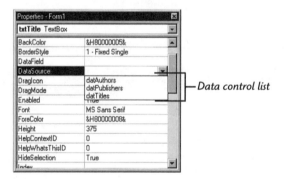

— *Data control list*

 TIP **You can only bind a control to a Data control on the same form.**
Data controls on other forms are not accessible to a bound control.

 TIP **Double-clicking the `DataSource` property steps through the** available Data controls on the form.

The basic controls

The basic controls are the ones that are directly linked to a single field in a recordset and do not require any additional setup other than specifying the field name. Table 29.2 lists these controls, the information they can handle, and the control property that contains the value of the database field.

Table 29.2   Controls and Associated Data Types

Control Name	Data Type(s)	Property
PictureBox	Long Binary	`Picture`
Label	Text, Numeric, Date	`Caption`
TextBox	Text, Numeric, Date	`Text`
CheckBox	True/False, Yes/No	`Value`
Image	Binary	`Picture`
Masked Edit	Text, Numeric, Date	`Text`
3D CheckBox	True/False, Yes/No	`Value`
3D Panel	Text, Numeric, Date	`Caption`

To use any of these controls, you select them from the toolbox and draw them on the form as you would for any non-database use. Then you set the `DataSource` property as discussed previously. After you have set the `DataSource` property, you can set the `DataField` property of the control. If you click on the arrow button at the right of the property in the Properties dialog, Visual Basic shows you a list of fields available in the recordset (see fig. 29.8). You can then select a field from this list.

Fig. 29.8
The selected field should be of a type supported by the control.

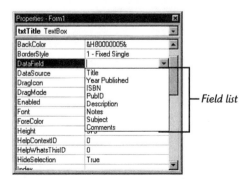

TIP **Double-clicking the `DataField` property steps through all the** available fields in the recordset.

CAUTION **Visual Basic does not perform any type checking when you assign** fields to a control. For example, you can assign a text field to a checkbox, which only supports Yes/No information. You will, however, get a `Type` `mismatch` error when you try to run your program.

These basic bound controls can be used to build any type of database application. These controls are the ones used to build the form in figure 29.1, shown at the beginning of this chapter.

Make your choice

Two other bound controls that are easy to use are the ListBox and the ComboBox. These controls allow you to handle text, numbers, dates, and other data just like a text box, except that they allow you to provide your users with a choice of values for the data field to which they are bound.

To learn more about the setup of the list box and combo box, see Chapter 9, "Allow More Input Choices with List Boxes and Combo Boxes."

Like the basic bound controls, you bind the list box or combo box to a field in a recordset using the `DataSource` and `DataField` properties. The field specified by the `DataField` property is the one that holds the value of the field. It is not the source of the choices in the list portion of the control. To place any choices in the list, you must use the `AddItem` method of the control as you would for an unbound ListBox or ComboBox.

If the database field contains a value that is not in the selection list, the list box shows no item selected, and the actual value is not shown. For the combo box, the value is shown in the text portion of the box but is not shown in the list portion.

Catch the bug

What is wrong with the following code used to set up a bound control?

```
Form1.txtTitle.DataSource = Form2.datTitles
txtTitle.DataField = "Title"
```

Answer: The code tries to bind a text control on one form to a Data control on another form. This is not supported in Visual Basic.

Advanced controls

In addition to the basic controls and the simple lists, there are three more advanced controls that you can use in your programs. These controls are the Data Bound ListBox, Data Bound ComboBox, and the Data Bound Grid. These controls are a little more difficult to set up than the previous controls, but they give you greater functionality than any other bound controls. These data-bound controls are custom controls that must be selected from the Custom Controls dialog box in order to be available for use.

Data-bound lists

Like their standard counterparts, the Data Bound ListBox and ComboBox are designed to present the user with a list of choices. The key difference is that the Data Bound ListBox and ComboBox controls get their list information from a recordset instead of from a series of AddItem statements.

You might use this to handle state code in a membership system. You could have a database that contains all the state codes and their full names. This database could be used as the source of a data-bound list that stores information in a membership database. Figure 29.9 shows the use of a data-bound list for state codes in a membership form.

Fig. 29.9

The data–bound list presents the user with choices that are contained in another recordset.

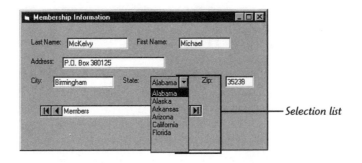

— *Selection list*

You set up the Data Bound ListBox or ComboBox by specifying five properties. These properties are described in table 29.3.

Table 29.3   Properties for Data Bound ListBox or ComboBox Controls

Property	Sample Case Setting	Description
RowSource	States	The name of the Data control containing the information used to populate the list.
BoundColumn	StateAbbr	The name of the field containing the value to be copied to the other table.
ListField	Statename	The name of the field to be displayed in the list.
DataSource	Members	The name of the Data control containing the recordset that is the destination of the information.
DataField	StateID	The name of the destination field.

You can set each of these properties by selecting the property from the Properties dialog box and choosing the setting from a drop-down list. Several notes must be considered when setting the properties of the data-bound list and combo boxes:

- The Data controls specified for the RowSource and DataSource properties can be the same control or different controls.

- The fields for the BoundColumn and DataField properties must be of the same type.

- The `ListField` property can be set to the same field as the `BoundColumn` property.

- All five properties must be set for the control to work properly.

Data-bound grids

The data-bound grid provides a means to view the fields of multiple records at the same time. It is similar to the table view used in Access, displaying information in a spreadsheet style of rows and columns. It can be used to display any alphanumeric information or pictures.

To set up the data-bound grid, you only need to specify the `DataSource` property to identify the Data control containing the data. After this is set, the grid displays all fields of all records in the recordset. If the information is larger than the area of the grid you defined, scroll bars are presented to allow you to view the remaining data.

Your user can select a grid cell to edit by clicking the cell with the mouse. To add a new record, the user positions the pointer in the last row of the grid indicated by an asterisk (*) and enters the desired data. You must specifically allow editing and record addition in the grid by setting the `AllowAddNew` and `AllowUpdate` properties of the grid to `True`. Figure 29.10 shows the data-bound grid used with the `BIBLIO` database.

Fig. 29.10

You can use the data-bound grid to display information from several records at once.

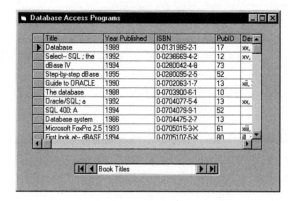

Title	Year Published	ISBN	PubID	Des
Database	1989	0-0131985-2-1	17	xx,
Select-- SQL ; the	1992	0-0238669-4-2	12	xv,
dBase IV	1994	0-0280042-4-8	73	
Step-by-step dBase	1995	0-0280095-2-5	52	
Guide to ORACLE	1990	0-0702063-1-7	13	xii,
The database	1988	0-0703900-6-1	10	
Oracle/SQL; a	1992	0-0704077-5-4	13	xx,
SQL 400: A	1994	0-0704079-9-1	52	
Database system	1986	0-0704475-2-7	13	
Microsoft FoxPro 2.5	1993	0-0705015-3-X	61	xiii,
First look at-- dBASE	1994	0-0705107-5-X	80	ill

Book Titles

Let Visual Basic build your forms

If you want to get a jump start on developing your database application, or just don't want to be bothered with handling all the links between the Data control and the bound controls, you can let Visual Basic develop your data access forms for you. Visual Basic comes with the Data Form Designer that will build a form to handle the data in a specified recordset.

Before you can use the form designer, you must first add it to Visual Basic's menu. To do this, select Add-In Manager from the Add-Ins menu. This will bring up the Add-In Manager dialog box (see fig. 29.11).

Fig. 29.11
The Add-In Manager lets you add new capabilities to Visual Basic.

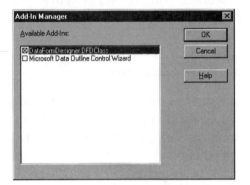

In the Add-In Manager dialog, you need to select the DataFormDesigner by clicking the checkbox next to the description. This will place an X in the box indicating that the add-in will be available for use. After selecting the add-in, close the dialog by clicking OK. If you look at the add-ins menu now, you will notice that the Data Form Designer has been added to the bottom of the menu. Choosing this option brings up the Data Form Designer dialog box (see fig. 29.12).

To use the Data Form Designer, you first need to enter a name for your form in the Base Form Name field. This can be any valid form name. (Note that the Data Form Designer will add the string form to the beginning of the form name when you choose to build the form.) Next you specify the type of database with which you will be working using the Connect String list box.

After you have set the form name and the connect string, you need to choose a database from which to obtain the data. You choose a database using the Open Database dialog which is accessed by choosing the Open Database button on the Data Form Designer dialog. When you select a database, its name appears in the Database Name field of the dialog, and the first table of the database appears in the RecordSource field of the dialog.

Fig. 29.12
The Data Form Designer allows you to choose the database and fields to include on your form.

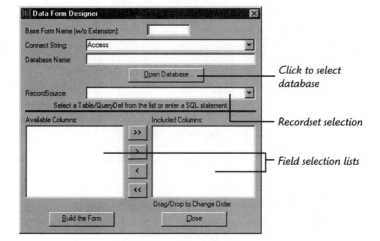

You can use this first table or choose another from the list of available tables and queries. When you choose a record source, the Data Form Designer dialog displays a list of fields from that record source in the Available Columns list. This list shows you all the fields that you can include in your data access form. You can select any or all fields from this list for inclusion on the finished form. To select all the fields, click the right-pointing double arrow indicated in figure 29.12. To select individual fields, click the field to choose it, then click the right-pointing single arrow.

As each field is selected, it is removed from the available columns list and placed in the included columns list. If you inadvertently include a field, you can remove it from the list by selecting it from the Included Columns list and clicking the left-pointing single arrow. To remove all fields, click the left-pointing double arrow.

After you have selected all the fields you want to include on your form, you can build the form by choosing the Build the Form button on the dialog. Figure 29.13 shows a completed dialog, and figure 29.14 shows the form built by the Data Form Designer.

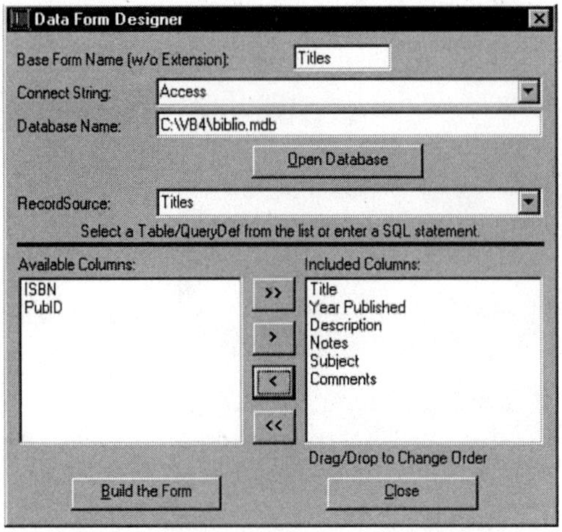

Fig. 29.13
The completed Data
Form Designer dialog
shows all the fields to
be included on the
data access form.

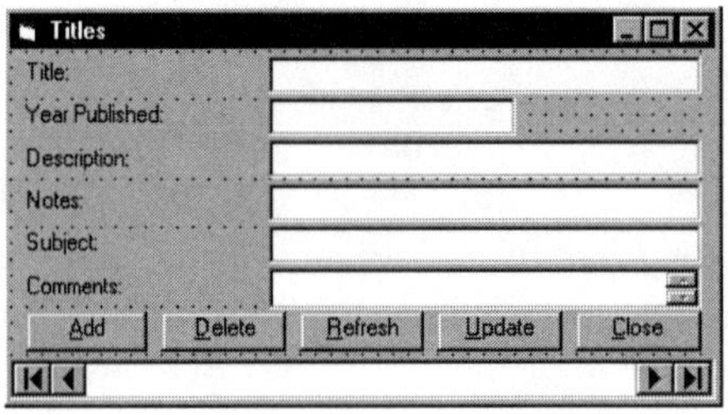

Fig. 29.14
The Data Form
Designer builds a form
with a Data control
and all the necessary
bound controls.

Summary

Using the Data control and the bound controls allows you to quickly and
easily build a data access application. And if you want an even easier way,
Visual Basic can build the form for you after you select the data to be
included.

Review questions

1 What does the Data control do for you?

2 What one property must be set for any bound control?

3 What is the difference between the standard list box and the data-bound
list box?

4 Where must the Data control to which a control is bound reside?

Exercises

1 Set up a form that shows the book titles in the BIBLIO database.

2 Set up a second Data control and a data-bound list to allow the user to choose the publisher by name.

3 Set up a data-bound grid to view all the author information.

30

Getting the Most from Your Database Application

● **In this chapter:**

● **How to add new records to a recordset**

● **Deleting records from a recordset**

● **Controlling the order in which records are shown**

● **How do I find a specific record?**

With program commands, you can add and delete records, or find a specific piece of data. . . . . ➤

T he Data control is an excellent way to set up database applications since it does the work of connecting you to the database and providing you with a means of moving between records in the database. However, a few things aren't included in the Data control. You'll want most of your programs to be able to at least do the following:

- Add new records
- Delete records
- Display records in a specific order
- Find a particular record

Writing code to enhance your database application

Since the Data control doesn't handle these things, how do you include them in your programs? Visual Basic provides additional methods for working with recordsets. These methods are applicable to any recordset, whether the recordset is part of a Data control or is created with the Data Access Objects (DAOs).

To learn how to set up the Data control, see Chapter 29, "Accessing Databases."

If you looked at creating a data access form with the Data Form Designer (refer to Chapter 29), you saw that the Form Designer included several buttons on the form in addition to the Data control itself. These buttons, as shown in figure 30.1, provided you with the capability to perform additional functions. In this chapter, you'll look at the code that makes these buttons (and others you'll add) work.

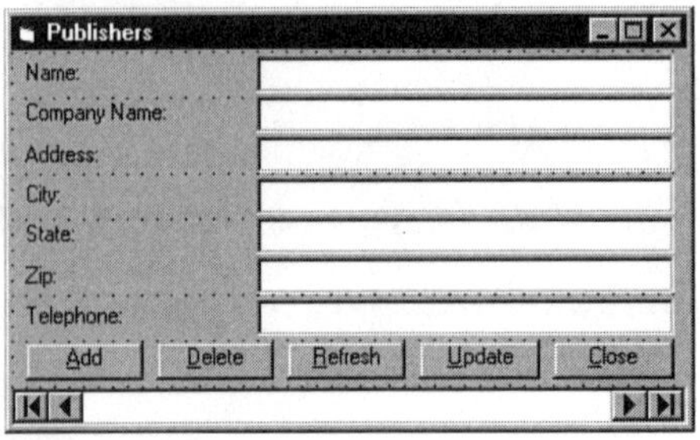

Fig. 30.1
A data access form created with the Data Form Designer includes buttons to let you add and delete records.

How do I add and delete records?

If you're like most people, the first thing you'll want to add to your database program is the capability to add new records or delete existing ones. These capabilities are easy to add to a program using the Data control. In fact, for adding records, the Data control does most of the work for you.

Adding data records

Adding a record to a recordset requires the use of the AddNew method. When you run the AddNew method, Visual Basic creates a blank record in memory; it's not added directly to the database. At the same time, the Data control clears all the bound fields on the form, allowing you to input information for the new record. After you've entered the information, the Data control will add the record to the database when you move to another record.

If you want to ensure that the information is added to the database without depending on the Data control to do it for you, you can add another button to the form that invokes the Update method. The Update method commits any changes to a record or the addition of a record to the database. The syntax of the Update method is similar to that of the AddNew method. This syntax is shown in the following line of code, where Member is the name of a Data control:

```
Member.Recordset.Update
```

Speaking of *AddNew*

The AddNew method is used in your program as follows:

```
datacontrolname.Recordset.AddNew
```

datacontrolname represents the name of the Data control to which you want to add a new record. The Recordset and AddNew keywords are required for working with a Data control. If you're working with the data access objects, datacontrolname.Recordset would be replaced by the name of the recordset object.

The data editing form shown in figure 30.1 now has two new buttons—one for updating the recordset and one for adding a new record (see fig. 30.2). The code for each of these buttons consists of a single line that invokes the appropriate method.

Fig. 30.2
You can add new records to a recordset with the *AddNew* method.

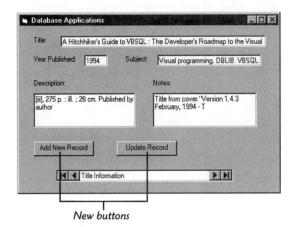

New buttons

Q&A **When I tried to add a record to my recordset using the AddNew method, I got the message, Feature not available. What happened?**

You probably set up the Data control to create a snapshot as your recordset type. Since a snapshot can't be updated, you can't add records to it.

Catch the bug

This code attempts to add a record to a data controls recordset. What is wrong with the statement?

```
Member.AddNew
```

Answer: When working with the Data control, you must include the Recordset keyword with the AddNew method. The following is the correct code:

```
Member.RecordSet.AddNew
```

Discarding data records

If you want to be able to add records, you probably want to be able to delete records as well. To delete records, you use the Delete method. This method is similar in form to the AddNew and Update methods. Listing 30.1 shows how to delete a record and update the screen.

CAUTION When you delete a record using the Delete method, it is gone from the database. You can't get the record back.

Listing 30.1   How to Properly Delete a Record

```
Member.Recordset.Delete
If Member.Recordset.EOF Then
    Member.Recordset.MoveLast
Else
    Member.Recordset.MoveNext
End If
```

The first line of the code invokes the Delete method to remove the current record from the database. Next, an If statement is used to determine whether the record pointer is at the end of file. If so, the MoveLast method is used to move the record pointer to the last record in the recordset. This has the same effect as clicking the far right button of the Data control.

If the record pointer is not at the end of file, the MoveNext method is used to move the pointer to the one immediately following the deleted record. Either of the Move methods will cause the Data control to update the bound

Speaking of *Delete*

The syntax of the Delete method is as follows:

datacontrolname.Recordset.Delete

As with the AddNew method, datacontrolname is the name of the Data control as assigned by the Name property. Also, as with the AddNew method, the Recordset keyword must be present.

controls. The reason for checking the end of file condition is to avoid an error that would occur if the MoveNext method were invoked while the pointer was already at the end of file. Figure 30.3 shows the Delete button added to the form and indicates the MoveNext and MoveLast buttons of the Data control.

Fig. 30.3
You can delete records from a recordset using the *Delete* method.

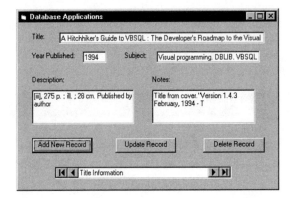

Q&A *When I tried to delete a record, the information was still visible in the bound controls on the form. Why?*

When you invoke the Delete method, it removes the record from the database, but it doesn't automatically update the information on-screen. The bound controls are only updated when you move the record pointer. However, if you try to edit the data after deleting the record, you'll get an error message.

Will the data please come to order?

When you work with a recordset using the Data control, the information is presented in the order in which it was entered into the database. This order is often referred to as the **physical order**. While this order may be fine for some applications, most times you'll want to present the data in a particular order, such as alphabetical order.

For example, imagine using a database for a Rolodex application. If you use the Data control by itself, the names in your Rolodex will appear in the order in which you entered them. This order would make it extremely difficult to find a particular record. So what's a developer to do?

You can set the order of the recordset created by the Data control in two ways. First, if you're using a recordset that is of the table type, you can use an index to set the order of the recordset. For you to use the index, though, it has to already exist.

For information on the creation of indexes using the Data Manager, see Chapter 28, "Creating a Database."

TIP **Using the Data Access Objects, it's possible to create an index** using program commands in the event that an index for the desired order is not available. However, the creation of indexes in this manner is beyond the scope of this book. Refer to Que's *Special Edition Using Visual Basic* to find out how to create these indexes.

Indexes, however, only work with table type recordsets. If you create a dynaset or snapshot type recordset, you must set the order when the recordset is created. You can do this in either of two ways. The first way is to set the Sort property of an existing recordset, then create the new recordset from the existing one. The second way is to use the ORDER BY clause of an SQL statement in creating your recordset.

Chapter 31 discusses creating recordsets using SQL statements and other conditions.

The only way to change the order of a recordset on-the-fly is to use a table type recordset and indexes. Assuming that you have created a table type recordset, you can change its order by setting the Index property of the recordset to the desired index.

Speaking of *Index*

To set the order of a recordset based on a table with an existing index, change its Index property as follows:

```
datacontrolname.Recordset.Index [= indexname]
```

As with the other methods, datacontrolname refers to the name of the control whose order you are trying to set. Recordset and Index are required keywords. indexname is a string that identifies the index to be used to control the order of the records. The expression may be a literal string enclosed in quotes, a string variable, or a string function. The value of the expression must be an index that exists for the current table; otherwise an error will occur. If you don't know what indexes exist for a table, you can find them by using the Data Manager to examine the structure of the database.

Figure 30.4 shows the command button for setting the order of the Titles table of the BIBLIO database to show the books alphabetically by title. Listing 30.2 shows the code to accomplish this change of presentation order.

Fig. 30.4
You can set the order of a table type recordset by changing its *Index* property.

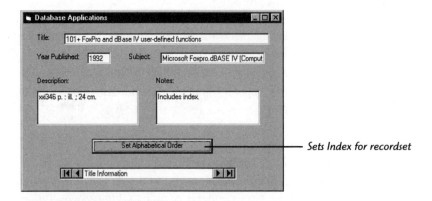

Sets Index for recordset

Listing 30.2   Setting the *Index* Property

```
BookList.Recordset.Index = "Title"
BookList.Recordset.MoveFirst
```

Q&A

Why can't I set the order of a table type recordset using the *Index* property in the Properties dialog box?

Unfortunately, there are two unrelated properties that use the same name. The Index property that you see in the Properties dialog refers to the index value of the Data control in a control array. This property will usually be blank, but if not, it will always be an integer. (See Chapter 16 for information about control arrays.) The index that controls the order of the records is a property of the Recordset object that is part of the Data control. This property is not accessible in Visual Basic's design mode. This also shows why you must specify the Recordset keyword when assigning an index.

How can I use this in the real world?

Depending on your application, you may need to have several recordset orders available. For example, in a library system, you would probably want to have the capability to present the information in order by title, author name, or subject. This would require three indexes and three command buttons to set the various orders.

How do I go about searching for data?

The last enhancement to the data access application that we'll discuss is the capability of finding a particular record in a recordset. As with setting the order, the method you use depends on the type of recordset with which you are working.

One thing to keep in mind with finding records in any type of recordset is the effect of indexes on your search. An index is absolutely required for finding a particular record in a table type recordset. Without an index, you can't perform a search. Many people don't know that appropriate indexes will also speed searches on dynaset and snapshot type recordsets. This is because the Jet engine will use any available index to optimize a search. Therefore, if you know you will be performing particular searches (such as a name or ID number) on a regular basis, it's a good idea to create an index for the search.

Finding records in a table

Other than using the brute force method of checking every record in a table one record at a time, the Seek method is the only way to search a table type recordset for a particular record. A Seek on a table is a very fast method of locating a record. However, the Seek method does have a few limitations:

- A Seek can only be performed on a table type recordset; it cannot be used with a dynaset or snapshot type recordset.

- A Seek can be used only with an active index. The parameters of the Seek method must match the fields of the index in use.

- A Seek finds only the first record that matches the specified index values. Subsequent uses do not find additional matching records.

To use the Seek method, you must specify the comparison condition and the comparison value. You must also specify the recordset on which the Seek is to be performed. The syntax of the Seek method is:

```
datacontrolname.Recordset.Seek compexpr, compvalue
[, compvalue2]
```

As with other methods shown in this chapter, `datacontrolname` is the name of the Data control that provides the link to the recordset being searched. `Recordset` is a keyword that tells the program that you're working with the Recordset object of the Data control. `Seek` is the keyword that tells the program what action to perform.

`compexpr` is a string expression that identifies the comparison operator to be used in the `Seek`. The comparison operator can be <, <=, =, >=, >, <>. The comparison operator must be either a literal string, enclosed in quotes, or a string variable containing one of the valid operators.

For more informa-
tion about these
comparison opera-
tors, see Chapter 20,
"Making Decisions
Based Upon Data
Comparisons."

`compvalue` is an expression that tells the `Seek` method what to look for. The type of expression used (i.e., string or number), will be determined by the field being searched in the index. If the field in the index is a text field, `compvalue` must be a string expression. If the index field is numeric, `compvalue` must be a numeric expression. The comparison expression must be a variable of the correct type or a literal expression with the proper delimiters (quotes for strings, # for dates, none for numbers).

`compvalue2` indicates an optional second comparison value. In actuality, you can include as many comparison values as there are fields in the index. Each comparison expression must be separated from the others by a comma, and must be of the correct type for the field. For example, if you had a membership table indexed on `lastname` and `birthdate`, you would need to make sure that the comparison expression was a string and a date, respectively. Also, the comparison expression must be in the same order as the index fields.

One frequent use of the `Seek` method is to find the information record of a particular person in a database. Depending on the setup of the index, you would search for a person's name or ID number. To illustrate this, we will perform an author search on the Authors table of the `BIBLIO` database. Figure 30.5 shows the form used to perform the search, and listing 30.3 contains the code used for the search. (Note: To run this example, you'll need to create an index in the Authors table on the Author field.)

Fig. 30.5
You can use the *Seek* method to find a particular author in the Authors table.

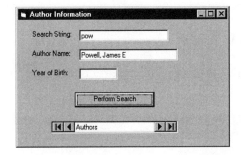

Listing 30.3   Find an Author Using *Seek*

```
datAuthors.Recordset.Index = "Author"
srchstr = txtSearch.Text
datAuthors.Recordset.Seek ">", srchstr
If datAuthors.Recordset.NoMatch Then
    MsgBox "Author not found"
    datAuthors.Recordset.MoveFirst
End If
```

The first line of the code sets the index for the search. Remember that an index is required for the Seek method. The next line retrieves the search criteria from the text box where the user would enter the name (or part of a name) to be located.

Next, the Seek method is used to perform the search. In this case, the > operator is used to find the first name that contains the search string. If you had used the = operator, the author's name would have to exactly match the search criteria for the Seek method to succeed.

After the search is performed, the NoMatch property of the recordset is checked to determine whether the Seek was successful. If the Seek located a record that matched the search criteria, the NoMatch property would be set to False. If the Seek fails, the NoMatch property would be set to True. For the code in listing 30.3, if the Seek failed, you would show the user a message indicating that the name was not found, then return to the first record of the table.

Catch the bug

The following code is used to find a particular record. What is wrong with the code?

```
datAuthors.Recordset.Index = "Author"
datAuthors.Recordset.Seek = "Smith"
```

Answer: *Two errors are present in the* Seek *method shown here. First, the comparison operator must be enclosed in quotes. Second, the comparison operator and the comparison value must be separated by a comma. The correct code follows:*

```
datAuthors.Recordset.Seek =, "Smith"
```

Finding records in a dynaset or snapshot

What the Seek method does for tables, the Find methods do for dynasets and snapshots. That's right, "methods" is supposed to be plural. There are actually four Find methods you can use to locate records in a dynaset or snapshot. These methods and their purposes are as follows:

- FindFirst starts at the top of the database and finds the first record in the recordset with the specified criteria.

- FindNext starts at the current location in the recordset and finds the next record down with the specified criteria.

- FindPrevious starts at the current location in the recordset and finds the next record up with the specified criteria.

The WHERE clause for SQL statements is discussed in Chapter 31 and gives you more information about the various comparisons that can be performed in the Find methods.

- FindLast starts at the bottom of the recordset and finds the last record in the database with the specified criteria.

The Find methods use a search criteria that is similar to the WHERE clause of an SQL statement. This can give you greater flexibility in locating records than was available for the Seek method. The search criteria for the Find methods can also look for fields that match a specific pattern as well as values that are greater than, less than, or equal to a specific value.

You can use the `Find` methods to locate each record that meets a specific criteria. If you are searching forward through a recordset, you would use the `FindFirst` method to locate the first record, then the `FindNext` method to locate all other records. If you want to search backward through the recordset, you would start with the `FindLast` method, then use the `FindPrevious` method to locate additional records that meet the specified criteria.

Speaking of *Find*

The syntax for each of the `Find` methods is the same. The following is the syntax of the `FindFirst` method. To use any of the other three methods, simply substitute the appropriate keyword for `FindFirst`:

```
datacontrolname.Recordset.FindFirst compexpr
```

`datacontrolname` and `Recordset` represent the same items as they did for the `Seek` method. `compexpr` represents a string expression that contains the comparison condition. This can be a literal string or a string variable. `compexpr` has the following syntax:

```
fieldname compoperator compvalue
```

`fieldname` is the name of the field to be searched in the recordset. The contents of this field will be compared to the comparison value. `compoperator` represents the comparison operator to be used for the search. The same operators that were used for the `Seek` method are valid for the `Find` methods (`<`, `<=`, `=`, `>=`, `>`, `<>`). In addition, the `Find` methods support the use of the `Like`, `In`, and `Between` comparison operators.

`compvalue` represents the value to which the field is being compared. As with the `Seek` method, this value must be of the same type as the field being searched. Also, any literal expressions must be enclosed in the appropriate delimiters (" for strings, # for dates, none for numbers). A note of great importance: When you are setting up a literal string for the `Find` method and are comparing a text field, the comparison value must be included in *single* quotes as shown in this example:

```
"Author > 'Smith'"
```

As with the Seek method, when one of the Find methods fails to locate a record matching the search criteria, the NoMatch property of the recordset is set to True. This allows you to easily create loops to find all matching records.

Listing 30.4 shows how to use a loop and the Find methods to list all titles that match a specific criteria.

Listing 30.4 *Find* **Methods Locate Matching Records**

```
findcrit = "Title Like '*database*'"
datTitles.Recordset.FindFirst findcrit
frmTitle.Print datTitles.Recordset("Title")
Do Until datTitles.Recordset.NoMatch
    datTitles.Recordset.FindNext findcrit
    frmTitle.Print datTitles.Recordset("Title")
Loop
```

The first line of the code sets up the search string. For this search, you are looking for any title that contains the word "database." To do this, you use the Like comparison operator and the wildcard (*) character. Note that the comparison value is enclosed in single quotes.

Next, you use the FindFirst method to locate the first title that matches the search criteria. That title is printed, then a loop is started that will run until the Find method fails to locate a matching record. Inside the loop, you use the FindNext method to locate successive records meeting the search criteria. As each record is found, the title is printed on the form.

How can I use this in the real world?

Working with a dynaset type recordset, you could use the Find methods to print a list of all titles in the recordset that contain the word "database."

Catch the bug

What problem will the following code cause?

```
findcrit = "Title Like '*database*'"
datTitles.Recordset.FindFirst findcrit
Do Until datTitles.Recordset.NoMatch
    frmTitle.Print datTitles.Recordset("Title")
    datTitles.Recordset.FindFirst findcrit
Loop
```

Answer: *This code will result in an infinite loop, since the* FindFirst, *not the* FindNext *method is used inside the loop. As long as at least one record in the recordset meets the search condition, the loop will run forever. This is an easy mistake to make if you use Copy and Paste operations to develop your code. I, for one, use Copy and Paste a lot to cut down on typos. The correct code line is as follows:*

```
datTitles.Recordset.FindNext findcrit
```

Returning to a specific record

In listing 30.3, you returned to the first record of the recordset if the Seek method was unsuccessful. But what if you want to return to the current record instead of the first record? That is, you want the record pointer to be moved only if the search is successful.

Visual Basic provides a recordset property that will allow you to "mark" a particular record, then return to it later. This property is the Bookmark property. To set a Bookmark and then return to a particular record, you set a variable (either a string or variant type) to the value of the Bookmark property prior to any operations that could move the record pointer (such as a Move, Seek, or Find method). After the operation, if you want to return to the original record, you just set the Bookmark property to the value of the variable. Listing 30.5 updates listing 30.3 to return the user to the original record if a search is unsuccessful.

Listing 30.5   The *Bookmark* Property

```
datAuthors.Recordset.Index = "Author"
srchstr = txtSearch.Text
bkmrk = datAuthors.Recordset.Bookmark
datAuthors.Recordset.Seek ">", srchstr
If datAuthors.Recordset.NoMatch Then
    MsgBox "Author not found"
    datAuthors.Recordset.Bookmark = bkmrk
End If
```

Summary

Methods such as AddNew, Delete, Seek, and Find all allow you to increase the capabilities of your database application, while still being able to use the Data control for the bulk of the work.

Review questions

1 How do you add a new record to a recordset?

2 How do you delete a record from a recordset?

3 What can you do to change the presentation order of a table-type recordset?

4 What method is used to find a record in a table?

5 What method is used to find a record in a dynaset or snapshot?

6 Which is the more flexible search method? Why?

Exercises

1 Change the program in listing 30.3 to search for the author ID instead of the name.

2 Change the program in listing 30.4 to scan the titles in inverse order.

3 Using the Pub_ID in the titles table and a second Data control, write a routine to find the name of the publisher for any given book.

31

Working with More Than One Table: Using SQL and the Data Control

● **In this chapter:**

● **No need to work with all the fields in a table**

● **So you only want to access the records that meet a certain criteria...**

● **How to make sure the records in a dynaset are in a particular order**

● **Can I change the record scope or order after the recordset is created?**

The Data control becomes even more powerful when you combine it with SQL statements . . . .

When you first start working with the Data control, you may think that you are limited to working with single tables. It may also appear that you must work with all the records in the table every time you open a recordset. Fortunately, this is not true. If you use a dynaset or snapshot type recordset, there are several options available that allow you to work with multiple tables and to limit the number of records and/or fields with which you work.

Doing more with the Data control

For information on setting up the Data control, refer to Chapter 29, "Accessing Databases."

In this chapter, you will take a look at some of these options. For many of the examples and figures, you will be using the data-bound grid so that you can see the effects of the different commands. Also, for most of the examples, you will make use of the `BIBLIO` database so you can recreate the examples. Just for starters, figure 31.1 shows part of the recordset that would be returned from the Titles table using the `RecordSource` selection list of the Data control.

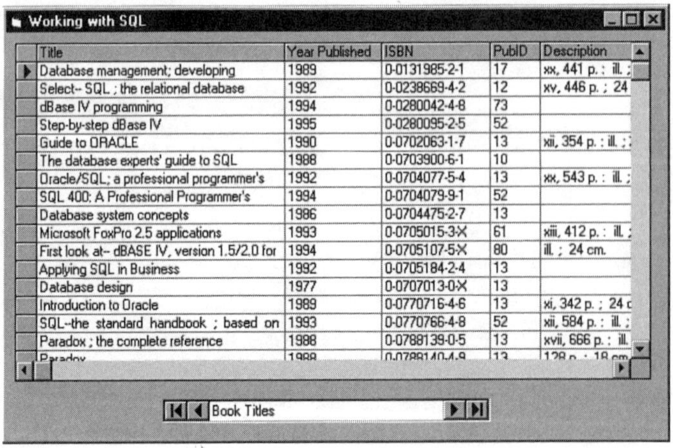

Title	Year Published	ISBN	PubID	Description
Database management; developing	1989	0-0131985-2-1	17	xx, 441 p. : ill. ;
Select-- SQL ; the relational database	1992	0-0238669-4-2	12	xv, 446 p. ; 24
dBase IV programming	1994	0-0280042-4-8	73	
Step-by-step dBase IV	1995	0-0280095-2-5	52	
Guide to ORACLE	1990	0-0702063-1-7	13	xii, 354 p. : ill. ;
The database experts' guide to SQL	1988	0-0703900-6-1	10	
Oracle/SQL; a professional programmer's	1992	0-0704077-5-4	13	xx, 543 p. : ill. ;
SQL 400: A Professional Programmer's	1994	0-0704079-9-1	52	
Database system concepts	1986	0-0704475-2-7	13	
Microsoft FoxPro 2.5 applications	1993	0-0705015-3-X	61	xiii, 412 p. : ill. ;
First look at-- dBASE IV, version 1.5/2.0 for	1994	0-0705107-5-X	80	ill. ; 24 cm.
Applying SQL in Business	1992	0-0705184-2-4	13	
Database design	1977	0-0707013-0-X	13	
Introduction to Oracle	1989	0-0770716-4-6	13	xi, 342 p. ; 24 c
SQL--the standard handbook ; based on	1993	0-0770766-4-8	52	xii, 584 p. : ill. ;
Paradox ; the complete reference	1988	0-0788139-0-5	13	xvii, 666 p. : ill.

Fig. 31.1
Selecting an item from the *RecordSource* list returns the entire table from the database.

Structured Query Language (SQL) to the rescue

In order to work with anything other than a single table in a Data control, you will need to enter a query in the `RecordSource` property of the Data control. A query in the `RecordSource` property is an **SQL** command.

 Plain English, please!

Structured Query Language is a set of programming commands that allow you to retrieve records from a database, edit records in a database, and even make changes to the structure of the database. These commands are used by many database management systems to handle record retrieval. **99**

To start our discussion, let's first define SQL. It is a specialized set of programming commands that enable you to accomplish the following tasks:

- Retrieve data from one or more tables in one or more databases

- Manipulate data in tables by inserting, deleting, or updating records

- Obtain summary information about the data in tables, such as totals; record counts; and minimum, maximum, and average values

- Create, modify, or delete tables in a database (Access databases only)

- Create or delete indexes for a table (Access databases only)

For working with the Data control, we will only be concerned with the first bulleted item, retrieving data from one or more tables in a database. The other capabilities of SQL are typically reserved for use with the Data Access Objects.

I only need one table

The simplest SQL statements are those that only work with a single table. The advantage of using SQL with a single table over just selecting the table from the RecordSource list is that you can limit the number of fields and records retrieved from the table. You can also control the presentation order of the resulting recordset.

The simplest form of the SQL statement selects all the fields from a single table. This statement is shown below for the Titles table:

```
SELECT * FROM Titles
```

This statement produces the same recordset as selecting the Titles table from the `RecordSource` list. Therefore, the results of this statement are the same as those shown in figure 31.1.

I only need a few fields

The first change that you will want to know about is selecting only specific fields from a table. Selecting specific fields produces a smaller recordset than retrieving the entire table, which means your program will use fewer resources and will perform better.

Speaking of *SELECT*

To retrieve records using an SQL statement, you use the SELECT statement. The basic form of this statement is as follows:

```
SELECT fieldlist FROM tablelist
```

In this syntax, the keywords SELECT and FROM must be included in the statement. These words are capitalized in the example to differentiate them from other parts of the statement. In practice, the capitalization is unimportant.

`fieldlist` is the list of field names that you want to retrieve from the table(s). Each name must exist in the table, and each name must be separated by commas. If you want to select all fields from a specific table, you may use the wildcard character (*) instead of the individual field names.

`tablelist` is the list of table names from which the fields are retrieved. The tables listed must exist in the database and must be separated by commas.

Table names and field names are not case-sensitive. Therefore, the capitalization of the names is not important.

As an example of retrieving specific fields, let's retrieve just the Title and Year Published fields of the Titles table. The following line of code would be entered in the `RecordSource` property of the Data control:

```
SELECT Title, [Year Published] FROM Titles
```

You probably noticed something a little funny about the statement above. The `Year Published` field name is surrounded by square brackets. These are required any time a field name contains a space. If these were not included, the query engine (which processes SQL statements) would assume that `Year` and `Published` were two different field names and would give you a syntax error because they were not separated by a comma. The results of the above statement are shown in figure 31.2.

Fig. 31.2

Specifying the fields to retrieve produces a smaller recordset.

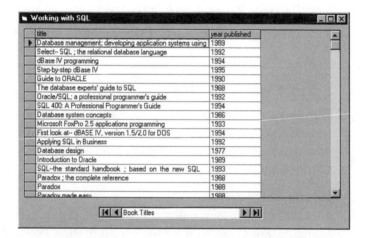

How can I use this in the real world?

One use of selecting specific fields is in generating mailing labels. Most applications that deal with information about people include the person's name, address, phone number, date of birth, and social security number, along with other information like job classification and date of employment. If you are producing mailing labels, the only information you need is the name and address of each person. By selecting only those fields when your recordset is created, you will produce a much smaller recordset and your application will run faster.

Catch the bug

Identify the error in each of the following SQL statements:

```
SELECT *

SELECT Lastname, Phone Number FROM Members

SELECT Lastname Firstname FROM Members
```

Answers:

1 *The table name is not identified.*

2 *The Phone Number field is not enclosed in square brackets.*

3 *No comma separates the field names.*

I don't want all the records

The other thing that you want to limit in order to produce a smaller recordset is the number of records. Limiting the number of records in a recordset requires the use of the WHERE clause of the SQL statement. This clause specifies a criteria that all included records must meet.

Simple comparison

A simple comparison is one that uses one of the six symbol comparison operators. For example, if you only want to show books that were produced in 1994, you could use the following statement:

```
SELECT title, [year published] FROM titles WHERE
[year published] = 1994
```

Speaking of *WHERE*

The WHERE clause in the SQL statement is added after the tablelist as shown:

```
SELECT fieldlist FROM tablelist WHERE condition
```

The condition expression consists of a field to be evaluated, a comparison operator, and the criteria to be met. The WHERE clause supports the use of the <, <=, =, >=, >, and <> operators as well as the IN, LIKE, and BETWEEN comparison operators. These are detailed in the following discussion.

Notice that the Year Published field is enclosed in square brackets both times that it is referenced. The results of the statement are shown in figure 31.3. If you want to include all books published in 1994 and later, you can change the comparison operator to >=.

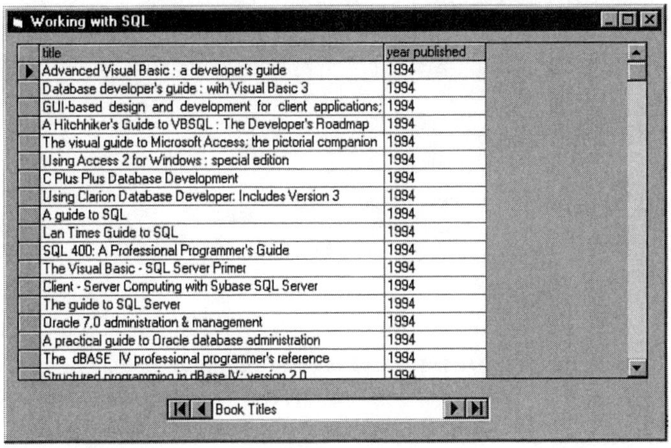

Fig. 31.3

You can retrieve records that match a specific value for a field.

IN the list

Another way to limit the selection of records is with the IN comparison operator. This operator compares the contents of the field to a list of choices that you want to have included. For example, you can include books published in 1990 or 1991 using the IN comparison as follows (see fig. 31.4). To use the IN comparison, the desired values must be enclosed in parentheses and separated by commas. As with all comparisons, the desired values must be of the same type as the field to which they are being compared. The following line of code selects all books that were published in 1990 or 1991:

```
SELECT title, [year published] FROM titles WHERE
[year published] IN (1990, 1991)
```

Records LIKE me

One very powerful comparison type is the LIKE comparison. This allows you to compare the contents of a field to a pattern of values. This means you can make selections such as last name starting with *S*, titles containing the word *database*, or zip codes starting with 3. The LIKE comparison can only be used with text fields and string expressions.

Fig. 31.4
You can retrieve records whose values for a field falls within a list of values.

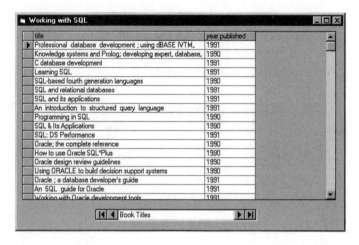

You define the patterns for the LIKE comparison using literal characters, wildcard characters, and character range lists. There are three wildcard characters that you can use. Table 31.1 shows the characters and some sample patterns.

Table 31.1   Wildcards Used in Pattern Matching

Wildcard	Used To Match	Example Pattern	Example Results
*	Multiple characters	S*	Smith, Sims, sheep
?	Single character	an?	and, ant, any
#	Single digit	3524#	35242, 35243

If you use character range lists, you need to make sure that the lists meet these criteria:

- The list must be enclosed within square brackets.

- The first and last characters must be separated by a hyphen.

- The range of the characters must be defined in ascending order (for example, a - z, and not z - a).

The following statement produces a list of all books whose titles start with the word Using. The results of the statement are shown in figure 31.5.

```
SELECT title, [year published] FROM titles WHERE title
LIKE "Using*"
```

If you want to find all the authors whose names begin with the letters A through M, you can use a character range list as shown in this line of code:

```
SELECT author FROM authors WHERE author LIKE [A-M]
```

Fig. 31.5
You can retrieve records whose values for a field match a pattern of values.

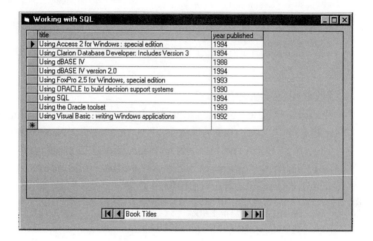

BETWEEN a rock and a hard place

The last type of comparison is the BETWEEN comparison. This checks the value of the field against a range of values. For example, to see the titles of books published between 1990 and 1993, you could use the following statement:

```
SELECT title, [year published] FROM titles WHERE
[year published] BETWEEN 1990 AND 1993
```

The BETWEEN comparison is an inclusive comparison, meaning that a record containing a field with a value equal to one of the endpoints will also be included in the returned recordset. As you can see in the example, the two endpoint values must be separated by the AND keyword. Figure 31.6 shows the results of the BETWEEN comparison.

Fig. 31.6

You can retrieve records whose values for a field fall between two endpoint values.

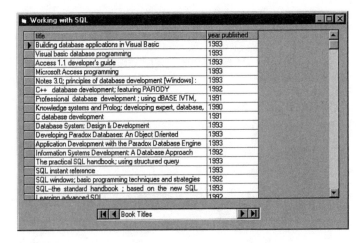

Multiple conditions

Because all the comparisons are logical expressions, they can be combined using the AND or OR keywords. This gives you even greater flexibility in the specification of the records to be included in your recordset. For example, the following statement returns the titles of all books with SQL in the title which were published in 1994:

```
SELECT title FROM titles WHERE title LIKE "*SQL*" AND
[year published] = 1994
```

Catch the bug

Identify the error in each of these statements:

```
SELECT title FROM titles WHERE title LIKE *database*
```

```
SELECT title FROM titles WHERE title BETWEEN "A" AND "F"
```

Answers:

1 *The pattern must be enclosed in quotes.*

2 *Trick question. This is a valid statement.*

May I take your order?

In addition to specifying which records should be included in a recordset, you can also use SQL statements to specify the order in which the records are to be presented. This is accomplished using the ORDER BY clause of the SQL statement.

As an example of the ORDER BY clause, the following statement sorts the book titles alphabetically for presentation:

```
SELECT title FROM titles ORDER BY title
```

The WHERE and ORDER BY clauses of the SQL statement are not mutually exclusive. You can use these statements in combination to control both the order of the records and the specific records included in your recordset. One condition that must be followed, though, if you use the two clauses together—the ORDER BY clause must follow the WHERE clause. The following statement shows the two clauses used together. Figure 31.7 shows the results.

```
SELECT title FROM titles WHERE title LIKE "*database*"
ORDER BY title
```

Speaking of *ORDER BY*

The ORDER BY clause in the SQL statement is also added after the `tablelist` as shown:

```
SELECT fieldlist FROM tablelist ORDER BY field1 [DESC]
```

`field1` is the name of the field that you want to use to control the order of the recordset. If you use just the field name, the sort will be performed in ascending order (for example, in order from a to z, 1 to 10, and so on). As an option, you can follow the field name with the keyword DESC which will reverse the order of the sort for that field. You can also include multiple fields in the ORDER BY clause. In this way, you can sort names by last name, then first name. There is no limit to the number of fields that can be included, but each field must be separated from the others by commas.

Fig. 31.7
The *WHERE* and *ORDER BY* clauses can be used together to control both the records to be included and the presentation order of the recordset.

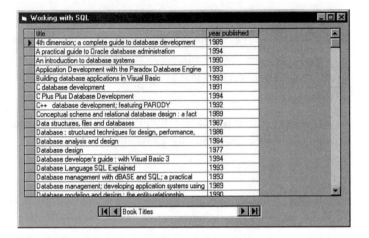

Catch the bug

What is wrong with the following SQL statement?

```
SELECT title FROM titles ORDER BY title WHERE title
LIKE "Using*"
```

Answer: *The* ORDER BY *clause must follow the* WHERE *clause.*

```
SELECT title FROM  titles WHERE title LIKE "Using*"
ORDER BY title
```

I need multiple tables

I said earlier that one of the biggest benefits of using SQL statements is that they allow you to retrieve fields from multiple tables. This is done using the SELECT statement that we have been discussing throughout this chapter. Each of the clauses that can be used for single tables may also be applied to multiple tables. However, there are two key items that must be specified when working with multiple tables:

- The table from which each field is to be retrieved

- The relationship between the tables

If you recall from Chapter 28, "Creating a Database," information is broken into tables to make the storage and management of the information more efficient. When this is done, specific fields are used to maintain the relationship between the tables. For instance, in the BIBLIO database, instead of including the publisher information for each book in the same table as the book titles, a publisher ID is assigned to each publisher. This ID is then placed in the title record to relate the book to the publisher. Doing this eliminates having to repeat all the publisher information multiple times.

But when you want to view the publisher information for each book, you want to see the publisher's name, not the ID. This means that during the retrieval process, you have to establish the relation between the tables. The following SQL statement shows how this works for the two tables. Figure 31.8 shows the results of the statement.

```
SELECT Titles.title, Publishers.[Company Name] FROM Titles,
Publishers _
        WHERE Titles.pubid = Publishers.pubid
```

Speaking of multiple tables

The basic syntax for selecting information from multiple tables is the same as for single tables, with a couple of slight differences:

```
SELECT fieldlist FROM tablelist relationship
```

When you are working with fields from multiple tables, each field in the field list should have an identifier that specifies from which table the field is to be retrieved. This takes the form of the following:

```
tablename.fieldname
```

As with retrieving fields from a single table, each field in the SELECT statement must be separated from the others by commas.

relationship represents a clause that specifies how the tables in the tablelist are tied together. One form of the relationship clause makes use of the WHERE keyword. This type of relationship is of the following form:

```
WHERE table1.field1 = table2.field2
```

This indicates that a key field exists in each table which controls the relation between the records in the two tables.

Fig. 31.8

You can retrieve fields from multiple tables by including the table names with the fields and specifying a relationship between the tables.

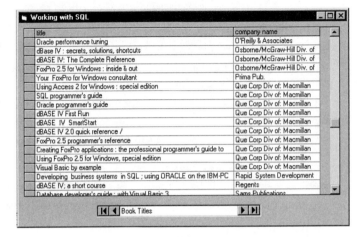

The first part of the statement says that you want to retrieve the book title of the titles table and the company name from the publishers table. Note that the Company Name field is enclosed in square brackets because the field name contains a space. The FROM clause specifies the two tables from which you will be retrieving fields.

The WHERE clause specifies the relationship between the two tables. This tells the program to get the book title from the title table, check the pubid field for that book, and retrieve the corresponding company name for that pubid from the publishers table.

 TIP The statement is broken onto multiple lines for purposes of presentation in this book. The statement should not have any breaks in it when used with the Data control.

You are not limited to combining information from just two tables. The following statement combines fields from the Titles, Authors, and Publishers tables. This combination is shown in figure 31.9.

```
select title2.title, authors.author, publishers.
[company name] _
    from title2, authors, publishers _
    where title2.au_id = authors.au_id _
    and title2.pubid = publishers.pubid
```

Fig. 31.9
You can retrieve information from any number of tables.

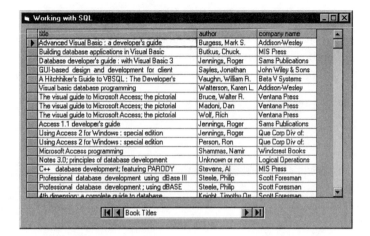

How do I change the recordset?

You can set up the initial recordset for a Data control by specifying an SQL statement in the RecordSource property of the Data control. But how do you change the recordset while the program is running? For example, how can you change the presentation order?

To change the recordset on-the-fly, you need to do two things. First, you must set the RecordSource property to the new SQL statement. Then you must use the Refresh method of the Data control to reset the control and show the results of the new SQL statement.

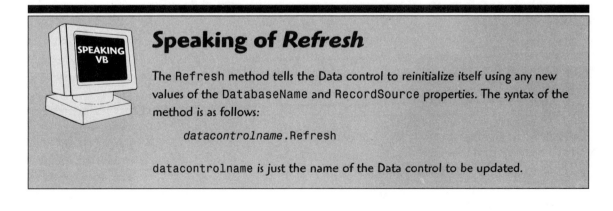

Speaking of *Refresh*

The Refresh method tells the Data control to reinitialize itself using any new values of the DatabaseName and RecordSource properties. The syntax of the method is as follows:

```
datacontrolname.Refresh
```

datacontrolname is just the name of the Data control to be updated.

The code listed below shows how a Data control containing a mailing list could be reset from the original order to the new address order as described in the "How can I use this in the real world?" section. Figure 31.10 shows the original order of the recordset; figure 31.11 shows the revised order.

```
Member.RecordSource = SELECT * FROM Members ORDER BY
zip, address
Member.Refresh
```

Fig. 31.10

The original order was established by the initial *RecordSource* setting.

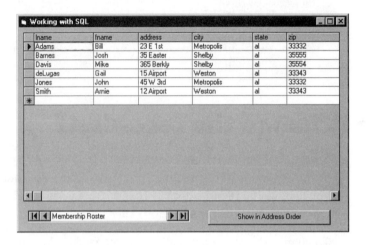

How can I use this in the real world?

You could use this method to change the order of a recordset for a membership database from alphabetical by member name to an order by address. The address order could be used in mailings to sort the members by zip code and save money by making use of the pre-sort savings.

Fig. 31.11
The new order was established by resetting the *RecordSource* property and issuing the *Refresh* method.

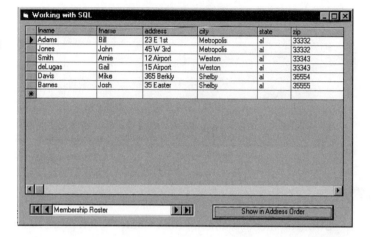

How can I test my SQL statements?

While you can enter your SQL statements in the RecordSource property and try running your code, this can be a frustrating way to set up and debug your SQL statements. A better way is to use the Data Manager Add-in.

The Data Manager has an area where you can enter SQL statements and execute them (see fig. 31.12). If the statement is successful, a form is displayed containing the data retrieved by the statement, as shown in figure 31.13. If the statement was unsuccessful, an error message is displayed. You can then edit your statement and try again. When the statement does what you want it to do, you can use the Copy and Paste operations of Windows to copy the statement to the RecordSource property of a Data control.

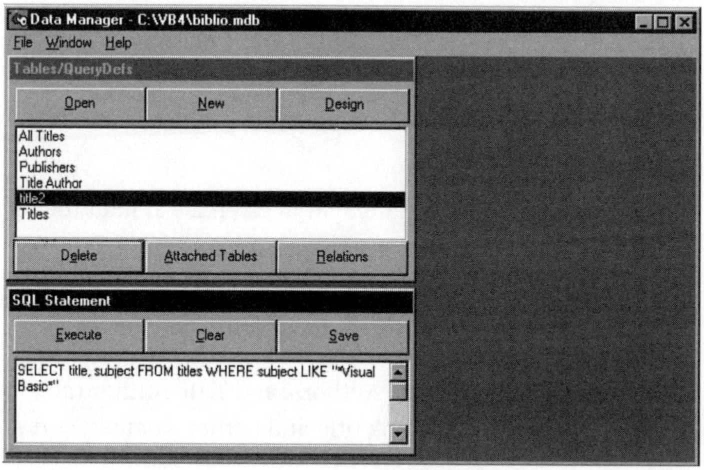

Fig. 31.12
The Data Manager allows you to enter and test SQL statements.

Fig. 31.13
A successful SQL statement displays a recordset containing the results.

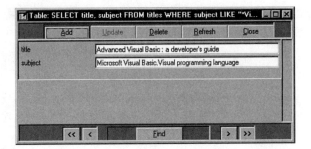

Summary

SQL statements make the Data Control even more flexible by allowing you greater control over the fields and records that comprise your recordset. You can even retrieve information from multiple tables.

Review questions

1 What must be specified for even the simplest SELECT statements?

2 How do you limit the records that will be retrieved for a recordset?

3 Which comparison operator allows you to compare a text field to a pattern?

4 How do you specify the order of a recordset?

5 What two things are necessary to retrieve records from multiple tables?

6 Name the two steps required to change a recordset after its initial creation.

Exercises

1 Create a SELECT statement to get the Title and Subject of each book in the Titles table.

2 Based on the statement in Exercise 1, limit the records to those dealing with SQL. Hint, use the LIKE operator.

3 Sort the recordset from Exercise 2 by the year in which the book was published.

4 Using the Titles, Authors, and Title Author tables, create a recordset that lists the book title and author's names, sorted by author.

32

Printing the Results of Your Programs

● In this chapter:

- How do I control where information is printed on a page?

- How do I use different text formats on the same page?

- Am I limited to printing just to the printer?

- Printing an entire form the easy way

Printed reports are still the most widely used way to distribute information. . . . . ➢

While Visual Basic gives you a variety of ways to display information on the screen, sometimes you just need to get something down on paper. This might be to send the information to someone else, or just for your own convenience in reviewing data. (It's easier to carry a ten-page report to the Little League game than to haul your computer there with you.)

For detailed information on fonts and font attributes, see Chapter 5, "Making Your Words Look Good."

But printing information involves more than just getting the bare facts on paper. If you are presenting information to others, you want to at least make sure that the information is well organized and easy to read. You might even want to make use of special effects to highlight particular pieces of information. For this, you will need an understanding of page layout and font characteristics. You can also use graphic elements to enhance your printing as you will see later.

To see how graphics can be used in your printouts, take a look at Chapter 33, "Adding Graphics to Your Programs."

In addition to printing out information on paper, most of the methods shown in this chapter can also be applied to presenting information on the screen. This provides you with the ability to present large amounts of information without having to use a large number of TextBoxes, Labels, or other controls.

All I really need it to do is just print!

The first thing to look at is the simple task of printing a set of values. The report doesn't need fancy text or effects; it just needs to print out some text and numbers for someone to read.

Where does my printing go?

When you use the `Print` method, you can direct the output of the method to one of four areas:

- Forms
- The printer
- PictureBox controls
- The Debug window

For the forms and picture box controls, the Print method outputs information to the background of the object. This means that the print will appear behind any controls that are placed on the form or in the picture box.

TIP **If you want to print to the screen, it is best to create a picture box** specifically for the purpose. This assures you of a clean printing area.

For more on fixing errors in your program, see Chapter 34, "Finding Bugs in Your Programs."

For the printer, the Print method directs output to the Print Manager to develop the pages. When you indicate that you are through printing, or when your application is terminated, the Print Manager sends the information you printed to the actual printer.

Printing to the Debug window is used to get information while a program is running. This is used to help track down errors in your programs.

Putting words on paper (or screen)

All printing in Visual Basic, whether to the printer or on a form or picture box, is done using the Print method. The Print method places the contents of a string or numeric expression on a line on the printer. Multiple expressions can be printed with a single print statement.

The information you print with the Print statement can be a single string or numeric expression, or can include multiple expressions and position definitions as follows:

```
expr1 [, ¦ ;] [Spc(n) ¦ Tab(m)] [, ¦ ; expr2]
```

Speaking of *Print*

The Print method is invoked using the following syntax:

```
[objectname.]Print [expressionlist]
```

In this syntax, objectname refers to the object where the information will be printed. This will be either the name of a form or picture box, the Printer object, or the Debug window. If the objectname parameter is omitted, the program assumes that the information should be printed to the currently active form. If the objectname is included, the dot must be included to separate the name from the Print keyword. expressionlist refers to the information to be printed.

expr1 and expr2 can be any numeric or string expressions. These can be literals, variables, or functions which return a string or number. If multiple expressions are included, they must be separated by either a comma or semicolon. If a semicolon is used, the second expression will begin printing immediately after the last character of the first expression. If a comma is used, the second expression is printed at the beginning of the next print zone. Each print zone is 14 characters wide.

The functions Spc and Tab can be used for additional control over the position of expressions on the print line. The Spc function tells the program to move a number of spaces (defined by n) before printing the next expression. The Tab function tells the program to move to a specific character position (defined by m) before printing the next expression. If included, these functions must be separated from other expressions by either a semicolon or a comma.

CAUTION **If you use a comma to separate the Spc or Tab functions from** other expressions, you may not get the desired results. Remember, the comma forces the printout to move to the next print zone.

Each time the Print method is used, it starts on a new line unless the semicolon is included after the last expression in the statement.

Listing 32.1 shows how to print a week's worth of daily sales data. The results of the code are shown in figure 32.1.

How can I use this in the real world?

One use of the Print command by itself would be to print two columns of information—for instance, daily sales figures. The prints are done using four different combinations of the comma, semicolon, Tab, and Spc functions to show you how these affect the appearance of the output.

Fig. 32.1
The *Print* method is used to display information on paper or on the screen.

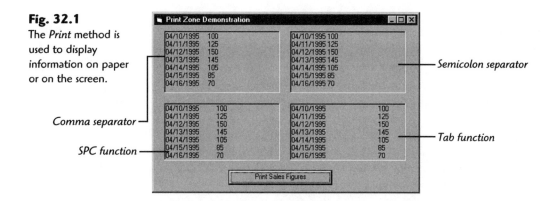

Semicolon separator

Comma separator

SPC function

Tab function

Listing 32.1   Separators and Position Functions Produce Many Effects

```
picPrint1.Print "04/10/1995", 100
picPrint1.Print "04/11/1995", 125
picPrint1.Print "04/12/1995", 150
picPrint1.Print "04/13/1995", 145
picPrint1.Print "04/14/1995", 105
picPrint1.Print "04/15/1995", 85
picPrint1.Print "04/16/1995", 70
picPrint2.Print "04/10/1995"; 100
picPrint2.Print "04/11/1995"; 125
picPrint2.Print "04/12/1995"; 150
picPrint2.Print "04/13/1995"; 145
picPrint2.Print "04/14/1995"; 105
picPrint2.Print "04/15/1995"; 85
picPrint2.Print "04/16/1995"; 70
picPrint3.Print "04/10/1995"; Spc(5); 100
picPrint3.Print "04/11/1995"; Spc(5); 125
picPrint3.Print "04/12/1995"; Spc(5); 150
picPrint3.Print "04/13/1995"; Spc(5); 145
picPrint3.Print "04/14/1995"; Spc(5); 105
picPrint3.Print "04/15/1995"; Spc(5); 85
picPrint3.Print "04/16/1995"; Spc(5); 70
picPrint4.Print "04/10/1995"; Tab(30); 100
picPrint4.Print "04/11/1995"; Tab(30); 125
picPrint4.Print "04/12/1995"; Tab(30); 150
picPrint4.Print "04/13/1995"; Tab(30); 145
picPrint4.Print "04/14/1995"; Tab(30); 105
picPrint4.Print "04/15/1995"; Tab(30); 85
picPrint4.Print "04/16/1995"; Tab(30); 70
```

Since the command for each date is the same in each of the blocks, we will only look at one line per picture box. In the code for the picPrint1, the date and the number are separated by a comma. This causes the program to print the number at the beginning of the second print zone; so, approximately four spaces are between the end of the date and the beginning of the number.

In the code for picPrint2, the semicolon was used as the separator. This causes the number to be printed immediately after the end of the date. The single space between the two fields is due to Visual Basic reserving a space for a negative sign when printing numbers.

The code for picPrint3 uses the Spc function to place a set amount of space (in this case, five spaces) between the two fields.

Finally, in the code for picPrint4, the Tab function is used to start the second column at a specific character position. In this listing, the number will be printed beginning in column 30.

TIP

As with documents in a word processor, it is better to use the Tab function than to use spaces to define the placement of fields. This is especially true when you are printing different strings where proportional fonts will affect the length of the string.

Syntax
Error

Catch the bug

The following code printed on the form instead of the picture box. Why?

```
Print "04/10/1995", 100
Print "04/11/1995", 125
Print "04/12/1995", 150
Print "04/13/1995", 145
Print "04/14/1995", 105
Print "04/15/1995", 85
Print "04/16/1995", 70
```

Answer: The Print *method did not specify the object to be used for the output. Therefore, the current form was assumed to be the desired output area. Each line should contain the name of the picture box as follows:*

```
picReport.Print "04/11/1995", 125
```

How can I liven up a dull report?

To learn more about displaying graphics, see Chapter 33, "Adding Graphics to Your Programs."

The `Print` method is a very effective tool for displaying information. However, by itself, it is a little boring. You want to be able to add excitement to your reports, to make certain information stand out and be noticed. (Of course, you may also want to make some information as inconspicuous as possible.)

Well, the `Print` method by itself can't handle this. It has no additional arguments that allow you to change fonts or font characteristics. Fortunately, there are ways to make it accomplish what you want in terms of text characteristics.

Can I choose another font?

The `Print` method will always use the current font and font attributes when it outputs information to the screen or printer. You can, however, change the current font to change the appearance of the text you are printing. The form, picture box, and Printer objects all contain the same font properties as are used by the text box and other controls. These properties are:

- `Font.Name`—determines which font to use.

- `Font.Size`—determines the height in points of the font.

- `Font.Bold`—determines whether the font is printed with heavy, dark strokes.

- `Font.Italic`—determines whether the letters are printed with a slant to the right.

- `Font.Underline`—determines whether a line is drawn under the text.

- `Font.StrikeThrough`—determines whether a line is drawn through the text.

These properties are changed using assignment statements in your code. For the forms and picture boxes, you can change the initial font settings using the Properties dialog while you are in the design mode. For the printer, the initial font settings are determined by the Print Manager in Windows.

The code in listing 32.2 shows how to add formatting to the report described in the "How can I use this in the real world?" section. The results of the code are shown in figure 32.2.

Fig. 32.2

Using different font attributes can highlight information in a printed report.

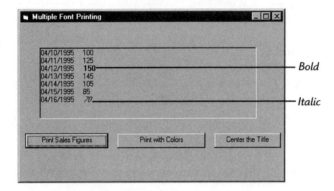

Listing 32.2 Fonts Can Be Changed In Code

```
picFonts.Print "04/10/1995", 100
picFonts.Print "04/11/1995", 125
picFonts.Print "04/12/1995", ;
picFonts.Font.Bold = True
picFonts.Print 150
picFonts.Font.Bold = False
picFonts.Print "04/13/1995", 145
picFonts.Print "04/14/1995", 105
picFonts.Print "04/15/1995", 85
picFonts.Print "04/16/1995", ;
picFonts.Font.Italic = True
picFonts.Print 70
picFonts.Font.Italic = False
```

Much of this code is similar to what was shown previously for the simple printout. The interesting lines of the code are the ones that print out

How can I use this in the real world?

Referring back to the example of printing out sales figures, you could highlight the top sales figure for the week by making that number appear in bold type. You could also point out the minimum sales by using the Italic property.

information for the 04/12/1995 date and the 04/16/1995 date. These are the figures that I chose to highlight with special font attributes.

The line that prints out the date for 04/12/1995 is basically the same as it was before, except that a semicolon was placed after the comma on the print line. This tells the program to move to the next print zone, and then print the next item starting at that point. If you had omitted the semicolon, the next Print statement would have started on a new line. After the date is printed, the Bold property of the font is set to True. This tells the program to use bold printing until the property is reset to False. You next print out the sales figure itself. This appears in Bold font. After printing the sales information, reset the Bold property to False, so the rest of the print continues in the normal font.

The same process is used for the minimum sales amount which is shown in italics. The date is printed, then the Italic property is set. Next the figure is printed, and the Italic property is reset to it original value.

While only the use of the Bold and Italic properties were shown in the example, you could have created other effects using the Name, Size, Underline, or StrikeThrough properties of the font. Remember that the Name and Size properties require a string and numeric value, respectively, while the Underline and StrikeThrough properties are set to either True or False.

TIP **If you are distributing an application to others, limit your font** selections to only those that are installed with Windows. They may not have the same additional fonts as you.

For information on the Common Dialog, see Chapter 15, "Use the Common Dialog for Specialized Information."

TIP **If you allow your user to select fonts, remember to use the** Common Dialog to get the font information.

Spice things up with a little color

If you are printing to a form or picture box, or are using a color printer, you can also affect the color of the text using the ForeColor property. Changing the ForeColor property only affects text that is printed after the property change. All other text remains as it was originally printed.

CAUTION **Do not change the BackColor property of a form or picture box** to which you are printing. You will wipe out any text that was printed before the color change.

TIP **The BackColor property is not applicable to the Printer object.**

Listing 32.3 modifies listing 32.2 to show how color can be used to achieve effects either by itself or in combination with other properties. Figure 32.3 shows the results of the use of color.

Fig. 32.3
Color can also be used to highlight information.

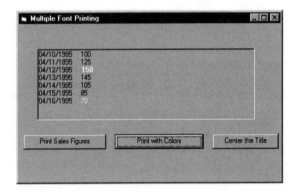

Listing 32.3   Change Text Color With the *ForeColor* Property

```
picFonts.Print "04/10/1995", 100
picFonts.Print "04/11/1995", 125
picFonts.Print "04/12/1995", ;
picFonts.Font.Bold = True
picFonts.ForeColor = vbWhite
picFonts.Print 150
picFonts.Font.Bold = False
picFonts.ForeColor = vbBlack
picFonts.Print "04/13/1995", 145
picFonts.Print "04/14/1995", 105
picFonts.Print "04/15/1995", 85
picFonts.Print "04/16/1995", ;
picFonts.ForeColor = vbWhite
picFonts.Print 70
picFonts.ForeColor = vbBlack
```

I need to make sure everything fits

So far, you have only looked at printing information in the print zones established by the `Print` method itself. For many situations, you will want even more control over the placement of text and graphical objects on the screen and the printed page.

Naturally, there are properties which allow you to set the absolute position of a piece of information anywhere in your print area. Working with layouts in this way is like arranging furniture in a room. When you arrange furniture, you need to know the size of the room and the size of each piece of furniture. You then work at making sure the pieces will fit where you want them, and arrange and rearrange pieces until you have a setup that is pleasing to you.

Visual Basic has several tools which help you determine the size of your space and the various pieces with which you are working. It also has tools to let you specify the exact placement of a piece.

How big is my print space?

Typically, we think of the printed page as a piece of paper 8.5 by 11 inches. Unfortunately, Visual Basic doesn't typically work with inches as its dimensions. Visual Basic works with a unit of measure called twips. (One inch equals 1440 twips.) Also, the size of the paper can be different from the standard 8.5X11, and we must account for whether the printer is working in **landscape** or **portrait mode**.

 Plain English, please!

> If you have not heard these terms before, **portrait mode** means that printing is done with the longest dimension being from top to bottom. **Landscape mode** means that the long dimension of the printing is from side to side.

If you are working with the printer, the dimensions of the object are controlled by the Print Manager and the printer itself. If you are working with forms or picture boxes, the dimensions of the print area are controlled by the initial design. Any resizing is done by the program.

The best way to determine the available space in an object where you want to print is to use the Height and Width properties of the object (see fig. 32.4).

Fig. 32.4
The *Height* and *Width* properties tell you the size of your print area.

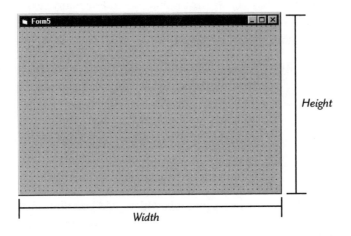

Height

Width

SPEAKING VB

Speaking of *Height* and *Width*

To obtain the value of the Height and Width properties for any object, use the following commands:

    resultHt = objectname.Height

    resultWd = objectname.Width

objectname is the name of the form or picture box for which the property value is desired. It can also be the Printer object. If objectname is omitted, the currently active form is assumed.

For the form and picture box objects, you can set the value of the Height and Width properties to change the size of the object as shown in the following lines:

    objectname.Height = value

    objectname.Width = value

value in each case must be an integer greater than zero.

When the size of a form or picture box is changed using the Height and Width properties, the top and left sides of the object remain fixed. The right and bottom sides adjust to accommodate the change (see fig. 32.5).

Fig. 32.5
Resize an object using the *Height* and *Width* properties.

This corner stays put

Changing Width *moves this edge*

Changing Height *moves this edge*

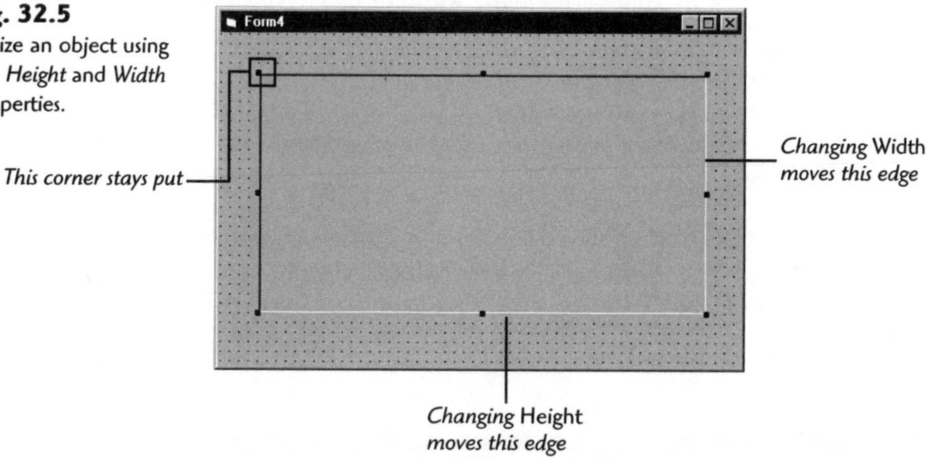

What size is the piece I need to print?

Now that you know how big your space is, you need to determine the size of the piece you want to print. This is necessary to determine whether the piece will fit and to determine how much space is left over.

The reason you need to determine whether something will fit is that the Print method is very simple-minded. It does not check to see whether the text is wider than the area where it is to be printed. Therefore, if the text is too wide, it simply disappears off the right edge of the print area, as shown in figure 32.6.

Fig. 32.6
Word wrapping would be useful here.

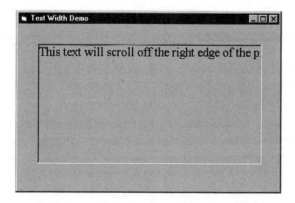

Since the `Print` method doesn't do this for you, you must do it yourself. The `TextHeight` and `TextWidth` methods can tell you the vertical and horizontal size of a piece of text.

When you want to determine the width or height of some text, you must supply a string expression to the `TextWidth` and `TextHeight` functions. The string expression can be a literal, a variable, or a function. If you are evaluating the size of a number, it must be converted to a string using the `Str` or `CStr` function. Also, remember that literal strings must be enclosed within quotation marks.

Listing 32.4 shows how to perform word wrapping on a string of text that is too long for a single line. The program takes a statement from the text box and prints it in a picture box in a larger font. The results are shown in figure 32.7.

Speaking of *TextHeight* and *TextWidth*

To use the `TextHeight` and `TextWidth` methods, you must supply a string to be evaluated. These methods are used as follows:

```
resultTxHt = objectname.TextHeight(stringexpr)

resultTxWd = objectname.TextWidth(stringexpr)
```

`resultTxHt` and `resultTxWd` are variables which will contain the values returned by the methods. `stringexpr` represents the string to be evaluated.

How can I use this in the real world?

One use of the `TextWidth` method is to determine how much of a line can be printed across the print area. If the text is too wide, you can use string manipulation functions to break the string up into smaller pieces. This process is very useful for printing large amounts of information and works the same way as your word processor.

Fig. 32.7

The *TextWidth* method can be used to handle word wrapping in a printout.

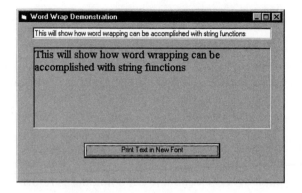

Listing 32.4   Perform Word Wrapping In Your Own Printouts

```
prntvar = txtInpt.Text
objwid = picWord.Width
Do
    endpos = 0
    txtlen = 0
    prntln = ""
    Do
        strtpos = endpos + 1
        endpos = InStr(strtpos, prntvar, " ")
        prntln = Left$(prntvar, endpos)
        txtlen = picWord.TextWidth(prntln)
    Loop Until txtlen > objwid Or endpos = 0
    If endpos = 0 Then
        prntln = prntvar
        prntvar = ""
    Else
        prntln = Left$(prntvar, strtpos - 1)
        prntvar = LTrim$(Mid$(prntvar, strtpos))
    End If
    picWord.Print prntln
Loop While Len(prntvar) > 0
```

The object of the code is to break the string at a space between words and place any text that doesn't fit on the current line onto another line.

The first line of the code gets the input string from the text box. The second line of the code determines the width of the output picture box using the `Width` property.

The third line starts the outer loop of the code. As you print part of the text on a line, you reduce the size of the remaining text contained in the `prntvar` variable. When the length of the remaining text is zero, the loop will terminate.

Each time the outer loop is run, three variables are initialized for processing the remaining text. This is done in the first three lines inside the loop. After the variables are initialized, the inner loop is started. This loop determines the largest text string within the remaining text that will fit on a print line.

The inner loop does its task by first looking for a space character in the text using the InStr function. If no space is found, 0 is returned by the InStr function and the loop terminates. If a number is returned by the InStr function, a string is created containing all the text up to the space. The length of this string is checked against the width of the print area. If the string is longer than the print area, the loop terminates. Otherwise, the loop goes back and looks for the next space in the text.

After the inner loop terminates, the string to be printed is determined. If the return value from the InStr function (stored in the variable endpos) is zero, the entire remaining text is stored to the output variable and the remaining text variable is set to a zero length string. If the value of endpos was not zero, the output variable is set to the portion of the text that will fit on the output line, and the remaining text is set to the string left over after the print text is removed.

Finally, the output variable is printed using the Print method.

Put it where you want it

Now you know all about how big things are. All that is left is to place them in the correct spots to achieve the desired effects. Two properties are used to determine or set the position of a piece of text on the print area. These properties are the CurrentX and CurrentY properties. These two properties define the upper left corner of the print position. When the Print method is issued, the text is printed down and to the right of this position.

To set the current print position, use the following syntax:

```
objectname.CurrentX = value

objectname.CurrentY = value
```

As before, objectname refers to the Printer object or the name of a form or picture box. value is a positive number that expresses the position in the current scale (usually twips).

CurrentX sets the distance of the print position from the left edge of the print area. CurrentY sets the distance of the print position from the top of the print area.

One use of the TextWidth method and the CurrentX and CurrentY properties is to center a title expression on the line. The code in listing 32.5 shows how this is done.

Listing 32.5   Center Text Using the *CurrentX* Property

```
objwid = picWord.Width
txwidth = picWord.TextWidth("Centering a Title")
cntrpos = Int((objwid - txwidth) / 2)
picWord.CurrentX = cntrpos
picWord.Print "Centering a Title"
```

This code determines the empty space available after the title would be printed. This is accomplished by subtracting the width of the text (obtained with the TextWidth method) from the width of the output area (obtained from the Width property). This remaining space is divided in two to allow equal space on both sides of the title.

The CurrentX property is then set to the value of half the empty space. This will cause the Print method to start at that point. The Print method then prints the title, and it is perfectly centered.

How can I control the printer?

When you are working with the Printer object, you not only have to tell it what to print and where to print it, you also have to tell the printer when to start a new page and when you are finished printing the document. You may at some time also want to terminate the print job being processed. Each of these tasks is accomplished with a method of the Printer object.

The NewPage method is used to start a new page on the printer. Its syntax is quite simple:

```
Printer.NewPage
```

When this method is used, the printer is signaled to eject the current page and start a new one. Also the values of the CurrentX and CurrentY properties for the printer object are each set to 0.

Catch the bug

The following code is intended to center a title. What is wrong with it?

```
prntwid = Width
titleinfo = Monthly Budget Projections
txtwid = TextWidth titleinfo
Form1.CurrentX = (prntwid - txtwid)/2
Form1.Print titleinfo
```

Answer: The error in the code is that the string expression to be evaluated by the TextWidth method is not enclosed in parentheses. Also, while it is not an error, the object names were not included for the Width property and TextWidth methods. This is fine if the current form is Form1 (the one used for the Print method). However, you can avoid errors and make your code more readable if you always include the object name. The correct code is as follows:

```
txtwid = Form1.TextWidth(titleinfo)
```

When you have finished sending information to the printer, you notify Windows by using the EndDoc method as shown:

```
Printer.EndDoc
```

This method tells the Print Manager that the current documents is complete, and the printout can be sent to the printer. Like the NewPage method, EndDoc sets the values of the CurrentX and CurrentY properties for the printer object to 0.

If you decide that you really didn't want to print the information, you can terminate the Print function using the KillDoc method.

```
Printer.KillDoc
```

This method tells the Print Manager to abort the print job and clear the information from the print buffer.

How do I clear the screen?

When you are printing information to a form or picture box, the Print method will keep right on creating lines and will eventually reach the bottom of the visible print area. I use the word *visible* because if another `Print` method is issued after the bottom is reached, the line will be printed, but it will be outside of the area you can see.

When printing to the screen, you want to be able to start back at the top of the print area after you have reached the bottom. Resetting the `CurrentX` and `CurrentY` properties to `0` will place the print position back at the top of the screen, but the `Print` method will just print over existing text. You also need to be able to wipe out the existing text before new printing is begun. Otherwise, you may see part of the previous text on your new screen.

This is done using the `Cls` method of the form or picture box.

The `Clear screen (Cls)` method clears the printable area of the object and resets the objects `CurrentX` and `CurrentY` properties to `0`:

```
objectname.Cls
```

As with the other methods, `objectname` is the name of the form or picture box to be cleared. There are no other arguments to be specified for this method.

I want to print it all

There is one final way to get information to the printer. There are times when the easiest way to present the information is to set it up on a form, and then print an image of the entire form to the printer. When this is done, all

Speaking of *PrintForm*

The syntax for the `PrintForm` method is:

```
[formname.]PrintForm
```

`formname` is the name of the form you want to have printed. If `formname` is omitted, the currently active form is the one printed.

`PrintForm` prints the contents of the form as it appears on the screen. It does not, however, print the forms borders, caption, or any control buttons (maximize, minimize, or control box).

controls on the form including labels, command buttons, pictures, and so on, are sent to the printer exactly as they occur on the screen. Even bitmap pictures are sent to the printer.

Printing a form is accomplished using the `PrintForm` method.

Summary

While the `Print` method is a simple command with limited capabilities, you can use the method and the properties of the Printer object (or form or picture box) to generate very complex reports. Ultimately, your only limit is your imagination and the amount of time you spend arranging your pages.

Review questions

1 Where can you direct the printed output from your program?

2 How do you force the `Print` method to start at a specific character location on a line?

3 How do you change the font or font attributes of the text you are printing?

4 How do you determine the size of your output area?

5 How do you determine the size of the text you are trying to print?

6 What happens if your text is larger than the print area?

7 How do you print to a specific location?

8 What commands do you use to get a clean print area?

Exercises

1 Change listing 32.2 to underline the minimum value.

2 Change listing 32.5 to align the text with the right edge of the picture box.

3 Write a code routine that prints a title down the left side of a picture box.

33

Adding Graphics to Your Programs

● **In this chapter:**

- **Draw lines and shapes with Visual Basic**

- **What kinds of objects can be drawn?**

- **Can the objects be solid or just out-lines?**

- **How are graphics methods different from the graphics controls?**

With its graphics controls, Visual Basic even lets you show your artistic side . . . .

While the term "computer graphics" may sound complicated, and some of the things done with computer graphics are quite complex, the basic concepts behind generating computer graphics are really quite simple. In the simplest terms, computer graphics is merely the placement of lines, shapes, and points on the computer screen or on the printed page. How you create those lines and shapes is the subject of this chapter.

You can use the techniques presented here to do complex tasks such as drawing pictures or designing buildings. However, there are also a number of simpler tasks that require a little knowledge of the graphics methods. For instance, if you draw a line on a report to show the total, you have used a graphics method. You can also use the methods to generate graphs like the one shown in figure 33.1. These graphs can help you analyze information.

Fig. 33.1
A graph drawn with the graphics methods can help you analyze information.

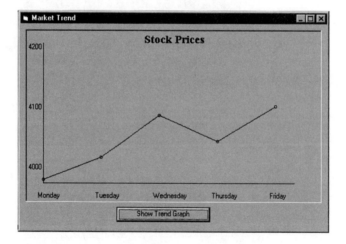

So what are the graphics methods, and what can you draw with them? There are six methods that are used to draw on the screen or on paper. They are as follows:

- Line method, which draws a line or a box on the screen or printer.

- Circle method, which draws a circle, oval, pie, or arc on the screen or printer.

- PSet method, which places a single point on the screen or printer.

- Point method, which returns the color of a specific point.

- `PaintPicture` method, which draws an image from another control onto the screen or printer.

- `Cls` method, which clears the output area of the screen.

Where can I draw?

For information on printing, see Chapter 32, "Printing the Results of Your Programs."

Like the `Print` method, the graphics methods can be used on a form, a picture box, or the printer. The methods are controlled by properties of the object on which they are used. For example, the `DrawStyle` property determines the line pattern used to draw the borders of objects. Table 33.1 contains a list of the properties that affect how the graphics methods work.

Table 33.1   Object Properties Control the Appearance of Lines

Property	Affects
DrawMode	Determines how the color used to draw the border of the object interacts with objects already on the screen.
DrawStyle	Determines the pattern used to draw the border of the object.
DrawWidth	Determines the width of the line used to draw the border of the object.
FillColor	Determines the color used to fill an object.
FillStyle	Determines the fill pattern used to fill an object.
ForeColor	Determines the primary color used in drawing the border of an object.

How do I add lines and boxes?

Probably the simplest to use of the graphics methods is the `Line` method. In its simplest form, it is used for drawing a straight line from one place to another. Don't let its simplicity fool you. The `Line` method can be used for a number of tasks, such as drawing grid lines for a table, drawing lines for a building design, or plotting trends on a data chart.

By changing properties and adding other arguments to the `Line` method, you can draw outlines or filled boxes. You can also change the pattern of the line and/or its color.

From point A to point B

To draw a line, use the `Line` method and specify the starting and ending points of the line.

For information on setting the value of the `CurrentX` and `CurrentY` properties, see Chapter 32, "Printing the Results of Your Programs."

The coordinates used for drawing lines are single type numbers that represent the distance of the point from the left side (x1) and top (y1) of the drawing area. The coordinates are specified in the current scale for the object, usually twips. If the `coordinate` pair is omitted, the drawing of the line will start from the `CurrentX` and `CurrentY` position of the object. If the pair is included, it must be enclosed in parentheses.

The hyphen in the method must be included. It precedes the pair of coordinates that mark the endpoint of the line.

The end point coordinates are measured the same way as the starting point coordinates. This coordinate pair must be included when drawing a line, or an error will occur. All the coordinates (x1, y1, x2, and y2) are numeric expressions which can include literals, numeric variables, numeric functions and equations.

When the line is drawn, the value of the `CurrentX` and `CurrentY` properties of the object are set to x2 and y2, respectively.

To illustrate the use of the `Line` method, listing 33.1 shows how to draw a triangle in a picture box. The result of the code is shown in figure 33.2.

Speaking of *Line*

To draw lines on the screen or to print them, use the `Line` method as follows:

```
objectname.Line [(x1, y1)] - (x2, y2)
```

`objectname` is the name of the form or picture box where the line will be drawn. `objectname` also can refer to the Printer object. If `objectname` is omitted, the currently active form is used as the target object.

x1 and y1 are the coordinates of the initial point of the line, while x2 and y2 are the coordinates of the end point of the line.

Listing 33.1   Drawing a Triangle With Code

```
objwid = picGraphDemo.Width
objht = picGraphDemo.Height
stx = objwid / 2
sty = 100
enx = 100
eny = objht - 100
picGraphDemo.Line (stx, sty)-(enx, eny)
enx = objwid - 100
picGraphDemo.Line -(enx, eny)
picGraphDemo.Line -(stx, sty)
```

Fig. 33.2

The *Line* method is used to place lines and draw objects on the screen.

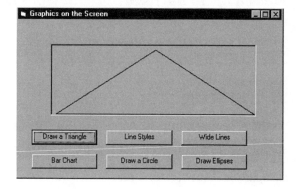

 In this example, draw a triangle that fills a large portion of the picture box. Therefore, you use the Height and Width properties of the picture box to help determine the starting and ending points of the lines that make up the triangle. In the first two lines of the code, the height and width of the picture box are stored to variables for further use.

In the next line, calculate the midpoint of the picture box to use as the starting horizontal position of the first line. Set the starting vertical position to 100 to make sure that it is not right at the top edge of the picture box. (A value of 0 would put the point at the top edge.)

Next, set the ending coordinates of the first line. The horizontal coordinate is set to 100, and the vertical coordinate is set to 100 less than the height of the box. After setting the values of the coordinates, use the Line method with the variables to draw the first line. In this case, specify both the starting and ending point of the line.

Next, set the coordinates for the end point of the line along the bottom of the picture box. After you set the value of the horizontal coordinate, again use the Line method to draw the line. This time, omit the starting coordinates, since the last line method set the CurrentX and CurrentY values to the end of the previous line, which happens to be the starting point of our current line.

Finally, use the Line method once more to draw a line back to the starting position to complete the triangle.

Q&A **When I tried to draw a line in a picture box, the line showed up on the form instead. What happened?**

You did not specify the name of the picture box with the Line method. If no object is specified, the current form is assumed.

Syntax Error

Catch the bug

What is wrong with the following code which attempts to draw lines?

```
picGraphDemo.Line (1500, 100)-(100, 1500)
picGraphDemo.Line (3000, 1500)
picGraphDemo.Line (1500, 100)
```

Answer: You must include the hyphen prior to the ending coordinates in the Line method. The correct code is as follows:

```
picGraphDemo.Line -(3000, 1500)
picGraphDemo.Line -(1500, 100)
```

Line patterns and widths

The lines used to draw the triangle above were solid lines. You can also draw lines with different patterns using the Line method. However, there is no parameter in the Line method which accomplishes this. In order to draw a line with a different pattern, you must change the DrawStyle property of the object on which you are drawing. The following table summarizes the values of the DrawStyle property and the types of lines that are drawn using these values. The effects of the different DrawStyle settings are shown in figure 33.3. The property may be set at designtime for a picture box or form using the Properties dialog. It can be set at runtime for any of the output objects using an assignment statement.

Value	Line pattern
0	Solid
1	Dash
2	Dot
3	Dash-Dot
4	Dash-Dot-Dot

Fig. 33.3

Different line patterns may be obtained using different settings of the *DrawStyle* property.

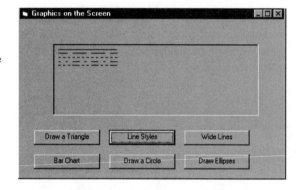

You can also set the width of the line to different values as shown in figure 33.4. The width is controlled by the DrawWidth property of the object.

Fig. 33.4

Different line widths may be obtained using different values of the *DrawWidth* property.

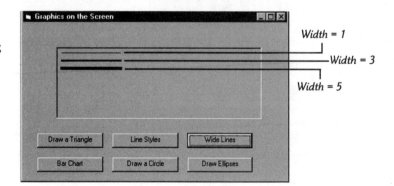

CAUTION **The DrawStyle property has no effect if the DrawWidth property is**
set to a value greater than 1.

Inside the box

The Line method can also be used to draw boxes by adding another parameter to the statement. The boxes can either be drawn as outlines or as filled boxes.

Q&A *I set the FillStyle to 7 (Diagonal Cross), but my box is drawn as a solid box. Why?*

You have probably done what I have done on numerous occasions, included the F parameter of the Line method. This parameter causes the box to be filled as a solid with the same color as the border, no matter what the setting of the FillStyle property is.

Half full or half empty

When a box is drawn with the Line method, the fill pattern can be selected using the values of the FillStyle property. The possible values of this property are summarized in the following table.

SPEAKING VB

Speaking of *Line*

To draw a box, use the following syntax of the Line method:

```
objectname.Line [(x1, y1)] - (x2, y2),,B
```

or

```
objectname.Line [(x1, y1)] - (x2, y2),,BF
```

If the first syntax is used, the box is drawn with the fill color and pattern controlled by properties of the object on which the box is drawn. The second syntax draws a filled box with a solid fill pattern, using the same color that was used to draw the border of the box.

Value	Fill Pattern
0	Solid
1	Transparent
2	Horizontal Line
3	Vertical Line
4	Upward Diagonal
5	Downward Diagonal
6	Cross
7	Diagonal Cross

These different fill patterns are shown in figure 33.5. The boxes showing the fill patterns were created with the following listing. As with the DrawStyle property, initial settings for the form and picture box can be made using the Properties dialog. Settings for any object can be made using assignment statements while the program is running. Listing 33.2 shows the code used to draw several different boxes with different shading.

Listing 33.2   Shading Controlled by *FillStyle*

```
frmBoxes.FillStyle = 0
frmBoxes.Line (200, 200)-(1000, 1000), , B
frmBoxes.FillStyle = 1
frmBoxes.Line (1200, 200)-(2000, 1000), , B
frmBoxes.FillStyle = 2
frmBoxes.Line (2200, 200)-(3000, 1000), , B
frmBoxes.FillStyle = 3
frmBoxes.Line (200, 1200)-(1000, 2000), , B
frmBoxes.FillStyle = 4
frmBoxes.Line (1200, 1200)-(2000, 2000), , B
frmBoxes.FillStyle = 5
frmBoxes.Line (2200, 1200)-(3000, 2000), , B
frmBoxes.FillStyle = 6
frmBoxes.Line (200, 2200)-(1000, 3000), , B
frmBoxes.FillStyle = 7
frmBoxes.Line (1200, 2200)-(2000, 3000), , B
```

Fig. 33.5
The *FillStyle* property controls the appearance of filled boxes.

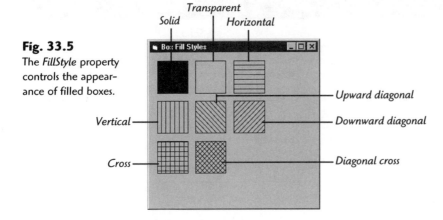

Solid

Transparent

Horizontal

Vertical

Cross

Upward diagonal

Downward diagonal

Diagonal cross

To draw a bar chart like the one mentioned in the "How can I use this in the real world?" section below, you can use the code in listing 33.3. Figure 33.6 shows how sales data for a week might be displayed using a bar chart.

Listing 33.3   Bar Chart Drawn With the *Line* Method

```
picGraphDemo.FillStyle = 0
picGraphDemo.Line (200, 1800)-(400, 800), , B
picGraphDemo.FillStyle = 2
picGraphDemo.Line (400, 1800)-(600, 1000), , B
picGraphDemo.FillStyle = 3
picGraphDemo.Line (600, 1800)-(800, 600), , B
picGraphDemo.FillStyle = 4
picGraphDemo.Line (800, 1800)-(1000, 500), , B
picGraphDemo.FillStyle = 5
picGraphDemo.Line (1000, 1800)-(1200, 1100), , B
picGraphDemo.FillStyle = 6
picGraphDemo.Line (1200, 1800)-(1400, 900), , B
picGraphDemo.FillStyle = 7
picGraphDemo.Line (1400, 1800)-(1600, 950), , B
```

How can I use this in the real world?

One of the most common uses of filled boxes with different patterns is in the creation of bar charts for business graphics. In bar charts, the height of the bar indicates the relative value of the data, while the different fill patterns are used to distinguish between data sets.

Fig. 33.6
Filled boxes with different fill patterns can be used to represent data in a bar chart and are used to help differentiate bars.

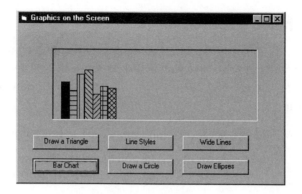

Catch the bug

The following code should draw a box on the screen. What is wrong with the code?

```
picGraphDemo.FillStyle = 7
picGraphDemo.Line (1400, 1800)-(1600, 950), B
```

Answer: *You must include two commas between the endpoint coordinates and the B option. There is an optional property of the Line method between these two parameters, and the second comma indicates that the property was skipped. The following is the correct code:*

```
picGraphDemo.Line (1400, 1800)-(1600, 950), , B
```

How do I add circles and curves?

You've seen how the Line method lets you draw lines and boxes. But how do you draw curves? The method for this is the Circle method. With it, you can draw circles, ellipses, arcs, and pie slices. You determine which is drawn by the parameters you include in the method.

Circles, ellipses, and pies can all be represented as outline drawings, or they can be filled. As with the Line method, the style and color of the fill is determined by the FillStyle and FillColor properties of the object on which you are drawing.

Perfect circles

In its simplest form, the `Circle` method draws circles on the screen or printer. All you have to define is the center of the circle and its radius. As with the `Line` method, the coordinates for the center and the length of the radius are specified in twips (or the current scale).

To draw the circle as shown in figure 33.7, use the following line of code:

```
picGraphDemo.Circle (900, 900), 750
```

Fig. 33.7
A circle is drawn using the *Circle* method.

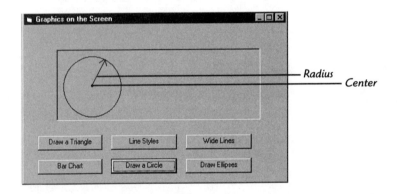

Speaking of *Circle*

To draw a simple circle, specify the center and radius of the circle in the method.

```
objectname.Circle (x, y), radius
```

`objectname` is the name of the form or picture box where the circle is drawn. It also can refer to the Printer object. `x` and `y` are the horizontal and vertical coordinates, respectively, for the center of the circle. The coordinate pair must be enclosed in parentheses. `radius` specifies the size of the circle. (If you don't remember geometry, the radius is the distance from the center to the edge of the circle.)

Not-so-perfect circles

An **ellipse** is a circle that has been stretched either horizontally or vertically. To draw an ellipse, you still use the `Circle` method, but you have to include an additional parameter. This parameter is the **aspect ratio**.

 Plain English, please!

The **aspect ratio** of an ellipse is the ratio of the vertical height of the ellipse to the horizontal width of the ellipse. An aspect ratio greater than 1 means the ellipse is longer in the vertical direction. An aspect ratio less than 1 creates an ellipse that is longer in the horizontal direction. An aspect ratio of exactly 1 yields a circle.

You can also draw an ellipse, using the following syntax of the `Circle` method:

```
objectname.Circle (x, y), radius, , , , aspect
```

The commas between `radius` and `aspect` represent other parameters for which values are not being provided. These four commas must be present in the statement. `objectname`, `x`, and `y` all have the same meaning for the ellipse as for the circle. `radius` for an ellipse specifies the distance from the center to the point farthest from the center on the border of the ellipse. `aspect` is a numeric expression defining the aspect ratio of the ellipse. Figure 33.8 shows two ellipses drawn in a picture box. These ellipses were drawn with the following code lines:

```
picGraphDemo.Circle (900, 900), 750, , , , 1.5
picGraphDemo.Circle (2700, 900), 750, , , , 2 / 3
```

Fig. 33.8
An ellipse is a flattened circle that can be drawn using the *Circle* method with an aspect ratio specified.

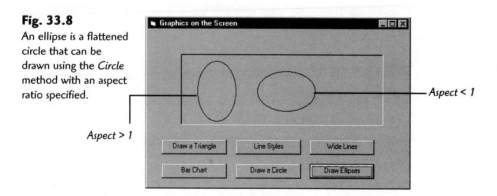

Want some pie?

You don't have to draw an entire circle or ellipse when you use the Circle method. You can also draw a part of a circle. The parts of a circle can be drawn in two ways—an **arc**, which is a portion of the edge of a circle, and a **pie**, which is basically an arc with lines drawn from the end of the arc to the center of the circle.

When drawing arcs using the Circle method, if the start or end point is a negative number, a line is drawn from the edge of the circle at that point, to the center of the circle. If the point is a positive number, no line is drawn from the center. In other words, to draw a pie, both the start and end points must be negative numbers. To draw an arc, both points need to be positive numbers. Figure 33.9 shows both arcs and pies drawn with the Circle method.

Fig. 33.9

Arcs and pies are drawn using the *Circle* method with start and end points specified.

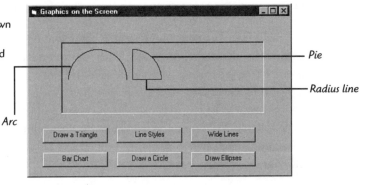

Pie

Radius line

Arc

Speaking of *Circle*

To draw pies or arcs, use the Circle method and specify the start and end points of the arc. The points are specified in radians. The Circle method is used as follows:

```
objectname.Circle (x, y), radius, , start, end
```

objectname, x, y, and radius are the same parameters as defined previously for a full circle. The start and end parameters specify the starting position and ending position of the arc. These values can range from 2 pi to –2 pi.

Listing 33.4 shows how the `Circle` method can be used to draw a pie chart for a home budget. It also uses a little trick to create what is called an **exploded piece**. Figure 33.10 shows the results of the code.

Fig. 33.10

An exploded piece of the pie is used to highlight the largest chunk of the budget.

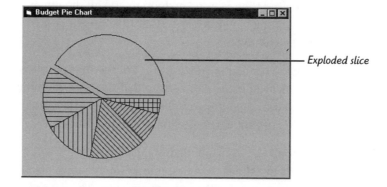

— *Exploded slice*

Listing 33.4   The *Circle* Method Used to Create a Pie Chart

```
Dim expns(1 To 6) As Single
pi = 3.14159
expns(1) = 1000
expns(2) = 400
expns(3) = 325
expns(4) = 375
expns(5) = 200
expns(6) = 100
totexp = 0
For I = 1 To 6
    totexp = totexp + expns(I)
Next I
stpnt = -0.00001
For I = 1 To 6
    frctn = expns(I) / totexp
    cirfrc = frctn * 2 * pi
    enpnt = stpnt - cirfrc
    If enpnt < -2 * pi Then enpnt = -2 * pi
    frmPie.FillStyle = I
    If I = 1 Then
        frmPie.Circle (2100, 1900), 1500, , stpnt, enpnt
    Else
        frmPie.Circle (2000, 2000), 1500, , stpnt, enpnt
    End If
    stpnt = enpnt
Next I
```

 **code** The first line of the code sets up an array to hold the expense amounts. The second line defines the value of pi. The next six lines set the values of each of the six expenses to be graphed and initializes the `totexp` variable.

The program then uses a For loop to add all the expenses together to get the total. The total is necessary so that the percent contribution of each expense can be calculated.

The next line sets the starting point of the first pie slice. The small decimal number is used instead of zero so that the line would be drawn from the center to the edge of the circle. If we had set the value to zero, it would not have been negative, and no line would be drawn.

The second For loop calculates each expense's fraction of the total, and draws the pie slices. The first line inside the loop calculates the fraction of the total expense for the current expense. The second line converts the fraction into a fraction of a circle. Next, the endpoint of the pie slice is determined by subtracting the fraction of the circle from the starting point. Using subtraction assures that all the points are negative. The next line is an error trap to make sure the end point is within the 2 pi to –2 pi range of the Circle method.

To learn more about data validation, see Chapter 35, "Error Handling: Anticipating Mistakes That Users Will Make."

Finally, you are ready to draw the pie slice. First, set the `FillStyle` property for the current slice. Since the `FillStyle` values range from 0 to 7, the loop index I (which goes from 1 to 6) makes a convenient value to assign. Next, use the `Circle` method to draw the pie slice. Notice that for the first slice (I = 1), a different set of coordinates for the circle's center is used. This is what gives you the exploding slice.

After the slice is drawn, set the starting point of the next slice to the ending point of the current slice. This ensures that there are no gaps between the slices.

What's the point?

The final method for you to look at is the `PSet` method. This method allows you to draw a single point on the screen or on the printer. Since a single point would be quite small, this method is mainly used to draw several points in a specific pattern to form symbols.

What can the graphics controls do?

For information on the graphics controls, see Chapter 12, "Other Controls You Should Know About."

You are probably wondering what the difference is between the graphics methods and the graphics controls? It is true that on the form or in a picture box, both the methods and the controls can produce some of the same visual effects. However, there are several advantages to using the graphics methods:

- The graphics methods can be used to draw on the Printer object; the graphics controls cannot.

- The lines, circles, and other objects drawn with the graphics methods can be added at runtime. Graphics controls can only be added during design.

- The graphics methods use fewer system resources because your program does not have to track the names and properties of the objects.

There is one disadvantage to using the graphics methods on a form. The effects of the graphics methods can only be seen at runtime. However, with the graphics controls, you can see the effects while you are still in design mode.

Summary

From within your Visual Basic program, the graphics methods provide you with the tools you need to draw charts, graphs, and objects on screen or printer.

SPEAKING VB

Speaking of *PSet*

To place a single point on the screen or printer, use the following syntax:

```
objectname.PSet (x, y)
```

objectname is the name of the form or picture box, or Printer object, where you are drawing the point. As always, if you omit the objectname parameter, the current form is assumed. x and y represent the horizontal and vertical coordinates for the location of the point.

Review questions

1 What property controls the line pattern used for lines and object borders?

2 What method is used to draw boxes?

3 What property defines the pattern inside a box or circle?

4 What method is used to draw curved objects?

5 What is the difference in the parameters used to draw arcs and pies?

6 To segregate blocks of information on a form, would you use the graphics methods or the graphics controls? Why?

Exercises

1 Use the `Line` method to draw two crossed lines.

2 Use the `Circle` method to draw a series of concentric circles on the screen.

3 Draw a picture of the Olympic rings on the screen.

4 Write the code to generate a graph similar to the one shown in figure 33.1.

34

Finding Bugs in Your Programs

● **In this chapter:**

● **Find errors in your program**

● **Can I find out the value of variables while the program is executing?**

● **What is the best way to test my program?**

● **Find out where the error occurred**

The debugging tools in Visual Basic make tracking code errors less of a chore. . . . . ➤

Keys to successful bug-hunting

No matter how long you have been developing programs or how good you are at what you do, you'll still have errors crop up in your program. Personally, I've been developing programs for over 20 years and still have some kind of error in my programs when I first write them.

It's easy to make mistakes. All it takes is a simple typo to make your program crash. There are also logic errors, where your program runs but it just doesn't do what you want it to do.

Because you will make errors, the key to successful program development is the ability to track down these errors, or **bugs** as they are often known, and kill them. Visual Basic provides you with a number of tools to help you find and eliminate bugs. If you have been programming for very long, you will appreciate the usefulness of these tools. Debugging with these tools is light-years ahead of having to place statements in your code such as "I got this far."

While there is no hard and fast procedure for debugging your programs, the following items should provide you with some good advice:

- Write your program in modules. Smaller pieces of code are easier to debug than large chunks.

- Test each module individually. This may not always be possible, but when you can, it narrows the scope of your search for errors.

- Place comments in your code. This is good programming practice and helps you keep track of the function that the code is supposed to be performing. This is also valuable for maintenance of your code.

Avoid syntax errors

One of the best ways to eliminate bugs is to prevent them in the first place. Visual Basic provides you with a syntax checker that checks each line of code as you enter it. If you have an error in the code, the checker alerts you to the problem as soon as you move to another line. The syntax checker looks for misspelled keywords and missing items in a statement, such as a parenthesis or a keyword. When you have a syntax error, Visual Basic shows the erroneous line in red and displays a message telling you the cause of the problem. Figure 34.1 shows how the syntax checker can alert you to a missing part of an `If` statement.

Fig. 34.1
The syntax checker looks for obvious errors in the commands you enter.

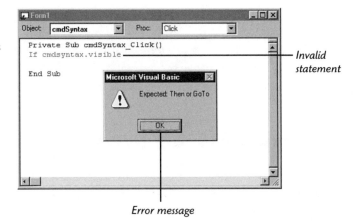

Invalid statement

Error message

The syntax checker is usually turned on when you first install Visual Basic. However, if for some reason it has been turned off, you can activate it by checking the Auto Syntax Check checkbox in the Environment tab of the Options dialog box (see fig. 34.2). The options are accessed by choosing Options from the Tools menu.

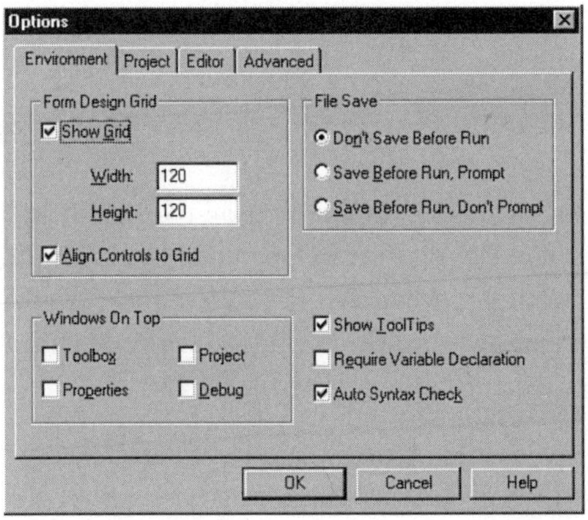

Fig. 34.2
The Environment tab of the Options dialog box lets you turn syntax checking on and off.

The other thing that Visual Basic does for you in the Code window is it properly capitalizes keywords and displays them in blue. This gives you another visual indication that you have correctly entered a command. Also, Visual Basic assures that property names are correctly capitalized.

TIP **If you enter all your control names and properties in lower case** and spell them correctly, Visual Basic capitalizes them. This indicates that you didn't make any typos.

TIP **If you don't like the default colors that are used in the code editor,** you can change them using the Editor Options dialog. This is another tab on the same Options dialog as the Environment Options.

When you encounter an error

While you are running your code from the Visual Basic development environment, you may encounter errors in your program. These errors can be one of the runtime errors listed in the Help files or the program manuals. When you encounter an error, you are shown an error message like the one in figure 34.3. The error message gives you the error number and a text description of the problem.

Fig. 34.3
An error message appears when you encounter a runtime error.

Notice that the message box has several command buttons on it. One of these buttons, the Debug button, provides you with the first line of assistance in tracking down errors in your code. If you choose the Debug button, you are shown the Code Editing window with the offending line highlighted by an outline box (see fig. 34.4).

Sometimes the error is obvious, such as mistyping a variable name or dimensioning the variable as the wrong type. Other times, though, you will need to dig deeper to find the source of the error.

Fig. 34.4
Choosing Debug from the error message box shows you the line of code that caused the error.

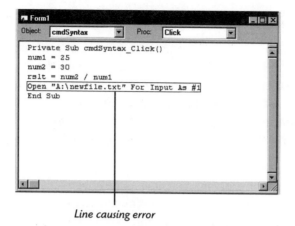

Line causing error

How the Debug window works

One of the primary tools for finding errors in your program is the Debug window. This window allows you to view the contents of variables, enter program commands, and trace which module you are in and the modules from which it was called. The Debug window is shown in figure 34.5.

Fig. 34.5
The Debug window provides you with many tools for tracking down errors in your code.

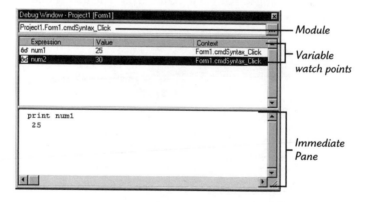

To help you understand how the Debug window helps you with error tracking, let's take a closer look at each of its parts.

You can determine a variable's value

Infinite loops are discussed in Chapter 22, "Conditional Loops: Keep Going Until I Tell You to Stop" and Chapter 23, "Counter Loops: How Many Times Will This Occur?"

Often when you encounter an error, it is because a variable contains a value that you did not expect. It may be that a variable had a zero value and was then used in a division operation. Or a variable that was supposed to contain the name of a file somehow had a number stored in it. You can also see how a variable changes as the program runs. Watching the change in a variable's value, or the lack of a change, is one of the major factors in finding infinite loops.

To debug your program, you have to be able to determine the value of the variables that are used in the program at different points in the execution. The top portion of the Debug window, called the Watch Pane, is used to show the value of variables as the program is running. Each look at a variable is called a **watch**. There are several ways to determine the value of a variable.

Adding watches to the Debug window

One way is to set a watch to observe a variable's behavior. To do this, you choose the Add Watch option from the Tools menu. This brings up the Add Watch dialog as shown in figure 34.6. The dialog allows you to enter the name of the variable to observe in the Expression field.

Fig. 34.6
The Add Watch dialog box lets you set up variables to observe during program execution.

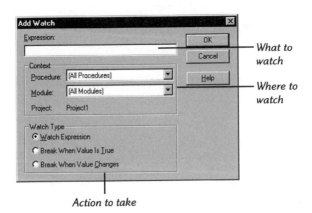

Action to take

The Add Watch dialog also allows you to specify where you want to observe the variable. These context settings let you observe the value of the variable during the entire program or just during a specific procedure.

Logical expressions are explained in Chapter 20, "Making Decisions Based Upon Data Comparisons."

The Watch Type options let you decide whether to just look at the value of the variable or to break (pause the execution of the code) when a specific condition exists. You can choose to have the program pause every time a variable changes or when the watch expression is True. This way you can determine when a variable reaches or exceeds a specific value. To use this type of watch, the expression must be a Boolean variable or a logical expression.

If at a later time, you want to edit the watch expression, you can double-click it in the Debug window. This brings up the Edit Watch dialog, which is basically the same as the Add Watch dialog but adds a command button that allows you to delete the watch.

In an instant

If you only need to find out the current value of a variable but do not need to track its value as the program progresses, you can use an instant watch. An instant watch displays a dialog that shows the name of the variable, its current value, and the procedure in which it is currently being used (see fig. 34.7).

Fig. 34.7
An instant watch provides a snapshot look at a variable.

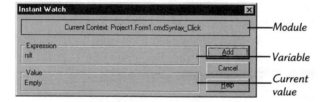

To use an instant watch, highlight a variable in the Code window while the program is paused. Then you can choose Instant Watch from the Tools menu to show the dialog. You can also run an instant watch by pressing Shift+F9 or by clicking the Instant Watch icon on the toolbar.

Q&A *The instant watch icon is dimmed and the option on the tools menu is also dimmed. Why can't I access the instant watch?*

There are several possible reasons. You may not have your program paused, or you may not have the code editing window active. Both of these conditions must be met before you can use an instant watch.

Another way to view variables

Watch points, whether instant or in the Debug window, only allow you to see the values of variables when the program is paused. If you want to observe the value of a variable while the program is running, you can use an assignment statement to tie the variable to a text box. This, however, is only useful if the variable will not be changing quickly because the speed of computers makes it nearly impossible to read each change of the variable.

Running commands

Another part of the Debug window is the Immediate Pane. This pane allows you to enter program commands which are executed as soon as you press Enter. From this pane, you can print the value of a variable, or even change the value of a variable, using an assignment statement. You can also use commands to change the environment of your program, such as the fonts on a form or the color of text in a text box.

The Immediate Pane allows you to enter any single line command. Loops and block statements (If blocks and Select Case blocks) are not allowed. If you issue the print command from the Immediate Pane, the results are printed on the line following the command. This provides another way to view the contents of a variable. Figure 34.8 shows how the Immediate Pane can be used to find the value of a variable or set a variable.

Fig. 34.8
You can run any code statement in the Immediate Pane.

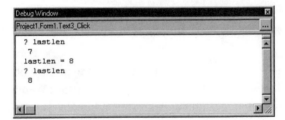

```
Debug Window                                    ☒
Project1.Form1.Text3_Click                      ...
? lastlen
  7
lastlen = 8
? lastlen
  8
```

How did I get here?

One final item you may need in debugging is the Code Pane. This pane tells you which procedure is currently executing. In addition, the pane has an ellipsis button that, when pressed, shows the Calls dialog for the procedure. You may also access the Calls dialog box from the toolbar.

This dialog shows which procedure called the current procedure (see fig. 34.9). It also shows the entire string of procedure calls from the initial procedure to the current one. These calls are listed from the most recent procedure (at the top of the list) to the initial calling procedure (at the bottom of the list). This list helps you determine how you got to the current point. This way, you will know if a procedure is being accessed from an area that you don't want.

Fig. 34.9
The Calls dialog box shows you the procedures that led up to the current procedure.

Current procedure

Stop it—Pausing the program's execution

Whenever Visual Basic encounters an error, it automatically pauses the execution of the program. There may also be times that you want to pause a program when there is no error. You would do this to check the value of variables at a specific point.

There are three ways to pause a program without an error having occurred.

- Set a watch to pause the program, either when a variable changes value or when an expression is True.

- Click the Break icon on the toolbar.

- Set a breakpoint in code to pause at a particular line.

A breakpoint in code is set while you are in design mode. In order to set the breakpoint, you must have the Code window open and be in the procedure containing the statement where you want the break to occur. At this point, you select the statement on which to break, and set the breakpoint by clicking the Toggle Breakpoint icon. You can also set the breakpoint by pressing F9 or by choosing Toggle Breakpoint from the Run menu. When a breakpoint is set, the code statement is highlighted as shown in figure 34.10.

Fig. 34.10
A breakpoint allows
you to pause the code
at a specific statement.

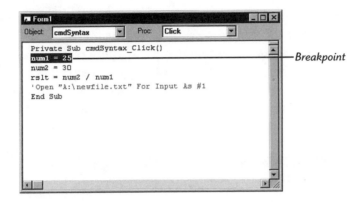

Each of the methods for setting the breakpoint actually toggles the breakpoint status of the line. This means that if the statement is not a breakpoint, it becomes one. Also, if it is a breakpoint, the breakpoint is removed.

One step at a time

In the previous sections, I have discussed how to pause the code, but in order for debugging to be effective, you have to be able to execute program statements and watch their effects.

After the execution of the program has stopped, you have several options for continuing the execution. You can do the following:

- Execute a single statement
- Execute a group of statements
- Resume normal execution of the code

To execute a single statement or group of statements, you need to be in the code editing window. To execute the program one statement at a time, you can press the F8 key. This executes the statement currently highlighted by the outline box and moves the box to the next statement. By repeatedly pressing the key, you move through the code a step at a time.

This method is extremely useful for determining which part of a conditional statement is being accessed. When the program encounters an If or Select Case statement, it evaluates the condition and moves immediately to the proper part of the block for the condition. For example, if the condition in an If statement is False, execution of the program immediately moves to the Else portion of the If block.

TIP **Clicking either of the step icons on the toolbar has the same ef-fect as pressing the F8 key.**

If the current statement contains a procedure call, pressing F8 or clicking the Step Into icon will cause you to go to the first step of the procedure. If you want to run the entire procedure and return to the next line in the current program, press Shift+F8 or click the Step Over icon.

If you're fairly certain that a block of statements is error free, you may want to execute the entire block at once instead of executing each statement individually. You can accomplish this by placing the cursor on the statement where you next want to pause the program execution and pressing Ctrl+F8. This method is useful for executing an entire loop after you have determined that the loop is not part of the problem.

Finally, when you think you have resolved the problem and want to finish executing the program, you can press the F5 key to allow the program to continue running normally. You can also do this by pressing the Continue icon (which also serves as the Run icon) on the toolbar.

Summary

Debugging a program requires time, patience, and the help of the debugging tools in Visual Basic. The tools help you find the erroneous statements and track the values of variables that led to a problem.

Review questions

1 Name three ways to determine the contents of a variable.

2 What can you do in the Immediate Pane of the Debug window?

3 What does the Calls dialog tell you?

4 How can you pause your program even if an error has not occurred?

35

Error Handling: Anticipating Mistakes that Users Will Make

● In this chapter:

- Can I prevent a user from making a mistake?

- Crash and burn —How do I prevent it?

- Do I have to write code to handle every possible error?

The best way to handle errors is to prevent them.......

No matter how simple your program is, or how well-written it is, sooner or later someone will enter an incorrect piece of data. Or they may press the wrong button at the wrong time. Either way, your user will be presented with that most dreaded object in the program, the error message. The error messages in Visual Basic do two things—they tell the user that a mistake was made, and they bring your program to a halt. Not a good way to make an impression on people, is it?

Now I'm not referring to the messages like you get when you enter an invalid name in a File dialog. These error messages, like the one shown in figure 35.1, give the user a chance to correct a mistake. The error messages that you want to avoid having your users see are like the one shown in figure 35.2. The only real choice the second error messages gives the user is to end the program.

Fig. 35.1

Good error messages give the user the ability to correct a mistake.

Fig. 35.2

The standard error message from Visual Basic programs forces the user to end the program.

Since mistakes are inevitable, what are you supposed to do? Setting up your program to handle users' mistakes requires a two-pronged approach. First, you want to try to avoid as many errors as possible. This is accomplished through the process of data validation, and through controlling the user's access to specific functions.

Second, in your program you need to include an error handler for the errors that can slip past validation routines. These errors include the `Drive not ready` error you get when you try to get a file from a floppy disk, but forget to put the disk in the drive. The error handler you include is what gives the user error messages like figure 35.1.

Only give people access to what they need

One way to avoid user errors is to only give the users access to the functions they need at any given time. This sounds like a simple concept, but it is one that is often overlooked by many developers (on occasion, myself included). Now, I am not talking about leaving features out of your program just to avoid errors, but to selectively activate features when they are ready to be used. For example, if you look at a program like Word, you will see that only part of the menu is visible if no document is open. Even when the entire menu is visible, several options, such as Cut and Copy, are only enabled when text is selected with which the commands can work. Figure 35.3 shows a menu with some of the choices disabled.

Fig. 35.3
Some menu choices are disabled until they are needed.

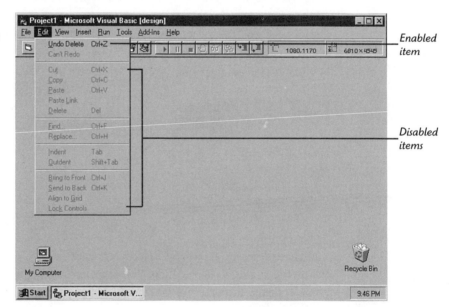

You can also choose to show or enable command buttons or any other control as they are needed.

Selectively showing or enabling controls gives you two advantages in your programs. First, it prevents a user from accessing a function that cannot be used at a particular time (limited menu choice with no open document). Second, it provides a visual indication to the users that they have not finished setting up for a particular function. (If Cut and Copy are not enabled, the user knows that nothing is selected.)

Start by disabling and hiding controls

Restricting a user's access to menu choices or controls is very easy to implement. Every control and menu item that you create has two properties associated with it to control access. These properties are the `Enabled` property and the `Visible` property.

The `Visible` property determines whether a control or menu choice is shown on the form. If the property is set to `False`, the control is not visible to the user. If the property is set to `True`, the control appears on the form.

The `Enabled` property determines whether the user can access the control even though it is visible. If the `Enabled` property is set to `False`, the control does not respond to any events, such as a user clicking a button. When the `Enabled` property is `False`, the `Caption` or text of the control (or menu choice) is shown in a subdued color, also known as **dimmed** (see fig. 35.4). When the `Enabled` property is set to `True`, the control responds to events, and the control is shown in normal mode (see fig. 35.4).

Fig. 35.4
Disabled controls are "dimmed" by Visual Basic.

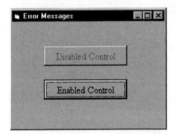

You can set the `Enabled` and `Visible` properties of a control through the Properties dialog at designtime. You can also set the properties of menu items at designtime through the menu designer.

To learn about menu design, see Chapter 13, "Enhance Your Program with Custom Menus."

The drawback with setting the properties at designtime is that this only sets the initial state of the control or menu choice. To selectively enable or disable options during your program's execution, you need to change the properties in code. Listing 35.1 shows the code that would be included in a File, Open routine to show the rest of the menu choices after a file was opened. The before and after screens for this listing are shown in figure 35.5.

Listing 35.1   Show a Menu Only After a File is Open

```
mnuView.Visible = True
mnuInsert.Visible = True
mnuFormat.Visible = True
mnuTools.Visible = True
mnuTable.Visible = True
mnuWindow.Visible = True
```

Fig. 35.5

After the *Visible* properties are set to *True*, the other menu choices are shown.

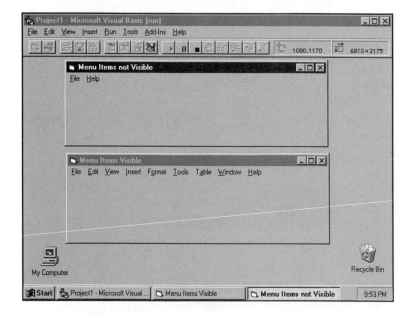

You could also include a routine in the File, Close part of your program to hide all the menu choices when no files are open. This would use the same statements as listing 35.1, except that you would replace True with False in each statement.

You can also prevent users from editing fields

In addition to limiting the use of command buttons and menu choices, you can also prevent the user from editing information on your form. What you are trying to prevent here is the accidental keystroke which would cause an error to occur. The need for this protection is greatest in database applications where the user may be moving through records with the Data Control. Until the user finds the specific record to be edited, you want to prevent the user from entering information.

For more on creating database applications with the Data control, see Chapter 29, "Accessing Databases."

As with command buttons and menu choices, you can set the Enabled property of the controls to False. However, this can make some of the information hard to read. For text boxes, the most used control for entering data, you can also set the Locked property to True. This has the effect of making the text box read-only without changing its appearance. Then, when the user finds the record to be edited, he or she can press a command button to "unlock" all the text boxes for editing. Figure 35.6 shows a database application form with locked text boxes and an edit command button. A disabled text box is also shown for comparison.

Fig. 35.6
You can lock text boxes to prevent the editing of their information.

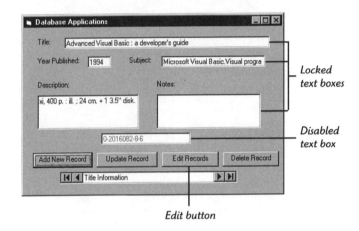

Edit button

For more about control arrays, see Chapter 16, "Creating Your Own Custom Dialogs."

To change the Locked property for all the text boxes, you could use a series of commands similar to the ones shown in listing 35.1. Another way is to make all of your text boxes part of a control array and use the code shown in listing 35.2.

Listing 35.2   Use a *For* Loop to Modify Control Array Properties

```
For I = 1 To 5
    txtMember(I).Locked = False
Next I
```

TIP   **Another trick I often use is to change the text color of fields when** they can be edited. This provides a visual cue to the user.

An ounce of prevention...

You have seen that there is much you can do to keep a user from accessing the wrong function at the wrong time. However, at some point, a user still needs to be able to enter information into the program. For further prevention of errors, it is a good idea to check the information that they enter before it is processed by your program. This is known as validation of the data.

The questions you need to address in data validation include the following:

- Is the data in the correct range of values?

- Did the user enter the right type of data (a number as opposed to a letter)?

If statements are covered in Chapter 24, "If I Go This Way, Where Will I End Up?"

These conditions are checked in program code after the data is entered. The most common form of data validation uses an If statement to check a piece of information, and allows processing to continue only if the information meets the criteria. If the information is invalid, a message can be displayed to the user to allow them to correct the problem, or you could present the user with a set of valid choices.

Is the data in range?

Range checking is one form of data validation. This usually involves checking numbers against an acceptable range, but can also be used to check dates and, in some cases, character information. Range checking uses either an If or Select Case statement to handle ranges of values.

Listing 35.3 shows how to check a person's age in a data entry screen and how to handle the possible errors.

Listing 35.3 Checking Age Ranges With *If* Statements

```
age = Val(txtAge.Text)
If age < 0 Then
   MsgBox "You cannot enter a negative age"
Else
   If age > 150 Then
      MsgBox "Are you sure the person is this old?"
   Else
      'Process information
   End If
End If
```

The first line of the code uses the `Val` function to assure that the information stored in the variable age is a number. Next, an `If` statement is used to check the value of age against the first condition, zero. If age is less than zero, a message is displayed informing the user of the invalid input. If age is greater than zero, the program moves to the `Else` part of the `If` statement.

In this section, a second `If` statement is used to check the value of age against 150. Again, if age is outside the desired range, a message is displayed informing the user of the error. If the age falls in the desired range, normal processing of the information is performed.

While an If statement was used in the example, you could use a `Select Case` block to perform the same function, as shown in listing 35.4.

Listing 35.4   Another Way To Check Ranges

```
age = Val(txtAge.Text)
Select Case age
   Case Is < 0
      MsgBox "You cannot enter a negative age"
   Case Is > 150
      MsgBox "Are you sure the person is this old?"
   Case Else
      'Process information
End Select
```

Wrong data types

One of the most common errors in handling data is where the user inputs the wrong type of information. This occurs when the user enters a character string where they were supposed to enter a number, or vice versa. There are several ways to handle the validation of data types.

How can I use this in the real world?

One check of valid numbers is in entering a person's age. Since it is impossible for a person to have a negative age, the number entered needs to be greater than zero. Also, check for any age entered that is over 150, since no one in recent time has lived that long.

First, you can check the actual type of the data using built-in Visual Basic functions like IsNumeric or IsDate. These functions will return a value of True if the variable is the correct type and a value of False otherwise.

To illustrate this point, consider the following example. A sales application allows the clerk to input an item number and a quantity. The program then calculates the total cost by multiplying the quantity by the cost (which is obtained from a data table). If the clerk accidentally enters a letter instead of a number, the computer would issue a Type mismatch error when the multiplication was attempted, and then halt execution. To avoid this, use the validation code shown in listing 35.5.

Listing 35.5 Making Sure a Variable is a Number

```
quantity = txtQuant.Text
If IsNumeric(quantity) Then
    totcost = quantity * itmcost
Else
    MsgBox "The quantity you entered was not a valid number."
End If
```

The other way to prevent the type mismatch error is to specifically convert the variable to a number using the Val function. If the variable contains a character string, a zero is returned. If the string contains numbers, the value of those numbers is returned. Applying this method to the total cost calculation would result in the following code:

```
quantity = Val(txtQuant.Text)
totcost = quantity * itmcost
```

Either method allows you to avoid errors caused by the user entering the wrong type of data.

Handling errors you can't avoid

Even though you restrict access to functions and include data validation in your programs, there are still some errors that occur. A common error is when the user forgets to put a disk in the drive before trying to read or write information. When your program tries to access the disk, the Disk not Ready error appears and your program comes to a halt.

You can try to avoid this type of error by displaying a message that tells the user to insert a disk and press a key when ready; but in the end, you still need to be able to handle the error as shown in the following sections.

The basic error handler

The method for handling errors in Visual Basic is to tell the code to branch to another area when the error occurs. The section of the code that you want to branch to is the error handler. The error handler evaluates the type of error that occurred and takes the appropriate action.

When you use the `On Error GoTo` statement, the keywords `On`, `Error`, and `GoTo` are all required for the statement. The `linename` represents a label of a line later in your procedure which starts the code section where errors are handled. The `linename` specified must be in the same procedure as the `On Error` statement.

At the start of the error handling routine, the `linename` must appear followed by a colon (:). All of your error handling statements for the procedure appear after this line label.

After you have processed the error message, you will want to return to the main part of your code. This is handled by the `Resume` statement.

```
Resume [Next]
```

By itself, the `Resume` statement causes your program to return to the line that caused the error. This has the effect of retrying the command. If you include the optional `Next` keyword, the program returns to the line immediately following the statement that caused the error. This has the effect of canceling the command. You can also have the `Resume` statement return to a specific line label by using a statement like the following:

```
Resume TryAgain
```

The code in listing 35.6 shows how a procedure is used to open a file on a disk and how the error is handled by the code.

Speaking of *On Error*

The way to branch to another part of your code when an error occurs is using the `On Error` statement. The following statement specifies a specific line where the program should go.

```
On Error GoTo linename
```

Listing 35.6   Error Handling in a Procedure

```
Private Sub cmdOpenFil_Click()
On Error GoTo FileErr
Open "A:\trident.txt" For Input As #1
Exit Sub
FileErr:
Select Case Err.Number
    Case 71
        retval = MsgBox("Insert a disk into drive A",
        vbOKCancel)
        If retval = vbOK Then
            Resume
        Else
            Resume Next
        End If
    Case 53
        msgtxt = "File 'Trident.txt' was not found.
        msgtxt = msgtxt & Insert the correct disk"
        retval = MsgBox(msgtxt, vbOKCancel)
        If retval = vbOK Then
            Resume
        Else
            Resume Next
        End If
    Case Else
        ernum = Err.Number
        msgtxt = "Error number " & Str(ernum) & " was
        encountered."
        msgtxt = msgtxt & Chr(10) & Chr(13) & "Error
        Message:"
        msgtxt = msgtxt & Chr(10) & Chr(13) & Err.Description
        MsgBox msgtxt
        End
End Select
End Sub
```

 The first line in the procedure sets up the error handler and tells the code to go to the line labeled FileErr if an error occurs. The next line attempts to open a file on the A drive. An error occurs if no disk is in the drive or if no file on the disk is named TRIDENT.TXT.

After the Open statement, an Exit Sub statement is placed to make sure that the program does not execute the error handling code if no error occurs. You should always place an Exit Sub (or Exit Function for a function) just before the label for your error handler.

The FileErr line label is after the Exit Sub statement. Note that a colon follows the label name. This label indicates the beginning of the error handling code. For our example, the error handler consists of a `Select Case` statement that can handle either a `Disk not ready` or `File not found` error condition. You determine which error occurred by checking the `Number` property of the `Err` object. This property is assigned a value any time an error occurs in your program. You can find a list of the error numbers in the Visual Basic manuals or the on-line help files.

The `Select Case` looks at the error number and determines whether it is one of the errors that your code can handle. If the error code is 71, `Disk not ready`, your error handler displays a message for the user to insert a disk. The user can then choose either OK to retry the operation, or Cancel to abort the operation. The `retval` variable contains the value of the button selected by the user. If the user chooses the OK button, the `Resume` statement is issued to cause the `Open` statement (which caused the error) to be retried. If the user chooses the Cancel button, the `Resume Next` statement is issued causing the Open statement to be bypassed. Figure 35.7 shows the custom error message resulting from this error handling routine.

Fig. 35.7

An error handler allows the user to correct the problem and retry a command.

A similar process is used to handle the `File not found` error. This `Case` statement checks for error code 53 and notifies the user to insert the correct disk.

Finally, if the error is not one of the two described, the error handler notifies the user of the error number and the error message, and then terminates. The text of the error message is contained in the `Description` property of the Err object.

Q&A   ***I have several procedures which can open a file. Can I have one error processing procedure to handle all of them?***

You can place all the condition statements (the `Select Case` statements) in a separate procedure that can be called by multiple procedures. However, you must include an error handler in each of your file open routines, which retrieves the error message and calls the central error handling procedure.

Catch the bug

What is wrong with the following error handling routine?

```
Private Sub cmdOpenFil_Click()
On Error GoTo FileProb
Open "A:\trident.txt" For Input As #1
Exit Sub
FileErr:
    MsgBox Error Number  & Str(Err.Number) &  occurred.
End Sub
```

Answer: *The label specified in the* On Error *statement does not match the line label of the error handler. The correct code line is as follows:*

```
On Error GoTo FileErr
```

You can ignore some errors

There are some instances where you may want execution of the program to continue, even if an error is encountered. You will only want to do this when the error will not bring the program to a screeching halt. Such is the case for errors such as Overflow or Division by zero. These errors will not halt the program, but may cause undesirable results.

If you want to continue execution after encountering an error, you may use a different form of the On Error statement. This form of the statement is as follows:

```
On Error Resume Next
```

This code line causes the execution of the program to proceed to the line immediately following the error. For example, the following code would normally produce an error message:

```
num1% = 0
num2% = 25
rslt% = num2% / num1%
```

By adding the `On Error Resume Next` statement, execution continues, though the results of the calculation are undefined. The modified code is shown here:

```
On Error Resume Next
num1% = 0
num2% = 25
rslt% = num2% / num1%
```

Summary

Restricting access to certain program functions, data validation, and good error handling routines should minimize the chance of your users ever seeing Visual Basic's internal error messages. This makes your program more reliable and useful to your users.

Review questions

1 What property determines whether a control is shown on the form?

2 What property do you use to make a text box read-only?

3 What does data validation do?

4 How do you determine if a variable is the right type for a function?

5 Describe the difference between the `Resume` and `Resume Next` statements.

6 How do you find out what error occurred?

Exercises

1 Starting from listing 35.6, add a case that handles the `File already open` error. This is error number 55.

2 Write an error handler to deal with numeric overflow or division by zero errors.

3 Write an error handler that handles type mismatch errors.

36

When One Form Isn't Enough

● **In this chapter:**

- **Can I have more than one form in my program?**

- **Telling the program which form to use when it first starts**

- **Customizing the design environment**

- **Is there any way to load custom controls automatically?**

- **I finished creating my masterpiece. Now what?**

When you run out of space on one form, you can add other forms, modules, and controls to your project . . . . ➤

Juggling multiple forms

You can cram a lot of controls onto a single form. You can even use container controls to create multiple pages on a form so you can cram more stuff on it. But even with the use of containers, you can only get so much stuff on a single form. Fact is, most of your programs will be made up of multiple forms.

Refer to Chapter 10, "Group Your Controls into Containers," to see how containers are used to create multiple pages.

One reason is, of course, the limitation of the amount of space on a single form. Another more important reason is that you will want to use multiple forms in your program to logically separate program tasks. For example, if you have a task in your program that is not performed very often, it makes more sense to put it onto a separate form than to try to squeeze it onto a single form with everything else. Also, loading and unloading forms as you need them saves system resources. In other words, your program will take up as little space as possible while it is running.

Some complex programs will require a large number of forms. The VISDATA sample application, for example, uses 37 separate forms.

Adding a new form

When Visual Basic first starts a new project, it typically loads one blank form as shown in figure 36.1. As you are designing your program, you add controls to this form and write code to handle events that occur on the form.

Fig. 36.1
New projects start with a single form.

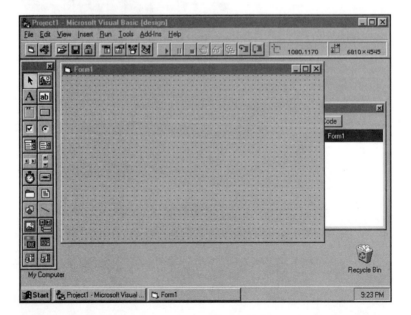

At some point in your design, you will decide that you need a second form (or third, fourth, etc.) to handle a new task or to provide space to relieve the crowding on the initial form. Adding a new form is simple. You can click the Form icon, or select Form from the Insert menu. This will place a new blank form on the screen which looks just like your first form initially did. If you did not rename your first form from the default of Form1, the new form will be named Form2 (or Form3, Form4, etc.). Otherwise, the new form will be named Form1.

After you have added a new form, you can place controls on it and write code for its events just like for the initial form.

Nothing but code

As you write more code to handle more events and more tasks, you will often find that you need to access the same procedure from a number of different places on a form or from multiple forms. If this is the case, it makes sense to store the procedure in a module file.

A module file contains only Visual Basic code. It does not contain any controls, pictures, or other visual information. When it comes time to add a module file to hold your procedures, you can do this either by clicking the Module icon or by choosing Module from the Insert menu. Either of these actions will add a new module to your project and place you in the code editing window for the module as shown in figure 36.2.

Fig. 36.2

Modules only contain program code; there are no visual elements.

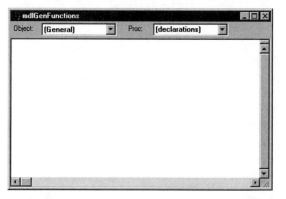

When you first open a new module, Visual Basic gives it the default name of Module1 (or Module2 for a second module, etc.). Like your forms and controls, it is a good idea to give the module a unique name. The module has a Name property just like a form does. To change the name of the module, access the Properties dialog box and change the value of the Name property.

Importing an existing form or module

As you develop more programs, you may find that you have standard procedures or forms that can be used in many of your projects. As an example, the custom dialog that was demonstrated in Chapter 16 can be used in many applications. You may have also developed custom procedures for getting the names and passwords of users, for opening files, or for any number of other tasks that are used in almost every program.

You could rebuild the form or rewrite the procedure for each program, but that would be a very inefficient way to do your program development. A better way is to reuse modules and forms that have been previously developed and fully tested.

Getting these modules and forms into your current project is a very simple process. By selecting Add File from the File menu, you bring up the Add File dialog (see fig. 36.3). This dialog box lets you locate and select files to be added to your current project. Unfortunately, the Add File dialog only lets you add a single file at a time. Therefore, if you have multiple files to be added, you will have to repeat the operation several times. You can use the Ctrl+D shortcut keys to avoid having to go through the menu each time.

Fig. 36.3
You can add program code and forms to your project which are also used by other programs.

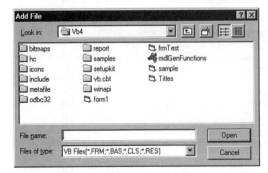

TIP **Files with an** `.frm` **extension are form files. Files with a** `.bas` **extension are module files.**

Working with the different forms

As you add forms and modules to your program, they are added to the Project window (see fig. 36.4). This window allows you to easily access any of the pieces of your program. You simply select a form or module by clicking its name in the Project window. For a form, you can then click either the View Form button to work on the design of the form, or the View Code button to edit the code associated with the form. For a module, only the View Code button is enabled, since a module has no visual elements. Double-clicking the name of a form has the same effect as clicking the View Form button. Double-clicking a module name has the same effect as clicking the View Code button.

Fig. 36.4

The Project window provides you easy access to all your forms and modules.

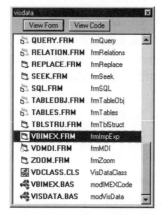

How do I display forms other than my startup form?

If you just add forms to your program and then try to run it, the only form that you will be able to access is the one that is shown when the program first starts. For all the other forms, you have to tell the program when to load and unload them, and when to show or hide them.

Two commands are used to place a form in memory and to remove a form from memory. These are the Load and Unload commands, respectively.

The Load command places the form in the computers memory so the properties of the form and its associated controls can be accessed. The Load command does not display the form. The Unload statement removes a form from memory. If the form is displayed at the time the command is issued, the Unload command will remove it from the screen before it removes it from memory.

Since the Load command only places a form in memory, you also need a way to display the form. This is the function of the Show method. If the form is not already loaded in memory, the Show method will first load it, then display it. The Show method can be used to display a form as either modal or modeless. This is controlled by the optional style argument. If the form is modal, no other forms in the program can be accessed until the modal form is hidden or unloaded. The message box is an example of a modal form. If the form is modeless, the user can switch back and forth between the current form and other forms in the program.

Also, there may be times when you want the form to be removed from view, but not from memory. If you want to remove a form from view, you use the Hide method. This method removes the form from the screen, but the form is still accessible through program code. This means you can still change the properties of the form and its controls. Hide does not unload the form from memory.

Making a new start

When you first start a programming project, Visual Basic assumes that the first form created is the one that will be displayed as soon as the program starts. While this will be the case for many programs, for others you will

Speaking of *Load* and *Unload*

The Load command is used as follows:

```
Load formname
```

formname is the name of the form to be loaded in memory. The name is the value of the Name property of the form.

To remove the form from memory, the Unload command is used as follows:

```
Unload formname
```

Catch the bug

What is wrong with the following statement that tries to display a form?

```
Form1.Load
```

Answer: First, Load is a command, not a method of the form. Therefore, the syntax is incorrect. Second, Load will place a form in memory, but will not display it. The Show method should be used as follows:

```
Form1.Show
```

want to start with one of the forms you create later in the development process. For some programs, you may not even want to start with a form at all.

Visual Basic lets you choose which of your forms will be the one shown initially by the program. This selection is made in the Project tab of the Options dialog box (see fig. 36.5). This dialog box is accessed by choosing <u>O</u>ptions from the <u>T</u>ools menu.

Speaking of *Show*

To display a form, the Show method is used. The Show methods syntax is as follows:

```
formname.Show [style]
```

formname is the name of the form to be shown. Show is the keyword that invokes the method. style tells the program how the form will behave once it is shown. The style can be either 0 for a modeless form or 1 for a modal form. If style is omitted, the form is assumed to be modeless.

The style setting has no effect on any other programs that may be running at the same time.

The Hide method removes a form from the screen but leaves it in memory. The syntax of the Hide method is as follows:

```
formname.Hide
```

Fig. 36.5
The Startup Form
drop-down list allows
you to choose which
form will be loaded
when your program
starts.

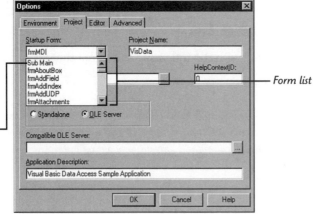

*Optional
start-up
procedure*

Form list

The Startup Form drop-down list includes all the forms contained in your project. In addition, the list includes the Sub Main entry. This is a reserved procedure name that allows your program to start without an initial form. If you choose this option, one of your module files must include a procedure called Main.

Take control of your environment

One of the nice things about the design environment is that you are not stuck with the settings that are installed by Visual Basic. You can control many aspects of your design environment through the Environment and Editor tabs of the Options dialog box.

How can I use this in the real world?

One reason to start your program with the Sub Main option would be for security. The Main procedure could use an input box to obtain a user ID from the person running the program. If the ID is valid, the program continues. Otherwise, the program terminates. You might use this for a payroll program where you want to restrict the access to the information to selected people.

The other reason to use Sub Main is if your program requires no user interaction. This type of program could be used to monitor a manufacturing process and record data.

Options to customize your design mode

Let's look at the options available in the Environment tab of the Options dialog box (see fig. 36.6).

Fig. 36.6
The Environment tab options let you control your design environment.

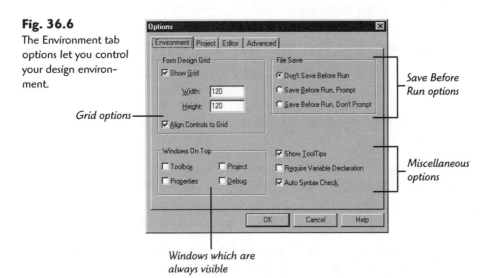

Grid options

Save Before Run options

Miscellaneous options

Windows which are always visible

First, look at the Form Design Grid options. The grid is the series of dots shown on the form at designtime that help you line up your controls. These options allow you to choose whether the grid is shown and how far apart the dots will appear. (The distance is measured in twips.)

In addition, you can choose whether controls should be aligned to the grid when they are drawn or moved. When this option is on, the upper left corner of a control is aligned with the grid dot nearest the starting point of the cursor when you draw the control. This makes it easier to assure that the left edge of a column of controls or the top edge of a row of controls are perfectly aligned. If the option is turned off, controls are placed exactly where you draw them, and they may not be perfectly aligned. These controls will remain unaligned, even if you turn the grid option back on.

The Windows On Top set of options allows you to choose which windows stay "on top." If you choose for a window to be on top, it cannot be hidden by the form when you move or resize the form. This is sometimes convenient for keeping track of the pieces of your environment, but can cause difficulties in accessing all the areas on your form.

The File Save options determine whether Visual Basic will save your project files before it starts running the program. The default behavior is to not save the files. You may also choose to have Visual Basic prompt you before the program is run or to save your files automatically. I usually leave the option set to not save the files since this slows down the initial loading of the program. If you do this, though, be sure to save your files after significant changes, just in case your program crashes the system.

The last three options control individual aspects of the design environment:

- The Show ToolTips checkbox determines whether the ToolTips (those little labels that identify an icon) will be shown if you leave the cursor on an icon.

For more on the declaration of variables, see Chapter 17 "Adding Variables to Your Programs."

- The Require Variable Declaration checkbox determines whether you must specifically declare a variable name before it can be used in a program. This option (when checked) has the same effect as placing the `Option Explicit` statement in every module and form.

Chapter 34, "Finding Bugs in Your Programs," discusses the use of syntax checking.

- Auto Syntax Check determines whether Visual Basic will check the syntax of your code as each line is entered.

In addition to the Environment options, Visual Basic provides you with the Editor tab (see fig. 36.7). This gives you the ability to control the fonts and colors used for the code editor which, in turn, allows you to customize the editor to your liking.

Fig. 36.7
You can control the color and fonts used in the code editing window with the options from the Editor tab.

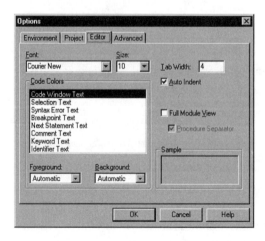

Saving your toolbox

When you first start Visual Basic, you will notice that a particular set of controls is loaded in the toolbox. You have also seen in other parts of the book that there are custom controls that can be added to the toolbox to accomplish particular tasks. But what do you do if you have a favorite control that you use in most of your projects? Or conversely, what if most of your programs don't need the data access custom controls (the Data Bound ListBox and ComboBox controls)?

You do have the capability to customize, to a degree, the control set that is loaded when you start a new project. Visual Basic contains a basic control set that cannot be changed (see fig. 36.8). However, you can choose which custom controls will be loaded.

Fig. 36.8

The toolbox shows you the available controls.

To change the initial control set, follow these steps:

1 Select New Project from the File menu.

2 Using the Custom Control dialog box, select the custom controls you want loaded for each new project.

3 Select Save Project As from the File menu.

4 Choose the file `auto32ld.vbp` as the file to save the project to. This file is located in Visual Basic's main directory. (For 16-bit systems like Windows 3.1, choose the file `auto16ld.vbp`.)

In addition to specifying the custom controls to be loaded, you can also include forms or modules that will be loaded as part of each new project. You can use this to automatically include a module of generic procedures, a custom input box, or any other generic program piece. To do this, follow the same steps as shown previously; but before you save the file, add the desired modules and forms using the Add File dialog box described earlier in this chapter.

Summary

This chapter contained a lot of odds and ends that didn't really fit well elsewhere in the book. The main point to be made is that in addition to being a powerful programming language, Visual Basic is also highly customizable to the needs and preferences of the developer, you.

Review questions

1 How do you add forms from another program to your project?

2 What command removes a form from memory while the program is running?

3 What command removes a form from the display but maintains it in memory?

4 What file determines which controls and forms are loaded for a new project?

Exercises

1 Add a previously created form to your project.

2 Create a program which uses Sub Main to start the program, then displays your form.

3 Customize your toolbox, and then save it to the proper file.

37

The Search for More Help Continues

● In this chapter:

- What other neat controls are available and where do I find them?

- Where to get more information about Visual Basic and help with programming problems

One of the most powerful features of Visual Basic is that the language can be extended through the use of custom controls and add-ins. . . . . ▸

There's no need to reinvent the wheel

As you have seen through the course of the book, the bulk of your Visual Basic programs are made up of controls. These controls are used to build your program like ignition systems, radios, and transmissions are used to build a car. And, just like a car, you can add optional equipment to your development environment. This is done in the form of custom controls and add-ins. You have probably already seen how a few of these are used as we covered the Masked Edit control, Tab control, RichTextBox control, and others in earlier chapters.

Some of these controls provide an enhanced version of a standard control. This is akin to replacing the basic radio in a car with the radio/cassette/CD combination. It still handles the basic functions but also provides you with more capabilities. Other controls provide completely new capabilities. This is like adding a sunroof to your car.

Controls you already have

While we have already touched on a few of the custom controls and add-ins that are included with Visual Basic, there are a number of others that you might want to have a look at. The following controls and add-ins provide additional capabilities to Visual Basic that allow you to build better and more complex programs:

- Crystal Reports control—This control provides you with an easier means of producing reports from information in a database. The Crystal Reports control allows you to set the location of the database fields, informational text, and graphics items such as lines and boxes. The control then takes care of sending all the information to the printer, and handles the task of word wrapping information in the fields.

- Desaware's Animated button control—You've probably noticed in many commercial programs that when you click an icon button (shortcut), the image on the button changes. This provides a visual indication of which button was pressed. The animated button control gives you an easy way to do this in your programs.

- Microsoft Comm control—This control provides most of the capabilities you need to send and receive data through the COM ports of your computer.

- Microsoft Grid control—This control lets you use a grid to display and edit information. With it, you can build an interface that looks like a spreadsheet or possibly an appointment scheduler.

- Pinnacle's Graph control—Need to be able to produce charts for data analysis and presentation? This control provides the means. It is capable of handling a wide variety of charts including bar, line, pie, scatter, and high-low-close.

You can find out more about these controls and others in Visual Basic's Custom Controls help file. The help file provides you with descriptions of the controls and their properties and methods. You will also find some usage examples. In addition to the help file, there is also a manual that explains the use of the custom controls.

One of other add-ins that comes with Visual Basic is the Report Designer. This add-in works with the Crystal Report control to set up database reports. The Report Designer lets you visually design your printed reports just like you design forms for your screen.

Other controls you can get

If the controls included with Visual Basic don't provide you with what you need, there are a number of companies that also produce controls that can be used with Visual Basic. There are controls out there to handle calendar functions, produce flowcharts, and create multimedia applications, just to name a few. Table 37.1 lists just a few of the companies that produce custom controls. With each company name is a contact address or phone number, and a partial list of the products they provide.

Table 37.1   Custom Controls To Use With Visual Basic

Company Name	Phone	Products
Crescent	(800) 352-2742	PowerPak Pro
Desaware	(408) 371-3530	Spyworks VB, Version Stamper
Farpoint Technologies	(800) 645-5913	Aware/VBX, Grid/VBX, Spread/VBX
MicroHelp, Inc.	(800) 922-3383	FaxPlus, MicroHelp VB Viewer

continues

Table 37.1 Continued

Company Name	Phone	Products
ProtoView Development Corp.	(800) 231-8588 x-90	Data Table, Interface Component Set, Visual Help Builder
Sheridan Software	(800) 823-4732	VBAssist, Data Widgets, Designer Widgets
Stylus Innovation, Inc.	(617) 621-9545	Visual Fax, Visual Voice
Visual Tools, Inc.	(800) 884-8665	First Impression, Formula One, Image Stream, Visual Speller, Visual Writer

Hungry for more?

Hopefully, this book has provided you with a lot of the information you need to develop programs using Visual Basic. Obviously, though, there is a lot of information that could not be squeezed into this book. Fortunately for you, there are a number of other sources available to teach you about advanced programming topics.

Printed material

The first source of additional information are books that cover advanced topics such as OLE automation and client/server programming. The following books provide more in-depth coverage of database development than was possible here:

- Que's *Special Edition Using Visual Basic*
- Que's *Visual Basic By Example*
- Que's *Visual Basic Expert Solutions*
- Que's *Building Windows 95 Applications with Visual Basic*
- Que's *Building Multimedia Applications with Visual Basic*
- Sams' *Database Developer's Guide with Visual Basic 3*

More printed material

In addition to books, there are a number of magazines that are dedicated to Visual Basic. These magazines provide descriptions of programming techniques, reviews of custom controls, and informative columns by noted authors. Table 37.2 lists several of these magazines along with their publishers and contact numbers.

Table 37.2 Magazines Devoted to Visual Basic

Magazine	Publisher	Phone
Visual Basic Programmer's Journal	Fawcette Technical Publications	(800) 848-5523
VB Tech Journal	Oakley Publishing Co.	(800) 234-0386
Inside Visual Basic	The Cobb Group	(800) 223-8720
Access/Visual Basic Advisor	Advisor Publications Inc.	(619) 483-6400

The on-line community

Finally, if you want information and you want it now, you might want to try on-line resources. Microsoft maintains a presence on CompuServe, Prodigy, America Online, GEnie, and the Internet. In addition, when the Microsoft Network goes on-line, you will be able to get information there as well.

The on-line services usually contain discussions, or **threads**, about problem solving, new products, industry trends, and general information. If you have a programming problem, posting a question on-line should yield quick and informative answers. Going on-line is a fast way to get help. In addition to the discussions, many on-line services have a library of files available to download. These files include reports pertaining to different aspects of Visual Basic, and demo and shareware versions of software and custom controls.

Also, many of the vendors of custom controls maintain a presence on-line. This allows you to get help with custom controls and to keep up with the release of the latest versions.

Summary

With the help of custom controls and information from other programmers, obtained through books, magazines, and on-line services, you can create programs with Visual Basic to accomplish just about any computer task you can imagine. I hope this book has been helpful. Happy programming.

Answers to the Quizzes

Chapter 1

1 Keys or key combinations that can be used instead of a menu command.

2 Look at the two blocks of numbers at the far right of the toolbar.

3 In the Visual Basic toolbox.

4 To select it directly from the File menu.

Chapter 2

1 There are seven steps listed on the first page of this chapter.

2 A plan helps you determine how you will build the program so that it is concise and organized, and the pieces fit together well.

3 You should include File, Edit, and Help menus, and probably a toolbar of common functions.

Chapter 3

1 A text box can display information and receive user input.

2 The Text property stores the information in a text box.

3 Controls require unique names so that they can be properly addressed in a program.

4 Both label controls and text boxes can handle text, numbers, and dates. Both can handle single words, sentences, or paragraphs. The key difference is that a user can edit a text box, but not a label.

5 An assignment statement sets the value of a property in a program.

Chapter 4

1 The MultiLine property set to True.

2 To indicate that there is text beyond the edges of the box, and to make it easier for the user to get to the text.

3 The MaxLength property.

4 The Mask property.

5 The Text property.

6 The Mask property should be set to AAA-###.

Chapter 5

1 Name, Bold, Italic, Underline, Size, StrikeThrough, Width.

2 8 to 12 points.

3 It will make your form look cluttered and confusing.

4 Red, Blue, and Green.

5 ForeColor and BackColor.

Chapter 6

1 The RichTextBox control supports the formatting of individual words, phrases, or segments of text.

2 The format of the selected text will be changed.

3 All new text entered after the property change will reflect the new property setting. No old text will be affected.

4 Rich Text Format codes are used to store the information in an ASCII text file.

5 The SaveFile method is used to store the information in a file; the LoadFile method is used to retrieve it.

Chapter 7

1 Forms, picture controls, and image controls.

2 Set the AutoSize property to True.

3 The picture is either compressed or expanded to fit the size of the control.

4 A picture control can be used as a container for other controls.

Chapter 8

1   To get a yes or no, true or false answer from the user.

2   The `Alignment` property controls whether the box is on the left or the right of the prompt.

3   0-Unchecked, 1-Checked, or 2-Grayed.

4   Every checkbox can be checked at the same time.

5   No, option buttons are only used in groups.

6   Only one option button may be selected from a group.

7   A container is used to segregate groups of option buttons.

Chapter 9

1   Using the `AddItem` and `RemoveItem` methods.

2   The `Columns` property.

3   Set the `MultiSelect` property to 1 or 2.

4   Use the `ListCount` property.

5   The `Style` property.

6   The list box uses the `List` and `ListIndex` properties to retrieve a selection. The combo box uses the `Text` property.

Chapter 10

1   The Frame control is the simplest container.

2   The controls in the container are hidden as well.

3   The picture box allows you to use a picture as the background for your controls.

4   The `Tabs` and `TabsPerRow` properties.

5   In order to have groups of option buttons, each group must be placed in a frame on the tab page.

Chapter 11

1 You set the range with the Min and Max properties.

2 You can only enter integers with the scroll bar.

3 The increment in a spin button is controlled by the code you place in the SpinUp and SpinDown events.

4 A scroll bar allows you to control the range of numbers that can be entered, and allows the user to enter numbers more easily.

Chapter 12

1 The AutoSize property determines whether a label control will change size to fit the text, and the WordWrap property determines if the text will be displayed on multiple lines.

2 A text box with scroll bars. The label control is limited by the space below and to the right of its original position.

3 Alignment, BorderStyle, and BackStyle.

4 The Default property allows you to specify a command button that is activated when Enter is pressed, and the Cancel property specifies the button that is activated if Esc is pressed.

5 By placing an ampersand (&) in front of the letter in the Caption property.

6 The Timer event.

7 A Frame control or Picture control. The Shape control cannot be used for this purpose.

8 The Slider control can be used to select a range of values.

9 The Max, Min, and Value properties.

Chapter 13

1 Trick question. You can only create and edit a menu using the Menu Editor.

2 The Checked property.

3 An access key is assigned by placing an ampersand in front of the letter in the items caption. A shortcut key is assigned by selecting it from the shortcut key list in the Menu Editor.

4 You can use the same access key for menu items in different groups, (i.e., the Close item in the File menu and the Copy item in the Edit menu).

5 Setting the Enabled property to False allows the user to see the item but not access it.

6 The standard menu is always present at the top of the form. A pop-up menu is only shown when invoked by your program code, and is only visible until the user makes a choice.

Chapter 14

1 The text argument (which contains the message text) is the only required argument.

2 By setting the options argument to the value of one of the four icons. These are listed in table 12.1.

3 You must use the syntax of the message box that returns a value. This value will indicate which button was pressed, as defined in table 12.4.

4 By checking the length of the returned string. If the length is not zero, the user entered a value and pressed the OK button. If the length is zero, the user either pressed the Cancel button or pressed the OK button with no value entered in the input field. In either case, if the length of the string is zero, no value was entered.

5 The user cannot enter data in response to the message. You can only display certain sets of buttons, you cannot define your own. You cannot use any icon but the four supplied.

6 You can only get one value from the input box. You cannot display any icons in the input box. You cannot specify any command buttons for the box; the OK and Cancel buttons are set up automatically.

Chapter 15

1 You set the `Filter` property with a description and filter for the files.

2 The `Flags` property determines whether screen fonts, printer fonts, or both will be displayed.

3 You call the dialogs `ShowPrinter` method.

4 The `FileName` property.

5 The fonts `Name`, `Size`, `Bold`, `Italic`, `Underline`, and `StrikeThrough` properties may be selected using the Common Dialog.

6 Set the `Flags` property to the constant `cdlCCRGBInit`, then call the `ShowColor` method of the Common Dialog.

Chapter 16

1 It allows you to get around the limitations of the message box and input box.

2 Load the form, set up the properties of the form and controls, and show the form.

3 A group of the same type of controls, all with the same name but with different index numbers.

4 A control array allows you to place additional command buttons on the dialog at runtime, and the Index provides you with the information about which button was pressed.

Chapter 17

1 Text, numbers, dates, OLE objects, or any other valid data type.

2 Explicit and implicit declarations.

3 No. If you omit the declaration, the variable will be assumed to be a variant type.

4 The main difference is that a constant cannot be assigned a new value after it is created, whereas the value of a variable may change.

5 You use the Const statement to declare and define the constant.

6 To make it easier for you to use the values of options for functions and properties.

Chapter 18

1 Literal numbers, numeric variables, and functions which return a number.

2 Floating-point division, integer division, and modulus or remainder division.

3 Parenthetical groups, exponents, multiplication and floating point division, integer division, modulus division, and addition and subtraction.

4 Group parts of the equation in parentheses, or use variables to hold intermediate results.

5 Only the addition and subtraction operators.

Chapter 19

1 Yes, but the concatenation operator (&) is recommended.

2 The RTrim or the Trim function may be used.

3 By using the Mid statement.

4 The Val and Str functions convert strings to numbers and vice versa. You can also use CStr, CInt, CLng, CSng, and CDbl.

Chapter 20

1 No. You must compare expressions of the same data type. You can, however, convert a number to a string or vice versa, and then use it in a comparison.

2 In most cases, no. However, if you have Option Compare set to Text, they are equal.

3 The And operator.

4 Xor requires that one and only one condition be True in order to return a True value. Or will return a True value if one or both conditions are True.

Chapter 21

1 Any data that can be stored in a variable, including numbers, text, and dates.

2 The index of the array.

3 Up to 60 dimensions.

4 Use the Dim statement.

5 Use the ReDim statement.

6 You can use a variable to specify dimensions with the ReDim statement.

Chapter 22

1 A Do While loop.

2 You place the condition in the Loop statement.

3 A Do While loop executes as long as the condition is True. A Do Until loop executes as long as the condition is False.

4 The Exit Do statement

5 Omitting the statement which changes the loop condition, and placing the change statement inside an If statement.

6 The DoEvents function lets the computer respond to system events.

Chapter 23

1 The For and the Next statements.

2 The default step size is 1.

3 Any numbers including decimal numbers and negative numbers.

4 Yes, if you change the value of the counter variable inside the loop.

5 Use the Exit For statement.

6 Add the `Step` keyword and a number for the step size to the `For` statement.

7 Set the step size to a negative number.

8 Working with multidimensional arrays.

9 You can use any combination of program structures when nesting loops and decisions.

Chapter 24

1 The `If` and `Then` keywords and a condition.

2 Use the block `If` statement with the `If` statement at the beginning of the block and the `End If` statement at the end of the block.

3 You can use the `Not` operator to change the `False` condition to `True`, or use the `Else` statement in the block `If`.

4 Multiple conditions can be handled with the `ElseIf` statement.

5 It returns one of two values supplied to the function based upon the value of the condition supplied.

Chapter 25

1 The statements compare a test expression defined in the `Select Case` statement to possible values in the `Case` statements. The program runs only the set of commands associated with the first `Case` statement that meets the comparison condition.

2 The `Case Else` statement.

3 Use the `To` keyword to specify a value between two points, or use the `Is` keyword and a comparison operator to specify a single-sided range.

4 When the condition to be evaluated is dependent on more than one variable.

Chapter 26

1 You can use the Procedure dialog box, or type the Sub statement in the (General) area of the code window.

2 You can use the Call statement, or just enter the name of the procedure. Remember to include any required parameters.

3 You can pass arguments to the procedure. These arguments or parameters have to have been declared in the Sub statement of the procedure. You can also define the variables as public variables.

4 Procedures can either be stored with a form or in a module file.

5 A public procedure is accessible from anywhere in your program. A private procedure is accessible only within the form or module where it was defined.

Chapter 27

1 Sequential data files.

2 Use the Append mode.

3 The Input # statement. The Write # statement.

4 It is used to read and write data in a random access file.

5 Use the Close statement without specifying any file list.

Chapter 28

1 Visual Basic uses the Jet database engine to access databases.

2 A table is a group of data items, each containing the same type of information.

3 To eliminate repetitive data and increase storage efficiency.

4 Use the Data Manager application.

5 The data access objects.

Chapter 29

1 The Data Control opens a database file and sets up the link to the tables in the file.

2 The `DataSource` property must be set for any bound control.

3 The standard list box gets its list of choices from a series of `AddItem` statements. The data-bound list box gets its choices from a table in a database.

4 The Data Control must be on the same form as the bound controls.

Chapter 30

1 Use the `AddNew` method.

2 Use the `Delete` method.

3 Set the `Index` property of the recordset object to an index that exists for the table.

4 The `Seek` method.

5 Any of the `Find` methods.

6 The `Find` methods are more flexible than the `Seek` method since the `Find` methods support the `Like`, `In`, and `Between` comparison operators.

Chapter 31

1 The names of the fields to be retrieved and the table name(s) from which they will be retrieved.

2 Use the `WHERE` clause.

3 The `LIKE` operator.

4 Using the `ORDER BY` clause.

5 You must specify from which table each field will be retrieved, and you must specify a relationship between the tables.

6 You must specify a new value of the RecordSource property and then invoke the Refresh method.

Chapter 32

1 To a form, a picture box, the Printer, or the Debug window.

2 Use the Tab function with the Print method to specify an absolute character position.

3 You change the property settings of the output object to the desired font and style.

4 Check the Height and Width properties of your output object.

5 Use the TextHeight and TextWidth methods of the output object.

6 The text is "printed" outside the print area and does not show up.

7 You set the CurrentX and CurrentY properties of the output object.

8 The Cls method for the screen and the NewPage method for the printer.

Chapter 33

1 The DrawStyle property.

2 The Line method.

3 The FillStyle property.

4 The Circle method.

5 The start and end points of an arc are positive numbers; those of a pie slice are negative numbers.

6 The graphics controls would probably be better since you can see how they would look on the form while you are designing it.

Chapter 34

1 Set a watch to view in the Debug window, use an instant watch, or assign the variable to a text box.

2 You can run any single line command, such as printing a variable's value or changing a control's property.

3 The Calls dialog box tells you the procedures that were accessed to get you to the current point in your code.

4 Click the pause icon, set a watch point to pause on a certain value of a variable, or set a breakpoint in code.

Chapter 35

1 The Visible property.

2 The Locked property.

3 Data validation makes sure that information is of the correct type and in the correct range of values for a particular task.

4 You can use functions such as IsNumeric or IsDate.

5 The Resume statement tries to re-execute the statement that initially caused the error. The Resume Next statement continues execution of the program on the line following the statement causing the error.

6 The Number property of the Err object will tell you which error occurred.

Chapter 36

1 You can use the Add File dialog box to include existing forms and modules in your project.

2 The Unload command.

3 The Hide method.

4 The auto32ld.vbp or auto16ld.vbp file.

Index

Symbols

, (comma), 560
! (exclamation) operator, 43
& (ampersand), creating access keys, 193, 219
& (concatenation) operator, 316-319
; (semicolon), 560
= (equal) operator, 44
| (pipe symbol), 254
32-bit controls, 202-204
   Progress bar, creating, 203-204
   Slider control, 202-203
3D Check box control (databases), 513
3D frames, 160
3D Panel control (databases), 513

A

Abs function, 311
access keys, creating, 193-194, 219
actual values (scroll bars), 178-179
Add-In Manager command (Add-Ins menu), 518
Add-Ins menu commands (Add-In Manager), 518
AddItem method (lists), 143
addition operators, 296-298
AddNew method (databases), 525-526
advanced mathematical functions, 311-313
aligning
   option buttons, 131

paragraphs (RichTextBox), 102-103
Alignment property, 47, 190
   checkboxes, 126
ampersand (&), creating access keys, 193, 219
AND keyword (SQL), 548
And operator, comparisons, 346
animated button control, 634
animation, copying pictures, 117
Appearance property (frames), 159
Append mode (files), 466
arcs, drawing, 590-592
array functions, 458-459
arrays, 352-368
   control arrays, custom dialogs, 271-273
   counter loops, 357-358
   Dim statement, 354-355
   dimensions, 354
   dynamic arrays, 448
   elements, 353, 355-358
   Erase statement, 367
   indexes, 353, 355
   lower bound, 359
   memory, 367
   multidimensional arrays, 361-363
   nested For loops, 402
   Option Base statement (starting indexes), 359
   passing to procedures, 448-450

   ReDim statement (sizing arrays), 364-365
   setup, 354-355
   sizing, 364-367
   starting indexes, 358-364
   three-dimensional arrays, 361
   To keyword (starting indexes), 360-364
   two-dimensional arrays, 361
   upper bound, 354
   variables (sizing arrays), 365-366
ascending order (lists), 145
ASCII (American Standard Code for Information Interchange)
   string comparisons, 339
   text format, 465
aspect ratios
   pictures, 113-114
   ellipses, 589
assigning values to control names, 44
assignment statements, 51
   assigning literals to variables, 288
   IIF function, 419-420
   variables, 279-281
Atn function, 313
attributes (fonts), 78-79, 87
   Common Dialog box, 257-258
   designing programs, 80-86
AutoSize property, 188-189
   picture control, 112-113

B

BackColor property, 565-566

backgrounds
Label controls, 190
pictures, 111

BackStyle property, 190

backward counting loops, 398-400

bar charts, creating, 586-587

BAS file extension, 451

base fonts, 78-79, 87
changing
at runtime, 83-86
controls, 82-83
Common Dialog box, 256-258
attributes, 257-258
Flags property, 256-257
default fonts, 80
designing programs, 80-86
Name property, 84
point sizes, 78-79, 85
printing, 563-565
properties, 83-86
RichTextBox, 97-98

BETWEEN comparision operator (SQL), 547-548

Binary datatype (Jet database engine), 485

bitmap files (pictures), 108

block If statements, 411-412

Bookmark property (databases), 537-538

Boolean datatype, 282

BorderColor property (Shape control), 201

borders (Label controls), 190-191

BorderStyle property, 190-191
custom dialogs, 265
Shape control, 201
Slider control, 203

BorderWidth property (Shape control), 201

bound controls (databases), 504, 512-517

BoundColumn property, 516

boxes, drawing, 584-587

breakpoints, pausing execution, 603-604

bugs, 596-605
breakpoints, 603-604
comments, 596
Debug window, 599-603
error messages, 598-599
modules, 596
pausing execution, 603-604
stepping through code, 604-605
syntax errors, 596-598

buttons (custom dialogs), 273-275

byte datatype, 282
Jet database engine, 485

bytes, compared to characters, 56

C

calculations (codes), 51-54

Call keyword, 445-446

Calls dialog box, 602-603

Cancel property (command buttons), 192-193

Caption property, 187-188, 194-195
adding label controls to programs, 46
checkboxes, 126
custom dialogs, 269
option buttons, 129

captions
command buttons
changing captions at runtime, 194-195
custom dialogs, 275
Tab control, 168-169

Case Else statement, 427-428

case sensitivity
Code window, 597
RichTextBox, 105

Case statement (Select Case), 424-437
Case Else statement, 427-428
If/Then/ElseIf block, 436-437
multiple comparisons, 429-436
multiple conditions, 434-436
ordering, 433
variables, 433

case-insensitive sorting, 342-343

Cdbl function, 331

centering text, 573

Change event (scroll bars), 178

character codes (Masked Edit control), 70-71

characters, compared to bytes, 56

Check box control (databases), 513

checkboxes, 124-128
Alignment property, 126
Caption property, 126
creating, 125-127
initial values, 127
justification, 126
prompts, 125
toggling, 127
Value property, 127

Checked property, 217-218

Chr function, 232-233

Cint function, 331-332

Circle method (graphics), 578, 587-592

clearing the screen, 574-575

Click events, adding code to menus, 217

ClipMode property, 74-75

ClipText property, 74-75

Clng function, 331

Close statement, 478-479

closing files, 478

Cls method (graphics), 579

code, 10-11

adding
to forms, 48-51
to menus, 217
as event activators, 50
calculation, 51-54
comment lines, 33
multiple forms,
623-624
pictures, 115-117
setting colors, 89-91
spin buttons, 182-183
syntax, 51
viewing, 20-21
**code modules,
19-20, 451**
debugging, 596
files, 623-624
local variables, 461
scope of proce-
dures, 460
selecting, 20
storing proce-
dures, 452
viewing, 20
**Code Pane (Debug
window), 602-603**
Code window
case sensitivity, 597
editing, 20
entering code, 49
color constants, 89-91
**color palette, setting
colors, 88**
**Color Palette
command (View menu),
88**
colors
Common Dialog box, 258-
259
designing programs, 87-91
foreground color (option
buttons), 130
scroll bars, 176
selecting for printing, 565-
566
**Columns property (lists),
147-148**
**Combo box control
(databases), 514-515**
combo boxes, 151-154
drop-down boxes
combo boxes, 152
lists, 151-152
input, 153

ListIndex prop-
erty, 153
simple combo
boxes, 152
Text property, 153
Comm control, 634
**comma (,), Print method,
560**
**comma-delimited data,
470-471**
**command buttons, 15, 191-
195**
accession order, 192
adding to forms
drawing, 48
label controls, 49
naming, 49
adding to message boxes,
235-238
Cancel property,
192-193
captions
changing at runtime,
194-195
custom dialogs, 275
changing captions at
runtime, 194-195
coding in message boxes,
239-241
creating access keys, 193-
194
custom dialogs, 266, 273-
275
Default property,
192-193
commands
Add-Ins menu (Add-In
Manager), 518
Edit menu, 12, 209
File menu, 209
Add File, 624
New Database, 493
New Project, 631
Open Database, 499
Save Project
As, 631
Help menu, 210
Insert menu (Module), 623
Run menu
start, 52
Toggle Break-point, 603
Tools menu, 210
Add Watch, 600
Custom Controls, 69, 96,
180

Instant Watch, 601
Menu Editor, 211
View menu, 210
Color Palette, 88
Window menu, 210
comments, 33
debugging, 596
**Common Dialog,
248-261**
adding titles, 250
creating instances, 249
file functions, 250-255
Filter property,
254-255
Flags property,
256-257
fonts
attributes, 257-258
functions, 256-258
printing, 259-261
selecting colors,
258-259
**comparison
operators, 338**
comparisons, 336-350
And operator, 346
equivalence comparisons,
337
multiple comparisons,
346-348
Not operator, 348-349
not-equal comparisons,
337
numerical comparisons,
336-338
Or operator, 346
parenthetical groups, 347-
348
Seek method, 531-534
string comparisons, 339-
345
Xor operator, 347
**concatenation (&)
operator, 316-319**
**conditional loops,
370-387**
comparing Do Until and
Do While,
379-380
Do Until loops,
376-380
Do While loops,
370-375
infinite loops, 382-384

long loops, 385-386
terminating early,
386-382
**conditional statements,
logical operations, 336,
409**
**Connect property (data-
bases), 509**
**Const statement,
292-293**
constants, 291-293
compared to variables,
291
defining, 292-293
containers, 158-171
Frame control, 134
frames, 158-163
option buttons,
133-134
picture boxes, 164
Picture control,
113, 135
tabbed dialogs,
164-170
**control arrays
(custom dialogs), 271-
273**
Control toolbox
controls, 14-18, 36
moving, 15
multiple forms,
631-632
viewing, 15
controls, 14-18
32-bit controls,
202-204
Progress bar, creating,
203-204
Slider control,
202-203
animated button control,
634
bound controls (data-
bases), 504, 512-517
changing fonts, 82-83
Comm control, 634
command buttons, 191-
195
Common Dialog,
248-261
containers, 158-171
Crystal Reports control,
634

custom controls,
635-636
Data Control (databases),
502-511
SQL statements, 540-556
deleting, 45
dimmed controls, 610
Enabled property (error
handling), 610
Graph control, 635
graphics controls, 199-202
Line control,
201-202
Shape control,
200-201
Grid control, 635
Label controls,
186-191
Masked Edit control, 68-
75
moving, 45
naming, 39-43
placing in frames,
160-161
properties, 41
responding to events, 50-
51
selecting, 37
colors, 87-91
fonts, 80-86
sizing, 45
text boxes, 36-37
Timer controls,
195-198
undeleting, 46
Visible property (error
handling), 610
**converting strings to
numbers, 331-332**
**coordinates (drawing
lines), 580-582**
**Copy command (Edit
menu), 12**
copying
files, 479
pictures, 117
Cos function, 313
**Counter datatype
(Jet database engine),
485**
**counter fields (databases),
492**
counter loops, 390-406
arrays, 357-358

counting backwards, 398-
400
For loops, 391-396
infinite loops,
394-395
nesting, 401-402
nested loops, 401-405
step sizes, 397
terminating early,
395-396
variables, 400-401
**Crystal Reports control,
634**
Csng function, 331
Cstr function, 331-332
currency datatype, 282
**CurrentX property, 572-
573**
**CurrentY property, 572-
573**
**custom controls,
635-636**
multiple forms, 631
**Custom Controls dialog
box, 96,
180, 631**
**custom dialogs,
264-276**
BorderStyle
property, 265
Caption property, 269
command buttons, 266,
273-275
control arrays,
271-273
forms, adding, 264
Height property, 269
Hide method, 270
icons, 271-273
Image control, 271
labels, 265
MaxButton
property, 265
MinButton
property, 265
Name property, 265
pictures, 271-273
removing, 270
running, 267-270
text boxes (input), 266-
267
Top property, 269
Unload statement, 270
**Cut command (Edit
menu), 12**

D

data
editing (text boxes), 65-66
inputting (text boxes), 56-64, 68-75
retrieving
Masked Edit control, 73-75
text boxes, 66-67
storing (variables), 278-290
validating, 450, 485-486
error handling, 613-615
range checking, 613-614
Data Access Objects (DAOs), 499-500
data comparisons, 336-350
Data Control (databases), 502-511, 524-538, 540-556
Data Form Designer, 518-520
data integrity, 485-486
Data Manager, 493-499, 555-556
data normalization, 488-490
data types, validating, 614-615
data-bound combo boxes, 515-517
data-bound grids, 517
data-bound list boxes, 515-517
DatabaseName property, 505-508
databases, 482-500, 524-538
accessing, 502-521
adding records, 525-526
AddNew method, 525-526
Bookmark property, 537-538
bound controls, 504, 512-517
Connect property, 509
counter fields, 492
Data Access Objects (DAOs), 499-500
Data Control, 502-511
SQL statements, 540-556

Data Form Designer, 518-520
data integrity, 485-486
data normalization, 488-490
data validation, 485-486
deleting records, 527-528
Exclusive property, 510
fields, 483, 487-488
adding to tables, 495-496
deleting, 495-497
editing, 496
selecting with SQL statements, 542-550
filters, 483
Find methods, 534-537
foreign keys, 491
indexes, 483, 529
adding to tables, 497-498
deleting, 497
Jet database engine, 484-486
key fields, 491-492
ordering, 528-530
physical order, 528-529
planning, 486-493
primary keys, 491
queries, 483, 507
RDBMS (Relational Database Management System), 482-484
ReadOnly property, 510
records, 483
limiting retrieval, 544-548
sorting, 549-550
recordsets, 503, 510-511
modifying at runtime, 553-555
RecordsetType property, 511
relationships, 498-499
restricting access, 510
searches, 531-538
Seek method, 531-534

tables, 483, 487-493
creating new tables, 494-495
defining, 490, 498-499
multiple tables, retrieving, 550-553
relationships, 491-492, 498-499
retrieving, 541-550, 544
Update method, 525
views, 483
DataField property, 513-514, 516
DataSource property, 512, 516
datatypes
double, 282
dynaset (databases), 510-511
integer, 282
long, 282
object, 282
single, 282
snapshot, 571
string, 282-288
table, 511
text, 485
variant, 282, 289-290
Yes/No, 485
recordsets (databases), 510-511
selecting default datatypes, 286-288
variables, 281-283, 474-475
date datatype, 282,288
date/time functions, 307-310
DateAdd function, 309-310
DateDiff function, 308-310
Debug window, 599-603
Code Pane, 602-603
Immediate Pane, 602
instant watches, 601
printing to, 559
variable values, 600-602
watches, 600-601
debugging, 596-605
breakpoints, 603-604
comments, 596

Debug window,
599-603
error messages,
598-599
modules, 596
pausing execution, 603-
604
stepping through code,
604-605
syntax errors, 596-598
**default datatypes,
selecting, 286-288**
**Default property (com-
mand buttons), 192-193**
defining
constants, 292-293
tables (databases), 490
variables (random file
access), 474-475
**Delete method,
527-528**
desktop, 11-18
menu bar, 12
Project Window,
18-23
toolbar, 13-14
toolbox, 14-18
dialog boxes, 14, 228
Add File, 624
Add Watch, 600
Add-In Manager, 518
Calls, 602-603
Common Dialog,
248-261
Custom Controls, 69, 96,
180, 631
custom dialogs,
264-276
Data Form Designer, 518-
520
Edit Watch, 601
Environment Options, 14-
15
Font, 81, 97
input boxes, 241-244
Insert Procedure,
444-445
Load Picture, 109, 168
Menu Editor, 211-216
message boxes,
229-230, 235-241
Object Browser, 292
Properties, 41-42, 81, 89,
109, 505-507

tabbed dialogs,
164-170
Dim statement
arrays, 354-355
scope of variables, 461
To keyword (array
starting indexes), 360-
364
**dimensions
(arrays), 354**
dimmed controls, 610
directories, paths, 253
**disabling menu items, 221-
222**
**division operators, 298-
301**
**Do loops, nesting,
403-404**
**Do Until loops,
376-380**
**Do While loops,
370-375**
compared to Do Until
loops, 379-380
**documentation
(designing programs), 33**
DoEvents function, 386
dot notation, 43-44
dot operators, 477
**DrawMode prop-
erty, 579**
**DrawStyle property, 579,
582-584**
**DrawWidth property, 579,
583-584**
**drop-down combo boxes,
152**
**drop-down lists,
151-152**
dynamic arrays, 448

E

**Edit Watch dialog
box, 601**
**Editor tab (multiple
forms), 630**
**elements (arrays), 353,
355-358**
ellipses, drawing, 589
Else statements,
414-416
ElseIf statements, 416-419
Enabled property, 221-222
error handling, 610

**Enter key (command
buttons), 192-193**
entering
codes (syntax), 51
list items, 142
**Environment Options
dialog box, 14-15**
**environments (multiple
forms), 628-632**
**equivalence comparisons,
337**
string equivalence
comparisons,
339-340
**Erase statement (arrays),
367**
error handling, 29, 608-620
access, 609-612
data type validation, 614-
615
data validation,
613-615
debugging, 596-605
editing restrictions, 611-
612
Enabled property, 610
ignoring errors,
619-620
On Error Resume Next
statement,
619-620
Visible property, 610
**error messages, debugging,
598-599**
events, 50, 440
Change, 178
coding controls to
respond to, 50-51
Load, 120
MouseDown, 120
MouseUp, 120
SpinDown, 181
SpinUp, 181
**Exclusive property
(databases), 510**
executable files, 20
**Exit Do statement, 380-
382**
**Exit For state-
ment, 396**
**Exit Sub statement, 450-
451**
Exp function, 312

explicit declaration
(variables), 283-284
exponential notation, 283,
301-302

F

feedback (custom dialogs),
275-276
field level validation
(databases), 486
fields (databases), 483,
487-488
  adding to tables,
    495-496
  counter fields, 492
  deleting, 495-497
  editing, 496
  key fields, 491-492
  selecting with SQL
    statements, 542-550
FileCopy state-
ment, 479
files, 464-480
  closing, 478
  comma-delimited data,
    470-471
  Common Dialog box, 250-
    255
  copying, 479
  deleting, 479
  EXE (executable), 20
  extensions, 20
  form, 20
  initialization files, 467
  opening, 466-467,
    475-476
  paths, 253
  project, 19-20
  random file access, 464-
    465, 474-477
  reading, 467-471, 477
  renaming, 479
  sequential file access, 464-
    473
  writing to,
    471-473, 477
FillColor property, 579
  Shape control, 201
FillStyle property, 579,
584-587
  Shape control, 201
Filter property (Common
Dialog box), 254-255

filters (databases), 483
Find command (Edit
menu), 12
Find methods, 534-537
fixed-length strings, 285-
286, 316
Flags property (Common
Dialog box), 256-257
floating-point division,
300-301
focus (option buttons),
131-132
Font dialog box, 81, 97
fonts, 78-79, 87
  changing
    at runtime, 83-86
    controls, 82-83
  Common Dialog box, 256-
    258
    attributes, 257-258
    Flags property, 256-257
  default fonts, 80
  designing programs, 80-86
  Name property, 84
  point sizes, 78-79, 85
  printing, 563-565
  properties, 83-86
  RichTextBox, 97-98
For loops, 391-396
  nesting, 401-402
  terminating early,
    395-396
ForeColor property, 565-
566, 579
foreground color (option
buttons), 130
foreign keys, 491
Form Design Grid options
(multiple forms), 629
forms, 9-10, 14
  adding, 622-623
    to custom
      dialogs, 264
  coding, 48-51, 623-624
  compared to message
    boxes, 230
  creating, 622-623
  custom controls, 631
  designing
    codes, 48-51
    label controls,
      46-48
    text boxes, 37-46
  dialog boxes, 228

displaying, 625-626
Editor tab, 630
environment control, 628-
  632
File Save options, 630
files, 20
font properties, 83-86
Form Design Grid options,
  629
graphics controls, 199-200
Hide method, 626
importing, 624
loading, 625
modal forms, 267
modeless, 267
module files, 623-624
multiple forms,
  622-632
pictures, 109-111
positioning/size, 13
printing, 559, 575-576
Project window, 625
scope of proce-
  dures, 460
selecting, 20
  colors, 87-91
  fonts, 80-82
Show method, 626
Startup Form drop-down
  list, 628
storing proce-
  dures, 451
syntax checking, 630
toolbox, 631-632
ToolTips, 630
unloading, 626
variable declara-
  tions, 630
viewing, 20
Windows On Top options,
  629
Frame control (option
buttons), 133-134
frames (containers), 158-
163
  3D frames, 160
  Appearance prop-
    erty, 159
  control placement, 160-
    161
  creating, 159-160
  multiple frames,
    161-163
  Name property, 159

functions
  Abs, 311
  array functions,
    458-459
  Atn, 313
  calling, 453
  Cdbl, 331
  Chr (carriage return/line
    feed), 232-233
  Cint, 331-332
  Clng, 331
  compared to procedures,
    452-453
  Cos, 313
  creating, 452-453
  Csng, 331
  Cstr, 331-332
  DateAdd, 309-310
  DateDiff, 308-310
  DoEvents, 386
  Exp, 312
  IIF, 419-420
  Input, 468-470
  InputBox, 242
  InStr, 323-325
  Int, 312
  IsDate, 615
  IsNumeric,
    289-290, 615
  LCase, 320-321
  Left, 327-329
  Len, 243, 326
  LoadPicture, 115-117
  LOF (length of file), 468-
    470
  Log, 312
  LSet, 321-322
  LTrim, 326-327
  mathematical functions,
    458
  Max, 458
  Mid, 327-329
  Min, 458
  MsgBox, 231-233, 236
  Right, 327-329
  Rnd, 312
  RSet, 321-322
  RTrim, 326-327
  Sgn, 312
  Sin, 313
  Spc, 473, 560
  Sqr, 312
  standard menu functions,
    209-210
  string manipulation
    functions, 320-331, 454-
    457
  Tab, 473, 560
  Tan, 313
  TextHeight, 570-572
  TextWidth, 570-572
  trigonometric functions,
    312-313
  Trim, 326-327
  UCase, 320-321
  Val, 243, 615

G

Get statement, 478
global variables,
  460-461
Graph control, 635
graphics, 107-121,
  578-594
  adding to forms,
    109-111
  aspect ratio, 113-114
  backgrounds, 111
  bitmap files, 108
  Circle method, 578, 587-
    592
  Cls method, 579
  code, 115-117
  controls, 199-202
    compared to methods,
      593
    Line control,
      201-202
    Shape control,
      200-201
  copying, 117
  creating bar charts, 586-
    587
  deleting, 116
  displaying, 114-115
  drawing
    arcs, 590-592
    ellipses, 589
    pie charts, 590-592
  filling boxes, 584-587
  icons, 108
  Image control,
    113-114
  inserting, 109-115
  Line method, 578-587
    coordinates,
      580-582
    drawing boxes, 584-587
    patterns, 582-584
  LoadPicture function, 115-
    117
  PaintPicture method, 579
  picture control,
    111-113
  Point method, 578
  properties, 579
  PSet method, 578, 592
  scroll bars, 111
  sizing, 111
  Windows meta-
    files, 108
Grid control, 635
grids (desktop), control-
  ling spacing of, 14

H

hanging indents, 94
Height property,
  568-569
  custom dialogs, 269
Help menu
  commands, 210
Hide method
  custom dialogs, 270
  multiple forms, 626
highlight bar (list boxes),
  141
horizontal scroll bars
  (text boxes), 60-63
HScrollBar, 175

I

icons, 229
  adding to message boxes,
    234-235
  custom dialogs,
    271-273
  pictures, 108
identifying inputs (label
  controls),
  46-48
If statements, 408-421
  block If statements, 411-
    412
  ElseIf statements, 416-419
  If/Else/End If block, 414-
    416
  IIF function, 419-420
  infinite loops, 384

nesting, 403
Not operator, 413-414
single line If statements, 409-411
If/Else/End If blocks, 414-416
If/Then/ElseIf blocks (Select Case statement), 436-437
IIF function, 419-420
Image control, 108, 113-114
arrays, 271-273
custom dialogs, 271
databases, 513
picture buttons, 118-121
Stretch property, 113
toolbars, 118-121
Immediate Pane (Debug window), 602
implicit declaration (variables), 284-285
importing forms, 624
IN comparison operator (SQL), 545
indents
hanging indents, 94
RichTextBox, 101
indexes
arrays, 353, 355
databases, 483
adding to tables, 497-498
deleting, 497
ordering, 529
infinite loops, 382-384
For loops, 394-395
INI files, 467
initial values
checkboxes, 127
option buttons, 130
initialization files, 467
Input # statement, 470-471
input boxes, 241-244
coding, 243-244
creating, 242
Input function, 468-470
InputBox function, 242
Insert menu commands (Module), 623
Insert Procedure dialog box, 444-445

instances, creating, 249
Instant Watch command (Tools menu), 601
instant watches (Debug window), 601
InStr function, 323-325
Int function, 312
integer division, 300-301
compared to rounding, 305-306
integrity of data, 485-486
interfaces, 9, 31-32
Interval property, 196-197
Is keyword (Select Case ranges), 432-433
IsDate function, 615
IsNumeric function, 289-290, 615
Italic property (fonts), 83-84

J-K

Jet database engine, 484-486
creating databases, 493-500
key fields (databases), 491-492
keywords, 279
AND (SQL), 548
Call, 445-446
Dim (scope of variables), 461
OR (SQL), 548
Private, 460-461
Public, 460-461
ReDim (scope of variables), 461
Static, 461
Step, 397
String, 286
Sub, 442
To (For loops), 392
Kill statement, 479

L

Label controls, 186-191
adding to forms, 46
backgrounds, 190
borders, 190-191
Caption property, 187-188
compared to text boxes, 187
databases, 513
identifying inputs, 46-48
justifying text, 190
resizing at runtime, 188-189
labeling
custom dialogs, 265
scroll bars, 177
LargeChange property (scroll bars), 177
LCase function, 320-321
Left function (strings), 327-329
Left property (option buttons), 131
Len function, 243, 326
LIKE comparision operator (SQL), 545-547
pattern matching, 345
Line control, 201-202
Line Input statement, 467-468
Line method (graphics), 578-587
coordinates, 580-582
drawing boxes, 584-587
patterns, 582-584
List box control (databases), 514-515
list boxes
AddItem method, 143
editing, 142-144
highlight bar, 141
List property, 141, 147
ListCount property, 150
ListIndex property, 147
MultiSelect property, 148-150

RemoveItem
method, 143
scroll bars, 141
Selected property, 150
setup, 141-142
sizing, 142
**List property (list boxes),
141, 147**
**ListCount property (list
boxes), 150**
ListField property, 516
ListIndex property
combo boxes, 153
list boxes, 147
lists, 140-155
AddItem method, 143
ascending order, 145
Columns property, 147-
148
combo boxes, 151-154
creating, 140-150
drop-down lists,
151-152
editing, 142-144
entering items, 142
RemoveItem
method, 143
selecting items,
146-147
Sorted property, 146
**literals, assigning to
variables, 288**
Load event, 120
**Load Picture dialog box,
109, 168**
loading forms, 625
**LoadPicture function, 115-
117**
locking text boxes, 612
LOF function, 468-470
Log function, 312
**logical comparisons, 336-
350, 409**
loops
conditional loops, 370-387
Do Until loops, 376-380
Do While loops, 370-375,
379-380
infinite loops,
382-384
long loops, 385-386
terminating early, 380-
382
counter loops,
390-406

counting backwards,
398-400
For loops, 391-396, 401-
402
infinite loops,
394-395
nested loops,
401-405
step sizes, 397
terminating early, 395-
396
variables, 400-401
spin buttons, 182-183
While...Wend
loops, 375
LSet function, 321-322
**LTrim function,
326-327**

M

**mailing labels, creating,
317-319**
**many-to-many relation-
ships (databases), 492**
Mask property, 70-71
Masked Edit control, 68-75
character codes, 70-71
databases, 513
place holders, 71-72
retrieving data, 73-75
**mathematical functions,
458**
**mathematical operators,
296-313**
addition/subtraction, 296-
298
advanced mathematical
functions,
311-313
creating calculators, 306-
307
date/time functions, 307-
310
exponents, 301-302
multiplication/division,
298-301
order of precedence, 302-
304
variable datatypes, 304-
306
Max function, 458
**Max property (scroll
bars), 176**

**MaxButton
property (custom
dialogs), 265**
**MaxLength property, 63-
64**
**Memo datatype
(Jet database engine),
485**
memory
arrays, 367
variables, 278-290
menu bar, 12
**Menu Editor dialog box,
211-216**
menus, 12, 208-226
adding
code, 217
menu items, 216
advantages, 208-209
Checked property, 217-
218
creating, 211-216
access keys, 219
menu items,
211-212, 216
pop-up menus,
223-224
separator bars, 214
shortcut keys,
219-220
submenus, 212-214
deleting menu
items, 216
Enabled property, 221-222
invoking pop-up menus,
224-225
moving menu
items, 216
planning, 210-211
pop-up menus,
223-225
standard functions, 209-
210
Visible property, 222
**message boxes,
229-230**
adding
command buttons, 235-
238
icons, 234-235
titles, 233
coding command buttons,
239-241
compared to
forms, 230

creating, 230-233
multiple lines, 232-233
setting default buttons, 238
methods, 143
AddItem, 143
AddNew, 525-526
Delete, 527-528
Find, 534-537
MoveLast, 527
MoveNext, 527
RemoveItem, 143
Seek, 531-534
Update, 525
Mid function (strings), 327-329
Mid statement (strings), 329-331
Min function, 458
Min property (scroll bars), 175
MinButton property (custom dialogs), 265
modular programming (procedures), 440-442
advantages, 440-441
compared to functions, 452-453
creating, 442-445
executing, 445-446
passing
arrays, 448-450
parameters, 446-448
private variables, 461
scope, 459-460
Static keyword, 461
storing, 451-452
terminating early, 450-451
Module command (Insert menu), 623
modules, 451
creating, 452
debugging, 596
files, 623-624
local variables, 461
scope of procedures, 460
storing procedures, 452

modulus division, 300-301
MouseDown event, 120
MouseUp event, 120
MoveLast method, 527
MoveNext method, 527
moving
controls, 45
menu items, 216
toolbox, 15
MsgBox function, 231-233, 236
MultiLine property, 59-60
multiple comparisons, 346-348
Select Case statement, 429-436
multiple forms, 622-632
code, 623-624
custom controls, 631
displaying, 625-626
Editor tab, 630
environment control, 628-632
File Save options, 630
Form Design Grid options, 629
Hide method, 626
module files, 623-624
Project window, 625
Show method, 626
Startup Form drop-down list, 628
syntax checking, 630
toolbox, 631-632
ToolTips, 630
variable declarations, 630
Windows On Top options, 629
multiple frames, 161-163
multiple lines of text
inputting into text boxes, 58-63
message boxes, 232-233
multiplication operators, 298-301
MultiSelect property (list boxes), 148-150

N

Name property, 41
adding label controls to programs, 46
custom dialogs, 265
direct access to, 41
fonts, 83-84
frames, 159
Name statement, 479
naming
controls
dot notation, 43
prefixes, 39-41
restrictions, 42
text boxes, 39-42
variables, 278-279
nested loops, 401-405
New Database command (File menu), 493
New Project command (File menu), 631
newval variable (spin buttons), 182
Next statements (For loops), 392
NoMatch property
Find methods, 536
Seek method, 533
Not operator, 413-414
comparisons, 348-349
numbers, converting to strings, 331

O

Object Browser dialog box, 292
OLE datatype (Jet database engine), 485
On Error Resume Next statement (error handling), 619-620
one-to-many relationships (databases), 492
Open command (File menu), 12
Open Database command (File menu), 499
Open Project dialog box, 22

Open statement, 466
opening
files, 466-467, 475-476
Common Dialog, 252-254
projects, 22
operators
BETWEEN comparision operator (SQL), 547-548
comparison operators, 338
concatenation (&) operator, 316-319
dot operators, 477
IN comparison operator (SQL), 545
LIKE comparision operator (SQL), 545-547
mathematical operators, 296-313
addition/subtraction, 296-298
advanced mathematical functions, 311-313
creating calculators, 306-307
date/time functions, 307-310
exponents, 301-302
multiplication/division, 298-301
order of precedence, 302-304
variable datatypes, 304-306
Not operator, 413-414
Option Base statement (array starting indexes), 359
option buttons, 129-132
Caption property, 129
containers, 133-134
focus, 131-132
foreground color, 130
Frame control, 133-134
grouping, 131, 133-136
initial values, 130
Left property, 131
lining up, 131
Picture control, 133, 135

Tab control, 170
text boxes, 130
Value property, 132
OR keyword (SQL), 548
Or operator (comparisons), 346
ORDER BY clause (SQL), 549-550
order of precedence
comparisons, 347-348
mathematical operators, 302-304
ordering
databases, 528-530
Select Case statements, 433
Orientation property, 203
output, 29
Output mode (files), 466

P

PaintPicture method (graphics), 579
paragraphs, aligning (RichTextBox), 102-103
parentheses ( )
comparisons, 347-348
order of precedence, 303-304
passing to procedures
arrays, 448-450
parameters, 446-448
Paste command (Edit menu), 12
paths, 253
pattern matching (string comparisons), 344-345
patterns
drawing lines, 582-584
filling boxes, 584-587
pausing execution, 603-604
percentages (scroll bars), 176
physical order (databases), 528-529
picture box
windows, 164
printing to, 559

picture buttons, 118-121
Picture control, 108, 111-113
AutoSize property, 112-113
containers, 113
option buttons, 133, 135
Picture property (listing 7.1), 120
pictures, 107-121
adding to forms, 109-111
aspect ratio, 113-114
backgrounds, 111
bitmap files, 108
code, 115-117
copying, 117
custom dialogs, 271-273
deleting, 116
displaying, 114-115
icons, 108
Image control, 113-114
inserting, 109-115
LoadPicture function, 115-117
picture control, 111-113
scroll bars, 111
sizing, 111
Tab control, 168-169
Windows metafiles, 108
pipe symbol (|), 254
place holders (Masked Edit control), 71-72
placing controls in frames, 160-161
planning
databases, 486-493
menus, 210-211
programs, 27-30
Point method (graphics), 578
point sizes (fonts), 78-79, 85
pointers, 503-504
pop-up menus, 223-225
primary keys (databases), 491

integrity, 486
Print # statement, 473
Print command (File menu), 12
Print statement, 471-473
print zones, 473, 560
printing, 558-576
  clearing the screen, 574-575
  Common Dialog box, 259-261
  controlling the printer, 573-574
  dimensions, 567-573
  forms, 559, 575-576
  landscape mode, 567
  picture box windows, 559
  portrait mode, 567
  selecting
    colors, 565-566
    fonts, 563-565
  setting text positions, 572-573
  Spc function, 560
  starting a new page, 573
  Tab function, 560
  terminating, 574
  to Debug window, 559
  word wrapping, 569-572
Private keyword, 460-461
Private variables, 444
procedures, 440-442
  advantages, 440-441
  compared to functions, 452-453
  creating, 442-445
  event procedures, 440
  executing, 445-446
  passing
    arrays, 448-450
    parameters, 446-448
  private variables, 461
  scope, 459-460
  Static keyword, 461
  storing, 451-452
  Sub procedures, 440
  terminating early, 450-451

programs, 18-23
  changing fonts at runtime, 83-86
  designing, 26-34
    colors, 87-91
    defining tasks, 27, 36
    desktop tools, 11-18
    documentation, 33
    fonts, 80-87
    forms, creating, 36-54
    interfaces, 31-32
    plans, creating, 27-29
  elements of, 9-11
  management of, 18-23
  opening, 22
  pausing execution, 603-604
  planning, 29-30
  running, 52
  saving, 53-54
  starting, 22
Progress bar, creating, 203-204
project files, storing program locations, 19-20
Project window, 18-23
  multiple forms, 625
prompts (checkboxes), 125
properties
  accessing specific properties, 42
  Alignment, 47, 190
  AutoSize, 188-189
  BackColor, 565-566
  BackStyle, 190
  BorderColor (Shape control), 201
  BorderStyle, 190-191
    Shape control, 201
    Slider control, 203
  BorderWidth (Shape control), 201
  BoundColumn, 516
  Cancel (command buttons), 192-193
  Caption, 46, 187-188, 194-195
  Checked, 217-218
  ClipMode, 74-75
  ClipText, 74-75

colors (designing programs), 87-91
Connect (databases), 509
controls, 41
  changing, 43
CurrentX, 572-573
CurrentY, 572-573
data-bound list/combo boxes, 516-517
DatabaseName, 505-508
DataField, 513-514, 516
DataSource, 512, 516
Default (command buttons), 192-193
DrawMode, 579
DrawStyle, 579, 582-584
DrawWidth, 579, 583-584
Enabled, 221-222
Exclusive (databases), 510
FillColor, 579
  Shape control, 201
FillStyle, 579, 584-587
  Shape control, 201
Filter (Common Dialog box), 254-255
Flags (Common Dialog box), 256-257
fonts, 83-86
  Common Dialog box, 257-258
  printing, 563-565
ForeColor, 565-566, 579
Height, 568-569
Interval, 196-197
ListField, 516
Mask, 70-71
MaxLength, 63-64
MultiLine, 59-60
Name, 41, 84
Orientation, 203
ReadOnly (databases), 510
RecordsetType (databases), 511
RecordSource, 505-508, 553-555

RowSource, 516
SelText, 67
setting database proper-
ties, 505-508
TabIndex, 192
Text, 42, 66-67, 73-75
TickFrequency, 203
TickStyle, 203
Value, 203
variables, 278-290
Visible, 222
Width, 568-569
WordWrap, 188-189
**Properties dialog box, 81,
109, 505-507**
accessing, 41-42
setting colors, 89
**Properties Window, 18
prototyping interfaces, 32
PSet method (graphics),
578, 592
Public keyword,
460-461
Public variables, 444
Put statement,
477-478**

Q-R

**queries (databases), 483,
507
random file access, 464-
465, 474-477
ranges**
data validation,
613-614
scroll bars, 175-176
Select Case multiple
comparisons,
430-433
**RDBMS (Relational
Database Management
System),
482-484
reading files,
467-471, 477
ReadOnly property
(databases), 510
record level validation
(databases), 486
records (data-
bases), 483**
adding, 525-526
deleting, 527-528

finding
in dynasets or
snapshots,
534-537
in tables, 531-534
limiting retrieval,
544-548
relationships, 492
sorting, 549-550
**recordsets (databases),
503, 510-511**
Bookmark property, 537-
538
Find methods,
534-537
modifying at runtime, 553-
555
ordering, 529-530
searches, 531-538
Seek method, 531-534
**RecordsetType property
(databases), 511
RecordSource property,
505-508,
553-555
ReDim keyword**
scope of variables, 461
sizing arrays, 364-365
**referential integrity
(databases), 486
Relational Database
Management System
(RDBMS), 482-484
remainder division, 300-
301
RemoveItem method
(lists), 143
removing custom dialogs,
270
renaming files, 479
Report Designer, 635
reports (Crystal Reports
control), 634
restricting**
access to data-
bases, 510
editing (error handling),
611-612
**retrieving records
(databases), 544-548
RichTextBox, 94-105**
accessing, 96
case matching, 105
compared to text boxes,
95

fonts, 97-98
formatting, 96-103
hanging indents,
94, 101
indents, 101
paragraph alignment, 102-
103
saving text, 103-104
text effects, 96-97
word formatting,
98-100
**Right function (strings),
327-329
Rnd function, 312
RowSource prop-
erty, 516
RSet function, 321-322
RTF (Rich Text Format)
files, 94-95
RTrim function,
326-327
Run command (Start
menu), 52**

S

**Save File As dialog box, 53
scope**
procedures, 459-460
variables, 459-461
screen
clearing, 574-575
printing to, 559
scroll bars, 174-179
Change event, 178
HScrollBar, 175
LargeChange property,
177
list boxes, 141
Max property, 176
Min property, 175
percentages, 176
pictures, 111
ranges, 175-176
setup, 175-177
slider bars, 175
SmallChange property,
177
text boxes, 60-63
value displays,
178-179
Value property, 176
VScrollBar, 175

searching
    arrays, 458-459
    databases, 531-538
    strings, 323-325, 457
Seek method
    comparison conditions, 531-534
    NoMatch property, 533
Select Case block, range checking (listing 35.4), 614
Select Case statement, 424-437
    Case Else statement, 427-428
    If/Then/ElseIf block, 436-437
    multiple comparisons, 429-436
    multiple conditions, 434-436
    ordering, 433
    variables, 433
Select statement (SQL), 541-550
    nesting, 403
    retrieving multiple tables, 550-553
Selected property (list boxes), 150
SelText property, 67
separator bars, 214
sequential file access, 464-473
setup
    arrays, 354-355
    list boxes, 141-142
    scroll bars, 175-177
Sgn function, 312
Shape control, 200-201
shortcut keys, 12, 46
    creating, 219-220
Show method (multiple forms), 626
Sin function, 313
Size property (fonts), 83, 85
slider bars (scroll bars), 175
Slider control, 202-203
SmallChange property (scroll bars), 177

snapshots, 534-537
Sorted property (lists), 146
sorting
    case-insensitive sorting, 342-343
    records (databases), 549-550
spaces, deleting from strings, 326-327
Spc function, 473, 560
spin buttons
    code, 182-183
    loop functionality, 182-183
    newval variable, 182
    SpinDown event, 181
    SpinUp event, 181
    text boxes, 181
SpinDown event (spin buttons), 181
SpinUp event (spin buttons), 181
SQL, *see Structured Query Language*
Sqr function, 312
statements
    assignment statements variables, 279-281
        assigning literals to variables, 288
    Close, 478-479
    Const, 292-293
    Exit Do, 380-382
    Exit For, 396
    Exit Sub, 450-451
    FileCopy, 479
    Get, 478
    If, 384, 408-421
    Input #, 470-471
    Kill, 479
    Line Input, 467-468
    Mid (strings), 329-331
    Name, 479
    Next (For loops), 392
    Open, 466
    ORDER BY clause (SQL), 549-550
    Print #, 473
    Print, 471-473
    Put, 477-478
    Select (SQL), 541-550
        nesting, 403
        retrieving multiple

tables, 550-553
    testing SQL statements, 555-556
    Type, 474-475
    WHERE clause (SQL), 544-550
    Write, 471-473
Static keyword, 461
Static variables, 444
Step keyword, 397
step sizes (counter loops), 397
stepping through code, debugging, 604-605
Stretch property (Image control), 113
Strikethrough property (fonts), 83
string comparisons, 339-345
    case-insensitive sorting, 342-343
    equivalence comparisons, 339-340
    pattern matching, 344-345
String keyword, 286
strings, 316-333
    concatenating, 316-319
    converting to upper- case, 320-321
    converting to numbers, 331-332
    deleting spaces, 326-327
    determining length, 326
    fixed-length strings, 285-286, 316
    length of, 326
    searching, 323-325, 457
    string manipulation functions, 320-331, 454-457
    variable length strings, 316
Structured Query Language (SQL), 541-553
    recordsets (databases), modifying at runtime, 553-555

retrieving
multiple tables
(databases),
550-553
single tables
(databases),
541-550
testing statements, 555-556

Style property (Tab control), 166

Sub keyword, 442

Sub procedures, 440

submenus, creating, 212-214

subtraction operators, 296-298

syntax checking, 596-598
debugging, 596-598
multiple forms, 630

system resources, 187

T

Tab control, 165-169
captions, 168-169
option buttons, 170
pictures, 168-169
Sheridan Tabbed Dialog, 169
Style property, 166
TabHeight property, 166-167
TabMaxWidth property, 166
TabOrientation property, 166
WordWrap property, 166-167

Tab function, 473, 560

tabbed dialogs (containers), 164-170

TabHeight property (Tab control), 166-167

TabIndex property, 192

tables (databases), 483, 487-493, 531-534
creating new tables, 494-495
defining, 490
relationships, 491-492
defining, 498-499

retrieving
multiple, 550-553
single, 541-550
Seek method, 531-534
SQL statements, 541-553

TabMaxWidth property (Tab control), 166

TabOrientation property (Tab control), 166

Tabs property, 165

TabsPerRow property, 165

text
ASCII text format, 465
centering, 573
fonts, 78-79
printing, 563-565
resizing Label controls, 188-189
RichTextBox, 96-97
setting text positions for printing, 572-573
string manipulation functions, 320-331
Tab control, 168
word wrapping, 569-572

text boxes
creating, 37
drawing, 37-39
label controls, 46-48
multiple text boxes, 57
naming, 39-42
editing data, 65-66
inputting data, 56-58
custom dialogs, 266-267
limiting input, 63-64
Masked Edit control, 68-75
multiple lines of text, 58-63
locking/unlocking, 612
retrieving data, 66-67
RichTextBox, 94-105
scrolling, 57-58, 60-63
spin buttons, 181
word wrapping, 60

Text property, 42, 66-67, 73-75
combo boxes, 153

TextHeight function, 570-572

TextWidth function, 570-572

TickFrequency property, 203

TickStyle property, 203

time/date functions, 307-310

Timer controls, 195-198

To keyword
array starting indexes, 360-364
For loops, 392
Select Case ranges, 430-432

Toggle Breakpoint command (Run menu), 603

toggling check-boxes, 127

toolbars, 13-14
display, changing, 14
Image control, 118-121

toolboxes
controls, 14-18, 36
moving, 15
multiple forms, 631-632
viewing, 15

Tools menu commands, 210
Add Watch, 600
Custom Controls, 69, 96, 180
Instant Watch, 601
Menu Editor, 211

ToolTips (multiple forms), 630

Top property (custom dialogs), 269

topics (database tables), 487-488

trigonometric functions, 312-313

Trim function, 326-327

troubleshooting
debugging, 596-605
error handling, 608-620

twips, 13-14, 567

Type statement, 474-475

U

UCase function, 320-321
undeleting controls, 46
Underline property (fonts), 83-84
Undo command (Edit menu), 12
Unload statement (custom dialogs), 270
unloading forms, 626
unlocking text boxes, 612
Update method (databases), 525
upper bound (arrays), 354
uppercase strings, converting to lowercase, 320-321
user access (error handling), 609-612
user feedback (custom dialogs), 275-276
user interfaces, 9
    common elements, 31
    designing programs, 31-32
    prototyping, 32

V

Val function, 243, 615
validating data, 450, 485-486
    data types, 614-615
    error handling, 613-615
    range checking, 613-614
Value property, 203
    checkboxes, 127
    option buttons, 132
    scroll bars, 176
variable arrays, 352-368
variable length strings, 316
variables, 278-290, 352-354
    assignment statements, 279-281

compared to constants, 291
datatypes, 281-283
    mathematical operations, 304-306
Debug window, 600-602
declaring, 283-288
    multiple forms, 630
explicit declaration, 283-284
fixed-length strings, 285-286
For loops, 391-394, 400-401
implicit declaration, 284-285
initializing, 281
naming conventions, 278-279
pointers, 503-504
Private variables, 444
Public variables, 444
random file access, 474-476
scope, 459-461
Select Case statement, 433
Static variables, 444, 461
variant datatype, 289-290
vertical scroll bars (text boxes), 60-63
View Code button, 20
View Form button, 20
views (databases), 483
Visible property, 222
    error handling, 610
VScrollBar, 175

W

watches (Debug window), 600-601
Weight property (fonts), 83
WHERE clause (SQL), 544-550
While...Wend loops, 375
Width property, 568-569

wildcards (SQL statements), 546
Window menu commands, 210
Windows
    long loops, 385-386
    message boxes, 229-230
windows
    code editing, 20
    code entry, 49
    Project, 18-23
    Properties, 18
Windows metafiles (pictures), 108
Windows On Top options (multiple forms), 629
wizards, 28
word formatting (RichTextBox), 98-100
word wrapping, 60, 569-572
    Label controls, 187-188
WordWrap property, 188-189
    Tab control, 166-167
Write statement, 471-473
writing to files, 471-473, 477

X-Y-Z

Xor operator (comparisons), 347
Yes/No datatype (Jet database engine), 485

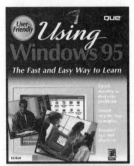
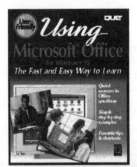

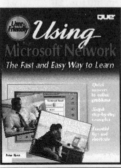